THE POLITICAL ECONOMY OF BRITISH CAPITALISM
A Marxist Analysis

THE POLITICAL ECONOMY OF BRITISH CAPITALISM
A Marxist Analysis

Sam Aaronovitch
and Ron Smith

with Jean Gardiner
and Roger Moore

McGRAW-HILL Book Company (UK) Limited

London · New York · St Louis · San Francisco · Auckland · Bogotá
Guatemala · Hamburg · Johannesburg · Lisbon · Madrid · Mexico
Montreal · New Delhi · Panama · Paris · San Juan · São Paulo
Singapore · Sydney · Tokyo · Toronto

Published by
McGRAW-HILL Book Company (UK) Limited
MAIDENHEAD · BERKSHIRE · ENGLAND

British Library Cataloguing in Publication Data

Aaronovitch, Sam
    The political economy of British capitalism.
    1. Great Britain—Economic conditions—
    20th century
    I. Title   II. Smith, Ron
    330.941′082   HC256   80-41153

    ISBN 0-07-084121-7

12345 B&T 84321

PRINTED AND BOUND IN GREAT BRITAIN BY
BUTLER & TANNER LTD, FROME AND LONDON

CONTENTS

NOTE ON CONTRIBUTORS

SAM AARONOVITCH is Principal Lecturer in Economics at the Polytechnic of the South Bank

JEAN GARDINER is Lecturer in Social Studies, Extra-Mural Department, Leeds University

ROGER MOORE is Industrial Tutor with the Workers Education Association

RON SMITH is Reader in Applied Economics at Birkbeck College, University of London

PREFACE

This book is an attempt to provide a coherent and consistent account, from a Marxist perspective, of how British capitalism reached its present position and where it is now. Such an analysis, which focuses on underlying forces, seems to us necessary in examining prospects and policies for the UK in the eighties. We have tried to write it in such a way that it can be used as a textbook and also by the more general reader. Works referred to in the main text are listed in full in the Bibliography at the end of the book.

We are more conscious now than when we began of the difficult task we set ourselves. Although each of us accepts responsibility for the chapters we have signed, the book is very much the outcome of collective discussion, even though differences remain and we have not just settled for a consensus.

Given the many areas covered by our book, we have been very dependent on the writing and research of many other economists in a large number of journals and institutions; we have a special debt to pay to those who have been working within the same broad theoretical framework and whose work is published in *Capital and Class* (issued by the Conference of Socialist Economists) and in the *Cambridge Journal of Economics*.

We have also benefited in particular from the help, criticism, and encouragement of many friends, including Dave Currie (who contributed a great deal to Part Three in particular), Pat Devine, Ben Fine, John Grahl, Francis Green, Laurence Harris, Linda Hesselman, Sue Himmelweit, Bob Rowthorn, Peter Samson, Frank Wilkinson, and Irene Brunskill who helped prepare the index.

Sam Aaronovitch
Ron Smith

ONE

INTRODUCTION

Ron Smith

The purpose of this book is to provide an account of the structure and development of the British economy from a Marxist perspective. Although the theoretical tools necessary to understand that structure and development will be introduced and explained, the emphasis will be on the concrete features of the economy that condition our lives.

At a day-to-day level we experience the economy through work and unemployment, through buying and selling, and through paying and receiving flows of money such as wages, pensions, grants, taxes, and so on. But at the level of economic analysis these familiar processes are transformed into dry statistics and esoteric concepts, often hiding behind initials like PSBR and M3, which seem to bear little relation to our experience. However, any treatment of economics that merely regards it as a set of technical relationships must be inadequate, because economic processes are rooted in a set of social and political relationships from which they cannot be separated. It is impossible to construct any pure economic theory that will produce a set of universal laws applicable to any society, since the form of economic relationships is specific to particular forms of the organization of society. Whatever orthodox textbooks may say, the economics of a peasant commune must be qualitatively different from that of an industrial city, because the prevalent values, social ties, motivations, and styles of life are so different. With different social organizations there go different criteria for rationality, success, and acceptable ways of treating others. Even within industrial society, differences in social relations between individuals influence what is thought of as the appropriate form of economic interaction. For instance, employers might be guided by different standards when giving money to their workforce compared with their family. However, with the growth of industrial society, more and more relationships that were once based on loyalty, kinship, and moral values are being reduced to purely monetary calculation. If the word 'political' is used in its wider sense—i.e., to cover not just party politics but the whole structure of power relations—then these social values and relationships that condition economic interaction are inherently political. One reason why the older term 'political economy' is used by many, including us, instead of 'economics' is to emphasize that the study of the economy cannot be separated from the politics of the society in which it operates. In order to examine the way in which the economy is rooted in a set of social and political relationships, we need some way to characterize these relationships and the organization of society associated with them. In this book the way that will be primarily used to classify societies is in terms of the structure of their class relations—i.e., the form of ownership and control of the means of production within them. On this basis the main feature of British society is that it is predominantly capitalist. Exactly what is meant by capitalism is discussed in Chapter 3; here it is enough to emphasize that our concern is with the economic processes associated with a specific form of social organization—the political economy of British capitalism—and that this concern will take us beyond the narrow definitions of economics and into wider political and social issues.

One main theme of the book will be that the characteristics of British economic development can only be understood in terms of the interaction between economic, political, and social phenomena, and that attempting to study economic phenomena in isolation can lead only to a misleading or superficial analysis. In particular, we shall argue that the structure of class relations in Britain has had important consequences for its pattern of development. Given this theme, Marxist theory provides a useful framework because, unlike orthodox economic theories, it integrates the social, political, and economic features of society into a single structure. An introduction to some of the main features of this structure is given in Chapters 3 and 4. As we have tried to use it in this book, Marxist analysis does not consist of a dogmatic exposition of what Marx said, but rather involves making use of a tradition of investigation employing techniques and principles pioneered by Marx. In addition, like any other theory, it does not provide all the answers, and there are a number of areas where Marxist, like orthodox, explanations of current events or patterns seem inadequate or speculative. But despite that, it seems to us that Marxist analysis provides the most coherent and comprehensive account of economic processes available. As with any intellectual tradition, Marxist economics is not monolithic and there are not unanimously agreed correct answers to every question. Rather there are a variety of disputes and controversies. While this is fruitful, since the analysis only develops through controversy and argument, it does tend to mean that there are heated debates about whether a particular argument is truly Marxist or not. Since our primary concern is to present a connected account of the British economy, we shall not devote much attention to discussing the Marxist credentials of each piece of analysis. Discussion of such credentials will be found in many works referred to in the text.

A second major theme of the book arises directly from the nature of Marxist analysis. The theme is that the use of orthodox static equilibrium modes of economic thought hinders understanding and that the analysis must be conducted in terms of the unstable and contradictory nature of the dynamics of economic development. An equilibrium is a position in which there are no forces or pressures for change. The bulk of orthodox economics is concerned with describing the mechanisms by which the system will be moved towards an equilibrium, and with analysing the properties that equilibrium will have. This also applies to much of what is called dynamic economics, where the object is to derive steady state, equilibrium growth paths. The alternative is dialectical analysis. Dialectics can be thought of as the logic of motion and change; it emphasizes the hidden tensions or contradictions within seemingly static institutions or situations which lead to their evolution into something quite different. For instance, during the post-war boom in all the advanced capitalist countries between 1950 and 1970, most orthodox economists came to regard continuous growth and relatively full employment as the normal state of affairs and provided theories that would explain why they should persist indefinitely. Marxists, on the other hand, emphasized the contingent nature of the boom, and how growth and full employment were themselves destroying the conditions necessary to maintain the boom. By virtue of their concern with the unstable nature of the dynamics of the prolonged boom and the contradictions within it, many Marxists predicted that the seventies would be a period of turbulence, recession, and conflict. Against this, it must be admitted that many Marxists have been over-hasty in predicting the imminent demise of capitalism.

This example raises a third major theme of the book, the extent to which the structure of the British economy has been conditioned by the pattern of development of world capitalism and the particular way that British capital has been integrated into the international economy. The form of this integration has created a contradiction between the international orientation and expansion of British capital and the relative stagnation of domestic production, both features created by the structure of class relations. The differences in the structure of class relations between Britain and its major capitalist competitors is discussed in Chapter 6. The contradiction between the international orientation and domestic development of British capital has been a major influence on British economic development and policy, and the ways in which this contradiction has manifested itself over the last century are discussed in Chapter 7.

Because a major argument of the book is that one cannot study the British economy without taking account of the social and political organization of the society, the international environment in which it operates, and the dynamics of its history, it means that we have to work on a very broad canvas, covering a vast range of topics. But in a book of this size we can do no more than provide a general introduction to many of the topics and some suggestions for further reading, and inevitably we have not had space to deal with much of the detail and some of the qualifications. In addition we have tried to write in such a way that our work would be accessible to a first-year student or a general reader with some knowledge of economics. Thus we have excluded much of the more technical material.

Our aim is to provide a broad and readable general introduction, and this has meant that we have had to sacrifice the detailed technical documentation of our position in a number of cases, and sometimes to treat highly controversial disputes somewhat cavalierly. We hope readers will be encouraged to question the account and pursue the matter further themselves.

The book is organized into five main parts:

Part One: Background
Part Two: The State
Part Three: International Capitalism
Part Four: Capital
Part Five: Labour

Part One, which provides the background, contains six chapters that give an overview of the major theoretical and empirical issues that will be treated at greater length in the rest of the book.

When the economy is analysed, it is through the use of a variety of concepts, relationships, and statistics, and to describe the economy in this way is to see it through a filter of economic theory. There is no alternative to this, for it is only theory that can provide the process of selection and abstraction that will reduce the vast mass of events and characteristics that make up the economy to some comprehensible structure. But, given the central role that economic theory plays in conditioning the way we perceive the economy, it is crucial to examine how this theory develops. This is the purpose of Chapter 2, which reviews the history of economic thought. The Marxist economic theory that will be used through most of this book is introduced in Chapters 3 and 4, which deal with capital and class respectively. Clearly it is impossible to do justice to the range of Marxist economic theory in such a short space, and the main function of the chapters will be to explain the main Marxist terms that will occur here and show how they are used. Since the bulk of the book is concerned with empirical material, it is important to consider how the theory and empirical evidence are linked. This is done in Chapter 5, which discusses the relation between the Marxist theoretical concepts and the available statistics, which are largely constructed on the basis of categories derived from orthodox theory.

With the benefit of this theoretical background, Chapters 6 and 7 provide an overview of the British economy, which attempts to identify the main features to be explained. To obtain an overview of this type requires some perspective, since the significance of particular features of the British economy cannot be established in isolation, but only relative to some standard of comparison. A different standard is used in each chapter.

Chapter 6 compares the UK with other advanced capitalist countries in order to highlight the similarities and differences, particularly in the structure of class relations. Chapter 7 compares the British economy with its past in order to identify the major factors in its development. In doing this, the chapter focuses on certain crucial periods during this century, at which strategic policy decisions were taken that determined the subsequent path. On four occasions, at roughly 25–year intervals, the choice has centred on whether to maintain the international aspirations of British capital or whether to foster domestic production and development. These choices were seen as the responsibility of the state, and the role of the state in the economy is analysed in Part Two. This section examines the main influences on government decision making, the extent of state intervention in production and society as a whole, and the main areas of policy. But state policy is constrained by the operation of international capital, because Britain is a very open economy dependent on trade, with large overseas investment, and is also the home of a major world financial market in the City of London. Thus to understand the development of the British economy it is necessary to examine the dynamics of world capitalism which has so much influence on it. This is done in Part Three. Chapter 12 considers the uneven nature of world capitalist development and the process of internationalization of capital, which has increasingly integrated world capitalism into a single system. Chapter 13 explains the reasons for the collapse of the long post-war boom and describes the crisis of the seventies. Chapter 14 describes how British capital is integrated into this world system.

Parts Four and Five examine in more depth the two main classes, capitalists and workers. A final chapter draws some conclusions and looks at current policy debates and the possibilities of an alternative economic strategy. Although the conventional economic phenomena that are the focus of so much concern—inflation, unemployment, balance of payments, etc.—appear again and again, our account, unlike many conventional treatments, is not organized around them. This is because it seems to us that they are better regarded as symptoms of more fundamental characteristics of the economy, in particular the structure of production and class relations. It is precisely because of their role as symptoms of these underlying structural features that orthodox relationships to predict or explain them are so prone to break down. The orthodox relationships and equations take structural features—such as the relative power of workers, capitalists, and the state—as fixed. But when the balance of class forces changes, the relationships will shift and the equations will seem to break down. This is true for many conventional economic relationships, and partly explains their low predictive power.

There are two general points to be made about Marxist method. The first is that Marxist theory is political in two ways. Not only does the analysis integrate economics and politics, it also provides a basis for political action.

Marx himself was a lifelong revolutionary and the purpose of his studies was not merely to understand the world but to change it. Marxism remains the basis of revolutionary political groups devoted to the overthrow of capitalism and its replacement by socialism, and within Marxist method the elements of theory and political practice remain tightly linked. The second point is that the theory should not be regarded as deterministic in any mechanical way; rather, it identifies the principal processes at work. The most common process is one of constraint. For instance, a certain structural characteristic of the system may make certain outcomes impossible or very unlikely, but not determine which of the feasible outcomes will in fact result. The actual outcome is then determined by factors not explicitly considered in the theory (political coalitions, individual actions or whatever) within a range set by the structural constraints. A simple example of such a constraint is the need imposed by competition for a capitalist firm to make profits. Competition makes it impossible for the firm to follow certain courses, but does not completely determine exactly how it behaves. A second important process is the generation of certain strong tendencies by the system—for instance, the tendencies towards the concentration and internationalization of capital. These pressures are not necessarily inexorable, and policy actions may reverse them for a time. But such policy actions would in effect be sailing against the wind, possible, but requiring great effort and likely to be temporary unless the structure itself is substantially changed. Thus the theory is not completely deterministic, in that it does not predict exactly what will happen in the future or say that what did happen in the past was inevitable and that nothing else could have occurred. The role of the structural constraints, pressures, and tendencies identified by the theory is to specify the likelihood or probability of certain outcomes, not their inevitability.

The book has been organized so that it can be read in a number of different ways. Although the chapters are separately authored, the linking material enables the work to be read straight through to provide a fairly comprehensive picture of the British economy. Alternatively, since each of the chapters treats its topic in a relatively self-contained way, individual chapters can be used as an introduction to a specific aspect. One consequence of trying to make each chapter relatively self-contained is that there is inevitably some repetition of material. A third way of reading the book is to use the index to trace a particular phenomenon, such as unemployment, through the book. Reading in this way may also highlight the differences in approach and emphasis between the authors. For although we have spent long hours reading and discussing each other's work, and think we have agreed a common analysis, some differences remain, and we felt it better not to suppress them.

The final point about reading the book is that it should be remembered that there is so much that is just not known about the economy that some explanations must be somewhat speculative and remain matters of opinion. In general, we have tried to indicate where we feel this to be the case. Nonetheless, we hope we can convince the reader that the Marxist framework provides the most complete and coherent structure for the analysis of British capitalism.

ONE

BACKGROUND

This section introduces the theoretical and empirical analysis that will be used throughout the book. Chapter 2 discusses the role and development of economic theory and the significance of its ideological component. Chapters 3 and 4 provide a brief review of Marxist economic theory. A major problem arises in economics, as in any science, in making a transition from theoretical concepts to observed or measured phenomena. The problems are even greater for Marxist economists because most available data is constructed within orthodox theoretical categories. These problems are examined in Chapter 5. Since the chapter also discusses the nature of the main data sources that will be used in the book, it involves more detailed and technical material. Chapters 6 and 7 provide an overview of the central characteristics of the British economy that need to be explained and of the main components in our explanation of the poor performance of the British economy. This explanation puts emphasis on the particular character of the structure of class relations that developed in Britain.

ECONOMICS

Ron Smith

2-1 BACKGROUND

In this book economics will be broadly regarded as the study of the processes
that determine the production of goods and services; their exchange through
purchase and sale; and the distribution of the value of the product as wages,
profit, taxes, etc., together with the study of the forces which give rise to
and change these processes. These processes will depend, of course, not
merely on what are usually regarded as economic phenomena, but also
political, social, and ideological factors, and these will be given due weight
in the analysis. However, it can be misleading to speak of one subject
'economics', since not only does there not exist any single generally accepted
theory but there is also disagreement about what the subject covers. Instead,
economics is composed of a number of competing doctrines or 'schools of
thought' which have different visions of the subject, conflicting analyses,
and contradictory policy recommendations. There is even further disagreement within these schools.

Many economics texts (e.g., Lipsey, 1975) begin with a distinction between
'positive' and 'normative' analysis or theory. Positive questions are those
that can, in principle, be settled by appeal to facts, while normative questions
can only be decided by personal, moral, or value judgements. Thus saying
that economists do not agree is a positive statement (one could investigate
whether or not it is true); saying that economists should agree is a normative
statement, a matter of opinion. This distinction between positive and
normative is usually followed by the argument that economics is (or should
be) scientific, in that it consists of positive theories tested by confrontation
with the facts. There are many problems with this account. Despite its
superficial plausibility, the positive/normative distinction cannot be maintained; the idea that there exist value-free 'facts' which will test theories is
too simple; and the historical description of how economics (or the natural
sciences) progresses is misleading. Normally the history of economic
thought, like much other history, is presented as a clear progression, a well-
defined path of discovery and advancement culminating in the satisfactory
state of current wisdom. This has the consequence that when current

wisdom changes, history has then to be rewritten. When this is done, once shadowy figures suddenly become important precursors, while others are condemned to an underworld of heretics who took dead-end paths (i.e., paths that do not lead to the current received wisdoms). But the history of economic thought can also be seen not as a neutral, value-free search for objective knowledge, which steadily progresses towards what is now known to be the truth, but as part of a system of thought, an ideology, reflecting economic development itself.

This can be understood by looking more closely at the relationship between the ideas and theories people formulate about society and the nature of society. The relationships into which people enter in any social system are shaped by the form of economic organization or the mode of production that is dominant in that society. Capitalism, feudalism, socialism are all modes of production, ways of organizing production, with associated structures of class relationships. The characteristics of a mode of production will be discussed in more detail in the next chapter, but it is the mode of production that determines the character of class relations and the character of class conflicts. For instance, in organizing production, people enter into social relationships with each other—such as capitalist/wage earner, land-owner/serf, master/slave—and these relationships, which are constructed by society in the course of development, exist independently of the choice of the individual concerned. The method of organizing production thus gives rise to particular relations between classes of people, which form the basis upon which society is organized; and the individual's pattern of life will be severely constrained by these relationships, as will their perceptions of the system.

These perceptions and the ideas and theories that develop may both reveal and obscure important characteristics of the society. But any class society requires the existence of a set of ideas that will contribute to the stability of that system, legitimize its structure, and support the position of the dominant class. Such systems of thought or ideologies may contain accurate descriptions of certain features of a society, but also play a political and economic role that reinforces the *status quo*. The class relations of a particular mode of production—feudalism, capitalism or socialism—then get taken for granted and appear as the natural organization of society. Despite their appearance of objectivity, the language and structure of orthodox economics are rooted in a system of thought that takes as natural the structure of capitalist or bourgeois society, thus helping to support and maintain that society. This is why Marxists often refer to the orthodox economics of the advanced capitalist world as 'bourgeois' economics. The concept of ideology is a controversial one, both within Marxist thought and between Marxist and non-marxists. It is sometimes, wrongly, thought of as being merely conscious self-justification, or apologetics for one's self-interest, on a level with propaganda. But it goes deeper than this.

The mode of production, the method of economic organization, and the form of ownership of the means of production generate a particular form of social consciousness. They create beliefs and perceptions that mirror the way society appears. These are taken for granted and naturally adopted by the participants, and then play a part in maintaining and reproducing that form of society and the mode of production itself. But these beliefs and perceptions may provide only a limited and inadequate vision of man and society. For instance, what 'bourgeois' economists take for granted as timeless features of man and society—greedy, acquisitive, profit-maximizing economic man in a market economy—are merely a set of relationships peculiar to one method of production: capitalism. Notice that this ideology is not necessarily wrong; economic man may be a perfectly accurate description of individual businessmen. But often it is merely a superficial, narrow perception, treating as fixed constants things that are variable. Such an ideology makes the system relatively stable, because once a society's dominant perception of itself is accepted, there does not seem to be any alternative. But the limited nature of these perceptions, which form the ideology of the society, may only become obvious when the society changes. Thus the objective of economics should not merely be to describe how the society appears at any moment, but to investigate the processes that made it what it is and cause it to change—the laws of motion of that society.

Orthodox economics fails to do this because it treats the institutions and relationships of the capitalist mode of production not as transitional phenomena of a particular stage of economic development, but as being natural and inevitable forms of economic organization—almost characteristics of human nature. Given that it takes so much of the system for granted, treating it as fixed, it has difficulty dealing with the processes that cause the system to change.

The next section considers how the development of orthodox economics was influenced by material factors—the structure of class relations and of production. The materialist interpretation of history will be discussed further in the next chapter, but some points must be made here. First, the account is a very brief one and, although it emphasizes the influence of the structure of production and class relations on the development of thought, it should not be interpreted as implying either that these were the only influences or that the process was completely deterministic. Hobsbawm (1975) uses the analogy of the influence of the wind on a yacht. The direction of the wind does not completely determine the direction in which the yacht goes, but it is a major constraint, which must be taken account of, which conditions the course followed, and which influences progress. Neither are individuals' thoughts completely socially determined, but the acceptance and spread of an economic theory is a social process, requiring the new ideas to appeal to a large number of people and to seem useful in dealing with the problems thrown up by a particular social context. Thus the acceptance and spread of a theory is historically conditioned: if the time and economic environment is not right, the idea will not spread. One example of this is provided by Gossen, who in 1854 published many of the ideas central to the marginalist revolution of the eighteen-seventies, discussed in the next section, which had no impact then. Second, although the account relates the theories to the interests of the ruling class at particular times, this does not mean that the theories are devoid of any useful analysis or that there is no dynamic within the theory itself. The theory developed to provide answers to questions posed by current events, but was conditioned not only by the existing economic organization and class relations, but also by the accepted ideas and systems of thought at that time. This is discussed in some detail in Dobb (1973).

2-2 MATERIAL FACTORS IN THE DEVELOPMENT OF MAINSTREAM ECONOMICS

The word 'economics' itself merely means housekeeping; an 'oikonomos' was the slave in ancient Greece who ran the household. Thus in the eighteenth century 'political economy' was the term used for national housekeeping. But this is a relatively recent use. Although classical and feudal writers such as Aristotle and Aquinas had speculated about such things as the 'just price', they did not indulge in any systematic analysis of what we consider economics. The development of such analysis was largely associated with the development of commodity production. With the growth of merchant capital, the discovery of America, and the expansion of trade in the sixteenth and seventeenth centuries, systematic observation of economic phenomena became more common. One of the first observations was by Gresham, a courtier of Elizabeth I, who gave his name to the law that 'bad money drives out good'. It was noticed that when a monarch debased the coinage—by reducing the gold content, for instance—people would hoard any of the original good coins they could obtain, and pass on the debased ones, so that rapidly only the new inferior coins would be left in circulation. These observations on the effects of debasing and the in-flow of New World gold also led to formulations of a quantity theory of money, relating the general price level to the money supply.

However, the main emphasis in seventeenth- and eighteenth-century England was on the economics of trade, and in particular, on the flow of gold and silver into and out of a country. The traders and merchant capitalists put pressure on the state to enact laws that would give them an edge over their foreign competitors and enable them to acquire more bullion. The English economists who tried to justify the laws to help merchants have become known as the mercantilists. France, in contrast, was then dominated by landlords, and the economists there, the physiocrats, reflected the system by explaining how all wealth derived from land. When, in England, the dynamic force became industrial production, economics followed suit, and Adam Smith provided the argument that through the 'invisible hand' private greed led to social good. Smith, together with Ricardo and Malthus, who followed him in the early nineteenth century, are regarded as the main classical economists. They developed a systematic analysis of the accumulation of wealth and of the distribution of income between wages, profits, and rent. Partly because of this emphasis on accumulation and distribution, class played an important role in their analysis; and they emphasized the benefits and dynamism of capitalist production. The theory then became a major weapon in the class conflict as the industrial capitalists tried to capture power from the then dominant group of landowners, the battles being over such issues as the Corn Laws. But the theories based on classes were also used against the capitalists by workers, initially by the Ricardian socialists and then by Marx. By the late nineteenth century, the conflict between capitalist and landowner having been settled to the former's advantage, the theoretical use of class was downgraded and economics was again transformed. This time the emphasis was switched from class relations to relations between individuals, and to how the harmonious operation of the market rewarded each in accordance with his contribution to production. This transformation in the early eighteen-seventies is known as the marginalist revolution in economic thought, and it provided the foundation for the theory often labelled 'neo-classical' that still dominates orthodox economics.

Although this development of orthodox economic theory was influenced by the interests of the ruling class, the dominant group in society, the interaction between ideas and society is more complex. The theory is not mere apologetics, but contains serious analysis, and Marx paid tribute to scientific bourgeois economics. The mercantilists had a grasp of balance of payments adjustment; the physiocrats, a relatively sophisticated picture of the input–output flows between sectors of the economy; and the transition between classical and neo-classical thought contained technical developments in the treatment of price determination as well as the development of the mode of production. There had been two strands within classical theories of the relative prices at which goods exchanged. On the one hand, the prices were seen as reflecting costs of production, in particular the labour time embodied in produced commodities, and on the other, as reflecting the forces of supply and demand in the market. The labour theory of value (discussed in the next chapter) was reformulated by Marx and made the centre of an extensive analysis of capitalism. The analysis of supply and demand was, however, hindered by confusion over the relationship of the utility or use value of a good to its price or exchange value. Adam Smith had pointed out the paradox of water and diamonds: water is of great use but very cheap, while diamonds are inessential but expensive. It was the neo-classical revolution that dealt with this paradox by reformulating the theory in terms of the marginal utility of a commodity, that is, the utility of the last unit purchased. This reformulation followed shortly after the publication of the first edition of *Das Kapital* in 1868. It was achieved almost simultaneously by three economists: Jevons in England and Menger in Austria, both writing in 1871, and Walras in Switzerland in 1874.

These three provided the basis of modern neo-classical economics. Within this tradition there have been differences in approach, in particular between partial equilibrium analysis, which looks at demand and supply in a single market, and general equilibrium analysis, which allows for the feedbacks between all of the markets. But despite the differences, all are derived from individual maximizing behaviour and share the objective of investigating the operation of the invisible hand. Neo-classical economics is primarily concerned with the process by which the self-interest of individual economic agents—firms maximizing profits and consumers maximizing utility—leads, through the operation of supply, demand, and exchange in a free market, to an equilibrium. Then it is shown how this equilibrium will be Pareto optimal (i.e., no one can be made better off without making somebody worse off); and how the prices and quantities traded are determined in the process by the initial endowments of goods, individual preferences, and the structure of technology embodied in the production functions that relate outputs to the inputs necessary to produce them.

This complete general equilibrium system has considerable intellectual appeal. The question is, does this construction give us any insight into the actual operation of the economy? One way of interpreting the results is that they show that the assumptions necessary to justify the invisible hand are so strong and so contrary to experience that there is no scientific basis for relying upon it for the allocation of goods and services among economic agents. What is clear is that Marxist and neo-classical theories are asking quite different questions. One is concerned to discover the laws of motion of the system, the other to establish the conditions under which an equilibrium would exist.

Although both Marxist and neo-classical thought has developed over the last century, each has retained its original objectives and vision of capitalism. Since these visions differ somewhat, one might have thought that a century of economic evidence might have decided between them, confirming one and relegating the other to a historical curiosity. That this is not so reflects both the characteristics of theory and the operation of ideology. Even in natural sciences, competing theories can coexist for long periods of time (e.g., wave and corpuscular theories of light) and different theories, although seeming to relate to the same subject, may look at different aspects so that their ranges of effective application may overlap very little. Nor do there exist crucial experiments that can discredit whole theories; rather the theories are extended to allow for the new information. Both Marxist and neo-classical theories have been faced with unexpected evidence—for instance, the neo-classicals with the slump of the nineteen-thirties, the Marxists with the long boom between the Korean and Vietnamese wars—but both adjusted to accommodate explanations. If the theory cannot be extended, sometimes the evidence can just be ignored. For instance, econometric evidence from the mid-thirties onwards showed that average cost curves were not in general U-shaped, a necessary condition for neo-classical theory to determine the size of the firm and to ensure that perfect competition was stable. Nonetheless, textbooks still retain their U-shaped cost curves and repeat the standard results.

The main adjustment made by bourgeois thought to the slump of the thirties was the 'Keynesian revolution'. Most neo-classical theory is derived at the micro level of the firm and the consumer, and has little to say about the movements of national income or aggregate investment. From the point of view of traditional neo-classical thought, this was unnecessary, since an implication of the micro results was that the economy would always move to full employment equilibrium and that changes in the rate of interest would bring desired savings and investment to the level required to achieve this. In his General Theory, Keynes proposed a macro theory that was not only capable of explaining fluctuations in the level of output and employment but that also seemed to provide the basis for post-war demand management policies. Keynesian thought was later largely reintegrated into the neo-classical approach by splitting the subject into micro and macro courses, and treating macro (Keynesian) theory as merely a practical tool of empirical use but little theoretical significance. The micro and macro courses in what Samuelson called 'the neo-classical–Keynesian synthesis' were, in fact, logically inconsistent. If the world behaved as it was described in the micro course, it would not show the aggregate phenomena taught in the macro course. Although this fudge persisted for some time, it was unsatisfactory, and generated two responses. On the one hand, a group labelled the monetarists argued that in fact Keynesian theory was wrong, and that the Depression had not been caused by any failure of the market mechanism but by government policy failure and workers' unwillingness to work at the equilibrium wage. On the other hand, attempts were made to restructure micro-economics within the same basic individualistic framework in order to explain Keynesian phenomena, such as unemployment.

Although during the fifties and sixties Keynesian economics became the orthodoxy in most of the capitalist world, it came under attack from a group centred around Milton Friedman at the University of Chicago. By the late seventies the monetarist position that Friedman and his followers put forward was itself established as the new orthodoxy. Friedman took the quantity theory of money, adjusted its interpretation somewhat in the light of Keynesian theory, and added to it a belief in the efficient operation of markets and the price system together with a hostility to state intervention.

Contrary to what many Keynesians seem to suggest, the analytical use of a quantity theory of money is not inherently reactionary, and it has been used by Marxists (e.g., Rowthorn, 1980). But the neo-classical/monetarist combination of theories used by Friedman did provide a powerful right-wing political ideology. The theory legitimated cuts in state expenditure and social services; lack of concern at rising unemployment (which was portrayed as being largely 'voluntary' on the part of workers who chose not to accept jobs); and inegalitarian shifts in income distribution (to improve incentives). In the troubled economic climate of the seventies the individualist monetarist theory, with its emphasis on the discipline of the market, appeared much more attractive to the ruling class than 'social democratic' Keynesianism, with its emphasis on the responsibility of the state to regulate society. References to this monetarist–Keynesian conflict will recur throughout this book, but first the more general limitations of orthodox analysis, whether monetarist or Keynesian, will be considered.

2-3 THE LIMITATIONS OF ORTHODOX ECONOMICS

Throughout this book it will be argued that orthodox economics suffers severe limitations with respect to both the scope of the questions it confronts and the methods of enquiry that it uses to provide answers. It starts from a set of conventional categories (prices, quantities, inflation, unemployment, etc.) and a set of standard relationships between them (supply and demand curves, and Phillips curves, for instance). From these theoretical relationships and observations on past values of the variables, the object is supposed to be to derive some understanding of how the system works; to use this to predict changes in those variables; and to design policies which will improve the functioning of the system. These endeavours have not met with great success and crucial variables in the system remained unexplained. For instance, the central question for the UK economy is why its growth rate is so much lower than those of its competitors. But there is no coherent and well-documented theory to explain differences in growth rates between countries. Instead most economists remain content with putting an unexplained time trend in their equations and labelling it 'technical progress' or the 'residual factor'; or otherwise have recourse to *ad hoc* and crudely formulated non-economic explanations—achievement motivation, national character, etc.

A large part of the reason for the failure of orthodox economics is that the variables they consider and the categories used relate largely to features that are symptoms of underlying forces and social relations that determine the development of the economy. To understand the symptoms requires analysis of the structural factors determining them. Orthodox economics fails to do this adequately by largely confining its scope to market relations and problems of individual maximization, giving little emphasis to the other social processes involved. This excludes from consideration a whole set of processes and relations that are central to the economic structure. Orthodox economics analyses economic phenomena, primarily the prices and quantities of commodities exchanged, under the assumption of some fixed set of political and social institutions with given technology and individual preferences. But the pattern of the economy, the organization of production, and the form of exchange relationships must influence political and social patterns and individual preferences. These in turn feed back onto the economic structure. There can be no justification for assuming away these causal links and analysing economic phenomena in isolation from the society within which they are embedded.

In orthodox economics the logic of market rationality is treated as being universal, applicable to Robinson Crusoe on his island or to peasants in the third world, not merely as a characteristic of a particular capitalistic society. Marxist analysis, by contrast, starts from the proposition that there are no universal general historical laws. Instead the analysis must always be conducted relative to a particular social structure or mode of production. For instance, the orthodox analysis of the post-war international monetary system was conducted in terms of anonymous trading partners, using an anonymous reserve asset, and presented as a general analysis. In fact, the system was determined by specific features peculiar to that historical situation. It was not irrelevant to the analysis that the dollar was the main reserve asset, because the choice of reserve currency has substantial political and ideological implications, which influence and are inseparable from the economic analysis. To convert a state's reserves from dollars to gold or roubles is not merely a technical economic adjustment but a major ideological challenge, which has political and economic repercussions (a fact that French policy exploited throughout the post-war period). To provide a complete economic analysis requires the integration of ideology and politics into the theory, and explicit treatment of the feedbacks between them and the economy.

Much of the method used in orthodox economics derives from equilibrium analysis, the investigation of the conditions that will lead to a position in which there are no forces or pressures for change. Marxist analysis emphasizes the conflicts, hidden tensions, and contradictions within seemingly static institutions or situations, which lead to their evolution into something quite different. This evolution through the resolution of the contradictions and tensions within the situation is rarely through a smooth, steady advance, but usually through an abrupt, conflict-laden transformation. Just looking at the history of capitalism—with its Industrial Revolution, its repeated transformation of technology and institutions, alternating booms and slumps, growth and decay of firms, ceaseless innovation and expansion—it seems unlikely that an analysis based on the tendency of this system to converge to a stable equilibrium will do justice to a process of development so rooted in change. The alternative is to identify the laws of motion of capitalism, which are generated by the unfolding of the contradictions of the structure, these conditions being embedded in the very character which defines the system.

For example, since 1945 the international monetary system has rested on US political and economic power. The dominance of the US allowed it to organize and regulate the system, while the strength of the dollar maintained its role as a reserve currency and the role of the US as banker to the capitalist world. This system appeared to be, and was presented as being, in stable, permanent equilibrium throughout the fifties and early sixties. But to maintain one pillar of the system, US political dominance, required massive foreign expenditure on wars, investment, support for client regimes, etc. This expenditure was paid for in dollars, which flooded the foreign exchange markets, destroying the other pillar of the structure, the strength of the dollar. The result was the collapse of the international monetary system into inflation, recession, and violently fluctuating exchange rates. The nature of the American dominance or hegemony that maintained the system contained within itself the contradictions that destroyed the system.

These features of the international system will be discussed in more detail in Chapters 12 and 13. Now, having argued that orthodox economics suffers severe limitations, it is necessary to present an alternative. This is done in the next chapter.

FURTHER READING

Readers who wish to place Marx's political economy within the wider framework of his life and times could read a biography such as McClellan (1973); for a much more detailed study of the way in which *Capital* came to be written, see Rodolsky (1977).

Standard accounts of the history of economic thought may be found in Roll (1973) and Blaug (1968). Less detailed 'radical' accounts are Routh (1975) and Deane (1978). Marx's own account of the classical economists can be found in his *Theories of Surplus Value* (Progress Publishers): Marxist histories can be found in Dobb (1973) and Rubin (1972 and 1979). Valuable historical analysis can be found in Meek (1967 and 1973).

THREE

CAPITAL

Ron Smith

3-1 INTRODUCTION

The purpose of this chapter is to provide a brief introduction to the Marxist terminology and analysis that will be used throughout this book. Much of this account will be rather abstract, but this arises from the need to explain the underlying principles for the most simple case before trying to extend the analysis to the complexity of actual societies. It should also be kept in mind that Marxist analysis is a tradition of investigation in which many issues are still matters of dispute. The immediate purpose of Marx's analysis was to understand the process of historical change, and the primary tool he used to achieve this was a materialist conception of history. The approach was materialist in the sense that it saw people's consciousness and ideas about society as deriving from the real world of social relations. The basis of these social relations was the mode of production, the organization of the way in which people produced and distributed among themselves the goods they needed to survive. For the most part, production has to be a social process; it involves groups of people interacting and working together, using the productive forces—labour power, raw materials, and available technology—within particular relations of production, which include patterns of control of the work process and of property ownership. The form of this interaction will be analysed in terms of the class position of the different groups—i.e., their relation to the means of production. What characterizes the dominant class is that they control the means of production (the material and resources needed to produce the necessities of life), and this gives them power over the other members of society. Since most societies produce a surplus (more output than the minimum necessary to reproduce itself), one form this power takes is the ability to acquire this surplus and control its disposition. Thus the mode of production can be thought of as the way in which surplus is produced and extracted by one class from another. For instance, in feudal society the lord controls the land, which gives him power over the serf. The serf may then have to surrender a proportion of the food he produces to the lord, or work part of the time on the lord's land. Thus the serf works so many hours to maintain himself, and the remainder is used to produce a surplus which is supplied to the lord. Here the process of exploitation—i.e., of extraction of the surplus—is very clear, as are the social relations of production. Other social structures and relationships—laws, religion, political organization—will then be conditioned by the social relations in production, whose influence will pervade the whole society.

Under capitalism the position is less obvious. The worker is not tied to the employer by any legal compulsion, as the serf is tied to the land, and there is every appearance of freedom on the part of the worker and competition between employers. Explaining the way surplus was produced and extracted under capitalism was a major focus of Marx's efforts. The position is further complicated by the fact that, although within any observed society there is a dominant mode of production, which conditions the main relationships, it may also contain other modes. Hence the class structure of any particular society will be more complex than the simple two-class system described above. When analysing practical problems or real societies it is necessary to take this into account, but in order to introduce the processes it is more useful to abstract from these complications and consider a pure capitalist mode of production.

A major condition for the development of the capitalist mode is the prevalence of commodity production. In simple societies, production is largely for use by the producer. In commodity societies, production is for exchange. The motive for production ceases to be the use value or desirability of the product to the producer, and becomes instead its exchange value, the amount of other desired commodities that can be acquired in return for the product. The product may be exchanged directly for other commodities, as in barter, or it may be exchanged for money, which is generalized value or purchasing power (i.e., the general power to acquire any commodity). Marx argued that the value of a commodity was determined by the labour required to produce it. In the case where the worker also used produced means of production in making a commodity, the labour embodied in the commodity produced could be divided into a direct component (the labour used on making it) and an indirect component (the labour used making the required means of production). This labour theory of value, as used by Marx, was not primarily a theory of price; it was a theory of the social relations involved in production and exchange. In fact, there will be a range of other factors that will influence the relationship between prices and values. The problem of specifying the exact form of this relationship, known as the transformation problem, has attracted considerable attention in Marxist economics. Since the principal concern at this stage is the social relationships rather than the determination of prices, we can abstract from these problems and assume for the moment that the conditions necessary for commodities to exchange at their values hold. The point of doing this is to try and understand exchange not as a relationship between things, the commodities that are exchanged, which is how it appears under capitalism, but as a relationship between people. This transformation of social relationships into commodity relationships, which Marx called commodity fetishism, has a major influence on how people perceive the operation of the system.

The value of any commodity is given by the socially necessary labour time embodied in it. The qualification 'socially necessary', meaning under the normal conditions of production and with the average degree of skill and work intensity prevalent at the time, is required since wasted or unnecessary labour does not contribute to value. The capitalist uses labour to produce commodities for exchange, and under ideal conditions competition between capitalists will ensure that these commodities exchange at their values. The capitalists organize production, since it is they that own and control the means of production, without which it is impossible to produce. Although the worker is free of the legal compulsions that existed under feudalism or slavery, the free labourer has no means of production with which to work; the bulk of the people having been separated from the means of production in the course of the development of capitalism. Thus under pure capitalism, although the worker is free to choose which employer to work for, he is not free to choose not to work, except at the cost of starving. In this the urban worker can be contrasted with the peasant, who still owns means of production (land), and can support himself even if he chooses not to work for someone else. The extent to which social security and other forms of state intervention have changed the picture is considered below, but let us remain with the pure capitalist system.

The capitalist who owns the means of production then hires workers to produce commodities; thus labour also becomes a commodity exchanged in the market. In fact, the commodity sold by the worker is not the work, labour, but the capacity to work, labour power. The form of the employment contract is different from that for most other goods. The labourer does not sell a specific service but the willingness to do what the employer requires of him. The employer then decides how the labour power should be exercised as labour in order to produce commodities. Since labour power is a commodity, its value is determined in exactly the same way as that of any other commodity—by the socially necessary labour time required to produce it. This will include the labour required to produce the wage goods, food, housing, etc., necessary to support the worker and his family. Since it is the socially necessary labour time, the value of labour power is not determined by some physiological subsistence level, but is historically determined and thus will also be a focus of class struggle. But although the capitalist buys labour power at its value, the value of what is produced by the worker is greater—i.e., labour is productive. This difference, called surplus value, is the source of profit, and is generated even when there are no monopolistic pressures or direct coercion on the workers. For in these circumstances the process of exchange cannot be the source of surplus value and profit, because free competition ensures that commodities all exchange at their values; while coercion of the worker cannot be the source, because the worker is free to sell his labour power at its value. The source of surplus value lies in production, where the value of what the worker produces is greater than the value of labour power required to produce it. To consider the role that the creation of surplus value plays in the system, the next section examines the process of production more formally.

3-2 THE PROCESS OF PRODUCTION

The capitalist starts out with an amount of money M; with this he acquires produced means of production with value c. In Marxist literature these are called 'constant capital'. The capitalist also buys labour power with value v, referred to as variable capital, and organizes the production of some commodity. The value of the commodity produced, however, is greater than the value of the capital (constant plus variable) used to produce it. Call the value of this excess s, the surplus produced by labour in the production process. The capitalist can then exchange the commodities produced for a sum of money M', which will be greater than his initial investment M by the amount of the surplus value.

Schematically the process can be described as money capital being used to buy productive capital $(c+v)$ and used to produce commodity capital with value $(c+v+s)$, which is converted back into money capital.

$$M=(c+v)\text{—Production—}(c+v+s)=M'$$

Constant capital just adds its value to the final output; without the labour no surplus would be produced. This process is sometimes abbreviated, and represented as a chain:

$$M\text{—}C\text{—}M'$$

with C standing for both the labour power and means of production purchased to provide productive capital, and for the commodities produced for sale. This formulation will be used in the next section, which considers the interaction of production and exchange.

The characteristics of the production process can be described by three ratios.

(a) The rate of profit r, which is the surplus produced in production expressed as a proportion of the capital advanced:

$$r=s/(c+v)$$

This is the return the capitalist makes on his investment.

(b) The rate of exploitation e, which measures the surplus produced relative to the value of labour power required to produce it:

$$e=s/v$$

When the term 'exploitation' is used, it will be used in this technical sense, and it will depend on such things as the value of labour power, the length of the working day, the intensity of work, and the degree of control the capitalist has over the production process.

(c) The organic composition of capital k, which measures the degree of capital intensity in the production process, i.e., the ratio of the values of constant capital (means of production) to variable capital (labour power):

$$k = c/v$$

Notice that c, v, and s are calculated in value terms, e.g., in days of labour time, for instance. If commodities do not exchange at their values, these ratios calculated from price magnitudes will not equal the ratios calculated in value terms. At this stage one of the assumptions necessary for commodities to exchange at their value can be introduced. It is that the organic composition of capital be the same in every industry. This, needless to say, is a rather strong assumption, and in practice one would expect deviations between prices and values. Since the purpose here is to understand the structure of production rather than to explain market prices, we shall continue to use values for a little longer.

Considering the rate of profit, it can be seen that if the top and bottom of the fraction are divided by v, the rate of profit is not changed, but it can be expressed in terms of the rate of exploitation and the organic composition of capital:

$$r = \frac{s}{v+c} = \frac{s/v}{(v/v)+(c/v)} = \frac{e}{1+k}$$

Marx argued that with increasing mechanization there was a tendency for the organic composition of capital to rise, so that if the rate of exploitation stays constant, the rate of profit will fall. The rate of exploitation may increase either by increasing the absolute surplus value extracted from the workers by increased work intensity or a lengthening of the working day, or by increasing relative surplus value by raising productivity. Marx's argument was that there are inevitable limits to increasing e, while there are no limits to increasing k. Thus, given that increased accumulation and mechanization were characteristic of capitalism, Marx argued that there was a tendency for the rate of profit to fall with its development. But he also pointed out a range of counteracting tendencies. For instance, the increased productivity of the production process will mean that machines can be built much cheaper, so that although there will be more machines, their value (the labour time needed to produce them) will be less. This may then stop the organic composition of capital rising with mechanization. The whole question of the tendency of the rate of profit to fall and the role of the counteracting tendencies is a controversial one in Marxist economics (see Howard and King, 1975, and Fine and Harris, 1979).

The term 'capital' has been used repeatedly above, but since it is a word with a variety of meanings it is important to explain the Marxist usage and contrast it with other uses. Capital is often used to describe any sum of money available for investment either in financial assets (stocks, shares, government securities), or in physical equipment like plant and machinery, or in holding goods produced and work in progress. Economists tend to confine their use of capital to the physical stock of plant and equipment that is used to continue production rather than for final consumption. In this sense, neo-classical economists treat it as a factor of production, like labour or land, which is an input into a technological production function determining the output produced from given inputs.

In Marxist terminology, capital is the use of money and commodities to produce a surplus for its owners, and labour power, when used by capitalists in production, becomes part of capital. The essence of the distinction between the neo-classical and Marxist concepts is that in one case capital is merely a thing, whereas in the other it describes a relationship between people. Contrary to the neo-classical position implied by the production function, production is not determined merely by technological factors independent of property relations. Rather it depends on the form of organization and the social relations between those involved. Thus the fact that wage labour is bought by capital in order to generate surplus value is central to understanding the organization and characteristics of production under capitalism.

3-3 PRODUCTION AND EXCHANGE

In the previous section the production process was abbreviated to

$$M—C—M'$$

The capitalist starts with money capital, converts it to an equivalent amount of productive capital, made up of constant (means of production) and variable (labour power) capital, uses this to produce commodities of greater value, which are exchanged for an equivalent amount of money M'. The process may then start all over again, so that a sequence is obtained:

$$M—C—M'—C'—M''—C''—M'''$$

and it is in the production stage (i.e., between C and M', C' and M'', C'' and M''') that value is created; elsewhere money and commodities exchange for equivalent amounts of value. In describing this circuit of capital through exchange and production, as it changes its form from money to commodities and back to money, the process has been started and ended with money capital. This is significant, for the capitalist is producing not because he wants the output itself, but so that he can exchange the output and acquire more money. This money capital is generalized value, which can be used to acquire any form of commodity or productive capital. The orthodox economic account is the reverse of this. An individual starts off with an initial endowment of resources (commodities including labour power). These he sells for money, using this money to buy a set of commodities he prefers, i.e., a circuit of commodity capital:

$$C—M—C'$$

Formally, this seems very similar to a section of the continuing $M–C$ chain pictured above, but there are two important differences. First, it emphasizes the exchange aspects (the worker selling labour power to buy goods, for instance) rather than production, and second, it has very different implications, when the exchange–production–exchange process is interrupted; when the chain is broken.

It will be clear that in the $C–M–C'$ chain there are very powerful pressures towards equilibrium. Individuals want to hold commodities, and they will only sell commodities when they want to buy other commodities. Thus for every sale there is a corresponding purchase, and it is impossible to have general excess demand or supply for all commodities. This is the basis of the argument for what is called Say's Law—every supply creates its own demand. With the alternative sequence $M–C–M'$, there are no such equilibrium pressures. Owners of capital only buy and sell commodities to expand their capital so that they can convert it back into money. Thus since the objective of capitalists is to expand their capital and transform it back into its most flexible form, money, there is no mechanism to ensure, at any particular time, that the demand for commodities will equal its supply. Suppose for some reason a capitalist firm finds its sales weak; it will tend to cut back on its own purchases of commodities for production, and hold money instead. This depresses the sales of other capitalist firms, who do the same. Thus a destabilizing feedback is generated.

This money circuit of capital emphasizes that the links in the $M–C–M'$ process are fragile, and that there is no reason to expect the value of the amount of money being advanced to necessarily equal the value of the commodities available. There is no mechanism to ensure that unemployment of workers, under-utilization of means of production, and gluts of produced goods that cannot be sold will not occur. In the long run the system will expand under the pressure of the need by capitalists to accumulate, because it is only by converting their money capital into commodity capital, by hiring labour power and means of production, and by producing that they can generate surplus value and increase their capital. But the process will be erratic, with recurrent crises at times when the circuit is interrupted and individual capitalists are unable to realize the surplus value extracted from the workers as money capital. For to realize the surplus value as profit, they must sell the output produced. The significance of this 'realization' problem that capitalists face in finding markets for their production is a matter of controversy among Marxists.

The stability of the process is further endangered by the need to maintain balance between the different sectors of the economy. The sectors are usually divided into Department I, which produces capital goods, the means of production; Department II, which produces wage goods, consumed by the workers; and sometimes Department III, which produces goods that do not contribute to the reproduction of the system, such as luxury goods consumed by the capitalists. For growth to progress steadily (for expanded reproduction to continue), the output of Department I must be just equal to the demand for the means of production by all three departments; and the output of Department II equal to the wages paid in all three departments. The question then arises of what mechanism there is to maintain the proportionality conditions necessary for demands and output to balance. Further, if capitalists throughout the economy are trying to cut their wage costs, this depresses the demand for the output of Department II, which will then cut back its demand for means of production, the output of Department I, which itself cuts back, sending the system into a deep slump. This contradiction between exploitation (which requires keeping down or cutting the cost of labour) and realization (which appears to require the workers as a market for the output) is a major, if controversial, theme in Marxist literature (Bleaney, 1976).

3-4 THE EXPANSION OF CAPITAL

In 3-2 it was shown that in the process of production capital took three forms. Money capital, the initial M and the final M'; productive capital, the labour power and means of production purchased; and the commodity capital produced. Three circuits of capital can be followed, corresponding to starting and finishing at any one form of capital. In the last section, the money circuit of capital ($M-M'$) was emphasized, how the capitalist starting with money bought productive capital in order to produce commodities to produce a larger quantity of money. The commodity circuit ($C-C'$) was also considered when discussing the orthodox approach. And if one is interested in the physical potential of the system, the productive circuit is central. That is, given fixed resources, labour, and means of production, how through production and exchange can they be transformed into a greater quantity of resources? But although particular analytical questions imply choosing starting and ending points, the circulation of capital through these stages is a continual flow, expanding value with every circuit.

Up to now, the circuit of capital has been described as if it had been organized by one vast capitalist or equivalently by capital in general—all capitalists operating simultaneously. But total capital is split into many blocks held by individual capitalists who are in competition. It is the operation of competition, the law of value, that enforces the logic of capital on each individual capitalist and determines many of the characteristics of the operation of the system. Whatever the characteristics of a capitalist as an individual—they may even be revolutionaries like Engels—they must make profits and expand their capital or be driven out of business. The individual employers or firms then must act as representatives of capital, since it is only by meeting the needs of capital, through exploitation and accumulation, that they remain capitalists at all. Competition is the mechanism that ensures compliance with the needs of capital.

In addition to capital being composed of competing blocks, different sectors of capital dominate different stages of the circuit. The production of commodities is the area of industrial capital, while their distribution and sale is the area of commercial, trading, or merchant capital. Further, the development of banking and credit creates a system where money resources are mobilized for loan to those who wish to use them as capital. This is the area of banking or financial capital. Although the development of these institutions aids the generation of surplus value in production, they do not, in general, produce surplus value themselves.

A point that will recur in this book is that the interests of industrial and financial capital can diverge. To the industrial capitalist borrowing money, production is profitable if the return he gets from investing in productive capital is greater than the rate of interest he pays on the borrowed money. For industrial capital, production is of prime concern, for it is the core of its circuit. But financial capital lends money and receives back money, and the profit may seem the same wherever it is gained. In so far as financial capital has a privileged position in the economy (as will be argued is the case in Britain), it can lead to a failure to recognize that neglect of the surplus producing sector will remove the basis for profitability anywhere in the system. Likewise, if profitability is low in production, industrial capital may divert spare funds into financial or commercial markets, reducing accumulation in production.

What has been called here 'financial capital' should be distinguished from 'finance capital'. The latter was the term used by Lenin to describe the fusion of banking and industrial capital. Such a fusion seems more characteristic of German or Japanese capitalism and the British pattern has been rather different.

As these circuits proceed, capital expands through accumulation. The only way to maintain and increase profits in competition with other capitalists trying to do the same is to accumulate further. The more successful capitalists get larger and larger, having greater concentrations of capital under their control. Their less successful or smaller competitors tend to be driven out of business or taken over, so centralizing the control of more capital in the hands of the successful firms. This process of concentration and centralization of capital as a result of competition and accumulation is the major characteristic of capitalist expansion. In the UK in 1909, the 100 largest firms produced 16 per cent of net manufacturing output; in 1972, 41 per cent. Production thus becomes increasingly monopolized. This may happen through the dominant position of large firms in the market, which makes it impossible for small firms to compete effectively. It may happen through a process of takeover or merger. It may happen because monopolistic firms can maintain barriers to entry to stop new firms invading their market.

At the same time that capital is being formed into larger and larger units, it is expanding into new areas. Initially these may be non-capitalist sectors within the same country, such as agriculture or artisan production. Capitalist organization replaces existing structures, such as peasant farming or craft production; the independent workers are turned into wage labourers; the techniques of production are revolutionized, freeing much of this newly created wage labour either to join a reserve army of unemployed or to work in capitalist industry. Subsequently, capital spreads internationally, drawing more and more parts of the world into the capitalist market and capitalist social relations. This internationalization of capital may take a number of forms. Initially it may take the form of trade, the exchange of commodities with non-capitalist parts of the world and extraction of raw materials from those areas; then flows of financial capital appear, as borrowing and lending between areas develops; finally, production plants are established. Through these flows of capital, peripheral areas become increasingly integrated into what becomes a world capitalist system. At the same time, as the non-capitalist world is becoming increasingly integrated into the system, competition within the system continues. In this process of expansion, individual nation states also compete to obtain preferential terms for the firms from their own country. The state may obtain preference in the exploitation of non-capitalist areas by colonization or the indirect use of its power; or it might defend home markets through protection. This process of inter-imperialist rivalry may even lead to war, but the internationalization of capital continuously reasserts itself.

This expansion is not a smooth and trouble-free process but a contra-dictory one. The expansion of capital also expands the size of the class of wage labour, so by its very success it creates an opposition to it. With the expansion goes an increasing socialization of production. The vast multi-nationals, with their international organization of production and exchange and their dominant role in many of the societies in which they operate, provide an example of social organization of production on a world scale. But this conflicts with the private appropriation of the surplus produced. Although the multi-nationals are highly planned and integrated organiza-tions, they must oppose the application of similar planning and organization to the economy as a whole, for this would threaten their profits and control. Thus increasingly the organization of the productive forces and the property relations on which that organization is based come into conflict. There also develops a contradiction between the international basis of capital and the national basis of the state. As firms expand and draw their profits from all over the world, their interests cease to be tied to any particular country. But the state functions necessary for that expansion continue to be provided by national governments. All three of these contradictions will play an important role throughout the book.

3-5 CONCLUSION

It is sometimes suggested that the simple model discussed above is of little use today, since the mixed economies of the advanced industrial world today are so unlike the system that Marx examined a century ago that it is misleading to use the same term for both. The basic characteristics of capitalism, as Marx described it, were that the mass of those who produce do not own the means of production, and in order to survive must sell their labour power (the capacity to work) to those who own the means of production: to capital. Capital is organized into separate firms which compete with each other for shares of the markets on which commodities are sold, for profitable fields of investment opportunities, for sources of raw material, etc. The different firms are then forced by competition to extort the maximum surplus value from the producers in order to accumulate more capital, which leads to mechanization, concentration and centralization of capital, alienation, and recurrent crises.

It can be argued that Marx's description of capitalism is in many ways more applicable to the late twentieth century than to the late nineteenth century, when many of the features that he emphasized—such as mechanization, the concentration of small firms into large monopolies, etc.—were still embryonic. Labour and capital remain antagonistic classes, accumulation of capital remains the motive force of the system, and the generation of profit still drives individual firms. Even the fact that a firm is nationalized may not change the capitalist nature of the labour process. Workers sell their labour power to it and are exploited (in the technical sense), while the firms are pressured to make profits in the market and to accumulate. The difference in ownership and the fact that the pressures on nationalized firms are both economic and political may therefore make little difference to the organization of the production process. The Marxist model, therefore, with elaborations that we discuss below, seems a useful basis for the analysis of current capitalism.

FURTHER READING

Many of the suggestions given for Chapter 2 are clearly relevant. But in the very first place must be the writing of Marx himself, in particular the three volumes of *Capital* (available in various editions including Pelican editions of Vols. 1 and 2, for which Mandel has written introductions). Two of Marx's short writings are *Value, Price and Profit* and *Wage Labour and Capital*.

Introductions to and overviews of Marxist economics can be found in Sweezy (1968), Dobb (1968), Mandel (1971), Fine (1975), Desai (1979), and Howard and King (1975). The two latter touch on the vigorous debate that has taken place on Marx's political economy in the light of Sraffa (1960), Morishima (1973), Morishima and Catephores (1978), and Steedman (1978). Further discussions of the issues raised can be found in Fine and Harris (1979).

Some aspects of Marx's theory of crisis are treated in Bleaney (1976). An important collection of essays on various aspects of Marxist economics can be found in Rowthorn (1980).

Applications of Marxism to contemporary capitalism are to be found in Baran and Sweezy (1968), Mandel (1975), and Cowling (1981) and in works listed earlier. See also material published in *Capital and Class*, *Cambridge Journal of Economics*, and *Economy and Society*.

FOUR

CLASS

Ron Smith

4-1 INTRODUCTION

The analysis in the previous chapter focused on the dynamics of capital as self-expanding value; but the evolution of capitalism as a mode of production is also determined by the struggle of capital with the workers whom it exploits and depends on for the generation of surplus. It is this struggle between the two main classes in capitalist societies that is the focus of this chapter. An individual's class position and the form of class relations depend ultimately on disparities in control over the means of production and over the labour process in which production takes place. Capitalists monopolize the means of production and control the production process, while workers are forced to depend on the sale of labour power for their livelihood, because they do not own the necessary means of production. Class position is significant because whether or not one depends on the sale of wage labour is a major determinant of position and status in society, and of the style and freedom in which one can live. Class relations are significant because they are a major determinant of the pattern of economic development. In the next section the analysis of class begins with an examination of the labour process, since roles within the labour process are central to class relations. In practice, the class structure in the UK, or in any other capitalist society, is more complicated than this pure two-class model with its simple capitalist–worker polarity, and the complexity of the actual structure must be considered. For instance, many managers, administrators, and other members of the new middle strata of white-collar workers do not fit easily into simple categories of worker or capitalist, and their contradictory class position requires analysis.

4-2 THE LABOUR PROCESS

The labour process is the term used to describe the productive activities by which people transform their natural environment in order to maintain themselves and reproduce the social formation in which they live. It includes both practices normally regarded as work, and a variety of practices that orthodox economic accounting tends not to treat as labour—e.g., housework, childcare, do-it-yourself. Orthodox economists base the distinction between productive and unproductive labour in national accounts not on the useful content of the labour—preparing food, looking after children, painting the house—but whether it becomes a commodity associated with a market transaction. Money payment associated with work becomes the only measure of its economic significance, and if there is no money payment the work does not appear as part of measured national product. What is important about the money payment for work, however, is that it corresponds to a specific social relation between buyer and seller of labour power. Thus labour processes can be categorized in two ways: according to the useful content of the labour, the use values produced; and according to the social relationships within which the labour is performed. While the cook in a restaurant and the housewife have in common the useful content of their activity (preparing food), the social relationships within which they work and the organization of the labour process are quite distinct. In the latter sense, the cook has more in common with the factory worker because they both work within capitalist relations of production and within a labour process that is subject to capitalist control. The domestic labour process of the housewife, and other non-capitalist labour processes in the society, while quite distinct and requiring separate analysis, are subordinate to the dominant capitalist mode of production. The organization of domestic labour will be influenced by the need of capital to sell commodities and the general development of the capitalist mode of production. It will change depending on the demand for women workers in production and the character of the commodities produced (such as labour-saving devices). To capital, the primary role of the family is to ensure the reproduction and supply of labour power; thus the character and type of workers required by industry will influence the organization and operation of the family. Many of the changes in the character of the family and domestic labour in Britain in the past two centuries reflect changes in the character of capitalist production.

To return to the capitalist labour process, orthodox economics usually regards its organization as determined by technology and market forces and has no concern for the form of social relations involved. However, these social relationships can be characterized by two features. The labourer works under the control of the capitalist to whom his labour power belongs, and the product is the property of the capitalist, not of the labourer, its immediate producer. Thus the relations are ones of domination—control of one group by another—and exploitation—the extraction of surplus labour in the form of surplus value by one group from another. Class antagonism thus arises directly out of the labour process, with conflict centring on control of the process of production and on the distribution of the product.

This dual source of conflict provides some clue to the contradictory position of some groups in society. For instance, as sellers of labour power, managers may be exploited, if they perform surplus labour. But they also have a substantial role in controlling the labour process, dominating others but being less controlled themselves. Thus in some respects they have a contradictory class location with regard to capitalists, who both own the means of production and control the labour process, and the core working class, who neither own nor control. But this contradiction generates polarization, and with the expansion of capital the managers and administrators are themselves becoming increasingly dominated. The spread of detailed corporate planning, together with control systems like Management by Objectives, reduces their freedom from control and also reduces their status. This is reflected in the spread of white-collar trade unions. Thus their class position is changing and influencing their class consciousness. This process of transformation is general; classes do not independently pre-exist, they emerge from conflicts generated by the economic process, and as the economy develops the class structure will change. A similar process of transformation is visible in the case of artisans and the self-employed. They are in the opposite position to managers. They own their own means of production and control their own labour power, but do not exploit or control others. Just as white-collar workers are being proletarianized by control systems within the firms, artisans were proletarianized by being driven out of business and forced to sell their labour power to capitalist firms.

At the same time as the capitalist labour process defines class relationships it defines associated areas of class struggle. Corresponding to the relations of domination and exploitation, class conflict arises over the control of the production process and the distribution of the output produced. The struggle over control and distribution takes place not merely at the level of production, but also at the level of politics (through organized class movements and pressure on the state) and the level of ideology (through the determination of class consciousness and the objectives of society). The political and ideological arenas of struggle will be returned to later in the chapter.

Within production, there are two dimensions to capitalist control: relative and absolute. Absolute control derives from the fact that by virtue of owning the means of production the capitalist ultimately has the freedom to close down the factory, dismiss the workforce, and move production somewhere else. The workers may, of course, oppose this by political pressure on the state, factory occupations to establish worker cooperatives, persuading other workers to 'black' or boycott the new production site, etc. The capitalist exercises relative control in determining the organization, pace, and methods of work within the plant—i.e., the use of labour power. The labour power purchased by the capitalist becomes variable capital, capable of performing a variable quantity of work and producing a variable quantity of output depending on the extent to which the capitalist can extract work from the labour power he has bought. The workers are intelligent human beings, guided by their own personal feelings and standards, which introduces an unpredictability into production. They are also alienated from the labour process in which they are dominated and exploited; they actively build organizations to resist management authority, and so threaten the organization of production. Thus discipline and supervision become necessary, and control of the labour process becomes the focus of struggle. The degree of control over the labour process that the worker is able to maintain will depend on the scarcity of any skills he or she has; labour market conditions, such as whether there is a large reserve army of alternative workers; and the strength of labour organization. These factors will determine a frontier of control over which conflict will centre, with capitalists continually attempting to extend their control, and workers resisting this. An essential craftsman who is difficult to replace will have much more control over the organization and pace of his work and the quality of the product produced than if the process is mechanized and subdivided, enabling it to be done by a series of limited operations carried out by unskilled workers. The power of the capitalist in this conflict derives from his control over the means of production, his ability to close down the operation, and the existence of a reserve army of labour with whom he can replace his workforce. The reserve army of labour plays a central role in conflicts over control and distribution, and deserves more careful examination.

4-3 THE RESERVE ARMY OF LABOUR

The worker's willingness to accept the discipline of capitalist production ultimately depends on the lack of an alternative. If he does not accept it, he will be fired and replaced; he may have difficulty finding another job, and even if he does, the new job will also involve accepting the same discipline. Thus the discipline depends on the capitalist having a source of alternative people willing to work, the reserve army, and the inability of the workers to maintain themselves and their families at an acceptable standard without work. What constitutes the accepted or reasonable standard will differ between societies and over time. While supplementary benefit is lavish compared with the workhouse, most people in the UK would regard it as woefully inadequate to maintain a family. To the extent that the reserve army becomes depleted or the alternative to work more attractive, labour discipline will break down and capitalists will have more difficulty in maintaining control of either the process of production or the distribution of the product. In the UK, the attractiveness of the alternative to work is largely determined by government social security policy and the policy adopted will reflect class conflict at a political level. This determines the extent to which pressures to minimize poverty and hardship can offset capitalist need to maintain the incentive to work. The battle is also fought at an ideological level, with tales of social security scroungers and the like.

The other disciplinary force, the reserve army, is inevitably depleted by the process of capital accumulation, which sucks more and more workers into production. But it is also replenished as labour requirements per unit output are reduced by restructuring of capital, mechanization, and automation, and as capital expands, destroying other modes of production, and releasing labour that can be used in capitalist production. The reserve army is not merely made up of the registered unemployed but of all the available sources of labour. Labour may be drawn from low productivity sectors, such as agriculture or small self-employment; women not working can be drawn into the labour force; and workers may be drawn from abroad. A major source of growth in the labour force in the advanced capitalist countries in the post-war period came from immigrants from poorer countries. These may become permanent residents, as tended to be the case in the UK, or merely temporary, able to be repatriated when employment demand turns down, as in the case of the German *Gastarbeiter* (guest workers). Women's participation rates also increased in most advanced capitalist countries in the post-war period; there was a substantial outflow of labour from agriculture in all countries except the UK and the US; and the proportion of self-employed in the workforce has also fallen. The ease with which this pool of potential labour can be drawn into capitalist production will vary, depending on political pressures and opposition by existing workers.

4-4 ARENAS OF CLASS STRUGGLE

The reserve army, with the threat of unemployment and replacement, is the major economic pressure that maintains labour discipline, but it is supplemented by ideological and political pressures. At the ideological level, if the political and economic system has acquired a certain legitimacy, and if the leadership of working class organization can be coopted and integrated into the existing power structure, labour discipline may be maintained with lower levels of unemployment. To maintain the apparent legitimacy of the system and working class compliance is likely to require that the working class obtain some reward from cooperation, such as growing real wages, social services, or other public benefits. For instance, it has been argued that the growth of revolutionary movements in the imperialist countries was inhibited partly because the working class in those countries were bought off with a share in the fruits of the exploitation of the colonies. Thus the working class in the advanced capitalist countries became an 'aristocracy of labour', with a material interest in maintaining imperialism.

If ideological or economic pressures do not maintain discipline, direct political force may be used to reduce the strength of working class bargaining power and organization. Such political measures may include legal restrictions, such as the Industrial Relations Act; the use of police to stop picketing; the use of the military to take over the running of services, etc. The relative balance between economic, ideological, and political methods of maintaining discipline varies substantially. In the fifties and the sixties in most of the advanced capitalist countries, high rates of growth and the strength of social democracy (the belief that social progress could be achieved within capitalism) as a political ideology among the working class created a widespread compliance with the system. In the seventies the trend was towards the maintenance of discipline by high unemployment and more direct repression. The reasons for these changes are examined later in the book.

All three methods of maintaining discipline are ultimately contradictory. High unemployment reduces the power of workers to attack the system, but it also depresses demand, preventing capitalists realizing the surplus extracted as profits. Cooption and integration of the workforce into the system can only go so far, for otherwise it threatens the capitalist control necessary for the maintenance of the system. These inherent limits mean that it is impossible to obtain real participatory democracy without threatening the system itself. In addition, while it may be possible for the system to provide real benefits, such as higher wages and better social services, to labour during a boom, in times of crisis to do so would severely damage profits. Hence at times when the system is under most strain it cannot provide the rewards necessary to legitimate it. Thus crisis re-creates the alienation of the workers from the system. At such times recourse is had to direct military or legal coercion, but this in itself is politically destabilizing, polarizing the mass of the workers against the state. It may also cause the state to be revealed as operating directly in the interests of capital, rather than appearing to represent society as a whole.

The effectiveness of each of these modes of discipline also depends on the strength of working class struggle against them. This struggle is carried on through a variety of organizations, most importantly the trade unions, but also political parties, pressure groups, and mass movements. Trade unions operate at all these levels. At the direct economic level in the workplace they battle with employers over wages and the organization of production. At an ideological level they are instrumental in creating class solidarity and consciousness. And at a political level they bargain with the government over economic policy and industrial relations. Their effectiveness at this level will depend on such factors as the form of their links with political parties and the contact of the leadership with the mass base. Although organized struggle proceeds through institutions such as unions and political parties, even if there are no such organizations struggle continues, since it is inevitably generated by the antagonistic form that social relations take within the labour process and society as a whole.

Under capitalism, working class organizations are themselves contradictory phenomena. On the one hand, they represent workers' interests in opposition to capital, thus threatening the structure of the system. But on the other hand, by bargaining, operating, and accepting, a role within the system, they stabilize and reproduce it. Thus in so far as it chooses to operate within the system, the Labour Party in government is forced to accept the role of administering and maintaining capital. Trade unions likewise may act as regulators of the production process, control the labour force, maintain order and discipline in industrial relations—all helping to provide the stable, compliant workforce needed by capital. Such 'responsible' unions are more common in the US and Germany but are not unknown in the UK. The main reason why such regulatory functions are less well developed in the UK seems to arise from the strength of the decentralized pattern of shopfloor bargaining organized around the shop steward as against the central union heirarchy. But given that these regulatory functions exist, it may be profitable for firms to support unions—e.g., by closed shop agreements—to encourage centralized disciplined bargaining. Unions may also be sectional, more concerned with the immediate interests of their members or a dominant group of their members than with the general interests of the working class as a whole. Thus the unions primarily represent the interests of the employed, not the unemployed, and of organized white males rather than women and blacks.

Many struggles within capitalist societies can be effectively analysed in class terms; in particular, patterns of economic policy, employment, accumulation, and distribution are determined by the antagonistic interests of capital and labour. But there are other antagonistic relations within society that cut across class boundaries. For instance, the subordination of black people and women that arises from the racist and patriarchal nature of the society gives rise to struggle by these groups against oppression. These other forms of oppression interact with class relations, and are influenced by the dominant capitalist relations of production, but they cannot merely be reduced to characteristics of capitalism or of class relations. The emphasis that will be placed on class relations and class struggle, as compared with these other antagonistic relationships, arises because, in the explanation of economic processes, class struggle and class relations—i.e., those deriving from the ownership and control of the means of production—play a central role. But this does not deny the importance of other forms of social conflict along racial, national, religious, or sexual lines. The pattern and extent of these conflicts will also have a great influence on class consciousness and solidarity.

4-5 CLASS CONSCIOUSNESS

Workers share real common interests, whether or not they are conscious of them, since they are all dominated and exploited by capital, and they are constituted into a class by virtue of their struggle against that domination. Many who do not work directly for capital, such as housewives or retired people, also share these interests and struggles since they are also forced to depend on the sale of labour power, either by other members of their family or at an earlier stage of their life. Class position is thus determined by the real material circumstances of people's lives, and the forces against which they struggle. These circumstances and forces will strongly influence, but not completely determine, people's perception of society. Thus class position and class consciousness need not coincide. Nor need class consciousness, which informs their judgement about community of interest in economic and political struggles, coincide with their perceptions of relative status, which governs their relations with others.

People rank themselves and others into groups (such as upper, middle, and lower class) on the basis of a variety of personal characteristics that they regard as important in determining relationships. The characteristics—such as income, education, accent, lifestyle, or occupation—that are regarded as important vary from person to person, and the way people perceive the structure of society also varies. It may be seen as divided into two antagonistic groups—them and us. If the division is into economic groups, they are likely to be referred to as classes, but the division may be on the basis of a racial, sexual, national, or age characterization. To the individual viewing society in these terms the determining characteristic of a relationship is whether it is with someone from their own group or the opposing one. Another subjective perception of society is in terms of a three-class model, which defines the person's relationship to those they may commonly deal with. People using this approach are likely to put themselves in the middle group, though the boundaries of the group will differ depending on the position of the person. To an earl, the groups might be royals, aristocracy, and commoners; to a craftsman, white-collar workers, skilled workers, and unskilled workers. Another view (often held by those whose status has changed) sees societies as made up of a large number of specialized groups, each with their own role and function, but which cannot be ranked in any simple hierarchical way. In the UK, official sources use the Registrar General's classification, constructed on the basis of occupation, and the ordering of these rankings may not mirror the classification by other characteristics or by income.

These perceptions, discussed above, derive from and organize people's relations to the community they live in, whereas class position derives from production relations. In some circumstances there may be very close correspondence between the two. For example, in isolated coal mining villages a common work experience, a homogeneous community, and family traditions all reinforce each other to create great solidarity and common perceptions and purpose. In a large city with a heterogeneous and mobile population working for many different employers, work relations and community relations do not correspond. Nor within any one individual need the various dimensions of class consciousness—such as militancy at work, political views, perception of personal relations within the community, etc.—match. The extent to which the working class is aware of and acts on the community of interests that arises from their common relation to the means of production depends on politics and ideology. But whether it is perceived or not, that community of interests arises directly from the organization of production.

A common explanation of Britain's poor economic performance puts the blame on the strength of the working class and, in particular, the trade unions. This does not seem plausible. Many of the characteristic problems of the British economy appeared in the late nineteenth century, before trade unions achieved their present position; and many of the differences between the UK and its more successful competitors (such as the organization of the financial system) have little connection with trade union strength. To examine these arguments requires a brief comparison of the UK with its competitors and a review of British economic history. This is provided in chapters 6 and 7. The position that will be taken in this book is that in explaining the British economy it is not just the question of trade union strength that needs to be examined, but the whole structure of class relations. This includes not only the organization of the working class, but also that of the capitalist class, and the relation between each of them and the state. It is in this whole structure, rather than just one aspect, that we can find some clues to Britain's poor performance.

FURTHER READING

Discussions of class from varying positions within a Marxist framework can be found in Hunt (1977), Poulantzas (1975a), Wright (1978), Therborn (1978), and Bottomore (1965).

Detailed material on class structure in Britain can be found in Westergaard and Resler (1975). For an earlier study see also Aaronovitch (1961).

An alternative Marxist view of the role of class struggle in determining the development of the British economy can be found in Kilpatrick and Lawson (1980).

FIVE

THE USE OF ECONOMIC EVIDENCE

Ron Smith

This chapter discusses the problems that arise in making the transition from the theoretical concepts used in the preceding chapters to empirical data. It also provides a brief introduction to the national accounts statistics that will be used throughout this book. Since some of the material is more detailed and technical, readers who wish to go directly to the main argument can skip this chapter and return to it for reference as required.

5-1 INTRODUCTION

Up to now the focus has been on theory, but for the rest of the book the emphasis will be on using the theoretical analysis to explain the empirical characteristics of the economy. In considering these empirical characteristics, a wide range of evidence will be used, including historical material, institutional descriptions, and, in particular, statistical data. Although of necessity a considerable use will be made of such economic statistics, they suffer from substantial problems, and great care and caution has to be exercised in their use. The purpose of this chapter is to introduce and to evaluate some of the main types of economic statistics to be used. For the purposes of a Marxist analysis, the main problem with much of the data is that they are constructed within an orthodox theoretical framework that is inappropriate for the problems being considered here. It is important to bear in mind that economic statistics, like the national output of a country, are not simple, direct observations, like that of the length of an object, but complex constructions based on a wide variety of assumptions and a specific theoretical structure. For instance, the construction of gross national product figures, as a measure of a country's output, derives from neo-classical and Keynesian theory, and if one had a different economic theory one would construct a different measure of economic output. Thus the Eastern European states use a quite different procedure for the measurement of output, based on the 'net material product system'. Given the close correspondence between the data and theoretical structures, the first problem that must be examined is the relation between theoretical Marxist categories and empirical measures. This relation will be illustrated by the case of the rate of profit.

5-2 MEASURING THE RATE OF PROFIT

Most of the discussion in the previous two chapters was conducted in value magnitudes: the value of any commodity is given by the socially necessary labour time embodied in it, either directly in the form of the labour expended on producing it, or indirectly through the labour time required to produce the means of production necessary to make it. What are observed are price or exchange value magnitudes. Except in special circumstances (when there is no exploitation or when the organic composition of capital is the same in each sector), the price and value magnitudes will be different. For instance, the rate of profit measured in values will not be the same as the rate of profit measured in price terms. This difference reflects a real feature of the capitalist economy, the complex relation between production and distribution. The surplus value produced depends on the labour power employed, while the amount of surplus value received depends on the capital advanced. To realize the surplus value produced, the capitalist has to sell the goods—i.e., exchange them for money. Since the capitalist will invest where the highest money return can be obtained, this will tend to equalize the money rate of profit between sectors. The process by which value magnitudes are transformed into prices thus corresponds to the social division of the surplus value produced, through exchange and competition. This process allows what are called 'prices of production' to be derived directly from values. Prices of production are themselves abstract concepts corresponding to the long-run or normal supply prices (i.e., when rates of profit are equalized) on which the capitalist bases calculations. Actual prices at which goods are exchanged may differ from these as a result of unexpected gluts or shortages, and the like. The abstraction of the theoretical concepts is not merely a characteristic of Marxist theory; the categories used in bourgeois theory are also not directly observable. Equilibrium wage, labour demand, and the expected rate of inflation are variables that relate only indirectly to observed magnitudes. What is required in both Marxist and orthodox empirical work is some correspondence relationship that specifies how the abstract theoretical category is related to measured magnitudes. Examples of such correspondence relations are assumptions that the labour market is in equilibrium and that observed employment is equal to both labour demand and labour supply; or that the expected rate of inflation is equal to the actual rate.

Within Marxist analysis, two main approaches have been taken to establishing the relationship between theory and statistical data. One approach is to construct direct statistical measures of the Marxist categories—rate of surplus value, organic composition, etc. The other approach is to use Marxist theory to explain the movements in the orthodox statistics. Wolff (1979) provides a good example of the use of the first approach and Weisskopf (1979) of the second, in both cases applied to an analysis of the rate of profit in the US. Throughout most of this book we shall use the second approach.

Wolff uses the inter-industry input–output matrix and labour inputs for each industry to derive direct and indirect labour required per dollar of output in each industry, labour values; and he uses consumption data to derive the value of labour power. From these the rate of surplus value can be calculated. Using other input–output data, the organic composition, the general rate of profit, and the prices of production can also be calculated. This was done for four years: 1947, 1958, 1963, and 1967. In each of these years over 90 per cent of the variation in relative prices of production was explained by the variation in relative labour values. Because of this close correlation, he found that empirically the general rate of profit (calculated using prices of production) was closely related to the value rate of profit. Construction of estimates of theoretical magnitudes in this way requires both a large amount of effort and resources plus various simplifying assumptions, some of which are controversial. This is true both for Marxist variables, like labour values, and orthodox ones, like national income. The difference is that the resources have been devoted to obtaining estimates of the orthodox variables on a very much larger scale. Thus by and large we are forced to use the orthodox measures, and to try to show the power of Marxist analysis in being able to explain estimates constructed under different theoretical assumptions. The method of doing this can be illustrated by using again the example of the rate of profit.

The value rate of profit was given as $s/(c+v)$, where s is surplus value, c constant capital (means of production), and v variable capital (labour power). The money rate of profit is usually given by P/K, where P is total money profits, and K the money value of the capital stock. There are thus two major differences. One is the transformation from value to price magnitudes; the other is the use of total capital stock, rather than the sum of constant plus variable capital. The degree of correspondence between the two measures is controversial among Marxist economists. Wolff's work on the US showed substantial correspondence between the value rate of profit, the general rate of profit in prices of production, and various orthodox estimates of the money rate of profit. Although there are not comparable comparisons for the UK, in general, our position is that the money rate of profit for the economy as a whole will be strongly influenced by the value rate. One can go a step further and decompose the rate of profit in terms of the major factors determining it. Suppose that, with full capacity working, the available capital stock can produce a level of output Q, and that the actual level produced in a period is Y (all the variables measured in price terms). Then

$$\frac{P}{K} = \frac{P}{Y} \cdot \frac{Q}{K} \cdot \frac{Y}{Q}$$

obtained by multiplying P/K by Y/Y and Q/Q and rearranging. This equation says that the rate of profit is equal to the product of the share of profits in income, the full capacity output–capital ratio, and the rate of utilization. The share of profit will reflect movements in the rate of exploitation, the capacity output–capital ratio, the organic composition of capital, the rate of utilization, the smoothness of the circuits of capital, and the extent of any realization problems. Weisskopf (1979) uses this decomposition (together with more complex ones) to identify the relative influence of changes in the rate of exploitation, rising organic composition of capital, and realization failures in causing the fall in the rate of profit and generating crisis.

But even if a procedure has been established for relating orthodox measures to Marxist categories, there is a further problem in that there are a plethora of different orthodox measures of the rate of profit. The orthodox literature on the appropriate measure of the rate of profit is large and controversial, and the issues raised by it will be returned to a number of times in the book. Here we shall pose some of the questions.

Measurement of the Money Value of Capital Stock (K)

Consider a machine owned by a firm. There are three ways it could be valued: the original cost, reduced for deterioration or depreciation; the price the firm would get were it sold; and its worth to the firm in terms of the present value of the future profits it generates. In general, the three values will not coincide, because of uncertainty, price changes, absence of extensive secondhand markets, etc. There are also problems in calculating depreciation: should the total depreciation set against profits over the lifetime of the machine equal the original cost of the machine (historic cost depreciation) or the cost of buying a new one when it collapses (replacement cost depreciation)? There is also a number of different ways of spreading the depreciation over the lifetime of the machine. For economic purposes the depreciation figures published in company accounts may be of little use, since they are set partly to minimize tax liability, and as tax laws change so does the way companies calculate depreciation. When one moves from trying to establish the value of an individual machine to estimating aggregate real capital stock, the problems multiply. In fact, except under very special and implausible assumptions, it is impossible to construct a theoretically consistent measure of aggregate capital stock. The problems are discussed in Harcourt (1972). Despite their questionable theoretical status, measures of aggregate capital stock are widely used, and there is a wide variety of estimates, which differ according to how depreciation is treated, and so on. Details on how the various official UK capital stock figures are constructed can be found in Griffin (1976); these differ from measures based on companies' own valuation of their assets.

Measurement of Total Profits (*P*)

Published figures on aggregate profits differ in a wide variety of ways. Coverage by sector varies, and profits in manufacturing move differently from services. The profits of financial institutions are often excluded from the coverage because of the difficulty of even defining their profits consistently. Measures that include the profits from North Sea oil move differently from those that do not. What is included in profit varies considerably (e.g., it makes a large difference whether profits from overseas operations are included or whether the figures are pre- or post-tax) and there are various different ways of allowing for the effects of inflation to obtain a measure of real profits. The figure might be net of depreciation either at historic or replacement cost; it might be net or gross of stock appreciation (the capital gain arising from the appreciation in the value of inventories of raw materials or finished products held by the firm); and it may or may not be corrected for the effect of inflation in reducing the real value of company debt. A discussion of some of the measures can be found in Chapter 18. Similar problems arise at the level of company financial reports, and there is great scope for creative accounting, which allows the published profit figure to be massaged within considerable limits.

In combination, the various definitions of profit and capital stock allow a vast range of measures for 'the rate of profit' to be constructed, and these measures may tell very different stories about what is happening to profitability. Given this, there are two points to bear in mind. Firstly, it is essential to check the exact definition used and note the coverage; the treatment of depreciation, stock appreciation, taxation, etc.; and the source of the numbers. Second, there is no unique correct measure; which measure is appropriate depends on the specific theoretical question concerned. For instance, a measure that reflects the real rate of return on capital advanced on production in the UK by a firm will be different from the measure of total surplus realized. The total surplus received by a firm will come from its activities not merely in the sphere of production, but also in the sphere of circulation, by buying and selling commodities and raw materials, borrowing and lending in financial markets, etc. Thus it may be earning healthy profits overall as a result of its speculative activities in financial, commodity, or property markets, but be earning nothing in production.

Bearing in mind the main points of this section—the role of theory in the construction and interpretation of statistical data, and the need for concern and scepticism about the details of their definition and construction—let us turn from profits to the major sourse of economic data, the national income accounts.

5-3 NATIONAL INCOME

The primary figure used to characterize the wealth or productivity of a country is its *per capita* national income. This is the average income, or production, or expenditure per person in the country. This equality arises because the national income accounts are centred around the identity that the total money value of supply (production or output) is equal to the value of demand (sales or expenditure), which is equal to total incomes (wages plus profit). This equality between total income output and expenditure provides three different ways of looking at the same total, although in practice measurement errors require 'residuals' or 'balancing items' to be added to the accounts to ensure that the three sides are equal. In addition there is a variety of different measures used (such as gross domestic product, net national product, etc.), depending on whether certain items are included or excluded from the totals. The relation between these various measures is discussed below, but first consider the variations between countries for one measure, gross domestic product (GDP). For comparability, each country's GDP is divided by its population and expressed in US dollars. The World Bank publication *World Tables* (1976) gives 1973 *per capita* GDP in US dollars for 145 countries. The UK, with a *per capita* income of $3060, ranked twenty-second, less than half the US figure of $6200. Since 1973 Britain has sunk further down the league table. Then the highest centrally planned economy, East Germany, ranked twenty-fourth, with a *per capita* income of $3000, although by 1977 it had overtaken the UK. India, with a *per capita* income of only $120, ranked one hundred and twenty-second.

Having introduced these figures, which are very widely used, some qualifications must be made, and such qualifications will apply in various forms to all the data used below. In comparing countries, we are looking at a snapshot recording a moment in time, and the measures can be very sensitive to the year in which the picture is taken. One country may be at a cyclical peak, another in a slump, so that the relationship between them may be atypical. In general, 1973 was a peak year for most industrial countries, and they were at roughly similar points in the cycle. Of course, for some variables—primary product prices, for instance—1973 would not be a good choice. Whether the year is typical or not, there remains the problem that taking just one observation may be misleading, because although two countries look similar in a particular year, they may be moving in quite different directions, with different histories and prospects for development.

A second problem is that international comparisons of monetary values have to be made in some common currency. Totals in rupees and yen are not directly comparable, and usually for comparison they are both converted to dollars, using some exchange rate that says how many rupees can be obtained for a yen. However, for many currencies, especially those of planned economies, there exist multiple exchange rates—different rates for different types of transaction. Tourists and exporters face different rates, for instance. This facilitates the planning and control of foreign trade and capital movements but causes statisticians trouble. Alternatively, the exchange rate may be pegged by the government at a level that does not represent a real comparison of the relative purchasing power of the two currencies, and maintained at that level by intervention in the foreign exchange market, protection, and exchange controls on the movement of funds. There may then exist a black market rate very different from the official one.

But even if there are not these problems, it is not clear what is being measured. Conceptually, the question is what someone with the average income of the country would have relative to the inhabitants of other countries were they all to convert their incomes into dollars. Whatever this measures, it is clearly not a measure of relative standard of living. In India a person with an income of $500 a year is relatively affluent; in New York $500 is not enough to keep body and soul together. Relative price differences further complicate matters. In the US, ownership of a car is very cheap and personal servants an expensive luxury—the reverse of the situation in India. The problems remain, although they are less extreme, when comparing industrialized countries. At official exchange rates, 1970 value added per employee was 48 per cent higher in West Germany than in the UK, while at purchasing power parity rates it was only 28 per cent higher (*National Institute Economic Review*, August 1976). In addition, the use of money flows may be a misleading indicator of welfare: higher incomes may be more than offset by worse pollution and a reduced quality of life, which are not reflected in the marketed output measured by GDP.

International comparisons of *per capita* income or the standard of living present the most difficult problems, partly because it is not clear what is being measured. Some other variables can be compared more easily, and sometimes the problems can be reduced by comparing not absolute levels but rates of growth or percentage shares of some total. Nonetheless, it is important to keep in mind the need to be sceptical about the type of economic and social data that will be used intensively throughout this book. Economists rely heavily on the analysis of aggregate statistical data, between countries or over time, but it is necessary to beware the pitfalls that surround these tools.

One might be justified in concluding that the problems involved are so great that it is pointless to attempt the exercise. However, if used with care, the data can provide some useful but limited information. What must not be done is to treat the figures as unproblematic facts. Figures on the national income of the UK are not direct observations but complex constructions based on neo-classical and Keynesian economic theory.

5-4   THE INCOME–EXPENDITURE ACCOUNTS

The structure of the accounts can be seen from Tables 5–1 to 5–4, which examine the composition of gross domestic product from the expenditure, income, and output sides respectively. The data are taken from the 1979 edition of *National Income and Expenditure* (the Blue Book).

Expenditure

Table 5-1 gives the components of expenditure. Item 2 is the current expenditure on goods and services (final consumption) by central government and local authorities (general government). Capital expenditure by the government (its investment) is included in gross domestic fixed capital formation (GDFCF); transfer payments, such as pensions and debt interest are not included, since they do not constitute a claim on resources by the government. Item 3 is gross domestic fixed capital formation, or total investment by public and private sectors. To make total expenditure equal total production, some allowance must be made for unsold goods held by firms. This is treated as a component of demand called 'stockbuilding'. It consists only of the value of the physical increase in the amount of stocks and work in progress. If, because of inflation, the value of a given amount of stocks increases, this is called 'stock appreciation'. The sum of the first four items is called 'total domestic expenditure', to which is added exports to give total final expenditure. But not all this expenditure corresponds to UK production, since the consumption, investment, etc., will be partly met from abroad, so imports must be subtracted to give gross domestic product at market prices. But this total still does not correspond to the value of production, since the amount people spend differs from what producers receive by the amount of any indirect taxes and subsidies. These are allowed for in the factor cost adjustment, item 8, which is taxes on expenditure less subsidies. This is subtracted from market price GDP to give factor cost GDP, the most commonly used measure of output or income.

Domestic measures correspond to income generated within the boundaries of the UK; to obtain national income—i.e., the total earned by UK citizens—one must add the income earned by UK citizens outside the UK, and subtract income earned within the UK by foreigners. The difference between the two, net property income from abroad, is positive and is added to GDP to give gross national product. All the figures considered so far are gross in that they include expenditure that merely goes to make good deterioration in the capital stock by replacement investment. If this capital consumption or depreciation is subtracted, net national product is obtained. The term 'national income' is sometimes used to refer specifically to NNP, or sometimes to any of the measures in general. In principle, NNP is the amount a nation could spend on consumption while keeping its real capital stock intact.

Reliability

The expenditure estimate of GDP is regarded as the benchmark, and a residual is added to the estimates of GDP from the income and output accounts to make them balance with the expenditure estimate. This is not to say that the expenditure estimate is more reliable than the others, and for some purposes a compromise estimate, an average of the estimates, is used. The reliability of the series varies—stockbuilding, for instance, is

Table 5-1 The expenditure account, 1978 (Current prices)

	£ billion	% GDP
1. Consumers' expenditure	96.086	67.7
2. General government final consumption	32.693	23.0
3. GDFCF	29.218	20.6
4. Stockbuilding	1.528	1.1
5. Exports of goods and services	47.636	33.5
6. Imports of goods and services	−45.522	−32.1
7. GDP at market prices	161.639	113.8
8. Factor cost adjustment	−19.640	−13.8
9. GDP at factor cost	141.999	100.0
10. Net property income from abroad	0.836	0.6
11. GNP at factor cost	142.835	100.6
12. Capital consumption	−18.310	−12.9
13. Net national product (NNP)	124.525	87.7

Source: National Income and Expenditure (1979).

much less reliable than consumer expenditure. Series that are obtained as the difference between two large numbers, like the balance of payments (exports minus imports) or savings (income minus consumption), will be likely to have large percentage errors. The accuracy of the figures depends on the source of information, and much of the data comes from tax records where respondents may have incentives not to be completely honest. The size of the 'black economy' of unrecorded transactions, usually made in cash to evade tax, has been estimated at between 5 and 10 per cent of GNP, although the figures are speculative. The quality of the figures also reflects administrative arrangements. In the mid sixties the Labour government reduced the paper work legally required of exporters. This led to a considerable volume of exports not being recorded, and the balance of payments appearing much worse than it was. Policy actions were taken on the basis of the incorrect payments figures, and the error was only discovered some years later, when inconsistencies between UK exports to certain countries and their imports from the UK appeared.

A further problem in using the data is that they are regularly revised, so that the estimate for GDP for 1970 will be different in each of the subsequent Blue Books. For some variables, the revisions can be very large and make a significant difference to any judgement about what was happening.

Income and Product

From Table 5-2 it can be seen that the major component of income is that from employment, wages, and salaries, which accounts for almost 70 per cent of GDP. Income from self-employment accounts for another 10 per

Table 5-2 The income account, 1978

	£ billion	% GDP
Income from employment	98.156	69.2
Income from self-employment	13.245	9.3
Gross trading profits of companies	17.055	12.0
Gross trading surplus of public corporations	5.412	3.8
Gross trading surplus of general government	0.184	0.1
Rent	9.842	6.9
Consumption of non-trading capital	1.283	0.9
Stock appreciation	−4.249	−3.0
GDP (income based)	140.928	99.2
Residual error	1.071	0.8
GDP (expenditure based)	141.999	100.0

Source: National Income and Expenditure (1979).

cent; profits of companies and nationalized industries 15 per cent; and rent just over 5 per cent. There are then various adjustments to make the accounts balance consistently. Because of all the problems of definition discussed in Section 5-2, the figure in Table 5-2 cannot be accepted uncritically as a measure of the share of profit.

Table 5-3 disaggregates output by industry. Included as an industry is ownership of dwellings, which is thought of as a type of production corresponding to rental income from dwellings. The financial adjustment corresponds to net receipts of interest by financial institutions. The energy industries that span the mining and quarrying and gas, electricity, and water categories accounted for 5.9 per cent of GDP, and this percentage is increasing rapidly with the development of North Sea oil.

Finally, Table 5-4 shows percentages of GDP and employment by sector in 1968 and 1978. The private sector accounts for over 70 per cent of both output and employment in both years, although its share has fallen slightly.

Table 5-3 Output account by industry, 1978

	£ billion	% GDP
Agriculture, forestry and fishing	3.715	2.6
Mining and Quarrying	4.467	3.2
Manufacturing	40.690	28.7
Construction	8.610	6.1
Gas, electricity, and water	4.772	3.4
Transport and communication	11.688	8.2
Distributive trades	14.687	10.3
Finance	11.268	7.9
Ownership of dwellings	8.578	6.0
Public administration and defence	10.197	7.2
Public health and education services	9.674	6.8
Other services	18.680	13.1
Total	147.026	103.5
Adjustment for financial services	−6.098	−4.3
Residual error	1.071	0.8
GDP at factor cost	141.999	100.0

Source: National Income and Expenditure '(1979).

5-5 PRICE INDEXES

Output is usually measured by 'real' or 'constant price' GDP. To construct this, the amounts produced or spent are revalued in terms of what they would have cost in some base year. The base year used in the 1979 Blue Book is 1975, and the estimate of what GDP would have been in 1978 had 1975 prices ruled was £100 billion, as compared with a figure in 1978 prices of £142 billion. The difference is accounted for by the inflation between 1975 and 1978. Formally, suppose production is made up of n goods, and production of each in 1978 is denoted by $q_1 \ldots q_n$, and their prices $p_1 \ldots p_n$. Then the total value of production in 1978 is

$$p_1q_1 + p_2q_2 \ldots p_nq_n = {}_i\sum p_iq_i$$

Table 5-4 GDP and employment by sector, 1968 and 1978

	% GDP		% employment	
	1968	1978	1968	1978
Private sector	73.0	70.4	74.2	70.4
Public corporations	10.8	11.6	8.3	8.3
Central government	6.6	7.5	7.6	9.3
Local authorities	8.6	9.7	9.8	12.1

Source: National Income and Expenditure (1979).

at 1978 prices. Similarly if $q_1^1 \ldots q_n^1$, and $p_1^1 \ldots p_n^1$ were the quantities and prices in 1975, $\sum p_i^1 q_i^1$ is the total value in 1975 at 1975 prices. These correspond to current price measures of GDP in 1978 and 1975 respectively. GDP in 1978 at 1975 prices is then

$$\sum p_i^1 q_i$$

It is a weighted sum of the quantities produced in 1978, weighted by 1975 prices. A measure of the extent of inflation between the two years can be obtained as the ratio of the current price to constant price measures for 1978:

$$\frac{\sum p_i q_i}{\sum p_i^1 q_i}$$

This is called the implicit price deflator and is an index number that compares the average level of prices in 1978 (the p_i) with the average level in 1975 (the p_i^1) using the 1978 quantities q_i as weights. Technically it is called a 'Paasche' index, one that uses current (1978) quantities as weights. An alternative widely used method is to construct a 'Laspeyres' index that uses base (1975) quantities as weights:

$$\frac{\sum p_i q_i^1}{\sum p_i^1 q_i^1}$$

The two indexes will in general differ. If relative prices and quantities are negatively related (i.e., if q_i/q_j falls as p_i/p_j rises, where i and j are different goods) because of substitution against goods whose relative price has risen, then the Laspeyres index will overestimate inflation and the Paasche underestimate it.

The fact that there exists a wide range of ways in which an index of prices can be constructed means that one can obtain a lot of different estimates of the rate of inflation. The estimates will differ according to the coverage of the index (i.e., which prices are included in it); the method of construction; which base year is used; and various other factors. For instance, between 1968 and 1978 the GDP deflator (the index of total home costs per unit output) rose by 206 per cent; the consumers' expenditure deflator 193 per cent; the retail price index by 202 per cent; and the food component of the retail price index by 259 per cent. A 200 per cent increase corresponds to prices tripling over the period.

5-6 FINANCIAL FLOWS

An alternative approach to the analysis of expenditure and income given above involves the consideration of the financial flows that result from differences between income and expenditure. In addition to an income–expenditure account, the public and private sectors have a capital account, which records their saving (the difference between income and expenditure) and their investment in fixed capital—dwellings, plant and equipment, etc. For each sector, savings and investment do not necessarily balance, leaving a surplus, which can be lent to other sectors, or a deficit to be covered by borrowing. Corresponding to this borrowing and lending is a transfer of financial assets, IOUs. So if a household lends to the government it acquires a financial asset in the form of a gilt-edged security. Deposits with banks also count as financial assets. There is also a sector labelled the overseas sector, which, although it does not save and invest in the same way, is involved in the transfer of financial assets, since a balance of payments deficit means that the rest of the world, the overseas sector, lends money to the UK by holding sterling—which is just another form of IOU.

The relation between these financial flows and this expenditure can be easily seen in a simple case where it is assumed that the only source of government tax revenue is an expenditure tax. Thus the income expenditure account can be written

$$Y = C + I + G - T + X - M$$

where Y is income, gross domestic product at factor cost; C private consumption; I private investment; G total government expenditure on goods and services; T expenditure taxes; X exports; and M imports. This is just a simplified version of Table 5-2 in symbols. It will be noticed that the balance of payments is just equal to the difference between income and domestic expenditure:

$$Y - (C + I + G - T) = X - M$$

This is what is meant by saying that a balance of payments deficit indicates that the UK is spending more than it earns. Private savings $S = Y - C$, income minus consumption, so the equation can be rewritten

$$S - I - G + T - X + M = 0 \quad \text{or} \quad (S - I) + (T - G) + (M - X) = 0$$

The three terms are net acquisition of financial assets (NAFA) by the private, public, and overseas sectors respectively. The equation says that all borrowing and lending cancels out, since for every borrower there must be a lender.

Private NAFA is the difference between savings and investment; public NAFA the government surplus $(T - G)$ and overseas NAFA the balance of payments deficit $(M - X)$. When there is a government deficit the government must borrow to finance it, (i.e., sell financial assets), and when there is a balance of payments deficit, the overseas sector must lend to the UK (acquire financial assets) to finance that. As always with economic accounts, there are a number of adjustments that have to be made to try to make the accounts balance. In particular, public sector NAFA differs somewhat from the public sector borrowing requirement (PSBR), the usual measure of the government deficit. This is largely because the borrowing requirement is the gross amount that must be financed, and the government also lends at the same time, and this lending is netted out in NAFA. There is also a substantial balancing item in the accounts to ensure that the three do add up to zero. Since the NAFA for any one sector is the negative of that for all the others combined, one can think of the sector that borrows as being financed by the others. At a theoretical level one might also ask what mechanism ensures that the amount that one sector wishes to lend or borrow just matches what the other sectors borrow or lend. This equality is usually described as being brought about by changes in the level of income, interest rates, or exchange rates, which change the decisions of the sectors and bring them into equilibrium.

Table 5-5 Net acquisition of financial assets (£m)

	1968	1973	1978
Personal sector	526	2305	11 007
Industrial and commercial companies	−39	−1308	−2183
Financial companies and institutions	−160	−270	−986
Total private sector	327	727	7838
Public corporations	−725	−774	−1093
Central government	970	• 173	−5436
Local authorities	−1189	−2057	−1348
Total public sector	−944	−2658	−7877
Overseas sector	242	934	−1032
Residual	375	997	1071

Source: National Income and Expenditure (1979), Table 13.1.

Table 5-5 shows financial surplus and deficit for each sector in 1968, 1973, and 1978. In all three years the personal sector was the major source of finance; the private sector was a net lender and the public sector a net borrower. In 1968 and 1973 the central government was in surplus and the balance of payments in deficit (the overseas sector a net lender); in 1978 the central government was in deficit and the balance of payments in surplus. Although this picture looks simple, there are substantial conceptual difficulties involved in interpreting these accounts, even within an orthodox framework. A major problem concerns the treatment of inflation, which reduces the real value of financial assets. Thus much of the saving recorded in these accounts merely represents an attempt to keep the real value of monetary assets constant in the face of rising prices, rather than an increase in the assets. If these wealth effects of inflation are taken into account, the government was running a surplus in 1978. This happens because inflation reduces the real value of the debt the government has to repay but not the real value of the assets it owns, like the capital stock of the nationalized industries, its land holdings, etc. These problems will be returned to in Chapter 15, when a Marxist interpretation of financial relations will be discussed. But now, having introduced some of the sources of information that will be used, we are ready to turn to our main task, the empirical examination of British capitalism.

FURTHER READING

Most standard macro-economic textbooks explain the structure of national income accounts, although usually in an uncritical way. Well-known texts are by Rowan, and Prest and Coppock (1978).

Parker and Harcourt (1969) provide a set of useful readings on the concept and measurement of income, and Usher (1968) of the meaning and significance of the numbers produced. A more general examination of the use of social statistics can be found in Irvine *et al.* (1979).

For the detailed statistical series see the annual Blue Books on *National Income and Expenditure, Economic Trends, Annual Supplement*, and other central statistical office publications.

THE RELATIVE DECLINE OF THE UK

Sam Aaronovitch

6-1 STRUCTURE OF CLASS RELATIONSHIPS

This book concerns itself with the characteristics and processes of British capitalism and the British economy. Inevitably, the first characteristic that must be examined is Britain's economic decline relative to other advanced capitalist economies. Some conventional statistics of this relative decline are set out in Table 6-1, which compares the UK with five other countries: Japan, France, West Germany, Italy, and the US. The first row gives the growth rates in real GDP for the period 1955–73; Britain's is the lowest. Data for 1973 are used in this Table because it marks the end of the long

Table 6-1 The relative decline of the UK: some indices

	UK	Japan	France	West Germany	Italy	US
Annual growth rate in real GDP 1955–73 (%)	2.8	9.9	5.6	5.4	5.2	3.6
Annual growth rate in real GDP 1973–9 (%)	1.1	4.3	3.3	2.5	3.9	2.5
Annual growth rate in manufacturing output 1955–73 (%)	3.1	13.9	6.6	6.8	7.2	3.6
Share in value of world exports of manufactures (%)						
1955	19.8	5.1	9.3	15.5	3.4	24.5
1973	9.3	13.6	10.2	20.3	7.5	16.1
Growth in labour productivity (%)						
Industry 1960–69	3.3	9.1	5.2	5.4	5.8	2.9
69–73	3.9	7.5	5.0	4.4	3.8	3.4
Total 1960–69	2.3	8.9	4.9	4.8	6.5	2.6
69–73	2.7	8.1	4.4	4.2	4.2	1.6
Share of Investment in GDP 1973 (%)	19.8	36.6	24.0	24.6	20.9	18.5
1973 *Per capita* GDP, US $	3060	3630	4540	5320	2450	6200

Source: OECD.

post-war boom, and it was a year in which all of these economies were at cyclical peaks. Row 2 indicates that for all the countries, growth rates were much lower during 1973–9, but that Britain's remained the lowest. The other feature to notice through the Table is that, except with respect to *per capita* income, there are great similarities between the UK and the US. As the Table shows, the UK not only had a lower growth of total GDP, but a lower growth of manufacturing output too; its share in world exports halved, while all the other countries increased theirs; it had a very slow growth in labour productivity; and a low share of investment. As a consequence of slow accumulation and lack of competitiveness, it increasingly became the poor relation of advanced capitalism. In explaining the differing patterns of behaviour among this group of countries, it is necessary to consider whether their different histories are related to differences in the underlying structure of society. The characteristic of the structure that we propose to examine here is that of their class relationships. How is this structure to be defined?

First, it is to be defined by the characteristics of the *dominant* class in the economy. These may be separated into (a) the direction or orientation of that class; (b) the relationship between the groups or fractions that constitute it; (c) the degree of political and organizational cohesion that it possesses and its influence on state policy and practice; (d) its relations with other classes, and especially to the working class and its organizations.

Second, it is defined by the role of the state, which in turn involves its relationship to the main classes of capital and labour as well as to other classes and interest groups. This will have an important influence on the objectives of the state and the character of its intervention in the economy.

Third, it is defined by the position of the working class in the labour–capital relationships; the supply and demand for labour; the degree of political and industrial organization of the working class; and cohesion of its (changing) components.

Analysing the structure of class relationships can, we suggest, throw light on the different course of development of advanced capitalist economies. Economists typically explain these differences in growth by factors like the rate of investment; but such factors may, in this context, be considered more as *proximate* causes. It seems clear, for instance, that the relationship between investment and growth is not invariant; investment seems necessary but not sufficient for growth. Rates of investment may be considered as 'embedded' in particular economic and class structures and can only be understood in those contexts.

We are not proposing to examine all these relationships in one chapter. In particular, detailed discussions on the state and on the working class will be found elsewhere in the book (Chapters 8 and 20). Nor can we examine *all* advanced capitalist economies. We consider here four other countries together with the UK. The group, which we shall call *The Four*, is made up of West Germany, Japan, France, and Italy—a group characterized by much higher average growth rates than the UK economy for the post-war period. *The Four* obviously have significant differences between themselves, but there are sufficient common features in contrast with the UK to help us illuminate the differences in growth and directions.

Our main concern is with the post-1945 period, but we have to consider—especially in the case of West Germany and Japan—deep-rooted forces and continuities with the period prior to 1945. In the case of France and Italy we observe breaks with the past that have made it possible to bracket these countries with West Germany and Japan in certain respects.

We have not chosen to contrast the UK with the USA; the two countries in fact show some interesting similarities. Both have much lower average growth rates of productivity than other OECD countries and correspondingly lower shares of investment. Capital in both countries is highly international by way of the multi-national companies and large foreign investments; and they both have imperialist traditions and high military expenditures. The international role of the US is examined in some detail in Chapters 12 and 13 and important similarities in the structure of class relationships will appear, even though they are at different stages in their relative decline.

6-2 CHARACTERISTICS OF THE DOMINANT CLASS

We look first at the direction and orientation of that class. Of course, in all these countries the general orientation is the same—i.e., towards profitable accumulation—but the way this goal is achieved does vary between countries.

Put in its broadest form, the thesis we are proposing is that the perspectives of capital in *The Four* were centred on domestic growth and accumulation, whereas in the UK the perspective of the dominant groups was focused on the world role of British capital (with the state operating to support this role politically, militarily, and ideologically).

In the course of time, the policies followed by UK capital and governments produced a severe conflict of interest between developing the productive base of the UK economy and the world-wide interests of British-owned capital. As is well known, towards the end of the last century Britain's world dominance in manufacturing and trade had already come under pressure and British capital was seeking to defend a world role and the industrial and financial structures that had been built up to buttress that role. That defensiveness has been a marked feature in all succeeding periods. The retreat from dominance was carried out in two main directions. One was the expansion of Britain's imperial role, where privileged access to markets was possible using formal or informal control. The other was the further development of the City of London and of allied services expressed in the growth of invisible exports (see Hobsbawm, 1969).

The Four, on the other hand (especially Japan and West Germany), had to *break* their way into the world market. In doing so they created (using the combined resources of capital and state) powerful modern industries which were the base for export of goods but not for capital export to the same extent. Such export-led growth had favourable effects because it generated income within the economy while stimulating investment and capacity expansion which could meet increasing domestic demand.

The situation was well put by W. A. Lewis (if in a rather voluntaristic style) when he wrote (in Shonfield, 1958, p. 259):

> The Germans had an irresistible urge to invest in steel, machinery, chemicals and such in the last decades of the nineteenth century, and broke into export markets, using whatever techniques were necessary. The British, by momentum and tradition, were otherwise occupied. In earlier decades, they had had an irresistible urge to invest in cotton and in iron, which had carried them breaking into world markets with the necessary techniques. The rate of expansion which this permitted slowed down after 1860, but rather than invest at home at the old rate in the newer industries, they slowed down home investment to the pace of cotton and iron and put their money instead into foreign investment in agricultural countries, where it financed sales of cotton and railway materials without adding to Britain's productive capacity.

Whereas Germany, for instance, concentrated on the markets of Europe, British goods and finance were directed mainly at the empire and spheres of influence. Not surprisingly, British capital pioneered the great multi-national companies concerned with exploiting raw materials and natural resources and therefore preoccupied with their overseas role (Unilever and Dunlop, the oil companies, the mining companies in Southern Africa, etc.; the financial conglomerates operating in Shanghai and Hong Kong, such as the Jardine Matheson group).

In the UK, nationalism was implicit (the effortless superiority of the English). In Japan, the conditions under which the Meiji restoration took place, releasing the conditions for Japanese capitalist growth, and similarly the unification of Germany under Prussian domination, produced and mobilized strong nationalist ideologies. These ideologies, attached to the idea of economic expansion, led to conscious decisions on systems of education and technical training directly geared to manufacturing and trade, with a heavy emphasis on the social standing of the businessman. It is a familiar charge that in the UK education tended to be anti- or non-scientific, that no comparable system of technical training and education existed, and that education for the ruling elite was directed at the civil service (home and colonial), and at finance, but not at business. In general, businessmen in manufacturing and trade, unlike the political dynasties and those in finance and the City, were not educated at public schools or universities (or, if they went to public schools, they left to go into business without 'wasting' their time at university). The fusion of aristocratic and business circles in Britain weakened the drive for industrial expansion and technological advance.

Second, we look at the relationships between the groups or fractions that constitute that class. Obviously, within the class of owners and controllers of capital there are many kinds of groupings and differing interests. But there is one difference—related to, though not identical with, the functional difference in circuits of capital as between financial and industrial capital— that seems to us of great importance in examining the differences in development between *The Four* and the UK. Financial capital, we recall, is capital concerned with the growth of credit by which money can be used as capital. Industrial capital is what it says: capital functioning in industry. The much greater degree of separation of financial from industrial capital in the UK as compared with *The Four* has often been noted. This separation reinforced the potential and actual conflict between national and international perspectives for UK capital. The export of capital from the UK started early (around the time of the Napoleonic Wars) and became massive by the First World War. United Kingdom manufacturing and trading dominance created a special place for sterling in the world financial and trading system. The City became very early a major economic force in its own right. As a result, the maintenance of conditions in which exported capital was safe, sterling defended, and international commercial and financial operations could freely function became the first priority in state policy. It can be argued that this operated *against* the expansion of the UK domestic economy from an early date, but especially when balance of payments problems began to emerge in the nineteen-thirties.

The UK financial system was not only orientated overseas towards foreign lending, etc.; its arm's length from industry was institutionalized in the concentration by banks on short-term loans and working 'capital'. This in turn had implications for the mobilization of financial resources for domestic expansion and the provision of risk capital for development, and helped to account for the exceptionally heavy dependence of UK capital on self-financing. We have to take care in attributing low growth to the separation of industry and finance (to some extent the phenomenon of low gearing in the UK is itself a consequence of relatively lower growth). Nevertheless, experience of other countries suggests that this more limited role of the clearing banks, in particular, has been a retarding factor.

In addition to overseas orientation and lack of close involvement by banks and financial institutions in industry, we must add the role of the enormous national debt. The capital market in the UK has been largely geared to the purchase and sale of government bonds and not to the provision of funds for industry. In influencing state policy, the institutions of the City— especially the Bank of England—with their powerful representation of UK capital operating overseas, have played an exceptionally important role. The composition of the Board of Governors of the Bank of England prior to and after nationalization makes this clear. The contrast with *The Four* in this respect is striking. In Japan and West Germany the connections between financial and industrial capital were and are extremely close. Writing about Japan, Professor Shigeto Tsuru (1968, pp. 234, 235) stated:

> ... the major portion of financial resources for industrial firms came in the first instance from commercial banks. Japanese industries traditionally depended for their funds—not only for operating capital but also for fixed capital—upon loans from commercial banks. ... This peculiarity of industrial firms depending on banks even for their long-term investment funds is, if at all more marked in the post-war Japan than in the pre-war.

A similar picture is given by Professor Shinohara (1970, p. 22). Japanese entrepreneurs, he argues, will increase their investment outlays as long as they can borrow from the banks. Even if the fixed investment is over and above their gross profits, the entrepreneurs will undertake investment as long as bank financing is available. In this sense, it may be considered that the foundation for the pushing vigorous investment lies in the pattern of financing or in the Japanese financial structure.

> In other words, Japanese commercial banks advance a large amount of funds for investment in plant and equipment, which would not seem to fall in line with the practices followed by their European counterparts. However, the lending tends to be preferential in nature concentrating on affiliated big companies than on a wide range of enterprises. As a result, the major companies are able to introduce large sized and efficient equipment.... But for these banks the enterprises would hardly have been in a position to finance the greatly expanded fixed investment with their own profits or by raising funds in the capital market.... Such a pattern of financing was supported ultimately by means of loans from the Bank of Japan. This so-called post-war phenomenon has, in fact, continued to exist since the end of the ninteenth century.

The main post-war groupings (eight or ten of them) are each centred on one of the major city banks. This closely resembles the position in Germany. Marshall, in his book *Industry and Trade* published in 1919, spoke of the exceptionally strong links between banks and industry. Shonfield (1965, p. 247) speaks of the German system in which 'the banks played from the beginning a major tutelary role. They were, perhaps the most powerful force making for the centralization of economic decisions. It is broadly true to say that what the great public and semi-public institutions are to the French economy, the big banks are to Germany.'

A 1960 survey found that 70 per cent of the capital of the main German companies was controlled by the banks. This arose both from voting power based on proxies and on direct ownership. The banks built up technical departments who could judge the scientific and industrial merit of requests for loans. In France and Italy, whatever the differing pre-war backgrounds, the post-1945 period was marked by a strong nationalized or semi-public financial sector which has played an active part in funding industry. In these countries, what private banking was unable to do, public and semi-public banking did through a mixture of informal or formal arrangements.

The Italian system of centralized credit control made it possible to channel large-scale investment funds into the public sector (where a great deal of industrial development has taken place).

The contrast with the UK is striking. The difference in gearing between the UK and *The Four* is illustrated in the following figures for 1972[1] (NEDO, 1975).

Japan	2.957
West Germany	0.741
France	0.923
Italy	1.579
UK	0.55

The relationship between financial and industrial capital is here again very different between the UK and *The Four*. What is the significance of this greater degree of separation between financial and industrial capital in the UK compared with *The Four*?

First, in the case of the latter, the power and profitability of financial capital was connected with the successful expansion of the domestic productive base, whereas in the UK the perspectives for UK financial capital were primarily overseas.

Second, where industry could depend upon long-term finance in the form of loans and equity (often at privileged rates of interest) firms could take a longer-term view of major investment programmes; they could take more risks without the worry of losing control. Long-term lending reduced the scale of repayments, whereas short- and medium-term loans raised acute problems for firms' cash flow. Furthermore, the involvement of banks in industry made available the widespread information and intelligence system that banks, of necessity, were in a unique position to acquire. This could be important where, for instance, rationalization in an industrial sector was required.[2] It made it easier to take a long-term strategic view.

The third characteristic is the degree of political and organizational cohesion of capital. The market alone does not and cannot provide the degree of coordination required for the steady expansion of capital. The contrast here is mainly between the UK and West Germany and Japan. In Italy and France, with their different traditions, the state has taken on the role of coordinator. Coordination of capital is not a direct function of the degree of centralization of ownership. British capital is probably under more centralized ownership than is the case in West Germany, yet the coordination of British capital is far weaker.

---

[1] Gearing is defined as short-term loans plus long-term loans divided by shareholders' interests.

[2] A useful summary of the differing relationships between financial institutions and industry in the UK and the other countries analysed here (except for Italy) can be found in Carrington and Edwards (1979).

The strength of coordination of Japanese industry and finance is, of course, well known through the so-called *Zaibatsu* (the main groups of capital that dominated Japan's economy pre-1939) and their reformation after the Second World War, especially around the big banks. Since 1966 an important role in this coordination has been played by *Sanken*, or Council for Industrial Policy, formed in 1966 and intended to change industry structure and assert the power of private capital. West Germany likewise has a powerful organized structure of business, with compulsory organization at regional level and the *Bundesverband der Deutschen Industrie* (BDI) based on manufacturing, a very powerful and politically involved organization. Pre-war the structure was buttressed by a formidable cartel system which has been partly reformed after the war. As Shonfield noted (1965) 'Industrial collaboration in pursuit of long-range objectives is fostered by powerful trade association in certain industries.'

In France the coordination of large firms has been partly by way of the associations in the course of the planning process. The role of the state itself and the larger public sector is more significant in France and Italy as compared with Japan and West Germany. But when we turn to Britain, the contrast is again very marked. No such powerful and semi-public organization of industry on a local and regional basis exists; there are much weaker and less effective chambers of commerce. The main organizations of employers have been built up on a purely sectional basis, concerned especially with wage bargaining and very jealous of their autonomy.

The Federation of British Industries (which became the Confederation of British Industries in 1965) excluded finance and trade as well as the nationalized industries. It lacked direction and influence, was without a policy on most questions, and was able to follow a unified line only in extreme emergencies.

Before the war it was the Bank of England, rather than the FBI, that played a significant role in the reorganization of industries that had run into difficulties, and since 1945, from time to time, the Bank of England has played a direct role in industrial reorganization. If anything, the CBI has been more involved in policy by Labour governments than by Conservative governments. The formation of the CBI in 1965, unifying three main organizations of employers and opening the way for an association with finance and the nationalized industries (though retail trade still refuses to take part), was partly a response to the need for restructuring British industry expressed in the policies of the 1964 Labour government.

It seems possible to explain the striking difference between the UK, on the one hand, and Japan and West Germany, on the other, only by taking account of this different focus of interests. The split between international and national concerns and between financial and industrial capital goes part of the way in accounting for the greater fragmentation of the interests of British capitalist groups. But in contrast, the Conservative Party presented at least a nominally unified political framework. The leadership of the Conservative Party, however, believed it knew what capitalism needed at least as well as the FBI or the CBI, and many of the leaders of the Conservative Party, such as Churchill or Macmillan, had only limited links with the main centres of large capital.

In the light of this account we wish to come back to the overseas 'orientation' of British capital. It is not a question of the degree of openness of the UK economy—i.e., the proportion that foreign trade occupies of total economic activity within the UK's state boundary. The UK in this latter sense is certainly a very open economy but it is not in a class of its own in this respect. If, however, we examine as indicators of this overseas orientation the stock of capital invested outside the UK in comparison with other countries and the proportion that net property income constitutes of GDP, we can see significant differences between the UK and *The Four*.

The major constituents of this international role are, in the first place, the City of London (used as a shorthand phrase for that massive complex of financial interests and services operating on a world scale); second, UK-based multi-national companies in manufacturing and trading; and finally, we should include substantial segments of capital that were originally 'based' on the UK but that have long since become detached and feature as South African or Far Eastern capital, even though the interconnections between these blocks and capital based on the UK remain strong. The *total* effect of UK involvement in the world economy made sterling the main world's trading reserve currency and the need to defend this role became a powerful force in UK economic strategy, as we have suggested. It fostered and supported the view that the UK had a world political and diplomatic role to play long after the strength to play this role had gone.

The Four have also striven for a world role; the tendencies for capital to expand across national frontiers is inherent in its nature. Major attempts to expand in this way by West Germany and Japan have been defeated in two world wars; both countries have been thrown back on the reconstruction of their domestic productive bases in the way we have indicated. Among *The Four*, the French economy had, prior to 1939, a far more pronounced colonial and international base, but the outcome of the Second World War, the setback caused by the German occupation, and the loss of her colonial empire also made (under the impact of the resistance movement and Gaullist nationalism) domestic expansion the major priority.

However, among *The Four*, West Germany and Japan, in particular, now show a dynamic growth in their export of capital, which is clearly shifting the balance towards their sections of capital operating overseas. In looking at the direction, cohesion, and internal relationships of the dominant class, a critical force is clearly that of the state and state policies, to which we now turn.

6-3 THE ROLE OF STATE POWER

However various the forms, the state is *always* involved in the development of capitalist economies from their earliest moments; but the degree of intervention and its main thrust has varied over time for any capitalist economy and as between such economies.

It is well established that the extent and success of West German and Japanese capital in industrializing and modernizing their economies has depended not only on a special relationship between financial and industrial capitals (as described by us earlier), but also on the active participation of the state, especially from the last part of the nineteenth century, a phenomenon that continued and developed in the twentieth century. That is also valid, we shall argue, for the post-1945 period in both countries. In the case of France and Italy, the pre-war histories are different, although France has had a highly centralized state accustomed to intervention and Italy had the experience of fascist 'corporatism'. In the post-1945 period, however, whereas in West Germany and Japan industrial and financial capital was strong and the working class and its organizations relatively weak, in France and Italy capital was much more fragmented and insecure and the working class and its industrial and political organizations much more powerful. In these circumstances the role of the state became exceptionally important as the only force that could enable capitalist reconstruction and modernization to be carried through.

Once again, the contrast between the UK and *The Four* is marked. From the middle of the nineteenth century, the British state's relatively non-interventionist role in domestic industry (except in war-time) was associated with the view that it has a *world* role to play based on UK capital's world interests and concerns. The British state had a built-in interest in free trade and, especially, the free flow of capital, and in the maintenance of Britain as a world imperial power. As we shall see, the contrast was carried forward into the post-1945 period.

In Japan—where, as we have pointed out, industry and finance were traditionally closely connected—the post-war state played a major role. As Tsuru wrote (1968, pp. 71–2):

> ... the role of the government cannot be abstracted from Japan's growth process in the fifties.... Especially after April 1952, when Japan regained her independence, it will be difficult to regard Japan ... as an example of an economy able to achieve a high rate of growth because of its competitive structure. Monopolistic practices came back early; and the government embarked on a gigantic industry-financing program through a number of governmental development cooperations, as well as introducing numerous tax-exemption or tax-relief measures aimed at specific industries and investment programs ... the level of treasury investments and loans has lately been of the magnitude fully comparable to the total and retained income of corporations.

As it happens, the shift from light to heavy industry in Japan was backed by the state, as was the massive export drive. Although draft plans existed in Japan, the state has played its part more informally than through a tight planning organization.

In many ways the situation in West Germany has been similar. The state to a large degree has 'left' industrial and financial capital, already closely intertwined, to get on with the business of accumulation and expansion. This position partly arose from the experience of German fascism, which imposed state controls not agreeable to all sections of business. But behind the scenes, the West German government practised substantial discriminatory policies and had substantial ownership stakes in fuel, steel, vehicles, and aluminium smelting, and held interest in some 3000 enterprises. Shonfield (1965, p. 297) reported that in its fiscal practice:

> Germany is much closer to France than to Britain. Subsidies, cheap loans provided by the state, and above all, discriminating tax allowances which support favoured activities, are used with an abandon that could only be acceptable in a society where the average citizen expects the state to choose its favourites and to intervene on their behalf.... The aggregate cost to the exchequer of (contributions to industry and commerce SA) is over three times as great in Germany as in Britain.

In using the Counterpart Funds (derived from Marshall Aid), the Germans in the fifties set up the *Kreditanstalt fuer Wiederaufbau* (KW), which worked under the direction of the Ministry of Economics to carry out a wide-ranging investment financing programme. In France, the state, through its planning programmes, through the activities of the Ministry of Finance, and especially through the close relationship between state officials and the executives of the giant firms, stimulated and financed the large-scale investment and reorganization of French industry. Economists who have had fun and games about unfulfilled targets of French planning have largely missed the point, since the essence of the exercise was the provision of the massive help and agreement on the broad strategies that fostered accumulation and growth.

In Italy, no state planning on French lines existed. There the greatly expanded public sector and its massive financing by and through the Italian Central Bank, plus the establishment of quasi-independent bodies, such as ENI and IRI, have made major contributions to growth.

Although the variations between *The Four* are substantial they nevertheless, even in respect to the role of the state, contrast with UK experience and practice. In all *The Four*, the state has an interventionist practice and, apart from West Germany, an interventionist philosophy. The British state, however, is one that has intervened at the micro-economic level with great reluctance—and this is true for both Labour and Conservative governments, who have been concerned above all with macro-economic management. In 1950 Sir Stafford Cripps set out the Labour government's view that 'the Budget itself can be described as the most important control and the most important instrument for influencing economic policy that is available to the Government'. In general, intervention at the micro level has been avoided, and after 1947 a determined effort was made to move away from such intervention.

The nationalized sector was used *not* for leverage in the economy but as a means of demand regulation (encouraging or checking investment spending, etc.). Little contribution was made to any system of industrial and technical training. The dominant role in economic policy formation was played by the Treasury and the Bank of England. And for both those organizations, the priorities were unmistakable; to 'put the pound first', to deal with problems of the balance of payments by deflating the economy whenever a threat existed. In this sense, the state was occupied with a policy that directly damaged the growth of accumulation within the UK itself. Between 1950 and 1969 every attempt to deflate the economy was triggered off by a sterling crisis.

As we show later, the British state has been driven into greater intervention, but even so, Conservative governments in 1970 and again in 1979 made determined efforts to reverse this process. The collapse of the 1970 strategy is now a matter of history.

6-4 THE POSITION OF THE WORKING CLASS

Within our theoretical framework, the capital–labour relationship is clearly the central feature in the structure of class relationships. Though we shall say much more about the position of labour in other parts of the book, we will state briefly the major contrasts between the UK and *The Four*. The strength of the working class will obviously be relative to that of capital and be affected by the supply of labour and the level and quality of its organization.

A first major contrast is that in *The Four* capital had large labour reserves available in agriculture and/or in neighbouring countries. This was not the case in the UK, where the proportion of the population in agriculture was already very small and where the overwhelming majority of the working people were wage or salaried employees.

The second major contrast was that in the UK the trade union movement emerged from the war far stronger and influential than it had been before. Moreover, trade unionists had created a massive system of shopfloor organization which extended shopfloor bargaining on a scale probably unique among all advanced capitalist countries. In West Germany, Japan, and Italy, the trade union movement had, of course, been destroyed by fascism and by Japanese militarism and had to be painfully rebuilt. In France, too, the trade union movement had to be rebuilt. In West Germany, France, and Italy the trade unions were disunited, divided on political grounds, whereas in the UK they remained within one single centre, the TUC.

In these circumstances, capital was able in *The Four* to achieve much higher rates of exploitation than was possible in the UK. Such a rise in exploitation is, of course, perfectly consistent with a rise in real incomes over time, just as a lower rate of exploitation is consistent with a lower rate of growth of real incomes.

In general, the strength of the trade union movement has therefore acted as a powerful bargaining force that has sought to share the gains of increased productivity with the owners of capital and to act defensively in blocking attempts to check the rise in real standards. This largely defensive posture has certainly interacted with the other conditions outlined above, which have contributed to the relatively lower growth rate of the UK, but this has been, in our judgement, a secondary rather than a primary factor.

6-5 CONCLUSIONS

The point of our brief comparative survey has been first to underline the importance of class and institutional relationships in economic growth. Matters like investment and productivity have to be analysed not as things that have the ability by themselves to change the growth rate of economies (it is clear that they have not) but as part of a dynamic structure.

The second main point is to underline the significance of the split between policies that primarily serve the expansion of the UK economy within national boundaries and policies formed on the basis of the world role both of the state and of dominant groups of capital. The further division between financial and industrial capital has for historical reasons served to aggrevate this conflict. The world economic, political, and military roles of the UK were the chief preoccupations of government and of the City. The balance of payments problems appeared to arise as constraints on pursuing world policies but they were also the products of these policies as well as of past history.

At almost every critical moment, economic growth within the UK was sacrificed to measures thought necessary to defend Britain's world financial and political position. The sacrifice of domestic growth to sterling, as it was often called, is no new theme in post-war economic analysis—it was the dominant theme of the analysis made, for instance, by influential observers such as Shonfield (1958) and Brittan (1964). Given this history, we must not be surprised if conventional investment functions—which, for instance, make new investment a function of previous rates of output—break down because of lack of confidence by British capital operating within the UK that such growth will be sustained by government policy.

Studying the comparative history of the five economies brings out the crucial nature of the fifties in setting Britain apart from *The Four*, especially during the period 1949 to 1955. Here is the point where the post-war advantages of the UK were 'thrown away' and growth paths inevitably diverged. A brief review of the period serves to illustrate the outcome of the difference in direction between the UK and *The Four*. In *The Four*, this was the period of reconstruction and modernization, with substantial foreign aid from the US. Once this was carried through there were immense opportunities for growth in trade as barriers were dismantled and high rates of growth of the domestic economies were sustained. But for the UK we could almost narrow down the critical moment from 1949 through to the early fifties: the rearmament programme carried out (or attempted might be the better term) under US pressure at the time of the Korean War. At a moment when the UK alone of all its main economic rivals (apart from the US) had the opportunity to take advantage of the immense postwar reconstruction and replacement needs, the heart of British manufacturing industry, engineering, was virtually pulled out of the operation. The rearmament programme cost the loss of two billion dollars from the UK's international reserves; represented the loss of one year's increment in national output; brought capital formation to a halt; led to a standstill or even a fall in productivity per man. The plan envisaged a million people on munitions and defence production with rearmament absorbing 10 per cent of GDP. A severe balance of payments crisis was created, with rising imports and falling invisible exports. Actual and potential customers had to turn to other economies for their needs. Consumers, hoping for continued expansion in real incomes now that the sacrifices of the war were behind them, found the growth in their living standards brought to a halt. So powerful was the ideology of Britain's world role that no special dollar help from the US was demanded or received. The British government was not so much giving way to US pressure as embracing it. This policy led to the split in the Labour Party (the resignation of Bevan and Wilson) that was the prelude to the Labour government's defeat in the 1951 elections.

But this was simply a repetition, regrettably not as farce, of the events of 1931, when the Prime Minister and the Chancellor of the Exchequer in the then Labour government (Ramsey MacDonald and Snowden, respectively) regarded inflation, the problem of Britain's external economic position, and the political situation in Europe as more decisive than 'domestic needs and aspirations' (Clay, 1957, p. 393).

FURTHER READING

Since this chapter attempts a brief comparative analysis of several advanced capitalist economies, a reading list would need to be very extensive. Useful studies of individual economies can be found in the series *Contemporary Economies* (Parts 1 and 2) published by Collins/Fontana, 1976; and some of the books referred to in the text would obviously be useful. Shonfield (1965) is particularly useful, in spite of its unjustified optimism.

Hobsbawm (1969) is the best introduction to UK economic history up to the mid sixties.

Statistical material can be found in the publications of the OECD and the EEC.

See also Cipolla (1976), in particular the article by Angus Maddison.

SEVEN

THE HISTORICAL DECLINE OF THE UK

Ron Smith

7-1 INTRODUCTION

Chapter 5 suggested that the economic performance of the UK relative to its major competitors can be explained in terms of differences in the structure of class relations. This chapter will provide a brief account of how this structure of relations arose and how it has conditioned the evolution of British capitalism. In summary our argument is that Britain's early industrialization led to the development of a mature working class with a strong political and economic organization before its competitors, while the early international expansion led British capital to focus on investment and operation abroad. The British ruling class thus became dominated by international and financial capital. The structure of production and social organization that arose in the course of this early start were initially very effective, but with the growth of competition from other industrial countries and the transformation of the technology of production they became increasingly inappropriate.

By the end of the nineteenth century these structures had become a major barrier to the expansion of domestic production and there developed a contradiction between the international orientation and interests of British capital and the growth of the British economy. To transform these structures required extensive state intervention in the organization of production and control of international trade and capital movements. Both of these were opposed by important sections of capital: the former because during the twentieth century the potential strength of working class organization meant that there was always a danger that state intervention might be used in a manner hostile to capital; the latter because control of trade and capital movements would endanger the freedom to pursue profitability on a world scale and endanger existing overseas investment. The control and intervention adopted were thus severely limited and as a result domestic production stagnated. This stagnation meant that Britain fell behind relative to her competitors and this deterioration generated recurrent crises.

The major crises occurred at roughly 25-year intervals in the early years of this century; after 1925, in the immediate post-war years, and in the mid seventies. Each of these crises, which are reviewed in this chapter, led to political pressure for some sort of control on trade and for state intervention. With the exception of the introduction of protection and some intervention during the thirties, when the crisis was world-wide, in each other case these pressures were resisted. Instead, the open and unplanned economy was maintained and the cost of adjusting to the crisis carried by the working class in higher unemployment and pressure on real wages. This argument will be illustrated by a brief review of the economic history of twentieth-century Britain.

7-2 BEFORE THE FIRST WORLD WAR

The late nineteenth century saw a transformation in the process of production that almost constituted a second industrial revolution. In Britain the first industrial revolution was centred around cotton, coal, and iron, and had been based on simple technology, small firms, and relatively small capital requirements. The second, centred around chemicals, electricity, and steel, was based on scientific developments, large-scale plants, and systematic organization, both through mass production and the 'scientific' management associated with 'Taylorism' in the US. These developments largely took place outside Britain, particularly in the US and West Germany, where the development of domestic industry was fostered by protection and state support, and the new, more scientific products and production methods were adopted.

Where the old style was still efficient—in finance, commerce, and, to a certain extent, ship-building—Britain retained her position. Elsewhere she lost markets to the new industrial competitors. The reaction of British industry to this challenge was essentially conservative. Driven out of the markets of their rivals, British firms tended to turn to the underdeveloped world, where Britain's long-standing financial, commercial, and political connections gave a decisive although temporary advantage, allowing them to produce the old products in the old way. The industrialization of Europe and north America did create new opportunities for finance and commerce and in the process London became the world's leading financial centre and sterling remained the dominant international currency. Invisible exports—payments for services abroad, foreign profits, etc.—were also crucial in offsetting the persistent balance of payments deficit in goods. As the most dynamic and profitable sector of the economy, commerce and finance, centred in the City of London, acquired a powerful and in some respects dominant position both economically and politically within the UK. The City itself was internationally oriented, and most of its energy was devoted to channelling funds into and out of Britain, rather than to the provision of finance for domestic industry. Consequently, Britain never developed a banking system of the Continental type, geared to providing long-term loans for capital investment.

This loss of markets and momentum was noticed at the time—late Victorian comments on the inadequacy of British industry have a very contemporary ring—and the issue came to a head in the debate on protection between 1903 and 1906. In this debate, as throughout the twentieth century, the issue was domestic development and employment versus the free movement of goods and capital. A campaign against free trade was launched by Joseph Chamberlain. His case was based on the marked trends in trade. Between 1872 and 1902 Britain's exports of manufactured goods to the US and Europe had dropped from £116 million to £73.5 million per year; while imports of manufactures from these areas had risen from £63 million to £149 million; and Britain's exports of manufactures to the colonies had risen by £40 million.

These trends reflected the displacement of British manufacturers by newly industrialized rivals, and the British retreat into the formal and informal empire. Chamberlain's proposals combined two aspects: a system of imperial preferences and protection for manufacturing goods that would enable British firms to expand their markets, improve their competitiveness, and maintain employment.

The campaign did not succeed; free trade was maintained, and the cost of the failure of British industry to restructure was imposed on the working class. Unemployment rose, real wages fell, and the period before the First World War was one of massive industrial unrest. Capitalists responded by increasing their investment overseas, and between 1905 and 1914 about seven per cent of national income was invested abroad, more than was invested in Britain. It was in this period that the dual character of the British economy was established. While British capital was a dynamic and expanding force, servicing the development of imperialism and operating profitably on a global level, domestic production failed to develop on the same scale. To British multi-national companies and international institutions the fact that the British industrial structure decayed as a result of the policies they advocated was of little concern, since those policies also guaranteed their international profitability.

7-3 THE INTER-WAR YEARS

At the end of the First World War Britain had lost her dominant position in the world economy. *Per capita* output was only 70 per cent of that of the US, compared with 90 per cent in 1914; sterling was no longer as good as gold; unemployment reached 11.3 per cent in 1921; and British industry was still suffering from its dependence on traditional organization, staple products, and the failure to develop new technologically based industries. However, the main concern of British policy, embodied in the report of the

Cunliffe Committee of 1918, was to restore the gold standard, which had been disrupted by the war, and to re-establish the old parity between sterling and gold. To do this required reducing the level of prices and wages, which had inflated substantially during the war. The indexes for the GDP deflator and money wage rates (both 1913 = 100) were 270.8 and 257 in 1920; by a policy of severe deflation, maintaining high unemployment, these were pushed down to 185 and 181 by 1925. Large as it was, this reduction in wages and prices did not force them low enough relative to the US to allow a return to pre-war exchange rates without making British exports uncompetitive. Nonetheless, the Chancellor of the Exchequer, Winston Churchill, announced the return to gold in April 1925. It seems likely, as Keynes vehemently argued at the time, that sterling was then about 10 per cent over-valued, requiring a further 10 per cent reduction in domestic costs relative to the world to make industry competitive and profitable. The return to gold at the pre-war parity was a City policy, based on their international financial interests; on their desire to discipline the working class; and on their political perception of Britain's world role. The cost of the policy was domestic stagnation, great damage to British industry, and high unemployment. Whereas the unemployment of the thirties was largely a result of the world collapse, that of the twenties in the UK was the consequence of economic policy, other countries having relative prosperity then. Nor was there much that British industry could do to expand production, given the depressed domestic market and the effect on its international competitiveness of the over-valued exchange rate. There was, however, some restructuring of production and an increase in concentration of industry.

Despite the effort that had gone into restoring the gold standard, it did not last long. The Great Crash on Wall Street in 1929, the general banking collapse, and the onset of the Great Depression in 1930 made it unsustainable. Sterling was allowed to float and free trade was abandoned. Protection and an improvement in the terms of trade arising from the falling prices of food and other primary products moderated slightly the suffering of the thirties. Bad though it was, unemployment in the UK was less severe than in the US. The UK peak was 15.6 per cent in 1932 compared with the US peak of 24.9 per cent in 1933. UK unemployment also fell more, reaching 9.4 per cent in 1935 and 5.8 per cent in 1939, as compared with the US, where it was still 17.2 per cent in 1939. (But it should be noted that there are severe problems in comparing unemployment rates, and more than one measure for each country). There were also important changes in the structure of British industry in the thirties: increases in size and concentration of firms; the growth of new industries with more technological base which catered to domestic demand, such as chemicals, cars, and electrical goods; and the end of dependence on the old staple industries. Despite the unemployment, the economy did grow. Protection and state intervention through the Bank of England were an essential component in this transformation, and the Second World War, spreading new technology and destroying old structures, extended it.

7-4 RECONSTRUCTION

When Labour took office in 1945, Britain was deeply in debt; there was a huge balance of payments deficit; industry had been run down during the war and was in need of massive investment, much remaining backward and inefficient; and the economy was still on a war footing, with a quarter of the labour force still directly employed in the armed services and arms production. On the other hand, most of Britain's competitors had been crippled by the war, and reconstruction of their economies would provide a large demand for British exports. Labour had also inherited the war-time planning and control mechanism, which could be used to direct resources into the areas where they were most needed.

In the light of Britain's later experience it is remarkable how successful the Labour government was in its first few years of office and how far it achieved these immediate objectives. Demobilization was carried through smoothly and efficiently, with nearly eight million people moving from military to civilian work by the end of 1946. Several key industries in urgent need of modernization were nationalized. Industrial production rose rapidly, recovering its pre-war level in 1946 and increasing by another 30 per cent over the next five years. Exports doubled in one year, reaching their pre-war level in 1946, and rising by a further 70 per cent in the next four years. Imports were held down by direct controls and remained well below their pre-war volume until 1950, with the result that the huge war-time balance of payments deficit on current account was eliminated by 1948. On the other hand, although there were many social reforms—the National Health Service, provision for National Insurance, etc.—working class consumption hardly increased and the period is rightly remembered as one of austerity. Even so, it seemed that the foundations were being laid for a successful welfare capitalism, and that a real attack was being made on the old problems of the British economy—industrial backwardness and the subordination of the domestic economy to international finance and world market pressures.

This transformation was never completed, and Britain entered the postwar period beset by many of the problems of old. Two factors underlay the failure of the Labour Party to sustain the transformation of British capitalism. First, the leading role of the state in planning the modernization and growth of British industry was prematurely abandoned. Second, Labour attempted to maintain Britain's role as an imperial power, imposing increasing burdens on the balance of payments by opening the economy, and distorting industrial production by rearmament for the Korean War.

Instead of trying to convert the war-time planning structure into a peace-time programme for modernization and development, like the Monet plan in France, the Labour Party was content to allow the system to be dismantled and to replace planning by demand management. This was still an era of 'cheap money', and it was fiscal rather than monetary policy that was seen as the main instrument of demand management. But fiscal policy was supported by an austere incomes policy and the 1949 devaluation. These policies left the crucial supply decisions of growth, investment, and trade to be increasingly determined by free market forces. The retreat from planning was symbolized by Harold Wilson's 'bonfire of controls' at the Board of Trade in November 1948. The retreat from planning was partly a response to the strength of the political opposition, which was much greater than in France, but there was little Labour struggle to defend planning in the UK. In addition, measures that were feasible in other countries, where working class strength and organization had been under-mined by fascism and occupation, posed a political threat to capital, given the balance of class forces in the UK.

The shift away from planning and control proved most damaging in the area of foreign trade. By 1950 a third of all imports were decontrolled, and when the European Payments Union was formed, Labour accepted a commitment to the removal of quantitative controls. This meant that the balance of payments would increasingly be determined by the decisions of individual firms once again, and that the government would have to rely almost entirely on deflation of domestic demand, with its dire consequences for production, to correct trade deficits.

The Labour government also subordinated internal policy to its world ambition to maintain Britain's special relationship as a junior partner of American imperialism. The benefits of this policy included Marshall aid, but the major cost was the Korean War rearmament. This raised military expenditure from 7.1 per cent of GDP in 1949 to 10.8 per cent in 1952, with catastrophic effects on investment, exports, and consumption. Engineering industries, in particular, were so heavily engaged in the rearmament drive that they were unable to meet export orders or provide for domestic investment needs. Given that Britain's competitors were well on the road to recovery by 1951, markets lost during the Korean War were never recovered. Indeed, as was suggested in the previous chapter, much of the relative decline of British capitalism over the subsequent 25 years may be due to the disruption caused by the military burden shouldered by the Labour government. Other countries maintained the impetus established during reconstruction after the war, and maintained their growth rates; Britain lost this impetus completely.

Post-war governments tried to come to terms with this loss of momentum through three main types of policy: attempting to manage aggregate demand in order to improve economic performance; attempting to influence supply through industrial policy and indicative planning; and attempting to influence the functional distribution of income (i.e., between wages and profits) by incomes policy. The performance of industrial and incomes policies are discussed in Chapters 10 and 22; here the history will be briefly reviewed within the context of demand management policies.

7-5 POST-WAR DEMAND MANAGEMENT

The alternative to planning for much of the post-war period has been demand management, the process by which the government attempts to ensure that the level of aggregate demand for goods and services (amount spent on consumption, investment, etc.) is in balance with the supply potential of the economy, determined by available labour force, capital stock, and technology. Since inflation and balance of payments deficits can be interpreted as symptoms of excess demand, and unemployment as a symptom of inadequate demand, it was hoped that by controlling the level of demand the government could maintain full employment, balance of payments equilibrium, and stable prices. Demand was to be managed primarily through fiscal and monetary policy—i.e., by adjusting government expenditure and taxation or interest rates and the controls on credit creation. However, when thought necessary these were supported by exchange rate variations (to correct fundamental disequilibria in the balance of payments) and prices and incomes policy. Once the government had provided the stable macro-economic environment it was believed that market forces would operate efficiently to deal with micro-economic allocation, and the creation of supply. Since history has not been kind to this optimistic view of demand management, it is necessary to return to the history of the period.

When the Conservatives came to power in 1951, in many respects their policies did not represent a major break, since they naturally continued the liberalization of trade and the dismantling of state controls that had been initiated by the Labour government. Thus by 1958 sterling was fully convertible into other currencies, while internationally negotiated tariff reductions and the removal of quotas were by the early sixties opening up British markets to overseas competition, particularly in the area of manufactured consumer goods. One difference in Conservative policy, however, was the more vigorous use of interest rates to influence the economy and protect the reserves.

In the fifties, the Conservative governments had various economic advantages. Resources could be released by cutting military expenditure from its Korean War heights, and the decline in primary product prices gave a favourable boost to the balance of payments. Nonetheless, this period was characterized by sharp swings in policy between expansion and deflation in response to the alternating stimuli of the fear of the electoral consequences of a sharp rise in unemployment and fear of a run on the reserves. This sequence became known as 'stop-go'. In response to high unemployment, tax rates and interest rates were cut, controls on hire purchase relaxed, and government expenditure increased, leading to a consumption-led boom, often—although not always—timed to precede an election (the 1959 'You never had it so good' Macmillan election campaign being the classic case). The boom led to a deterioration in the balance of payments, the fiscal stimulus was reversed, and interest rates rose sharply to prevent speculative outflows of money capital.

This pattern was an early indication of the structural problems of the British economy. Loss of competitiveness, a consequence of low productivity growth, caused a weak underlying balance of payments position; while integration into international financial markets and the major role of sterling as a reserve currency made the UK vulnerable to speculative pressures from international financial circles. Investment suffered because the booms were led by consumer demand, and tended to be over by the time the extra investment had started to catch up. Thus, although resources were then available for investment, there was little expectation of demand growth to motivate it. Without extra investment, at the next boom there would be inadequate capacity, so imports would be sucked in to meet demand, causing further deterioration in the balance of payments. Keynesians also held this lack of investment to be responsible for the low rate of growth of productivity and real output.

It was against this background of frustratingly low growth that Maudling, the Conservative Chancellor of the Exchequer, launched the first 'dash for growth' in 1963. This was based on the theory that high growth in demand would stimulate investment, raise productivity, and thus enable the expansion to become self-sustaining if the stimulus to demand were maintained for long enough. The difficulty was that the inevitable balance of payments deficit had to be financed during the lag between the initial expansion of demand and the consequent improvement in trend productivity and competitiveness. However, this was not a problem that the Conservatives had to face, since the 1964 boom did not lead to an election victory.

Many economic advisers argued that the Labour government should devalue to deal with the balance of payments problem, inherited on taking power in 1964. But this was regarded as unacceptable. It seemed a political liability for Labour to be seen as unable to protect sterling, having devalued once before in 1949. Devaluation also seemed likely to damage the confidence that was central to sterling's role as a reserve currency and to the City of London's financial activities; while the US opposed devaluation because sterling was the first line of defence against speculation against the dollar. The decision not to devalue conditioned economic policy for the next three years and condemned the National Plan, with which Labour hoped to solve the structural problems of the British economy, to oblivion.

Attempts were made to deal with the balance of payments by an import surcharge and deposit scheme, as well as by public expenditure cuts and a credit squeeze, but the position was unsustainable, and in November 1967 the pound was devalued from $2.80 to $2.40. The political pressures had also changed, since the City had diversified into the Eurodollar market, which had rapidly expanded in the sixties and was no longer so dependent on the role of sterling. Giving up the reserve role of sterling and the special relationship with the US also seemed more attractive in the light of attempts to persuade De Gaulle that the British were good Europeans who could be allowed into the EEC. Callaghan, the Chancellor associated with the refusal to devalue, resigned and was replaced by Jenkins, who in 1968 introduced a strongly contractionary budget. Devaluation and deflation brought the balance of payments back into surplus in 1969, at the cost of high and rising unemployment. Throughout the Labour government, an incomes policy of one sort or another was in force, but this broke down completely in 1969–70, when the price increases caused by devaluation led to wage demands by workers trying to protect their real incomes. Jenkins' reign as Chancellor also saw more attention paid to monetary factors, as a result of the influence of the IMF. The Labour government entered the 1970 election campaign with a depressed economy, rising unemployment, inflationary pressures, but a strengthening balance of payments, and were defeated by the Conservatives.

At first Conservative policy was one of continued tight restraint, with cuts in government expenditure to leave room for tax cuts, and a firm commitment to no formal incomes policy, except through public sector wage settlements. But with unemployment rising and topping a million in early 1972, a rapid policy reversal occurred. The Budget of 1972 cut taxes sharply and fiscal policy became strongly expansionary, reinforced by a rapid growth in the money supply, partly in consequence of a reform of a monetary system called 'Competition and credit control' introduced at the same time, which left banks with excess reserves. Barber, the Chancellor, floated sterling in mid 1972, partly on the view that this would remove the balance of payments constraint on domestic expansion. This shift in policy launched the UK on a repetition of the 'dash for growth' experiment of 1963–4.

However, in 1972–3 international conditions were even less favourable, since the rapid expansion of all the advanced capitalist countries after the Smithsonian meeting at the end of 1971 had boosted the demand for primary products, raising commodity prices and the import bill. Expansion, adverse movements in the terms of trade, and exhaustion of the competitive advantage gained by the 1967 devaluation all helped generate a massive balance of payments deficit. Added to this, the fall in sterling, coupled with the domestic expansion, generated inflationary pressures that put great strain on the incomes policy the Conservatives had been forced to introduce. The fourfold increase in oil prices by OPEC in November 1973 and the confrontation with the miners over pay marked the end of another attempt at growth.

7-6 PLANNING

In examining the history, the lack of effective state intervention has been emphasized. Since this does not accord with the common impression of 'meddlesome' British governments, it is necessary to review the few attempts at coherent intervention at an economy-wide level.

In the late forties and early fifties the detailed planning mechanism that had been used to organize production and allocate resources during the war and demobilization was dismantled, and for most of the fifties economic policy was seen as being primarily a matter of demand management. By the late fifties, however, concern at stop-go, lack of competitiveness, and low growth relative to other European countries, combined with the example of successful French planning, led to a renewed interest in planning, supported even by the Federation of British Industries at its 1960 conference. A distinction was made between imperative or command planning of the Eastern European type, where the state directly controls the decisions of the enterprises, and indicative planning of the French type. With indicative planning, the state, in consultation with firms and unions, generates a set of consistent feasible target levels of future output for each industry; it then considers what government policies and industry decisions are necessary to attain these targets, and what bottlenecks need to be removed. The state then provides guidance, finance, and other assistance to enable the targets to be met. The idea is that the government should simulate the role that futures and contingent markets play in economic theory. Such a framework should reduce the uncertainty faced by firms; increase their confidence in market prospects and thus their investment; and ensure that their various investment decisions are consistent, stopping the development of excess or inadequate capacity in particular areas. Thus efficiency, investment, and growth would be increased.

Whether French planning ever operated in this way or not is a separate question, but this perception of the role of planning had a substantial impact on British policy in the sixties. This was particularly true of the belief that if people could be persuaded that a higher growth rate was feasible, production would be planned on that basis, and if the individual plans were coordinated through a national plan, the higher growth rate would be achieved. To implement this belief, the Conservative government set up the Neddy machinery: the National Economic Development Council (NEDC), where representatives of government, unions, and firms could meet to formulate a nationally coordinated strategy, and the National Economic Development Office (NEDO), which would prepare reports on targets, bottlenecks, and implementing the strategy.

After 1964, the Labour government extended the system, setting up the Department of Economic Affairs to provide a bureaucratic force supporting long-term growth policies, against the Treasury's short-term mentality, and to produce a National Plan. Neddy also started breeding Little Neddies (Economic Development Committees), representing individual industries and regions, having a similar function at the micro level. Neither the NEDC/NEDO system or the DEA/National Plan approach managed to raise the rate of growth, and their target growth rates were rapidly overtaken by events. By the seventies planning was regarded as yet another faded economic fashion and the DEA was abolished, although NEDC/NEDO survived as useful institutional shells for functions unconnected with planning.

There are two elements in the explanation of this failure. First, the process was not one of planning but of wishful thinking. What was done was to say, 'Suppose the economy were to grow at, say, 3.8 per cent and suppose firms were to invest enough, what would happen to output in each industry?' But no mechanism was provided to make the suppositions come true. The government would not maintain the growth rate in the face of the inevitable deterioration in the balance of payments, and firms would not invest because they, correctly, did not believe that the government would maintain the growth rate. No mechanism was provided either to insulate domestic growth from the balance of payments or to ensure that private capital took the required investment and production decisions. The same problem was to beleaguer the industrial strategy of the 1974–9 Labour government. In its original form, proposed in opposition, this included import controls to insulate domestic growth, and a planning agreement structure that gave the state leverage over private firms. It was implemented without either, becoming merely a channel for passing money to industry, as will be seen later

The reason for the failure to provide a mechanism or teeth to the attempts at planning was political, in that, irrespective of whether it proved effective or not, a powerful planning apparatus with the means to pressure and control private firms was a major threat to capital in the UK. In France there was no danger that the planning mechanism would be controlled by groups hostile to capital even in the politically unstable fifties. There was no such confidence in the UK. Consequently the contradiction in the Labour Party's position was that the logic of their policies required considerable powers of state control of private decision making, which political forces stopped them taking. What the consequences of vigorous state intervention in decision making would have been is open to question; the point is that it was never attempted. Instead the intervention largely took the form of providing money to industry, in the hope either that firms would use it wisely or that by changing the relative costs faced by firms the government could push their choices in particular directions.

7-7 CRISIS MANAGEMENT

The years 1973 to 1977 represented a period of major crisis for the British economy. Between 1973 and 1976 industrial production fell 8 per cent and the unemployment rate doubled, reaching almost 6 per cent at the end of 1977. The rate of profit in British manufacturing fell sharply, and there was a major financial collapse following a sequence of secondary bank failures. This happened within the context of an international crisis, with rising inflation and unemployment throughout the advanced capitalist world in the aftermath of the OPEC price increase. The world-wide picture is discussed in more detail in Chapter 13. While it seems reasonable to describe this period as one of crisis, the term has been so over used that it has become the standard cliché to describe the perpetual state of the British economy. In this respect the metaphor is misleading. The term crisis was originally used to denote the point in the progress of a disease at which an important change takes place, leading either to recovery or death. In many ways such a definition does not apply to British economic performance, which in medical terms would reflect a chronic rather than an acute condition. The run-of-the-mill British economic crisis over sterling, inflation, the money supply and the like tend to be treated rather like the British weather, disapproved of but stoically taken for granted. The real economic crises, on the other hand, represent major turning points at which important structural readjustments are made that enable the system to survive. In the UK these adjustments have been made in response to the pressure of external events, at critical moments. The middle seventies was such a critical moment and it is worth examining the management of the crisis in some detail.

The Labour government that returned to power in early 1974 after the three-day week had one advantage in that it appeared that the balance of payments had ceased to be a constraint. The deficit, which was £3.6 billion in 1974, could be financed by the large capital account inflows that the newly enriched OPEC producers invested in sterling. But this was only a short-term expedient since such 'hot money' could easily flow out again. This it was to do within two years, worsening the crisis of 1976.

At the beginning of 1976 sterling had been worth two dollars. It was thought within the Treasury that at this rate it was over-valued, and that some decline in the rate was necessary to make British exports competitive. Although since the middle of 1972 the exchange rate for sterling had not been formally fixed, under the regime of 'dirty floating', government policy about what the rate should be, and foreign exchange market estimates of what government policy was, played a major role in determining the exchange rate. In March 1976, just before Callaghan replaced Wilson as Prime Minister, the policy of nudging the pound down was implemented. There were rumours of the conversion of Nigerian oil revenues from sterling into dollars; a cut in the MLR (minimum lending rate, equivalent to the old Bank Rate, the crucial government-controlled interest rate) and a discreet withdrawal of support for sterling. Instead of a gentle devaluation, the market fell out of control, and the exchange rate collapsed, touching $1.71 in June 1976. To defend the pound, Britain obtained a $5.3 billion standby loan from other countries, and in July the Chancellor, Denis Healey, introduced a mini Budget that deflated the economy by about £2 billion. The loan was only intended by the other countries, in particular the US, to be short term, and had the condition attached to it that, if Britain could not repay all of the money it had used within six months, it must borrow from the IMF. Any IMF loan would have strict conditions attached to it.

In September, further pressure on the pound developed, the Bank of England withdrew support (that is, stopped buying pounds with dollars to keep the rate up), and the pound collapsed again, reaching a low of $1.55 in October. At the end of September, the government approached the IMF to negotiate a loan, and the MLR was raised to 15 per cent; it had been 9 per cent in March. After some political battles, the terms were agreed, and announced in December. In return for the loan of $3.9 billion, Britain agreed to make public expenditure cuts of £2.5 billion, which together with the sale of part of the government holding of British Petroleum shares, would reduce the PSBR (the public sector borrowing requirement, roughly the government deficit) by about £3 billion. In addition, there were to be limits on the future growth of M3 (a measure of the money supply) and DCE (domestic credit expansion).[1]

Although to Britain these terms were very restrictive—increasing unemployment, disrupting public services, and forcing down real incomes–by comparison with the terms the IMF imposes on other countries they were rather mild. Despite the fact that this was the largest single loan in IMF history, the initial terms proposed were less draconian than in comparable cases, and in the final event the IMF accepted £1 billion less deflation than it initially proposed.

One point to notice is that, contrary to the way this crisis is often presented, it was not a balance of payments crisis. The balance of payments was improving, and the deficit in 1976 was very much smaller than it had been in the previous two years. In 1974 the deficit had been £3.6 billion, in 1975 £1.7 billion and in 1976 it was £1.4 billion. As percentages of GDP, these were 4.84 per cent, 1.83 per cent, and 1.28 per cent respectively. But despite this the effective exchange rate against a weighted average of other currencies had been steady during 1974, and declined much less in 1975 than in 1976.

---

[1] DCE is roughly the change in M3 minus the balance of payments. If Britain is running a balance of payments deficit, this corresponds to foreigners lending money to the UK, and so is counted as a source of credit expansion in addition to the extra credit that comes from the growth in the money supply.

The crisis was over the exchange rate, which is determined by government behaviour and movements of 'hot' money in the market, and in the short run both of these are determined more by political than economic considerations. Even if the balance of payments is in surplus, international bankers and corporate treasurers who object to government policies can cause an exchange rate crisis by converting their cash into another currency. Given the volume of international short-term capital, the central bank has little power to offset these movements. On the other hand, the central bank does have the power to precipitate a crisis by selling its own currency on a falling market, or indicating that it thinks the rate too high when the underlying market is not firm. It was suggested that the timing of the fall in sterling, initially engineered by the Treasury and the Bank of England, was influenced by the desire to convince the TUC, with whom the government was negotiating Phase 2 of the social contract, of the precarious economic position.

The character of economic crisis in Britain reflects not only the failure of British capitalism to make the fundamental structural readjustments necessary to meet changed circumstances, but also the operation of political forces. The British state operates under two main constraints, imposed by the domestic working class and by international financial capital. The working class can influence the government through electoral pressure, its trade union representatives, and mass action (as, for instance, against the Industrial Relations Act). International finance brings its pressure to bear through the markets for foreign exchange and government debt, as well as through international institutions like the IMF and EEC. It should be remembered that capital can go on strike just as effectively as labour, by transferring money, stopping investment, closing factories, withholding credit, etc. The objectives of the two groups are quite different. The working class are concerned with advancing employment, income, and social policies; capitalists with advancing profits, maintaining unhindered movement of capital and trade, and stopping anything that smacks of socialism. When the economy is going well the minimum aspirations of both groups can be met, but when it is in difficulty there is no feasible policy that the state can follow that is acceptable to both. Given the relative power of the two groups and their contradictory demands, the state loses freedom of action. However, the generation of a crisis atmosphere eases these constraints and restores to the administration in power some freedom of manœuvre, allowing it to appear as an 'honest broker' and to play on the fears that each side has of the other. In particular, a Labour Prime Minister can pressure the TUC and left-wing representatives in Parliament with the threat that unless they compromise and accept wage restraint, increased unemployment, cuts in social services and the like, the consequences will be much worse. In 1976 these consequences were painted as a flight of capital, national bankruptcy, and a takeover by the IMF. Likewise, Callaghan could threaten the international bankers that unless they accommodated the government, left-wing pressures within Britain would lead to import restrictions, with dire consequences for the rest of the world trading system, and to withdrawal from international responsibilities, such as NATO, etc. Given the crucial role that Britain still maintains in the international system, these are serious threats. In the face of this, the representatives of the working class compromise, the bankers moderate their demands, and the administration can put together an acceptable policy package that will allow it to survive another couple of years. This is the material of short-run politics, and in the short run these tactics were successful. By international standards, the IMF terms were mild, and the working class accepted a fall in real earnings, increased unemployment, and cuts in public services. In the longer run these tactics were disastrous because they perpetuated the pattern of short-term crisis management without any attempt to solve the structural defects of the British economy. It was this pattern of policy that produced the crisis in the first place, and the state adopted this pattern of policy because it was constrained by the structure of class relations within which it had to operate.

There was an alternative economic strategy available, and 1976 also was the culmination of a major debate on economic policy within the Labour Party. The choice was between two strategies. One emphasized the use of import controls to insulate the UK from international financial movements and to provide the protection necessary to implement a major restructuring of British industry; this was linked with extensive state intervention to effect the restructuring through planning agreements, public ownership, directed investment, etc. These measures would be supported by worker participation in companies, in an attempt to replace industrial conflict with industrial democracy. The other choice, the policy that was adopted, rested on maintaining the freedom of international trade and monetary movements, and dealing with the problem through an attack on the working class. It was this policy that was maintained through the rest of the seventies.

The deflationary policies adopted in 1976, and the commitment to fixed targets for PSBR and money supply, took effect, and unemployment rose and real consumption fell during 1977. Although the policy of restraint on monetary aggregates and public expenditure was maintained by Healey, the Labour Chancellor, output and consumer expediture were allowed to grow more rapidly in 1978, encouraged by tax cuts. This had little effect on unemployment, however, and economic survival became increasingly dependent on the flow of North Sea oil. The restrictive incomes policy and the damage such policies had done to real living standards caused an increase in industrial unrest and money wage increases in the winter of 1978–9. Inflation, which had fallen from over 25 per cent a year in late 1975 to under 9 per cent in mid 1978, started to increase, fuelling this pressure to maintain living standards.

After a general election in May 1979, Labour were replaced by a

Conservative government, which maintained the restrictive monetary policy. The Conservative Chancellor, Howe, did switch from direct taxes (on income) to indirect taxes (on expenditure) in his first Budget. From early 1979 the exchange rate started to appreciate, largely as a result of short-term capital inflows, motivated by a distrust of the dollar and by the effect of the oil price rises. These were similar factors to those generating the inflow in 1974–5, and could be equally easily reversed, given the onset of another world recession in 1980–81, and the precarious state of the British economy. The government's strong pound policy not only damaged British exporters—it also increased unemployment, and constituted one more pressure to increase labour discipline. At the same time the abolition of foreign exchange controls on capital movements in mid 1979 increased the ease with which capital could move and thus the potential instability.

FURTHER READING

Hobsbawm (1969) has already been mentioned; this could be supplemented by Pollard (1969), which provides more detailed information for the period since 1914. Glyn and Sutcliffe (1972) provide in their introductory chapters a different Marxist perspective on the development of the British economy. For the post-war years see Pritt (1963), Dow (1965), Blackaby (1979), Beckerman (1972), Brittan (1970), and Panitch (1976).

THE STATE

The review of British economic history in Chapter 7 emphasized the role of state action and the significance of certain crucial policy choices. It will also have been clear that these choices, and state policy in general, were themselves constrained by the structure of class relations and the pattern of capitalist development. Therefore our first task is to examine the role of the state in more detail, and to consider its influence on the economy, the determinants of its actions, and the form of its economic interventions. The basic theoretical issues are discussed in Chapter 8, while Chapter 9 examines the structure of state income and expenditure. This chapter is primarily concerned with looking at the statistics and contains more detailed material. The areas of state activity that will be the focus of our attention are the role of the state in regulating production, discussed in Chapter 10, and its role in ensuring the reproduction of capitalist society, dealt with in Chapter 11.

EIGHT

THE ROLE OF THE STATE

Ron Smith and Roger Moore

8-1 INTRODUCTION

For many economic issues government policy and state intervention are
central questions. Therefore it is important to examine the role of the state
and try to understand how it operates. That is the purpose of this chapter.

The pervasiveness of state influence on the lives of UK citizens needs
little emphasis. They are likely to be born in state-run hospitals, educated
in state schools, watch television on a state-financed channel, and obtain
work through state employment exchanges. Many live in state housing, and
the design of the buildings they work in will be determined by state
regulation. A range of goods and services like water, sewage, gas, electricity,
transport, and perhaps the petrol and oil for their cars are supplied by
state-owned institutions. The term 'state' is a general one, covering a
heterogeneous collection of institutions—the Cabinet and government in
power; the legislature, Parliament; the judiciary, the courts; the administration, civil service, local authorities, police; the military; the nationalized
industries; and many other semi-autonomous institutions like the BBC,
which either are ultimately under state control or have some state functions.

At its most general level one can think of the state as a set of public
institutions that meet certain collective needs of society. Such a definition,
however, does not provide much help, because what counts as the needs of
society depends on the class character of the society and the political forces
at work; and these needs can only be expressed through institutions that
themselves condition the needs that are expressed. Moreover, the control
of these institutions (e.g., the army) provides power, which gives those
individuals who dominate them a certain freedom to follow their own
interests. Although the need for collective institutions to maintain and
reproduce a society is fundamental to any community beyond the very
simplest, the form of those institutions will be constrained by the mode of
production and class relations of that society. Originally the state developed
because substantial advantages accrued to societies (or at least to the ruling
class in those societies) with some central power that could defend and then
extend its borders, while maintaining internal order within those borders.

These functions were carried out by military force, an army, and the need to pay the army led to the state providing coinage and raising revenue, while control of the army provided the state with the power to force people to supply that revenue.

Orthodox economists often begin from exchange and the market as the basic socio-economic institutions, but forget that these can only develop if there is some state authority to make them feasible. Why exchange or buy goods, when you can steal or loot them? For exchange to operate freely and for markets to work efficiently requires a legal system to prevent theft, to govern the transfer of property, and to enforce contracts. It also requires reasonable security to pursue agriculture and production and to retain property, and an acceptable and guaranteed means of exchange. Thus commodity production and exchange demand some form of state apparatus. As production develops and becomes more complex, the state becomes increasingly involved in the organization and regulation of trade, until now in advanced industrial societies a large part of its activities are directly geared to the needs of the productive system, and a large part of the productive system is geared to the operation of the state. The needs of this system take different forms depending on the dominant form of organization or mode of production, and in the UK they are largely the needs of a capitalist system.

It should be emphasized that one cannot formulate any general theory of the state, since, as was argued above, the character of the state in any society will be dependent on the mode of production and the nature of exploitation within it. Thus the theory of the state must be historically specific. Within the capitalist mode of production the state has certain characteristics because of the specific nature of production and class relations. For instance, because production relations are not based on force (as they are under feudalism and slavery), the state's near monopoly of force acquires significance. Likewise the importance of competition under capitalism leads to the development of sectional interests, fragmentation of the capitalist class, and the need for a relatively autonomous institution to promote their common affairs. The extent to which the state is able to do this will be examined more closely below. The central point is that the discussion of the state below refers to the state in a capitalist society, since certain of the characteristics assumed (e.g., the sharp division between economics and politics) are specific features of the capitalist mode of production. Further, although the discussion refers to the capitalist state in general, there is not just one state, but many individual nation states, which have different types of state forms and between which there is substantial rivalry. In this chapter, however, the emphasis will be on the domestic rather than international role of the state.

8-2   THE OPERATION OF THE STATE

Understanding the state involves some theory of the process that governs the interaction between the state apparatus—the set of institutions including legislature, judiciary, and administration—and society in general. This process of interaction is pictured schematically in Fig. 8-1. The linkages between these four elements take a variety of forms. For instance, the economy influences not only the form of government institutions but the political process itself. The political power of different groups depends partly upon their economic resources and control over the means of production (although it will also reflect their mass base and ideological hold), while the performance of the economy dictates a substantial part of the political agenda. Partly in response to economic pressures, the state apparatus is organized in such a way that it is designed only to perform certain tasks and express certain types of need, thus defining the range of what is regarded as politically possible. Thus the economy influences the political process and the form of the state apparatus, while the political process makes demands on the state apparatus that may give rise to a

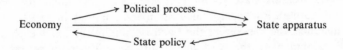

Fig. 8-1

policy response affecting the economy. The policy then causes consequent changes in the economy which feed back onto the state apparatus and the political process.

Different theories of the capitalist state can be characterized in terms of how they model each of these interactions. The orthodox economic approach assumes that the political process (reflecting some well-informed democratic consensus) leads to the expression of preferences in the form of some social welfare function that embodies the objectives of that society. Social welfare tends to be regarded in the literature as a function either of the utilities of each of the individuals in that society or of economic variables such as inflation, unemployment, the distribution of income, and the provision of public services. The state apparatus is then treated as a set of neutral institutions, which choose policy instruments, such as tax rates and government expenditure, to maximize the social welfare function subject to the constraints imposed by nature or by the economy (scarcity of resources, the structure of technology, and the pattern of private demands). The state apparatus is thus treated as a black box whose only function is to maximize social welfare, and the main feature of the political process that tends to be examined is the efficiency of alternative voting schemes in revealing the social welfare function. Through most of this literature there also runs the strong presumption that free enterprise and the operation of the market will tend to maximize efficiency; thus a necessary condition for state intervention to be desirable becomes the failure of the market. For instance, the market may fail to provide an acceptable distribution of income, or appropriate amounts of collective or public goods which cannot be allocated by price. Notice that within this theory market failure is not a sufficient condition for state intervention, for even if the market does not provide an optimum, the state may not be able to do any better. In contrast to the economic theories of the state, bureaucratic theories tend to emphasize the autonomy of the state apparatus, arguing that the civil servants who operate the institutions are relatively unconstrained by the political process or economic pressures and are thus able to use the power the state commands to pursue their own interests.

Below, each of the elements in the process linking the economy, politics, and the state are examined in turn, but it should be remembered that explanations of state policy cannot be reduced to dependence on any one element; it is the interaction that is crucial. Some Marxist writers have tended to take a reductionist position—i.e., reducing state action merely to the expression of capitalist class dominance—or a functionalist position—treating state action as a direct and immediate response to the needs of capital. But much policy cannot be analysed in such a simple way. For instance, the passage of the Factory Acts in the nineteenth century or the development of the National Health Service cannot be explained just in terms of a direct response to the immediate needs of capital. It is also necessary to take into account the role of class struggle, the political alliances formed among the various groups within society, the nature of the existing state institutions and who operates them, and a number of other historically specific factors. Emphasizing the interaction between the elements, while less simple and elegant, provides a more realistic framework within which to analyse the development of policy.

8-3 THE ECONOMY AND THE POLITICAL PROCESS

In the context of our argument that the UK economy is best understood as being capitalist, it is necessary to ask what the capitalist mode of production requires in order to survive that cannot be provided by capitalist firms. Some of the requirements for production, exchange, and distribution to proceed have already been mentioned—security, legal structures, money, etc.—and they are provided by the state for capital in general (rather than for the benefit of particular capitalists). It is in this sense that the state can be seen as the administrative committee of the bourgeoisie, meeting essential collective needs of capital, although the process of meeting those needs is not a simple functional one. The collective needs can be summarized (Gough, 1979, p. 158) as:

(a) Establishing the conditions of production, such as transport, energy, and infrastructure.
(b) Establishing the conditions for the reproduction of labour power, such as education and health services.
(c) Establishing the general conditions for the reproduction of capitalist relations, through general administration, justice, police, defence, etc.

The first set of needs is straightforward, and is discussed further in Chapter 10. The significance of the second set, discussed in Chapter 11, is that the central requirement of capitalist production—available labour power—is produced outside capitalist relations of production. Labour power is initially the product of the family, and the role of domestic labour in the production of labour power is discussed in Chapter 19. In traditional societies, to the extent that health, education, and welfare services were provided, they were provided by the family. This system was disrupted by urbanization and industrialization, which broke down traditional family structures. The production process also required better educated, fitter, and more specific types of worker, who were disciplined to accept the rhythms of industrial employment. Thus increasingly the reproduction of labour power was socialized, with the state taking a major role. Starting with the provision of public health services and education, extending into housing and social services, the state's responsibility for organizing the supply and quantity of labour has steadily increased.

To persuade the people so carefully nurtured to sell their labour power and work under capitalist control, the state orchestrates a system of ideology and coercion. Added to the primary coercion, that workers must sell their labour power to maintain their standard of life, is the system of police, courts, and military power to maintain domestic order, protect property, and prevent riots, revolution, and disruptive or general strikes. In the nineteenth century the role of state power in minimizing working class threats to the system was explicit. Today, this role is to a large extent implicit, and the public emphasis is on the integrative and cohesive role of the state in creating the perception of a shared national interest, and on minimizing the appearance of the society as a class-divided and alienating structure. This change was associated with the displacement of some aspects of class struggle from the factory to Parliament through the extension of the franchise; a displacement that was not merely of ideological significance, but that had economic and political effects, in particular through its influence on the form of working class organization.

It is important to distinguish the requirements of the capitalist system from the needs of individual capitalists. The requirements discussed above, such as the supply of labour power, are long-term necessities for the reproduction of the system. Capitalists also have short-term needs, such as maintaining the rate of profit in the face of wage demands, inflation, stagnation of markets, and the like. These short-term needs, which are the focus of most economic discussion, are central to the health, although not necessarily to the survival, of the system. Of course, pointing out needs does not indicate how, or whether, the state responds to them; that requires specification of the intermediate processes.

During the Industrial Revolution, one of the main needs that capital had of the state was the removal of the legislation that had been developed in the interests of feudalism and mercantilism, which had become an obstacle to the free accumulation of capital and to the growth of a supply of free and fragmented labour power. This was achieved only after major political conflict, but then the rapid expansion of capital itself raised further barriers to accumulation, which the market mechanism was inadequate to remove, creating the need for further state action to promote the reorganization of capital. The restructuring of capital, which under competitive capitalism had been achieved by crisis, bankruptcy and mass unemployment, became, with the growth of giant firms, a function of the state. Through industrial policies, provision of finance, and contracts, the state now plays a major role in the organization of production and the maintenance of profitable demand for the products of capitalist firms. With the internationalization of capital, the state must also protect and defend British capital abroad in competition with capital from other countries, and cooperate in attempting to create a stable international monetary and trading system.

It must be emphasized that listing capitalist needs in this way does not provide an explanation of state activity. There is no automatic mechanism to ensure that policy corresponds to needs. The needs may be contradictory: distributional policies to increase profits at the expense of wages may provoke working class resistance that threatens domestic order and stability, depresses demand, and prevents the realization of surplus as profits, or that hinders the introduction of higher productivity techniques. Likewise in the UK the policies necessary to maintain the interests of international British capital have hindered the restructuring and growth of domestic production. Not only do the needs of different sections of capital diverge, but the interests of capital in general, as expressed through the state, need not coincide with those of individual capitalists. To say that the state responds to the requirements of capital does not mean that it does what individual capitalists want. No individual capitalist wants to go bankrupt, and will plead and beg for the state to rescue the sinking firm, but for the health of capital as a whole bankruptcies are necessary, driving out the inefficient and unlucky and leading to the reorganization of excess capital and capacity in the industry.

Even when the needs are not contradictory, there is no magic process by which the state recognizes and responds to the hidden needs of capital; the specific needs must be expressed through the political process. The measures demanded may then be opposed by the working class, either in Parliament, through trade unions, or through industrial action. The political process then becomes a battleground and the outcome will depend on the specific class implications of the policy and the relative power of capitalists and workers—the balance of class forces. The political process does not merely consist of voting and Parliament, but of a whole range of struggles through a variety of institutions, ranging from mass action (like that in the early seventies against the Industrial Relations Act) to battles to make firms and institutions more responsive to democratic pressures. The outcome of these struggles can rarely be classified simply as a victory or defeat. To achieve substantial nationalization after the Second World War was a major advance for the working class movement, but at the same time the bureaucratic and hierarchical form in which it was implemented posed no threat to capitalism. The end result was thus not merely the product of the needs of the system or of the class struggle, but of the interaction of the two. This was reflected in the contradictory nature of the nationalized industries.

The complexity of the political process is increased because few societies are composed merely of two classes. In addition to capitalists and workers there are peasants, landlords, petit bourgeois groups, and various other sections with more complex relations to the means of production. Thus the balance of class forces within a society will vary with its class composition; with the alliances formed between workers and capitalists and other groups; with the degree of repression; with the power of the dominant ideology; and with the strength of the political perception of their class interest by the various groups. In many European countries the peasantry formed a conservative social group which provided the political base for right-wing parties like the Gaullists, who supported capital. Thus nationalization and planning in post-war France posed much less of a political threat than in the UK, since the mass working class vote and political pressure were partly offset by that of the rural areas. In addition France had a tradition of a much more powerful state and bureaucracy, while the political power of large business was reduced by the reaction against their widespread collaboration with the nazis during the Occupation. It is noticeable, however that as the left-wing vote grew in France, partly reflecting the shift of labour from agriculture, there was also a shift away from direct state intervention and planning toward the UK pattern of demand management. Planning is efficient for capital when it is under capitalist control, but it can be a dangerous threat when that control cannot be guaranteed. The power of religious ideology (the basis of the Christian Democrat parties in Europe) and the effect of Stalinism and the Cold War in splitting working class movements also shifted the balance of class forces against the working class in post-war Europe.

8-4 STATE APPARATUS AND POLICY

Even if the demands of capital have been clearly expressed through the political process and working class opposition has been overcome, the form of the state institutions may still influence the implementation of policy, and there may be limitations to the state's ability to deal with the problems or meet the needs of capital. Within the state there is a great heterogeneity in the form of organization; the National Health Service and the army, for instance, have quite different structures. The structures of the institutions, which have developed in response to economic and political pressures in the past, may have great conservatism, allowing them to change only very slowly. Thus the institutions may be mere fossils of past pressures, quite unsuitable for meeting current needs, and such failures of the state to respond to new demands are a major source of political crisis. There may be similar heterogeneity in the groups who run the state. The state in the UK is capitalist, in that the institutions developed in response to the needs of capitalism and to maintain that system, but the people who operate and control the institutions may not be capitalists—as was true of the British government through much of the nineteenth century when it was still controlled by landowners. Thus at times political and economic power may not match—although, since economic power can buy control of the media, advertising, and the support of powerful individuals, there is a tendency for the two to converge.

However, while it is wrong to see state actions as completely determined by economic requirements in purely functional terms, neither can the state be seen as a neutral institution independent of the economic structure, which can be taken over and used for any purpose. Imagine a left-wing party taking power in the UK and trying to implement a radical programme of reform. There would be opposition from civil servants, making implementation difficult; the measures would be likely to threaten profitability, causing a collapse in stock market prices and a reduction in investment and employment by firms; there would be a movement of money capital out of the country, causing a foreign exchange crisis; relocation of production by multi-national companies; and non-cooperation or retaliation by other capitalist states. Notice that none of this requires a conspiracy by capitalists. Each individual firm is merely taking prudent precautions to protect profitability. But the consequence of the logic of the system has the appearance of a massive failure by the socialist state to manage the economy. The structural constraint that the state faces, irrespective of the subjective beliefs and class allegiance of the politicians in power, is that in a capitalist economy success requires that capitalists be kept happy so that they will continue investing and employing in that country. The operation of these economic contraints goes some way to explain the similarities in policy followed by both parties in the post-war period, despite the difference in their ideologies. Recognizing the economic constraints deriving from the structure of the system does not mean that it is impossible to change the structure. This could be done by a determined government with mass popular support; the point is that to deal with the problems requires major changes in the structure and organization of the state apparatus and economy. It is impossible just to use the existing apparatus to implement radically different policies.

The manner in which the state now influences the economy takes a wide variety of forms. Goods and services it provides can be allocated either through the market, as with nationalized industries; by right, as in the case of education; on the basis of need as assessed by the state, in the case of supplementary benefit and other means-tested benefits; or on the basis of queuing, as in the case of health. The state also influences the economy through regulations and laws on matters such as safety, industrial relations, and trade, enforced through the courts or special tribunals. Its incidental powers obtained through the purchase of goods and services, provision of grants and allowances to firms, and control over building and location can be used to put pressure on economic agents to follow certain courses, as in the case of sanctions to enforce pay policy. Finally, it has substantial moral and ideological power to influence people's behaviour by propaganda and publicity even when there is no direct intervention. The form of provision and intervention are not matters of indifference since the way policy operates in practice will depend to a large extent on the institutional form chosen.

In evaluating policy, it should be recognized that the manifest or claimed objectives of the policy may give little guidance either to its true purpose or its true effect. In the process of implementation, a policy that has a particular purpose as its avowed objective may be so transformed that, while retaining its name, it does something quite different. An example is regional policy, the avowed objective of which was to reduce unemployment in the depressed regions. However, for much of the post-war period, regional policy was implemented by a system of investment grants and allowances. These were subsidies to capital which reduced the price of plant and equipment relative to labour, thus encouraging the siting of highly capital-intensive processes in the regions, which did very little for employment. Nor should it necessarily be thought that simply because a group of measures is linked together and called a policy, they are linked by a consistent structure or a coherent strategy. Politicians have talked about UK energy policy, transport policy, and industrial policy, but what has characterized the substantial intervention in all three areas is the lack of any coherent framework. Adding together all the government does in an area does not constitute a strategy.

The divergence between the manifest or apparent purpose of a policy and the form of its implementation, on the one hand, and the tendency of much government intervention to be *ad hoc* rather than part of a coherent strategy, on the other raises questions about the mechanisms by which the state monitors and controls the implementation of policy. This issue came to the forefront with the debate on the public expenditure cuts in 1976–7, when public expenditure was represented as running out of control. Within the market sector, control over expenditure and production are enforced by profitability and competition, at great social cost, through bankruptcy, redundancy, and plant closures. Within government, if control is to be enforced, it must be through the political process, and the programme of cuts represented a major attempt to reassert the control and discipline of capital over the production of public sector output. This involved a shift in the level at which control was maintained, from the level of real output to the level of money expenditure.

The public production process can be thought of as having three levels, in terms of real outputs, real inputs, and money expenditures. The real outputs are the end products—the number of hospital beds, provision of benefits and welfare services, defence capabilities—what the state actually provides. Most legislation is expressed in terms of outputs, and the highly complex Treasury PESC (Public Expenditure Survey Committee) system maintained relatively effective control in this area. The second level is in terms of real inputs—the number of civil servants, doctors, nurses, or soldiers, or the amount of construction required to provide a given level of real output. This will depend on the productivity of the public sector labour process and on the external environment. The real service may be providing every child with an education, but the number of teachers required depends on pupil–teacher ratios and the number of children in each age group. The third level is the money expenditure, which will also depend on the wage levels of public sector workers, the general rate of inflation and the level of unemployment. It is this money total that determines taxation and borrowing requirements. Errors in forecasting wages, inflation or unemployment are then reflected in deviations of expenditure from target.

In the early seventies the planning system emphasized control in real terms; then, with the large increases in unemployment and inflation, money expenditures grew unexpectedly fast, even though the real provision of goods and services (public expenditure in volume terms) remained on target. In response to this and to substantial political pressure, PESC was supplemented by a system of cash limits, which imposed controls on the money totals. The consequence was that adjustment to unexpected movements in inflation and unemployment was taken not by the borrowing requirement but by the provision of real services—hospital beds were taken out of use, classrooms became more crowded, and local authorities had to cut back on their activities. When cash limits bite, programmes have to be stopped unexpectedly, causing disruption and inefficiency in provision as well as considerable hardship. The issue is thus what level bears the cost of adjustment, and the battle over the cuts was over the attempt to restore market discipline, money control, at the expense of planning real output and the use values provided.

Control is complicated by the contradictory position of the Treasury. On the one hand, planning expenditure requires it to forecast the cost of services, inflation, and unemployment; on the other hand, these are macro variables that it is trying to influence, and Treasury forecasts have political implications. For instance, when planning expenditure it may seem appropriate to allow for likely increases in unemployment and inflation, but such forecasts may cast current policy in an unfavourable light, and be politically damaging to the government.

The description above was given in terms of the production of public sector outputs, but in many cases (e.g., taxation and the payment of benefits) the policy merely involves the transfer of money. In such cases the efficiency of the process depends on how well the transfer meets the intended goals and the administrative cost of the programme. Usually the only administrative cost measured is that incurred in the public sector, but most programmes also impose a cost on the private sector, the rest of society. These costs include travelling to government offices to collect benefits, answering questions and filling out forms, keeping records for VAT and other taxes, and certain losses of freedom. These are rarely included in the cost of the policy. For instance, great weight is attached by some writers to the fact that in the US income tax seems to be much more cheaply administered than in the UK, but this is largely because in the US taxpayers have to calculate their own tax, while in the UK this is done by Inland Revenue. In the US every spring, shop-front accountants blossom forth in every town to help to fill out tax returns for a fee. These resources should be included in any calculation of relative administrative costs. Having considered the determination and control of policy, the next issue is its consequences.

8-5 THE ECONOMIC CONSEQUENCES OF POLICY

In trying to judge the effects on the economy of particular government intervention, there are many ways to categorize the outcome. For instance, the policies may influence the relative degree of control that workers and managers have over the process of production; the international division of labour and production; the flexibility of the economic system to adjust to change; or the quality of the environment and the depletion of non-renewable energy resources. However, orthodox analysis of policy considers the consequences in terms of five categories of variable:

(a) Macro variables like inflation, unemployment, growth, and the balance of payments.
(b) The supply of inputs available for production—capital, labour, raw materials, etc.

(c) The relative prices of inputs or outputs.

(d) The efficiency of the productive system.

(e) The distribution of income and wealth.

In practice any policy is likely to influence each of these. For instance, consider selective employment tax, a tax on each employee of a firm, charged at different rates in different industries, introduced in 1966 and abolished in 1972. It was designed to shift labour from the low productivity growth service sector to the higher productivity growth manufacturing sector, thus increasing the average growth rate. But since manufacturing demand did not expand proportionately, it instead increased unemployment. These are category (a) effects on growth and unemployment and (b) effects on the supply of labour to manufacturing. The differential tax rates changed the relative price of labour between manufacturing and services, a category (c) effect. Firms claimed that their efficiency (d) was reduced by the tax-related administrative work, classifying their activities, etc., and since the tax was a fixed amount per worker for each industry, it was a proportionately larger burden on low paid workers, tending to discriminate against them, so having distributional effects (e). Thus any particular policy is likely to have implications for each of the categories.

Rather than adopt this framework, we shall analyse the economic consequences of state policy largely in terms of their relation to the needs of capital, discussed in section 8–3. Chapter 10 will be largely concerned with the role of the state in production, Chapter 11 with its role in the reproduction of society. Other aspects are dealt with elsewhere in the book. For instance, macro-economic policy was discussed in Chapter 7, and distribution will be considered in Chapter 22. More generally, the issues raised by the economic consequences of state policy pervade the book because it is impossible to neatly partition the interaction between state, capital, and labour into separate components.

8-6 CONCLUSIONS

The discussion above has tried to emphasize the pervasive nature of state influence on the economy, because it provides the structure and environment within which capitalist firms can operate. But at times of crisis, merely providing the framework within which the economy can operate from day to day becomes inadequate, and then the state must intervene and organize directly. It may do this by taking over and running an important firm in danger of collapse (Rolls-Royce or British Leyland); using troops to maintain services or supplies; or directly controlling the use of resources through rationing or legislation, as during the three-day week in 1974. Another example of such direct organization when market operation failed was the formation of the 'lifeboat' by the Bank of England in December

1973, which over the following year provided £1200 million for failing 'secondary' banks, and involved the banking subsidiary of Slater Walker becoming part of the Bank of England. As Gordon Richardson said in evidence to the Select Committee on Nationalized Industries in January 1978:

> We had as our purpose protecting depositors, and the purpose of protecting depositors was simply to avoid a widening circle of collapse through the contagion of fear. The danger was real and, of course, we had seen it in the past. We saw it, for example, rage through the American banking system in the early 1930's, when hundreds and hundreds of banks were closed and finally a total closedown of the banking system was involved. (Quoted in Reid, 1978, p. 27).

The guarantee of state intervention and organization in the event of a massive market failure provides an essential stability and insurance against disaster. This is not, of course, to say that such intervention and organization will always be forthcoming or effective; this will depend on the political and economic forces involved in particular cases. In the case of the international banking crisis of 1973–4—with the failure of the Herstatt Bank in West Germany, the Franklin National in the US, and London and Counties Securities and other secondary banks in the UK—there was some danger that a major global breakdown would not be averted. The severity of the crisis arose partly from the fact that, while capital and these banks were international, each of the states operated only within one nation. Each country had a 'lender of the last resort' to guarantee the stability of its domestic banking system, but there was no lender of the last resort for the 'offshore' international Eurodollar market. The international nature of capital is discussed in Chapter 12.

The next few chapters will concentrate on the normal organization of the domestic economic framework by the state. But in examining this, two points should be remembered. First, in crisis the state can always supplement its normal operation with direct intervention. And second, there is a major contradiction between the national character of the state and the international character of capital.

FURTHER READING

Marxist thinking on the state has been much influenced by Karl Marx's *Critique of the Gotha Programme* and Lenin's *State and Revolution*.

Jessop (1977) provides a survey of recent Marxist theories of the state and gives many references. Useful discussions can be found in Miliband (1969) and in Poulantzas (1975b and 1980).

See also Holloway and Picciotto, S. (1978). A systemic presentation of Gramsci's views can be found in Buci-Glucksmann (1979). Important issues are raised in Hunt (1979).

Collections of articles that deal with the operations of the state in Britain are: Urry and Wakeford (1973) and Crouch (1979).

Orthodox treatments of economic policy may be found in Brown and Jackson (1978). An important aspect of state activity is explored in Hall *et al.* (1978).

NINE

STATE INCOME AND EXPENDITURE

Ron Smith and Roger Moore

The chapter provides a critical summary of the main features of government expenditure and taxation. It is primarily a factual review, and readers may wish therefore to use it for reference and proceed directly to Chapter 10.

9-1 INTRODUCTION

The purpose of this chapter is to provide a short empirical summary of the monetary magnitudes of state involvement in the economy. However, 'the state' is a theoretical concept, to which there is no corresponding accounting category in the published data. The closest approximation in the data is what is called the 'public sector'. This comprises three main components: central government, local authorities, and public corporations (essentially nationalized industries). The first two components, central government and local authorities, are often grouped together to form the category 'general government'. These definitions reflect administrative arrangements that may not correspond to actual functions. For instance, until 1969 the Post Office was formally part of central government, and then became a public corporation, but the change in form did not reflect any change in function.

The data on government income and expenditure must be treated with care and in general they are unable to provide straightforward answers to such questions as 'What is the share of the state in the economy?' One problem is that the question is not specific enough and can have a large number of answers, depending on the precise definitions used. Even a much more specific question such as 'What is the share of public expenditure in national income?' will still have many possible answers, depending on which definition is used, as Table 9-1 shows. In the Table, the various figures are expressed as percentages of GNP at factor cost, but GNP at market prices or some other national income aggregate could have been used. If market price GNP had been used in the denominator, all the percentages would have been lower, and if the balance of indirect taxation were to change, the size of the relative movements would also be affected. The first two rows which use general government expenditure on goods and services measure total government use of the resources of the country, through employing workers or through purchasing goods from the other sectors for government consumption or investment. In current prices this share was just over a quarter of GNP and stable over the period. In constant prices it fell by over three per cent of GNP. The difference between the two is the result of what is known as the relative price effect. According to the figures, the implicit price of government goods and services rose by much more than that for the output of the whole economy. Between 1968 and 1978 the price index for government rose 245 per cent against 206 per cent for GNP. Thus, since the government faced rising relative prices, a constant share of the money total brought a smaller real share. Suppose the total value of government expenditure is G, and income Y, both in current prices; and the price index for government expenditure is PG and for all output PY. The share in

Table 9-1 Shares of public expenditure in GNP

	£m		Percentage of GNP	
	1968	1978	1968	1978
General government expenditure on goods and services:				
current prices	9 844	37 161	25.98	26.02
1975 prices	24 687	27 047	29.90	26.67
General government, total expenditure,				
current prices	18 289	71 351	48.27	49.95
Expenditure of public corporations,				
current prices	7 058	31 552	18.70	22.09
GNP at factor cost:				
current prices	37 890	142 835	—	—
1975 prices	82 554	101 406	—	—

Source: National Income and Expenditure (1979).

current prices is then G/Y and in constant prices $(G/PG)/(Y/PY)$, i.e., the current price share times PY/PG. If PG inflates faster than PY the real share then falls relative to the current share. There is, however, a problem, because most goods and services provided by the government are not sold, thus we do not observe any prices from which to construct an index PG. Nor are there any measures of the volume of output produced by the government, since it mainly provides services. In practice it is assumed that the volume of output is proportional to the volume of input (e.g., the number of civil servants), which is equivalent to assuming that there is no productivity growth in the government sector. The constructed price index for the government then increases in line with rises in wages and salaries, whereas for the economy as a whole it is reduced by the rate of growth of productivity. It is difficult to tell whether this measured productivity differential is a real phenomenon or merely a statistical artefact without evidence of the real output produced by the government.

The third row of Table 9-1 gives total general government expenditure at current prices. This includes government expenditure on transfers (pensions, unemployment benefits, debt interest, etc.) as well as expenditure on goods and services. This is the figure that is used in common discussion of the share of government expenditure; it accounts for about half of GNP and rose by 1½ per cent of GNP between 1968 and 1978. Transfer payments do not involve a claim by the government on output, but merely a redistribution within the private sector. When the government buys goods or hires workers it is directly using resources that could be used for something else, but when it pays unemployment benefit or interest on the national debt there is no corresponding demand for goods or services until the recipient spends the money, and it then appears in the national income accounts as part of private consumption or investment. Thus it is possible for government expenditure, including transfer payments, to be greater than national income even though there exists a large private sector. For completeness the fourth row gives expenditure by public corporations. This cannot be added to general government expenditure to give total public sector expenditure since this would lead to double counting, subsidies to public corporations having already been included in general government expenditure.

9-2 THE STRUCTURE OF EXPENDITURE

Total government expenditure can be disaggregated in two main ways: by programme or function (what the expenditure is used for) or by economic category (what type of expenditure it is). Table 9-2 gives the general government expenditure account using both presentations, for 1968 and 1978. The largest components of expenditure are social security benefits, health, education, housing, and defence. Interpretation of these expenditure figures poses difficulties, and they may not be good indicators of how much money the government devotes to a particular area. The case of housing provides an illustration. For a variety of reasons the UK government provides help towards the cost of housing, but this help comes in two forms. For owner occupiers it is a tax allowance on mortgage interest and an exemption of the increase in the value of the house from capital gains tax. For council house tenants it is a direct subsidy. The former is a tax concession by the government, the latter is an expenditure that appears in the Table. Although the 'help' provided is of a similar nature in each case, they are treated quite differently in the accounts. Similarly, capital formation in the UK has been encouraged at times either by investment grants, which are a direct expenditure, or by investment allowances, which reduced the tax paid by firms making investments. In the 1979 Public

Table 9-2 Composition of public expenditure and percentages of total expenditure

	1968	1978
By function		
Defence	13.36	10.53
External relations	1.61	2.76
Roads and transport	6.85	3.99
Employment, industry, and agriculture	11.93	7.15
Housing, environmental services, etc.	10.59	11.17
Law, order, and protective services	2.56	3.33
Education	12.29	12.78
National Health Services	9.05	10.67
Personal social services	0.80	1.95
Social security benefits	18.26	22.12
Tax collection, records, and other services	1.66	1.86
	88.96	88.31
By Economic Category		
Current expenditure on goods and services	40.55	44.36
Gross domestic capital formation	12.05	6.34
Subsidies	4.89	5.04
Current grants to personal sector	20.11	25.02
Current grants abroad	0.98	2.38
Capital grants and net lending to private sector	3.84	2.15
Capital transfers and net lending to public corporations	6.24	3.12
Other	0.30	−0.10
	88.96	88.31
Debt interest	9.81	10.23
Non-trading capital consumption	1.23	1.46
	100	100

Source: National Income and Expenditure (1979), Table 9.4.

Expenditure White Paper (Cmnd 7439) a list of such 'tax expenditures' is published, giving the value of the reliefs, allowances, etc., given to special groups. In 1978–9, the estimated cost of mortgage interest relief was £1110 million, and exemption of owner-occupied houses from capital gains tax cost £1500 million, although the latter figure is particularly tentative. The estimated subsidy to council house tenants in the same year was £1589 million.

The second part of Table 9–2 shows that the bulk of government expenditure was on current purchases of goods and services, followed by current grants to the personal sector; and that capital expenditure fell as a proportion of total expenditure. Capital expenditures tend to be the easiest to cut when economies are required. The data in Table 9-2 comes from the national income accounts and are presented by calender year. The other main source of information is the annual public expenditure White Paper, which gives data for financial years. The White Paper definition of public expenditure differs somewhat from that for general government total expenditure. The White Paper also gives planned expenditure for future years, although changes of circumstances and government cause these plans to be regularly revised. As an illustration, Table 9-3 gives the composition of public expenditure by programme for 1977-8 and the composition

Table 9-3 Public expenditure by programme

	1977–78[a]	1980–81 Labour[b]	Cons[a]
Defence	11.52	11.29	11.40
Overseas payments	2.80	3.06	3.10
Agriculture, fish, food, and forestry	1.63	1.27	1.40
Industry, energy, trade, and employment	3.75	4.87	4.06
Government lending to nationalized industries	−0.36	1.22	1.27
Roads and transport	4.61	4.37	4.12
Housing	8.40	8.40	7.18
Other environmental services	4.98	4.82	4.54
Law, order, and protective services	3.49	3.33	3.59
Education, science, arts, and libraries	14.29	13.56	13.07
Health and personal social services	13.39	13.02	13.00
Social security	25.32	24.62	27.27
Other public services	1.48	1.40	1.41
Common services	1.56	1.70	1.54
Northern Ireland	3.13	3.06	3.04

[a] 1980–81, Cmnd 7746, November 1979.
[b] 1979–80 to 1982–3, Cmnd 7439, January 1979.
Sources: The Government's Expenditure Plans.

planned for 1980–81 by the Labour government in January 1979 and by the Conservative government in November 1979 respectively. The published figures are given in 'survey prices', i.e., those ruling at the time that public expenditure was surveyed and the plans were made. At 1979 survey prices the Labour government's plans were about three per cent higher than those of the Conservative government, and whereas Labour planned public expenditure to rise slightly between 1979–80 and 1980–81, the Conservatives planned that it should fall. Comparison between the two is complicated by the different assumptions that were made in each case about likely income growth, public sector pay levels, and pensions.

Expenditure in each category reflects a variety of factors. On the demand side, there are demographic pressures—increases in the number of children in the population will push up education spending; increases in the number of old people will push up health and pension expenditure. There are also pressures from the economic or physical environment—more unemployment requires spending on benefits, more pollution puts pressure on health expenditure. Political pressures will influence the level of benefit or service per client, and the priority the government attaches to particular areas. On the supply side, expenditure will be influenced by the wage rates paid to public sector employees and the ability of these employees to defend the level of provision.

The orthodox neo-classical explanation for state expenditure is in terms of a response to market failure. This derives from the normative criteria that the state should produce, regulate, or subsidize goods where the price mechanism fails to provide optimal amounts of them. One example of market failure is 'public goods', where access to the good cannot be rationed (i.e., people cannot be excluded from use of the good) and consumption of it by one person does not reduce the amount available for consumption by others. The example usually given of such a good is defence. It is difficult to imagine a pricing system that would allow each individual to buy their preferred amount of defence in a free market, since if a country is defended all inhabitants benefit to some extent. A closely related market failure arises from externalities, where the consumption or production of a good by one individual influences the welfare of others. Thus there are spill-over effects of individual choices, causing public and private costs and benefits to diverge and the amount of the good generated by free market choice to differ from the social optimum. Spill-over effects arise from public health measures like vaccination. If decisions are made privately, 'economic man' balances the benefit of the reduced risk of the disease against the cost of the vaccination and any possible side effects, but does not take into account the benefit to others that arises from his vaccination in the form of the reduced risk of transmitting the disease. Although market failure is a pervasive phenomenon, it does not seem an appropriate basis for an explanation of state expenditure. In practice, the state becomes involved in production, distribution, and exchange for a whole variety of political, ideological, and economic reasons, and using some hypothetical perfect market as a point of departure does not seem helpful.

9-3 TAXATION

Table 9-4 gives data on general government revenue in 1968 and 1978. In 1968 income and expenditure taxes each produced about 30 per cent of total receipts; by 1978, while the share of income taxes had remained fairly steady, the share of expenditure taxes had fallen to under 25 per cent. This trend was reversed by the 1979 Conservative Budget, which switched the burden from direct to indirect taxes. Indirect or expenditure taxes include

Table 9-4 General government receipts (£m)

	1968	1978
Taxes on income	5 846	22 321
Taxes on expenditure	5 261	17 545
Rates	1 548	5 693
National insurance contributions	2 161	10 023
Rent, interest, surplus	1 389	5 343
Non-trading capital consumption	224	1 039
Taxes on capital	437	898
Receipts on financial account	1 423	8 489
Total	18 289	71 351

Source: National Income and Expenditure (1979), Table 9.1.

VAT, the duty on alcohol and tobacco, and the tax on petrol. The income tax total includes corporation tax and petroleum revenue tax on North Sea oil production. Although the revenue from the latter was still quite small in 1978 (£183 million), it will become a major source of government income in the eighties. The component labelled 'Rent, interest, surplus' includes the rents paid to local authorities on council houses, gross trading surplus, and interest and dividends paid to the government. The receipts on financial account largely consist of the money the government borrows to finance its deficit. The deficits and borrowing requirement are given in Table 9-5. In 1968 central government was in surplus (shown as a negative deficit). The total financial deficit is equal but of opposite sign to PS NAFA (the public sector net acquisition of financial assets). The government has to borrow to finance not only the deficit, but also its lending to the private sector; thus the public sector borrowing requirement (PSBR) is larger than the total deficit in both these years.

Table 9-5 The public sector deficit and borrowing requirement (£m)

	1968	1978
Financial deficits		
Central government	−970	5 436
Local authorities	1 189	1 348
Public corporations	725	1 093
Total (minus PS NAFA)	944	7 877
Net lending, etc.	351	461
Borrowing requirement	1 295	8 338

Source: National Income and Expenditure (1979) Tables 9.1 and 13.9.

To return to the tax system. Although the formal incidence of a tax is usually clear (i.e., who is responsible for paying it to the Customs and Excise or Inland Revenue) the actual incidence (i.e., who actually bears the cost) is rarely clear. For example, in terms of formal incidence, retailers pay VAT to the revenue authorities, and workers have income tax deducted from their wages under PAYE. But the retailer increases prices to cover VAT, so the burden is passed on to the consumer; while the worker may be able to obtain a wage rise to offset any increase in tax, thus transferring the incidence. Similar problems surround judging who benefits from tax allowances, since these may also change prices, for instance by being capitalized into asset values. Giving a tax advantage to owner occupiers makes a house a more attractive investment and increases demand, causing prices to rise. This rise in prices provides a capital gain to present owners but reduces the value of the tax allowance to new buyers, who have to pay higher prices. One consequence of these problems with assigning incidence and benefit is that the conventional classification of taxes in terms of whether they are direct (on income) or indirect (on expenditure), or in terms of whether they fall on persons or corporations, is of little significance.

One function of the tax system is to redistribute income, and its effectiveness in doing this is often judged by how progressive it is. A tax is progressive if the total tax paid as a proportion of income (the average tax rate) increases with income. This will happen if the marginal tax rate (the rate on the last or highest unit of income) is above the average rate. With a progressive tax system, the post-tax distribution of income will be more equal than the pre-tax one. In analysing the degree of progression it is important to consider not just taxes but also how they interact with the social security system. Many benefits provided by the state in the UK are means tested—e.g., rent and rates rebates and family income supplement. As income increases, these benefits are withdrawn, imposing an implicit tax on income. The marginal tax rate thus generated by means testing can be over 100 per cent, so that for a £1 increase in income the family loses more than £1 worth of benefits. This is the notorious poverty trap. In the UK, the marginal tax rate for income-related taxes and benefits is a U-shaped function of income. There are high marginal rates at low incomes, as a consequence of the means-tested benefits; a minimum representing the standard rate of income tax and proportional national insurance contributions; and then increasing marginal rates on higher incomes. Throughout the range, the marginal tax rate is above the average, so the net effect of the social security/income tax system is broadly progressive. With indirect taxes the position is less clear. For instance, they appear to be regressive if indirect taxes paid are expressed as a proportion of original income (i.e., before taxes and benefits) but slightly progressive as a proportion of final income: Consider a person with a very low original income who lives largely on grants from the state, such as a pension. The total value of the indirect taxes they pay on their expenditure may be larger than their original income, giving an average tax rate over 100 per cent. But if the taxes are related to their final income (including benefits), the average tax rate might be quite small. The tax paid will also be influenced by the composition of consumption, which varies greatly between different income groups.

A major factor influencing the average tax rate in the post-war period has been the rate of inflation. The income tax system operates by giving each person a set of allowances reflecting family and other circumstances and taxing any income over the value of those allowances. The allowances thus set the threshold income at which the person enters the tax net. Before the Second World War the threshold was set at such a level that only about a fifth of workers paid income tax. During the war the government set up PAYE, extending the tax net; and after the war inflation, by reducing the real value of the allowances and thus the threshold, drew even more within income tax. A married man with two children under 11 earning the average wage would have paid no income tax in 1948 and only become liable for tax in the mid fifties. Yet now for some households the threshold is below the poverty line as defined by the level at which supplementary benefit is paid. With inflation, even if real incomes are constant, people will be moved above the threshold, or into higher rates, so the average tax rate will rise and more people will be drawn into the net. This 'fiscal drag' allows the Chancellor to appear to cut taxes by raising allowances by merely offsetting the effects of inflation. By 1979 some allowances had been indexed, but over much of the post-war period low income groups have been moved out of the tax system, as the Chancellor raised allowances, only to be dragged back as inflation reduced their value, to be let out again at the next give-away Budget.

The system of corporate taxation is in many ways even more involved than that for persons. The complexity has arisen partly from the difficulty of determining the appropriate measure of profits to be taxed and partly because the system keeps being changed. The changes have reflected such factors as a desire to harmonize with the EEC; to close loopholes; to encourage investment or regional development; and in response to whether the fashion is to encourage firms to retain profits or pay them out in dividends. The net effect has been that the effective rate of tax paid by companies (as distinct from that paid on dividends, which is effectively income tax) has steadily declined, until in 1977–8 it was nearly zero. The main factor reducing liability for tax in recent years was the introduction of tax relief on stock appreciation in 1974 as a response to the major profits crisis. The consequence of this was that, despite quite high nominal rates, the tax has become virtually voluntary.

This divergence between effective and nominal rates of tax is quite a common phenomenon within the system. People and firms adjust their behaviour to minimize tax, and with adequate allowances and loopholes they may be able to avoid all tax. A distinction is made between avoidance, which is legal, and tax evasion, which is not. In causing people to adjust their behaviour, the taxes generate a variety of economic distortions and inefficiencies and considerable employment for tax lawyers and accountants.

Economists objecting to the anomalies and distortions of the present tax system have proposed several alternative structures: a lifetime expenditure tax, a negative income tax, a tax credit scheme, and so on. But tax systems evolve not in response to some clearly formulated economic and social principles but as the product of short-term revenue requirements, political pressures, administrative convenience, the need to close loopholes, and the desire by the state to encourage or discourage particular activities. The structure that results is thus very involved, and its net effect difficult to determine. Good discussions of the system as a whole can be found in Kay and King (1978) and Field *et al.* (1977).

9-4 INTERNATIONAL COMPARISONS

Across countries there are wide differences in the share of taxation and public expenditure in income; in the composition of public expenditure; and in the structure of the tax system. Some data for a selection of advanced capitalist countries is given in Tables 9-6 and 9-7. Across countries there tends to be a positive relation between the share of taxes or expenditure and *per capita* income, but the scatter is large and the relationship does not seem stable. There does not seem to be any relationship between the share of taxes and the growth rate; the US with a low growth rate and Japan with a high growth rate both have a low share of taxes. As always, there are qualifications to be made about the data. The figures may be distorted by differing institutional arrangements; the use of other denominators than GNP may change the rankings; and there is a variety of different definitions of both taxes and expenditure that could be used. But allowing for all this, during the sixties and seventies the result tended to be that Britain lay

Table 9-6 Taxation as a percentage of GNP in 1975

	Direct taxes	Social security contributions	Indirect taxes	Total taxes
France	8.2	16.7	16.0	40.9
West Germany	13.2	14.1	14.5	41.9
Italy	8.2	15.4	10.6	34.2
Netherlands	18.7	21.0	13.2	52.9
Sweden	25.6	10.2	16.3	52.0
US	14.2	7.9	10.0	32.1
Japan	10.5	5.6	7.0	23.1
UK	18.2	7.3	14.4	39.9

Table 9-7 Government Expenditure as a percentage of GNP in 1975

	Goods and services	Current grants	Subsidies	Total expenditure
France	20.5	21.8	2.2	44.4
West Germany	28.4	17.5	1.5	47.4
Italy	18.3	22.1	2.8	43.2
Netherlands	24.4	29.5	1.9	55.8
Sweden	33.2	19.1	2.4	54.6
US	23.4	12.9	0.3	36.7
Japan	18.3	7.5	1.5	27.4
UK	29.6	11.2	4.2	45.0

Source: Ward and Neild (1978), Tables B2 and B3.

somewhere in the middle, below the Scandinavian and some other European countries and above the US and Japan. Britain differed from most other European countries in raising a smaller proportion of revenue from social security contributions. It also differed in that, up to 1979, the top rates of income tax tended to be higher, although easily avoided.

The data give average tax shares, but for many purposes marginal tax rates are more significant. Consider what happens when the standard rate of tax is increased. First, this reduces workers' real income, which may encourage them to work longer hours—through more overtime, say—to make good this fall and maintain their standard of life. This is a positive 'income effect' on work, which depends on the average tax rate. But at the same time it reduces the marginal return to an extra hour's work, making it less attractive relative to leisure. This is a negative 'substitution effect' on work which depends on the marginal tax rate, the rate on an extra hour's work. The net influence of taxation on work depends on the relative magnitude of these two effects, which offset each other. There is, however, very little hard evidence on their relative size, which will in any case depend on the incomes of the individuals concerned, on their ability to change their hours of work, and on a whole range of other social factors. Although this 'incentive' argument has great political currency, there is little evidence on its importance.

9-5 THE 1980 BUDGET

In principle, a budget involves balancing income and expenditure, and making the necessary adjustments to assets and liabilities. In practice, until 1980 the Budget presented by the Chancellor of the Exchequer to Parliament in the spring of each year has been almost entirely concerned with taxation. Expenditure plans were outlined in the public expenditure White Paper, published earlier in the year. Although the tax proposals were formulated in the light of the prior expenditure plans, it was very difficult for analysts to mesh the two. For a variety of reasons, including some difficulty in formulating expenditure plans, in 1980 the Budget and expenditure plans were submitted simultaneously, on March 26. The details are given in the *Financial Statement and Budget Report 1980–81* (the Red Book) and *The Government's Expenditure Plans 1980–81 to 1983–84* (Cmnd 7841). Not only did the government provide taxation and expenditure proposals within a common framework at the same time; they also introduced another innovation, a 'medium-term financial strategy'.

The elements of the strategy are set out in Table 9-8. It involves setting targets for total expenditure, receipts, the PSBR, and money supply growth for the next four fiscal years, 1980–81 to 1983–4. Implied by these targets

Table 9-8 Conservative financial strategy

	1979–80	1980–81	1981–82	1982–83	1983–84
Total expenditure	74.5	74.5	73.0	71.0	70.5
Total receipts	−66.0	−67.5	−67.5	−69.5	−71.0
Implied fiscal adjustment	—	—	—	2.5	3.5
General government borrowing requirement	8.5	7.0	5.5	4.0	3.0
PSBR	8.0	6.0	5.0	3.5	2.5
PSBR % mkt price GDP	4.75	3.75	3.0	2.25	1.5
Range for growth of money stocks (£M3) %	7–11	7–11	6–10	5–9	4–8

Note: Unless otherwise stated, figures are £ billion, 1978–9 prices.
Source: Financial Statement and Budget Report 1980–81, HMSO, 1980.

are fiscal adjustments of (in 1978–9 prices) £2.5 billion in 1982–3 and £3.5 billion in 1983–4. These mean that if the targets are met taxation or the borrowing requirements could be reduced by the equivalent of £2.5 billion or expenditure increased by that amount in 1982–3. The Conservative preference would seem to be for tax reductions prior to the next election, which might be expected in 1983–4. The strategy involves real public expenditure falling steadily, taxation increasing, and both the PSBR as a percentage of GDP and the rate of growth of the money supply (on the £M3 measure) falling. These targets involve some judgement about likely growth in GDP, and the assumption is that it will be at roughly the same rate as over 1973–9, around 1 per cent a year. This is rather lower than the pre-1973 average rate of between $2\frac{1}{2}$ and 3 per cent a year. Such forecasts are, of course, beset with uncertainty, and the government mention various factors that could significantly change the growth rate of the economy and hence the finances of the public sector. In such circumstances they insist that there would be no question of departing from the money supply policy set, and that expenditure, taxation, or interest rates would have to adjust.

Any economic evaluation of this financial strategy depends on some judgement about the influence of the money supply on inflation, the influence of the PSBR on the money supply, and the relative effects of expenditure and tax changes on the PSBR and on the economy. The implied government argument is that the cuts in public expenditure and taxation will both stimulate private output and demand and reduce the PSBR. The cut in the PSBR will reduce the rate of growth of money supply and this will reduce the rate of inflation. But not only are the mechanisms behind these links obscure, there is also little evidence in favour of them. For instance, the proposed cuts in public expenditure by deflating demand may increase unemployment, reduce revenue, and actually make the deficit larger than it would otherwise have been. Although the PSBR and the change in money supply are linked by an identity, the movement of the other factors in the equation—such as bank lending and sales of public sector debt to the private sector—have been such that there is little empirical association between PSBR and the change in £M3. Nor is there much evidence that control of £M3 influences inflation. In terms of class interests these monetarist policies may represent a rational response by a capitalist state, in ways that are discussed further in Chapter 23, but in terms of the purported economic argument they seem largely a matter of faith.

There are also a number of technical problems with the projections. In terms of past history, the assumed 1 per cent GDP growth may seem pessimistic, but in the light of the expected drop in output of $2\frac{1}{2}$ per cent during 1980–81, it appears optimistic, since it is not clear what will subsequently stimulate growth. The reduction in the PSBR also depends heavily on a transformation in the financial position of the nationalized industries, who are expected to switch from net borrowing of £2.3 billion in 1979–80 to net repayments of £0.4 billion in 1983–4. Since their total capital requirements are expected to rise by £0.65 billion over the period, their prices will have to rise very rapidly or their costs be cut. The Budget does not discuss either the scope for cost cutting or likely inflationary effects. It has also been argued in the financial press that the implicit assumptions about North Sea oil revenues are ultra-conservative, and the implied fiscal adjustments should be substantially bigger. The proposed turn around may also put severe strains on corporate finances.

The aspect of the Budget that achieves the most publicity is the tax changes. This Budget contained a very large number of them, the bulk of which were merely adjustments made necessary by inflation. In total the proposals involved a reduction in income tax worth just under £1.2 billion and an increase in specific duties (on cigarettes, alcohol, petrol, etc.) of a little over £1.2 billion. On the basis of the rates of taxation ruling in 1979–80, therefore, it was broadly neutral. Compared with what revenue would have been had the 1979–80 tax rates been fully adjusted for inflation, it was deflationary, raising revenue by an extra £1.6 billion. The effects of inflation on income tax and specific duties appear exactly opposite. To keep effective tax rates constant in times of inflation, specific duties must be raised (inflation makes them a smaller percentage of value), while income tax must be reduced (allowances raised). The effective rate of value added tax, which is a direct percentage of expenditure, is not influenced by inflation. The 1980 Budget reversed some of the switch from direct to indirect tax in the 1979 Budget, since effective income tax rates were increased by the abolition of the 25 per cent lower rate bands, and the specific duties were not fully increased to offset past inflation.

In total, the Budget reduced the 1980–81 PSBR by £810 million, made up of a £235 million increase in revenue and a £575 million reduction in expenditure. The projected expenditure changes would keep expenditure in real terms constant between 1979–80 and 1980–81, with a projected fall thereafter to a level 4 per cent lower in 1983–84 than in 1979–80. This means that expenditure in 1982–3 would be $11\frac{1}{2}$ per cent (9 billion in 1979 survey prices) below that planned by the previous Labour government In the Cmnd 7439 figures used above. Over the survey period to 1983–4 expenditure on defence, law and order, health, and social security is projected to rise; that for industry, energy, trade and employment programme, housing, and education to fall substantially. All these changes are relative to 1979–80 levels.

Table 9-9 shows projected public expenditure by programme in 1979–80 and 1982–3, and the proposed changes from the previous government plans. The largest change is in expenditure on housing, a reduction of £3.3 billion. Neither the Budget statement nor the expenditure White Paper makes it clear how this cut, which is equivalent to a reduction of 48 per cent, is to be achieved. Unlike Cmnd 7439, it only gives the total planned and not the breakdown into capital expenditure, rent subsidies, etc. Thus there is no indication of the extent to which the target is to be met by rent increases as against reduced house building. In this and a number of other cases the distinction between expenditure and taxation in the government accounts has little meaning. Increases in council house rents, prescription charges, nationalized industry prices and the like are all equivalent to tax increases, although they are presented by the government as expenditure reductions.

Table 9-9 also brings out the need to be specific about the base when discussing expenditure changes. It would be legitimate to say either that the Conservative government intended to cut public expenditure by £3.4 billion and raise social security spending by £0.61 billion by 1982–3, or that they intended to cut public expenditure by £9.65 billion and cut social security by £0.5 billion. The former uses the 1979–80 figures as a base, the latter the

Table 9-9 Expenditure plans, 1980

	1979–80 £m	1979–80 %	1982–3 £m	1982–3 %	Changes from Cmnd 7439 £m
Defence	7 723	10.3	8 490	11.8	+ 260
Overseas contribution	794	1.1	680	0.9	− 330
EEC contribution	919	1.2	1 300	1.8	+ 430
Other overseas services	432	0.6	400	0.6	− 30
Agriculture, fisheries, food, and forestry	944	1.3	900	1.3	− 50
Industry, energy, trade, and employment	2 969	4.0	1 910	2.7	− 1 490
Govt lending to nat. inds.	1 900	2.5	− 150	− 0.2	− 1 150
Roads and transport	3 073	4.1	2 690	3.8	− 470
Housing	5 372	7.2	3 250	4.5	− 3 290
Other environmental services	3 273	4.4	2 920	4.1	− 590
Law, order, and protective services	2 446	3.3	2 670	3.7	+ 30
Education and science	9 654	12.9	8 850	12.3	− 970
Health and personal social services	9 067	12.1	9 410	13.1	− 400
Social security	18 890	25.1	19 500	27.2	− 500
Other public services	1 014	1.4	950	1.3	− 90
Common services	1 047	1.4	1 080	1.5	− 150
Northern Ireland	2 200	2.9	2 070	2.9	− 210
Total programme	71 716		66 900		− 9 000
Contingency reserve	84	0.1	1 500	2.1	− 1 250
Debt interest	3 300	4.4	3 300	4.6	+ 600
Total public expenditure	75 100	100.0	71 700	100.0	− 9 650

Note: All money totals are at 1979 survey prices; percentages may not add to totals because of rounding.
Source: The Government's Expenditure Plans 1980–81 to 1983–84, Cmnd 7841, Tables 1.6 and 5.8.

Labour government's plans for 1982–3. Both these sets are in 1979 survey prices; if one allows for price changes one can get other estimates. In any event, the figures refer to plans and intentions, although the government go to some length to insist that their 'strategy' is not a 'plan'. Whether or not government policy goes through a U-turn, it is almost inevitable that the outcome will be very different. Quite apart from the technical problems of economic forecasting, the political feasibility of the projections must be questionable, although that will depend partly on the strength of the resistance to them.

FURTHER READING

Comprehensive, if conventional, treatment can be found in Brown and Jackson (1978). The official statistical material is to be found in the *National*

Income and Expenditure Blue Books, *Economic Trends*, etc., all of which have already featured.

An interesting discussion from a Marxist viewpoint can be found in O'Connor (1973), although the focus is on the US.

A full introduction to the economics of the UK tax system can be found in Kay and King (1978). Ward and Neild (1978) examine the role of the Budget. Field *et al.* (1977) shows in detail the regressive nature of much of British taxation.

Valuable material on income distribution and wealth can be found in Atkinson (1974), Atkinson and Harrison (1978), and the various reports of the Royal Commission on the Distribution of Income and Wealth.

TEN

THE STATE AND PRODUCTION

Sam Aaronovitch

10-1 INTRODUCTION

The relationship between the state and the economy was discussed in broad terms in Chapter 9. It can be argued that the state has always been in different ways involved in the economy not only as an external influence but directly engaged in economic activities. Even so, leaving aside two world wars, the state has become increasingly intertwined with the economy in all advanced capitalist countries. The dimensions of this involvement include the legal structure within which production takes place and the infrastructure (roads, utilities, basic services, etc.) that needs to be created and regulated. It includes the immense growth in the money-raising and spending power of the state and its influence on the private sector through subsidies, taxation, and other forms of transfer. It includes the direct employment and control of resources, including those sectors of industry that are state owned.

Given that state intervention is a political response to pressures produced by the interaction of class struggle with the needs of capital, subject to a variety of constraints, it is inevitable that the outcome will be complex and contradictory and cannot be reduced to a single monocausal explanation. What is required by capital and by labour may conflict and what the system can provide may not match the expectations of either. Further, capital faces a special problem with any extension of state control: the possibility that a strong labour movement may become the governmental power and use the levers in a way hostile to capital.

In the post-war period, and especially from the fifties, we can see a number of powerful forces that have necessitated the extension of the state's role in the economy. First is the onset of critical problems facing the UK economy, expressed in relatively low rates of growth, frequent balance of payments crises, and structural failures affecting entire industries and communities. The second factor is the growth in the scale of firms, with rising concentration and growing internationalization. Within the labour movement these two sets of forces became the grounds for a more radical programme of state intervention and public ownership as shown in the

Labour Party programme of 1973. The third force was the degree of trade union organization and shopfloor influence and its impact on the workings of the labour market, reducing the disciplinary powers of management. This was not an easy field for state intervention but both Conservative and Labour governments have attempted to limit working class bargaining power.

All these forces taken together have required increased effort at regulation and coordination even though UK governments have been reluctant interventionists, as we suggested in Chapter 7. The 1979 Conservative government has made a determined effort to reverse the character of state intervention and coordination in the economy, using state power to intervene in such a way as to discipline the labour force through unemployment, direct economic pressures, and through amending trade union law. This is a change in the form of intervention, not the refusal to intervene that the government claims.

In the rest of this chapter, we discuss in Section 10-2 the influence of the state on the decision of private firms; in Section 10-3 the direct control of production through nationalization; and in Section 10-4 the response of governments to the problems of rising concentration and the dominance in most markets of small numbers of large firms.

10-2 INDUSTRIAL POLICIES

By the end of the fifties, the then Conservative government and the Federation of British Industries (the forerunner of the CBI) began to acknowledge the consequences of the much higher rates of growth of Britain's main rivals and the belief grew that this was not the result of any deficiency of demand but a failure of the productive system—i.e., a supply failure. It therefore seemed appropriate to consider some kind of planned restructuring of the system to improve the underlying rate of productivity. Influenced by French planning experience, the Conservative government, supported by the FBI, set up the National Economic and Development Office (NEDO), with Conservative Ministers declaring that they were not afraid of planning.

The modernization of the UK economy, if it was to be carried through within the framework of capitalism, clearly required a weakening of the bargaining power of the unions as well as breaking up a number of established positions and market structures. Sections of business felt that the Conservative government would not be able to carry this through and this contributed to the 1964 Labour victory in the general election. Labour's programme was presented as one of modernization and technological change; a series of new initiatives and institutions was devised. In particular, a National Plan, with the objective of putting the economy on a $4\frac{1}{2}$ per cent growth path, was prepared and put in the hands of a Department of

Economic Affairs, while NEDO was put into hibernation. A Ministry of Technology was created; the Industrial Reorganisation Corporation was formed to help rationalize and merge UK firms so that they would be larger and more able to compete on an international plane. A National Prices and Incomes Board was set up to examine the productivity and performance of the firms it investigated. The National Plan, was, however, only a set of targets, and its expansionist philosophy collapsed within a year when the government, confronted by a balance of payments crisis, began a restrictive and deflationary policy. The IRC undoubtedly contributed to the large-scale merger boom of the sixties which increased the rate of concentration and altered the structure of a number of industries (the period of the formation of British Leyland and the merger of GEC with AEI and English Electric). In the circumstances, the activity of the IRC became just another restructuring of capital with government help.

Restructuring the labour market proved to be a difficult task for the government and it failed to carry through any major change in the legal position of trades unions.

With the Conservative Party victory in 1970, the Heath government set about a reversal of the trend to increased state intervention, abolishing the NPBI, the IRC, the Ministry of Technology, and the DEA. The problems faced by the government led it, however, to make a dramatic U-turn: as part of its counter-inflationary policy, it intervened directly on prices (establishing a Price Code) and on wages, dividends, and rent; and in 1972 it put through the Industry Act, which gave it wide powers of intervention, assistance to industries and regions, etc. In 1971 it nationalized Rolls-Royce and had to rescue the yards that formed the Upper Clyde Shipbuilders.

The 1970 Conservative government did, however, push through legislation weakening the legal position of the trades unions; in doing so it faced growing resistance and the restrictions were repealed by the 1974 Labour government.

During this period of Conservative government, a growing debate had been taking place in some circles of the Labour Party and union movement, which enabled the national executive of the Labour Party to move towards a far more radical programme than the Labour Party had presented previously. The rethinking was based on a recognition of the growth of monopoly and of the increased power of the multi-nationals. The programme envisaged a state holding company that would take a major stake in the 20 or 25 largest firms in the UK, and compulsory planning agreements between the government and the largest 100 or so firms and the major nationalized industries, moves that could lead, alongside other measures, to an 'irreversible shift in power to labour'. This radical programme, however, was little understood within the Labour movement generally and found only a faint echo among millions of electors.

In the event, the 1974 Labour government, confronted with a renewed economic crisis, brushed aside any radical version of the 1973 Labour Party programme. In the 1975 Industry Act, the powers and money given to the NEB were very limited and it became little more than the 'holding body' for the casualties that dropped unwanted and unloved into the state's lap (British Leyland, Rolls-Royce) plus a number of relatively small-scale investments. Planning agreements were not made compulsory and in the event only one was signed (with Chrysler, which received very large sums of public money although the planning agreement was never made public). In the same year, the Prime Minister, in response to a major attack on Benn, removed him as Minister responsible for the Department of Trade and Industry and put him in charge of the Ministry of Energy.

In the attempt to limit direct state intervention, NEDO was revitalized and in 1975 the slogan of an 'Industrial Strategy' was presented, with the creation of 39 sector working parties, composed of representatives of the leading firms, trade unions and Ministries, serviced by NEDO staff.

The sector working parties, however, proved to be limited instruments for several reasons. In the first place, they were attempting to influence the behaviour of firms and unions in investment and productivity and improving the industry trade balance in a situation where the government could not and would not offer any firm macro-economic framework. In the second place, the firms, in many cases if not most, were multi-nationals, operating on a global scale with global strategies. The requirements of the British government or of the UK economy were necessarily a secondary matter. And finally, the trade unions were being asked to stimulate productivity in a period of rising unemployment, faltering investment, and declining confidence in the future. But if the kind of purposeful, growth-directed intervention was missing, a great deal of intervention nevertheless took place.

There have been incentives to encourage capital accumulation (investment grants, investment allowances, accelerated depreciation, etc.); taxes and subsidies on employment (selective employment tax, regional employment premium, temporary employment subsidy, etc.); and financial support for, or government provision of, research and development, innovation, and technical training. Different regions have received financial assistance at different rates to encourage development in the depressed areas, and individual private companies in difficulty have received special aid. There is also a variety of direct controls, such as those on location through the need for industrial development certificates. The provision of government contracts, the approval of price increases, and other incidental powers of the state have been used to encourage firms to comply with policy objectives.

All of these instruments have been used at one time or another, and in the process the government has provided large amounts of money to industry. In 1978–9 regional support and regeneration cost £686 million; industrial innovation £358 million; general support to industry (including the NEB, selective assistance, and investment grants) £396 million; support for the nationalized industries £157 million (this does not include net lending to them, which came to £1100 million); international trade (export promotion and export credit support) £454 million; and labour market services (including industrial training and redundancy payments) £974 million. These figures came from *The Government's Expenditure Plans 1979-80 to 1982-83*, Cmnd 7439, and are at 1978 survey prices. A large proportion of this expenditure takes the form of direct payments to industry.

What is striking is that, despite the large expenditure and the variety of policy tools available, the rate of growth of trend productivity remained stubbornly unchanged at a little under three per cent through most of the post-war period up to 1974. It then fell to around one per cent over the 1974-9 period. Unemployment increased substantially over the period, and while regional policy did create jobs in the depressed regions, they only seem to have just balanced the jobs being lost at the same time, with no net effect on relative unemployment levels.

Of course, as always in economics, one could argue that the policy measures did have a substantial effect and that without them growth and regional disparities would have been much worse. But throughout the period there was never any coherent planning strategy to guide the interaction of the individual instruments, with the consequence that policies often offset each other. This partly reflected the lack of any clear theory about what the government was trying to do, and partly reflected real political contradictions. For example, productivity growth requires change, innovation, restructuring of capital, and the adjustment to new forms of organization, new markets, and new technologies. The question is then what mechanism should the state support for effecting such change. The main choice is between the market, competition, and direct intervention. Competition enforces change at substantial social cost: redundancy, bankruptcy, and the transfer of production overseas. Direct state intervention requires the subordination of the management and property rights of private firms to central planning. Given the political pressures upon them, British governments have, up to the 1979 Conservative government, been unable to accept the implications of either free competition or determined state intervention. Thus the adjustment has been minimal.

The Conservative government that took office in May 1979 (as far as one can judge in February 1980) cannot, however, be regarded as a repeat of Heath's 1970 government. It is a matter we discuss much more fully in our concluding chapter to this book, but at this stage it is sufficient to say that the 'radical right' won control of the Conservative Party in the period leading up to 1979. Its central concern, overriding all others, has been to break trade union influence in the labour market and on business policy, and this is where the main thrust of state intervention was to be felt. But in other respects the Conservative government has advocated a policy of systematic withdrawal of the state from direct productive activity, except that which cannot be made profitable; to open up functions that had become part of a welfare state system to private operations (as in private health); and to abolish all constraints on movement of capital across national frontiers. (We deal below with the nationalized industries and with competition policy.)

Industrial strategy as a slogan has been explicitly repudiated by 'Thatcher' government on the grounds that the market must decide. Undoubtedly, pressures will continue to force the government to spend substantial sums on aid to industry and carry forward many existing instruments that affect the private sector, even though it has clearly stated its intention to reduce government subsidies to the private sector.

10-3 NATIONALIZED INDUSTRIES

Nationalization is one possible response to a variety of economic pressures and needs. There are some sectors of industry that produce goods and services necessary for the reproduction of the system that cannot be provided either effectively or profitably by competitive private capital. Typical of this category are both large infrastructural industries like railways, which are subsidized and controlled by government in all advanced industrial countries, and natural monopolies like postal and telephone systems. There are also other sectors that require massive restructuring, involving scrapping of old equipment, changes in the techniques of production, capital investment, relocation of plant, redundancies, and redeployment of labour on such a scale that only the state has the power and resources to effect the transformation. But nationalization is not an inevitable response to such pressures. They can often be met by subsidizing or regulating private firms rather than by direct state control. In the US, utilities are regulated rather than nationalized, and restructuring effected by state aid to private firms rather than by takeover. The outcome will depend on class struggle, and the pressure the labour movement and trade unions bring to bear to achieve nationalization.

Nationalization in the UK has taken place in two main waves: the first between 1945 and 1951, by the post-war Labour government, the second in the seventies by both Labour and Conservative governments. The main exception to this pattern was steel, which was nationalized in 1949, denationalized in the fifties by the Conservatives, and renationalized in 1967. The first wave can be characterized as part of the reconstruction process carried out after the war, with the support of a massive Labour majority. The second wave was characterized by the rescue and rationalization of firms and industries under intense international pressure, and was a response to the structural crisis of the system.

The first-wave industries tended to provide essential services and infrastructure, especially energy and transport. They were not on the whole profitable areas, nor were they in competition with private industries or engaged in international trade. They did, however, have large capital investment requirements and were in need of restructuring. Many of the utilities had been owned or controlled by local authorities and all had been subject to substantial government control during the war. Thus nationalization was not a major break for most of them. The exception was steel. In most respects it was similar to the others. It provided an essential input, fundamental to British production; it was in need of large capital investment and restructuring of the industry; and it seemed unlikely that the private owners, protected by a powerful cartel, would be willing to rationalize and modernize production. The difference, and the source of the powerful political opposition, was that it was profitable. This opposition to nationalization was successful, and in consequence the restructuring, when it did come after renationalization, was that much more painful and took much longer.

The second wave of nationalization was mainly in manufacturing. It embraced the Rolls-Royce aero engine company; British Leyland; the entire ship-building and two-thirds of the ship-repairing industries; the aircraft and guided missile manufacturing industry; and Alfred Herbert (Britain's largest machine tool producer). A Conservative government took over the first of these and a Labour government the remainder. For many of these, the alternative to nationalization was liquidation. The state also has shareholdings in private firms, including (up to 1979) a majority stake in British Petroleum. Most of the nationalized industries are organized as public corporations. In 1975 the public corporations contributed 11 per cent of UK gross domestic product (GDP), employed 8 per cent of the labour force, and accounted for 19 per cent of total fixed investment. The nine main nationalized industries accounted for 84 per cent of the output and employment and 72 per cent of the fixed investment of the public corporations.

Neither post-war Labour nor Conservative governments regarded the nationalized sector as instruments of a general planned reconstruction or regeneration of the economy. The corporate plans developed by many of the nationalized industries (e.g., coal, gas, electricity, railways) in the fifties, as well as later, did not become part of any overall industrial strategy, or even coherent energy or transport policies. But they were used for macro demand management. The consequent stop-go policies and switchback instructions on capital spending were especially damaging for industries with long time horizons in investment planning. Their prices were also kept down for anti-inflation purposes, causing large deficits. Since many of the nationalized industries were effective monopolists, the size of the realized surplus or deficit was largely determined by pricing policies. The early deficits were aggravated by the character of their capital structures (great dependence on loan capital with heavy burden of interest charges plus compensation payments to former shareholders).

The nationalized sector did in general make profitable accumulation in the private sector easier; it was kept from competing with the private sector; and where the possibility existed of hiving off a profitable section (as with road transport) this was in fact done. But from the end of the fifties the general rise in state spending coincided also with the deficits of the nationalized industries. Concern grew at the burden of rising state spending. The demand for improving costs and efficiency in the nationalized industries became stronger. The 1961 Plowden Report (*Control of Public Expenditure*, Cmnd 1432) led to the incorporation of the investment plans of the nationalized industries into the public expenditure survey committee system (PESC). This control was tightened after 1975, with the application of cash limits in 1976. In terms of the actual objectives of the first-wave nationalization, the two influential White Papers were first the 1961 *Financial and Economic Obligations of the Nationalised Industries* (Cmnd 1337) and the 1967 *Nationalised Industries: a Review of Economic and Financial Objectives* (Cmnd 3437). The 1967 White Paper remained the main published guidelines until they were superseded by the *Nationalised Industries* (Cmnd 7131) in March 1978. The background to this White Paper can be found in the renewed efforts to use the nationalized industries in the anti-inflationary fight, first by holding their prices down so that they ran increasing deficits, and then by allowing massive price increases that dramatically increased profits of, for instance, British Gas and PO Telecommunications). The demand for 'efficient' restructuring of the nationalized industries became more strident, and the boards of the public corporations themselves became restive at the inconsistent demands imposed on them by government policies. In addition, the very principle of public ownership came increasingly under attack by those who saw it as a threat to capital and who were able to use the widespread feelings of many who experienced the bureaucracy and insensitivity of the public corporations (including many employees in these organizations).

The 1978 White Paper laid down the importance of (a) financial targets based on a three- to five-year period; (b) the objective of a five per cent real rate of return before tax on new investment; and (c) the publication of non-financial performance indicators so that the public could monitor the progress of the public corporations. There is no need at this stage to present a critique of the White Paper (for this see, e.g., Rees, 1979) because of the changes set in motion by the Conservative government in 1979, but one important strand in the White Paper has been given a further drastic twist, namely, the importance of cash limits and the generation of cash by the public corporations from their own operations. This trend, begun by the Labour government, was powerfully reinforced by the 1979 Conservative government and has been a major element in the crises in British Steel and a number of other nationalized industries.

However, this insistence on cash limits and the determination by the 1979 government to operate them severely has to be seen as part of the overall political programme envisaged by that government. This includes: first, the sale of substantial amounts of state-owned assets and the creation of conditions under which sections of nationalized industries may be hived off; second, a sharp reduction in the powers and resources (already meagre) of the National Enterprise Board, confining it to 'casualties' (hopefully able to recover and walk away), and of regional development in England, and some support for new ventures in high technology; third, significant reduction in the powers of the BNOC and the involvement in it directly of the major oil companies; fourth, enforced rationalization of steel, British Leylands, ship-building, and other such industries, through use of cash limits, etc.

10-4 COMPETITION POLICY

Unlike the US, whose 'anti-trust' policies date back to the eighteen-nineties, until 1948 Britain had little legislation to promote competition. But in the post-war period a variety of influences produced a series of Acts.

Political hostility to big business and the powerful cartels organized in the thirties had developed during the war and persisted; therefore action against monopolies seemed likely to forestall the development of pressure for their nationalization. There was also the belief, encouraged by conventional theory, that while competition would generate optimal allocation, monopoly caused market distortions and welfare losses. Finally, the rigidity, lack of innovation, and low productivity growth of much British industry was also widely attributed to lack of competition. These changes were also supported by elements within the business world who saw the potential for new markets and profits in the destruction of existing arrangements made by dominant firms and powerful cartels. These pressures produced a variety of legislation.

In 1948 a Monopolies and Restrictive Practices (Inquiry and Control) Act was passed; in 1956 the Restrictive Practices Act was passed, setting up the Restrictive Practices Court. In 1964 the Resale Price Act abolished retail price maintenance; in 1965 mergers were brought within the scope of the legislation, and the various amendments culminated in the Fair Trading Act of 1973, which brought the agencies together and established an Office of Fair Trading. A new Restrictive Trade Practices Act was passed in 1976 and supplemented in 1977. Since 1948 competition policy has advanced at roughly ten-year intervals, but its consequences have been contradictory.

The *main* thrust of state policy and practice has in fact been to strengthen the tendencies to monopoly based on concentration and centralization, reinforcing what is already a trend within the system. Accumulation under capitalism leads to concentration and tendencies to monopoly, for monopoly is the outcome of competition. Thus even measures that foster competition will, unless other steps are taken, promote concentration. However, it is important to distinguish those measures concerned with current monopolies and proposed mergers, that can be used to limit the extent and growth of monopolies, from those that prohibit price agreements or similar restrictive practices, which, when not evaded, promote rivalry leading to further concentration.

State action against monopolies and mergers has been timid, and the main presumption embodied in legislation and implementation is that the restructuring of industry (which involves merger and concentration) is likely to be beneficial, and is only to be challenged if damaging to some vague concept of the public good. As a consequence, only a small fraction either of mergers or of dominant market positions by a firm or a group of firms has been investigated. It could be argued that the legislation and the few actions taken work as a deterrent. Given the growth in concentration and the number of mergers over the period, this is implausible.

It can be argued that the Restrictive Practices Act of 1956, which set up the Restrictive Practices Court, was and is the most effective of the instruments created by competition policy. Agreements between competitors became matters of law; the agreements as defined here were presumed to be against the public interest unless the Restrictive Practices Court could be convinced that they passed one or more of the various tests ('gateways') that would offset the damage done to the public interests. By the end of 1966 it was thought that the thousands of agreements that had been in existence had been abandoned. Up to the end of 1972, only 27 agreements were contested, and of these, 11 were approved.

It would seem, therefore, a very successful enterprise in ending price-fixing and similar agreements and permitting the wind of competition to blow vigorously through the economy. In addition, the Resale Prices Act of 1964 made retail price maintenance illegal, although this system was in fact already breaking down under the pressure of the aggressive multiple and supermarket chains. One consequence of the abolition of restrictive agreements was an acceleration in mergers, since price (or any other) agreements between different parts of the same firm were not illegal. Firms also found ways of circumventing the law, through the use of parallel pricing and price leadership, and a number of illegal agreements persisted (e.g., in ready-mixed concrete). The restrictive practices law also came into conflict with other forms of industrial policy, since in trying to restructure an industry the state might wish to encourage agreements which would otherwise come within the range of the Restrictive Practices Court.

In this field, the Conservative government elected in 1979, in its determination to cut back the public sector, to remove many of the controls and levers that influence the private sector and to proclaim the supremacy of the 'market', has been obliged, if only for reasons of ideology, to state its intention to challenge constraints on competition. It added further powers to the Office of Fair Trading by means of the Competition Act, which gives the Director General of Fair Trading power to define anti-competitive practices and initiate investigations.

However, if the economic analysis made in Chapter 17 is at all valid, then either the state must greatly reinforce its legal pressure on big business and especially against mergers of all kinds, which seems unlikely from such a government, or the further unleashing of competitive forces will reinforce the tendencies towards increased private concentration, accompanied by the destruction of many UK firms that cannot cope with the intensified rivalry from multi-national and multi-product firms.

FURTHER READING

Useful accounts of state intervention in the UK economy can be found in Devine *et al.* (1979), Morris (1979), Young and Lowe (1974), Crouch (1979), Smith (1979), and Vernon (1974) (the last also carries useful material on other countries).

For a review of the historical record since 1960 see Blackaby (1979b) and Beckerman (1972). For a 'market-orientated' critique of ideas and experiences of UK planning, see Budd (1978) and Leruez (1976).

Bacon and Eltis (1978) raised major issues which have been keenly debated.

On the nationalized industries see Pryke and Rees (1976).

On competition policy, see Cowling *et al.* (1980), HMSO (1978 and 1979), and the last chapter of Aaronovitch and Sawyer (1975b).

For running commentaries see the annual *TUC Economic Review*, *Labour Research* (monthly, LRD).

ELEVEN

THE STATE AND SOCIETY

Ron Smith and Roger Moore

11-1 INTRODUCTION

In Chapter 8 it was argued that an important need of the capitalist system was to establish conditions that would ensure the reproduction of labour power and the reproduction of capitalist property relations. The manner in which the state responds to this need is the topic of this chapter.

The reproduction of labour power requires not merely the provision of workers, but the support of non-workers (children, students, old people, etc.). This is the area of state social policy, and Section 11-2 discusses a variety of factors that influence social policy. The next section contains a short discussion of the main areas of social policy—health, education, poverty, and housing—together with a discussion of the mechanisms of social control. The reproduction of specific capitalist property relations requires not merely the maintenance of working class tolerance of the system by ideology, coercion, or concessions; it also requires the maintenance of stable international relations. These and the significance of the military expenditure that supports them are examined in the final section.

11-2 THE DETERMINANTS OF SOCIAL POLICY

As was mentioned above, a fundamental requirement of capital is the availability of suitable labour power. But with the increasing complexity of technology and sophistication of production, capital needs not merely the brute force of a labourer but a skilled, healthy, educated, and appropriately motivated workforce. Of course, better health and education are also demanded by workers for their own benefit, and this raises the question of the relative extent to which the improvements in health, education, social services orchestrated by the state over the last century are responses to the needs of capital or to working class struggle. Clearly, the improvements will reflect both; and policies, services, or institutions introduced in response to one pressure may be transformed in response to the other. In orthodox jargon the question is often posed as being whether these services are consumption goods (giving benefit merely to those who receive them) or capital goods (improving the efficiency of the productive process).

It should be remembered that when it is said that state actions are a response to 'needs of production' or 'class struggle', these terms are no more than abstract shorthand ways of referring to complex processes. Any particular area of social policy involves a variety of interrelationships, and this chapter will be unable to do more than sketch in the main features.

Given the inequality in the distribution of power and property within capitalist systems, there is always a danger that those who benefit least from the system (primarily the working class) will try to overthrow it. In attempting to minimize those threats, the state has three possible instruments: coercion—the use of police or army to compel acquiescence; ideology—the promotion of a set of beliefs and practices that maintain the legitimacy of the system; and reforms or concessions that do not change or endanger the basic structure of society. As Gladstone put it: 'Please to recollect that we have got to govern millions of hard hands; that it must be done by force, fraud, or goodwill; that the latter has been tried and is answering' (quoted in Fraser, 1973). Much social policy then appears in a dual form: it meets a need of capital generated by the development of the productive system and it is a concession to working class pressure in order to maintain the system in the face of a threat to its stability. The interaction of these may lead to the appearance of a coincidence of interests. Reforms fought for by the working class, when adopted, seem to strengthen rather than undermine capitalism. The threat of a powerful working class movement may overcome differences of interest among capitalists and galvanize the ruling class to think more cohesively and strategically, and to restructure the state apparatus to this end (Gough, 1979, p. 65). Wars often have the same effect; thus the Crimean, Boer, and First and Second World Wars were all followed by extensions of state intervention, relative to the preceding peace-time practice. There will, however, be economic limits to the concessions that are available; what is feasible in a prosperous, profitable, fast-growing society, would itself be a threat in a poor, stagnant one.

Typically the development of social policy follows a pattern, beginning with the recognition of a 'social problem' that poses a threat to the system. The problem itself—poverty, public health, malnutrition, educational failure, poor housing, etc.—is rarely new, but it is only recognized as a problem when it represents a threat. For instance, in the case of public health, the Industrial Revolution had generated a growth in urban population in areas without proper water or sewage facilities. The consequence was high infant mortality and low expectation of life for the working classes living in insanitary housing in crowded cities. This in itself did not generate government action, but resulting cholera epidemics, which also struck the middle classes, did attract attention to the problem. Recognition of the phenomenon as a problem is also aided by the development of a vocal pressure group or mass movement. Thus the threat of working class revolt posed by the Chartist movement in the eighteen-forties was a major factor in generating an environment more favourable to social reform. Once the threat forces recognition of the problem and the need for the state to respond to it, some administrative apparatus follows. The administrative apparatus then becomes the focus of pressure and struggle, which tends to extend state responsibility. Given the central role that the apparatus then takes in dealing with the problem, the form of organization adopted is of great significance. Victorian social policy was largely administered through local government and voluntary groups (e.g., religious schools) because of the concern among the ruling class about the implications of centralized state power. In the twentieth century, the organization of education after the 1944 Act embodied a division into public, grammar, technical, and secondary modern schools that reflected both the structure of the British class system, and the perceived needs of the productive system for different types of workers. The schools were designed to produce, respectively, administrators, white-collar workers, skilled craftsmen, and a mass who need have little more than the rudiments of the three Rs. In fact it seems likely that this perception of the needs of the productive system was better suited to the late nineteenth century than to the mid twentieth. Nonetheless, the contemporary perception of productive needs influenced the organization of education. Subsequently, the struggle for comprehensive education changed that organization. In examining the form of organization used, one needs to examine the form of control embodied in it—whether private, democratic, or hierarchic; the extent to which its objectives are geared to the needs of the system or the needs of the people it is meant to serve; and on what criteria it distributes resources and benefits.

The form of organization adopted for state intervention will also be conditioned by previous institutional arrangements. Thus the structure of the National Health Service reflects the administrative tradition of the Poor Law hospitals and the war-time emergency medical services, as well as the conflict between the working class political pressures for a universal system and the power of the doctor's lobby. While economic needs of the system generate pressure for state provision of health services, they do not determine the form of organization that will govern that provision. This will depend on political factors and the balance of class forces. The contrast between the US and UK is illuminating here. In the US there were also strong economic pressures towards state provision of health services. The poor quality of care that most received had consequences for production, while the profitable development of the health industry was constrained by the distribution of income—poor and middle income people could not afford it. But the political power of the doctors and the health business was such that direct state control could be prevented. Instead, the state merely provided the money. By 1976 the government (federal, state, and local) share of health expenditures was close to 40 per cent. This is through the finance of hospital building, research, medical training and the Medicare (for the old) and Medicaid (for the poor) programmes. Thus there is large-scale finance without control, a response to the economic need quite different from that in the UK.

The next section contains brief reviews of four of the main areas of state social intervention: health, education, poverty, and housing. To a greater or lesser extent, all four of these areas are in crisis. Cutbacks in expenditure, inadequate organization, and increased demand have led to a deterioration in the services and quality of provision. On the one hand, this is one consequence of the general cuts in government expenditure to reduce the burden on a capitalist sector suffering a severe crisis. But on the other hand, the crises represent the outcome of real contradictions of the production processes taking place within each of these sectors. Whether it is the production of commodities (as in the case of housing), use values (as in the case of health and education), or the organization of money transfers (as in the case of the social security system), there are distinct and specific labour processes involved in each.

The contradiction is that these labour processes, with the partial exception of house building, are largely not under capitalist control, yet are constrained by the capitalist relations of production within which they operate. State provision of these services partly arose as a consequence of realization crises—i.e., workers could not afford to buy from capital commodities that had become necessary for the reproduction of labour power. The significance of this for production is that these services are important determinants of the value of labour power, the socially necessary labour time required to produce the goods and services needed to maintain the worker. The value of labour power depends on the physical amounts of goods and services needed and their value, the labour time necessary to produce them. The fall in the value of labour power, through the reduction of the time needed to produce consumption goods, achieved by mechanization and reorganization, is a major dynamic of the capitalist system. But these state sectors, while providing essential elements for the reproduction of the workforce and thus influencing the value of labour power, are not under capitalist control. Not only is there not the scale of mechanization and restructuring that would reduce the labour time needed to produce the necessary output, but the labour process is partly conditioned by the professional and ethical considerations of workers who refuse to treat health, education, and social work as productive processes. The form of the labour process within these sectors and the lack of a direct mechanism to restructure it are thus a major obstacle to reductions in the value of labour power, and a source of political crisis. This argument is developed for the case of housing in Ball (1978). The control of the labour process under capitalist relations of production has been widely studied, but there has been less analysis of the dynamics and mechanisms of control in state production.

11-3 AREAS OF SOCIAL POLICY

Health

Over the past century and a half there has been a substantial improvement in the health of the British population. Infant mortality rates have fallen (from about 10 per cent of live births at the beginning of the century to under 2 per cent now) and expectation of life has increased. The major factor in this transformation is more and better food—diseases now regarded as inconsequential will kill the poorly nourished. The second factor is better public amenities. The municipal provision of clean water, drainage, and sewers was a major factor in reducing the spread of disease. This was aided by improvements in the quality of housing—again, partly the responsibility of local government. Preventive medicine—food, housing, and amenities, supplemented by vaccination, which became common against smallpox during the nineteenth century—was the major factor in the improvement in health. Therapeutic medicine—the treatment of illness by doctors—played a minor role in the improvement until the thirties, and even after that the net effect of curative rather than preventative medical treatment on general health is controversial. Just as in the nineteenth century the main determinants of ill health were environmental, it is argued that environmental factors remain dominant. Inappropriate eating habits and lifestyles are linked to heart disease; chemicals in food, atmosphere, and tobacco are linked to cancer; and accidents on the roads, in the home, and at work are a major source of ill health. Much ill health thus arises directly from the expansion of production. Although medical problems such as these are better treated by prevention or care the main focus of recent health policy has been on the curative services—doctors, hospitals, etc.—within the National Health Service.

The state has been involved in providing health services for well over a century—originally through local government and Poor Law administration—and the administrative organization of these services has always been a problem. The National Health Act of 1946 set up a tripartite structure made up of: hospitals; general practitioners and other services (dental, ophthalmic, and pharmaceutical); and local authority health and welfare services (including vaccination and immunization, health visiting, etc.). This structure, which reflected arrangements evolved in the past, fragmented treatment of patients between different structures. The system was reformed in the early seventies, setting up health authorities that controlled both hospitals and community health services, at the cost of an extra administrative layer.

In 1978/9 general government expenditure on health was £6.8 billion, of which £5.2 billion was on hospitals and community health services and £1.5 billion on family practitioners (£0.8 billion of which was for drugs, £0.4

billion for general medical services, and £0.2 billion for dental). £145 million was raised by charges—largely for dental work.

In 1975 expenditure on the National Health Service was 5.5 per cent of GNP, as compared with national health expenditures in the US of 8.4 per cent of GNP. Of course, to the UK NHS expenditure should be added all the money spent by individuals on branded non-prescription drugs, for headaches, coughs, colds, etc.

The establishment of a free and universal health care system after the Second World War was a major achievement, even though shortage of staff, expenditure cutbacks, growing waiting lists, and the difficulty of obtaining NHS treatment at all in dentistry and some other areas have eroded the benefits. Despite the universal provision, there remain large variations between groups in society, both in health and in access to health care. For instance in 1974–5 the rate of chronic sickness was over twice as high among male unskilled manual workers between 15 and 64 as among those in the professional group. This partly reflects differences in living and working conditions, but also less health care. The benefits of the National Health Service, although free, tend to be distributed in a fashion reflecting the same skewed distribution of income and influence.

State control of the process of production also has substantial influences on the distribution of that production by changing the distribution of market power. For instance, with the private provision of health services, the patient faces substantial disadvantages in the bargaining over the cost of treatment, drugs, etc. The patient lacks information, is relatively dependent on suppliers with monopolistic powers, and is probably not feeling very well either. Under a national health service the state acts as a monopolistic buyer of these services, supplying them to the patient. As a result, it can bargain over the prices of drugs and the salaries of the doctors, and the doctors are less likely to be influenced by the profitability of the treatment as opposed to the need for it when prescribing or operating. International data for industrialized countries seems to indicate that the cost of health services as a proportion of GNP is not highly correlated with output measures such as expectation of life and infant mortality, but is highly correlated with the pay of doctors relative to the average wage.

Education

In the mid nineteenth century, education came to be seen as the most effective antidote to the ideas of the 'agitators' who were spreading subversion in the rapidly growing poor urban population.

Initially the state confined itself to helping voluntary schools, in particular religious ones, and the 1870 Education Act established in principle the right of every child to some form of schooling. The passage of this Act is usually linked to the Second Reform Act of 1867, which extended the vote to some of the working class for the first time, and the consequent need by the ruling class to 'educate our masters'. State-financed education developed and remained under the control of local authorities, although working within a detailed national framework set down by central government. Elementary education became general after the First World War, and secondary education after the Second.

The distribution of education expenditure in 1978–9 is shown in Table 11–1.

Table 11-1 Education expenditure, 1978–9

Schools	£ million[a]	%
Under fives	223	2.6
Primary and secondary	5110	61.4
Universities	692	8.3
Further education and teacher training	1048	12.6
Student support	593	7.1
Libraries, research, and other services	649	7.8
Total	8315	100.0

[a] 1978 survey prices.

Source: The Government's Expenditure Plans, 1979–80 to 1982–83, Cmnd 7439, HMSO, 1979. Reproduced with the permission of the Controller of Her Majesty's Stationery Office.

In 1978 education accounted for 6.3 per cent of GNP. The expenditure is heavily influenced by demographic factors—the number of school-age children—which can vary substantially. In 1978–9 there were about 5 million primary school pupils as compared with $5\frac{1}{2}$ million in 1973–4 and a projected 4 million in 1982–3. Just as with health, access to education varies with social class and income. Sixty per cent of children of fathers in non-manual occupations are likely to continue in education beyond 16, compared with only 32 per cent of children of manual workers. In 1973, although manual workers made up 64 per cent of economically active males between 45 and 59, their children only obtained 26 per cent of acceptances to universities.

Any evaluation of education must recognize the conflicts between the functions the system has. It must provide workers with the skills needed by industry, commerce, and the productive system in general. It must sort out and label children in terms of the skills and abilities they possess, so that employers can recognize the candidates with the required qualifications. It must inculcate socially responsible attitudes, develop the discipline required in the workplace, and ensure that its products have expectations that conform to the structure of existing society. These objectives are in themselves contradictory. For instance, given the pace of economic development, the speed at which techniques of production are changing, and the flood of new products, it is economically much more effective to have managers and employees who are flexible, able to think for themselves, and willing to question traditional practices and adjust to new environments. However, it is likely to be much more difficult to persuade such people to accept existing social structures without question. Given this conflict, British industry and education seem to have preferred people who will go on doing things in the old way.

Poverty

Public responsibility for poverty had been a feature of English social policy since at least Tudor times through the provision of the Poor Laws. The objectives of these laws were not primarily charitable—that was the concern of individual conscience—but to prevent public disorder, and in particular to inhibit vagrancy. In the nineteenth century there was a major development with the Poor Law Amendment Act of 1834, which imposed some central control and uniformity on the diverse local systems of poor relief, encouraged the establishment of workhouses rather than the use of outdoor relief (the payment of allowances to the poor), and cut the cost of the system. Parts of the Poor Law remained on the Statute book until 1948, and its operation covered, and still influences, the whole development of a social security system. The Poor Law existed as a guarantee against starvation, yet the terms on which it offered relief were made socially unacceptable to the recipient to ensure that paupers were in a worse position than workers.

Throughout the nineteenth and twentieth centuries, at regular intervals there were repeated rediscoveries of poverty. For instance, there were the famous studies by Charles Booth on London between 1889 and 1903 and Rowntree on York in 1901 showing that about a third of the population lived at or below the poverty line defined as the minimum necessary for physical efficiency. These studies were reinforced by reports of the numbers of potential army recruits for the Boer War who were rejected on health grounds, and resulted in the 1906 Act that empowered local authorities to feed schoolchildren who needed it. At a practical level it was seen that poverty and the consequent malnutrition reduced the efficiency of the population both to fight and to work, and that poverty provided a fertile breeding ground for disruptive movements. The potential for disruption was of concern at the time because of the growth of the new unions, and the electoral success of Labour candidates in Parliamentary elections. The surveys also indicated that the bulk of the poverty was not the consequence of personal failure but of economic and social factors—old age, sickness, large families, low wages, and unemployment.

Current social security policy originates in the Beveridge Report of 1942. This proposed a system of family allowances and a state social insurance scheme that would provide flat rate subsistence benefits in return for universal flat rate contributions. This national insurance scheme—which would provide benefits to cover sickness, old age and unemployment—would be supplemented by a 'safety net' of means-tested national assistance. These proposals were largely embodied in the National Insurance Act of 1946 and the National Assistance Act of 1948. These, together with the health service and the use of Keynesian techniques to provide full employment, were regarded as providing the basis of the welfare state.

Yet once again in the sixties poverty was discovered to be alive and well and living in the UK. Surveys again showed substantial numbers living at or below the poverty line—now defined as the income at which supplementary benefit (the renamed national assistance) was paid. The major causes of this poverty were the low level of either wages or national insurance

Table 11-2 Social security expenditure, 1978–9

	£m	%
Retirement pensions	7 509	48.9
Other pensions	2 327	15.1
Supplementary pensions	662	4.3
Other supplementary benefit	380	9.0
Child benefit (net cost)	1 292	8.4
Family income supplement	25	0.2
Sickness, injury, maternity benefits	778	5.1
Unemployment benefits	657	4.3
Other national insurance benefits	100	0.6
Administration	631	4.1
Total	14 361	100.0

Source: The Government's Expenditure Plans, 1979–80 to 1982–83, Cmnd 7439, HMSO, 1979. Reproduced with the permission of the Controller of Her Majesty's Stationary Office.

benefits received by the family. Nor had the means-tested national assistance/supplementary benefit system escaped the stigma attached to relief by the Poor Law, and many entitled to benefit refused to claim. Furthermore, the interaction of a range of means-tested benefits with wage income created the poverty trap, by which low income families could become worse off after a wage increase because they lost so many benefits. Until recently the system was made worse by the wage stop, which ensured that people could not get more in benefits than in their last employment—further penalizing low wage workers.

In 1977 social security expenditure was 10.7 per cent of GNP, largely made up of transfer payments, an outlay of £13.2 billion, compared with national insurance contributions of £9.4 billion. The range of these transfer payments can be seen from Table 11-2, and the largest part of them go to the elderly.

As starvation and malnutrition in the UK have ceased to be the primary concern of policy, the focus for attention has shifted from the issue of poverty as such to the issue of distribution (of income, wealth, consumption, public benefits, etc.) in general. There has also been a renewal of the traditional notion that poverty is the product of personal choice or failure, with publicity and administrative attacks on 'social security scroungers'. But the evidence remains that most poverty is caused by economic and social factors outside the individual's control. What is more, the economic and social structures, including the social services, tend to reinforce rather than reduce poverty and inequality, as Townsend (1979) documents. As a consequence, poverty remains a major problem in the UK, and by the official definition around a quarter of the population lived in households that were in or near poverty during the seventies. This number will be increased by rising unemployment, cuts in public expenditure, and reductions in the real value of benefits.

Housing

As with health and education, state involvement in housing dates from the mid nineteenth century, and was largely the province of local authorities, the earliest involvement arising from public health concerns. The outcome of this involvement was the large-scale building of council housing, so that local authorities took over from private landlords the provision of rented accommodation (see Table 11–3).

Table 11-3 Great Britain: distribution of dwellings by tenure (%)

	1947	1961	1971	1975
Owner occupied	26	43	50	53
Rented from local authority or new town	13	27	31	31
Rented from private landlord or other	61	30	19	16

Source: Lloyds Bank Review, October 1977.

The housing and land markets were also regulated through planning and building controls, compulsory purchase powers, and the like, together with a variety of Rent Acts guaranteeing the rights of private (although not council) tenants.

In 1978–9 total expenditure on housing by general government was £5 billion. This included both housing subsidies and capital expenditure on house building. The relative subsidy to public tenants (through lower rents) as against owner occupiers (through tax relief and option mortgages) is complicated. Government figures for 1977–8 suggest a subsidy of £227 per dwelling for public sector housing and £208 per mortgaged dwelling for owner occupiers, but notes that direct comparisons are misleading. There seems no doubt, however, that tenants in private rented accommodation receive less subsidy than either public sector tenants or owner occupiers.

Despite a substantial programme of improvement grants, many houses still lack basic amenities or are structurally substandard. In addition, much of the council building of the fifties and sixties is rapidly turning into slums because of poor design, poor maintenance, and rigid and unresponsive local government policies.

Social Control

Most of the social policies considered so far have consisted of the government doing things for people—providing them with education or health services, housing subsidies, pensions, etc.; although it has been emphasized that the motives for providing these may not be altruistic. The needs of the productive system, the need to assuage dangerous discontent, or the interests of producers may be behind social policy. Nevertheless, these policies do provide benefits that tend to be welcomed by the recipients. There are, however, sets of policies that involve the government doing things to people that may not be welcomed. These are the social control elements.

The most obvious instruments of social control are the police and the judicial systems. In 1978–9 general government spent £2.1 billion on 'Law, order, and protective services'. This included the court services and legal aid, which cost £272 million less £83 million revenue from fees and fines; £328 million for the 'treatment of offenders' (prison and probation); £1220 million for police and £291 million for fire services. It can be argued that both the structure of legislation, with its emphasis on the protection of property rights and the maintenance of existing social relations, and the pattern of enforcement, as reflected in the rate of prosecution of different income and racial groups, suggest substantial class biases in the administration of justice.

Social control is also maintained through the creation of an ideology in the education system, political life, and the mass media.

The ultimate source of social control is, of course, military power, and this is discussed in the next section.

11-4 MILITARY EXPENDITURE

In 1979 the UK expenditure on military defence was £9.1 billion, 5.5 per cent of GDP at factor cost. As a share of GDP, military expenditure has tended to fall over the post-war period, while remaining higher than in other European countries, although lower than in the US. This military expenditure has a strategic role in providing the resources to create the political and military superstructure necessary to defend the prevailing system of economic relations, but it also has direct consequences for the structure of the economic system itself. Each of these features will be examined in turn.

The strategic element has four dimensions. First, the capitalist states as a group must defend the system, 'the free world', from the threat posed by the communist world as represented by the Soviet Union and China. Behind the Cold War rhetoric it is perfectly realistic for the administration of a capitalist state to perceive communism as a threat and to prepare to fight it. Furthermore, since capitalism is a highly integrated international system, it is also realistic for the various states to try to coordinate their activities through organizations such as NATO. This does not mean that capitalist military policy will be monolithic. Perceptions of the appropriate response differ; there are rivalries between capitalist states, as there are between communist states; and individual capitalists, defence contractors, bureaucrats, etc., may in the short run have power to direct policy in their own interest in ways that diverge from the long-run interests of the class. The Sino–Soviet hostility also creates opportunities for tactical alliances that cross the capitalist/communist divide.

Second, military force is an integral part of the mechanism through which the relationships between the imperialist powers and the less developed world are maintained. This involves supporting client regimes and military governments and countering revolutionary national liberation movements. The military in third world countries tend to be a major conduit for the transmission of imperialist ideology and power relations and this influence is maintained through the supply of weapons, training, and advisors. Since the Second World War, the third world has been the scene of almost continuous conflict. Regional hostilities and anti-imperialist struggles have become enmeshed with the confrontation between the superpowers to generate a sequence of long and bloody struggles in Africa, Asia, and the Middle East.

Third, among the capitalist states themselves, inter-imperialist rivalries and the ability of a hegemonic state to organize the system depend on military power. The US nuclear umbrella over the other capitalist states and its capacity for global military intervention were major supports for its hegemonic position, discussed in Chapter 12. To maintain the influence it obtained by economic and financial leverage it had to exhibit both the ability and the willingness to use force to deal with challeges to the system it represented. While it maintained this role of world policeman effectively during the fifties and sixties, it gained considerable benefits and influence over other states in the system, although the cost was large. Under the umbrella of American power, other Western states have not needed to arm to the same extent, and have therefore been able to devote additional resources to investment and growth, increasing the economic power of Europe and Japan against the US and ultimately threatening US hegemony itself.

Finally, within a state, military expenditure provides an insurance against internal threats to the existing order, both through the ideological role of militarism as a social system and the potential for domestic coercion provided by military power itself. Military values can be emphasized to develop feelings of national identity, prestige, and sovereignty in the hope of fostering a national rather than a class consciousness among workers. A large military budget can create a group of employees of military contractors who have a vested interest in militarism, even at the expense of their class interest. The military are also used for internal control activities and running industries or services during strikes.

Within the context of these four strategic factors one can explain the high levels of military expenditure in the post-war period in terms of the large variety of threats the system faced. The threats included the existence of a rival mode of production in Asia and Eastern Europe; the strength of national liberation movements in the periphery; and the potential for conflict with the proletariat in the metropolitan countries. The distribution of military expenditure between the advanced capitalist countries was determined by the inter-imperialist rivalry between them and by the hegemonic position of the US. Although such an explanation of military expenditure in terms of its role in creating the political and ideological preconditions for the maintenance of the economic system seems adequate, much Marxist writing tends to explain it in terms of its direct economic consequences. This involves the functionalist argument that the purpose of military expenditure was to produce those consequences rather than to meet political and ideological needs. The most common of these arguments is of an under-consumptionist type—that high military expenditure is necessary to offset realization crises and to prevent capitalism relapsing into stagnation and slump. The economic consequences of military expenditure can be examined through its effects on the process of circulation, on the structure of production, and on the relations of production.

In the sphere of circulation, the most obvious effect of military expenditure is in increasing total demand. Hence if the system faces a structural problem in absorbing the surplus produced, this may be solved by higher military expenditure. However, this increase in demand is subject to constraints, in particular the requirement that the reserve army of labour is maintained at levels adequate to preserve labour discipline. To the extent that military expenditure diverts surplus from accumulation, it may also reduce the organic composition of capital, or stop it rising so rapidly, and thus reduce the downward pressure on the rate of profit. Table 11-4 gives data for 14 OECD countries for the period 1954–73, for the shares of military expenditure and investment in output and the rates of growth and unemployment. The pattern is that there is no significant association between the share of military expenditure and the rate of unemployment, but a significant negative association between the share of military expenditure and both the share of investment and the rate of growth. What seemed to happen was that the necessary size of the reserve army and the rate of unemployment were fixed independently by the need to maintain labour discipline; increases in military expenditure were then met by reductions in investment, with consequent negative effects on the growth rate.

The main way in which it has been argued that military expenditure has influenced the organization of production is through state intervention. The state may finance military research and development, which has spin-off effects on civilian technology and productivity, or it may reorganize and restructure defence-producing industries, either for strategic reasons or because of their political influence. While the articulation of state and

Table 11-4 Investment, military expenditure, unemployment, and growth: Mean values, 1954–73 (%)

	Share of investment	Share of military expenditure	Unemployment rate	Growth rate
UK	16.6	6.1	2.7	2.9
US	16.4	8.3	5.0	3.9
France	22.5	5.5	1.3	5.6
West Germany	24.4	3.8	1.0	6.1
Italy	22.3	3.6	4.7	5.3
Japan	33.4	1.1	1.2	10.1

Source: OECD National Accounts Statistics

private capital within the military–industrial complex is undeniable, the economic implications of this articulation are less obvious. Although there are examples of very large profits being made on defence contracts, there is evidence that dependence on the military market creates substantial inefficiency within companies, causing them to be less profitable and less viable. Military contracts then become a way in which the state subsidizes outdated capacity and production techniques. Likewise, although there are examples where technology developed under military contracts has spun off to general production, during the post-war period it has been more common for military R and D to preempt scarce technical and design resources.

The third influence of military expenditure on the economy is through its effect on the relations of production. Militarism and a powerful military force may be used by the state to increase the rate of exploitation, either through its coercive or ideological use, and thus to increase the rate of profit. It is also sometimes argued, particularly for less developed countries, that the military may be an important modernizing force, destroying traditional social relations and patterns of life and enabling accumulation to proceed. Although within the advanced capitalist states the role of the military tends to be stable, well defined, and taken for granted, it still raises fundamental questions. Control of military power is basic to the maintenance of dominant patterns of social relations; military production is characterized by very close links between state and private capital; and the internationalization of military production is very advanced. Furthermore the increase in international tension in 1979–80 and the general escalation in nuclear capability and weapons stocks make it central to survival.

Within the UK between the mid fifties and the late seventies military expenditure in real terms was either roughly constant (if the GDP deflator is used) or fell slightly (if the official deflator for military defence is used). But this apparent stability is the product of recurrent conflicts between over-ambitious strategic aspirations and economic constraints. Attempts were made to resolve the conflicts by a series of defence reviews, which nibbled away at the global commitments Britain had inherited from its imperial role and which cancelled the expensive prestige projects like the TSR2 aircraft.

The major symbol of Britain's international pretensions, the strategic nuclear deterrent, was retained. The basis of this deterrent is four submarines armed with Polaris missiles, commissioned between 1967 and 1969. In 1980 the Conservative government announced that it would replace them at a cost of around £5 billion, by the US Trident system. It remains questionable, however, whether the UK will be able to afford Trident, and it is likely that economic pressures will force cancellation. The other major defence commitments are air/sea defence of the UK and eastern Atlantic; the provision of forces in the central region, which together with the nuclear forces comprise the UK contribution to NATO; and fighting the civil war in Northern Ireland. Given the extent of the current arms race and the rapidly escalating cost of military hardware, the UK is unable to meet these commitments effectively. Very much larger increases than those proposed by the Conservative government would be needed to change that position. Even within orthodox strategic terms, British military policy is a mess—incoherent, ineffective, and expensive. But worse than that, the policy diverts resources from productive uses and may actually reduce the real security of the British people.

FURTHER READING

Official statistics can be found in *Social Trends*, published annually by HMSO.

A general Marxist discussion of state social policy can be found in Gough (1979), and an analysis of the operation of local government in Cockburn (1977). The history of the welfare state can be found in Fraser (1973).

On specific areas see: Doyal and Pennell (1979), Blackstone and Crispin's chapter in Blake and Ormerod (1980)—which also contains brief articles on housing, health, personal social services, and social security—Ball (1978), and Lansley (1979).

A vast amount of information on poverty in Britain is to be found in Townsend (1979) and in the many publications of the Child Poverty Action Group. See also Townsend and Bosanquet (1980).

On military spending see R. Smith (1977), which discusses the economics, and D. Smith (1980), which discusses the political and strategic aspects.

THREE

INTERNATIONAL CAPITALISM

The last part of Chapter 11, on military expenditure, highlighted the strategic aspect of Britain's relations with the rest of the world. But developments in the rest of the world influence the British economy in a variety of other ways. In fact, the importance of these influences makes some understanding of the laws of motion of the world capitalist system as a whole a necessary precondition for any analysis of the British economy. Chapters 12 and 13 provide a survey of the main characteristics of international capitalism. Chapter 12 begins with a discussion of the instability of the process of growth and proceeds to analyse the main characteristics of the process. These are the contradiction between the national nature of most state regulation and the international nature of capital; the inherently uneven character of development; and the continued process of internationalization of capital through the integration of commodity and money markets and of production across national boundaries. The seventies saw the end of a long period of rapid growth in world capitalism, which had lasted from the end of the Second World War, and the relapse of the system into turmoil and crisis. Chapter 13 examines the origin and form of this crisis in some detail. The international scene having been set in the previous two chapters, Chapter 14 examines the way in which British capital is integrated into world capitalism and the significance of this international orientation.

TWELVE

PATTERNS OF GROWTH IN WORLD CAPITALISM

Ron Smith

12-1 INTRODUCTION

A major purpose of this chapter will be to explain the main characteristics of the period 1945–73, the 'long boom'. This label is apt, since this period was one of sustained and rapid economic expansion at a pace faster than in any earlier period of capitalist development. Moreover, this advance of prosperity was general: while some economies did grow much faster than others, all showed a rise in their growth rate compared with earlier experience. Accompanying this expansion was a general rise in the price level, so that secular inflation became a widespread phenomenon, deserving debate and analysis. However, inflation rates were very mild, and the predominant feeling was that it was an acceptable price to pay for a period of unprecedented expansion. Analysts, particularly monetarists, have since suggested that this mild inflation necessarily generated the rapid inflation following 1973, but this view seems founded largely on hindsight. In fact, the long boom represented a period of remarkable stability. While strains obviously did emerge, these were mild and easily rectified, even for the British economy, which for various reasons shared much less in the general period of post-war expansion. It seemed at the time that rapid economic growth was a natural state of the international capitalist economy.

This view continues to colour present-day thinking. Thus one frequently encounters the view, explicit or implicit, that the disturbances and crises of the international economy in the seventies are in some sense abnormal, a departure from the natural state of expansion, to be viewed as an unfortunate interlude. Table 12-1 presents a rather different picture, suggesting an alternating pattern of long phases of relative expansion and contraction. Thus the high growth rate, low unemployment, and absence of serious recession in the post-war period contrasts with the inter-war period, which saw low growth, high unemployment, and a collapse of world trade as powerful protectionist blocks were established.

Even before the period covered in the Table the world capitalist economy appeared to go through alternating phases of high and low growth, lasting

Table 12-1 Phases in capitalist development

	1870–1913	1913–50	1950–70	1970–76
Average output growth rate	2.5	1.9	4.9	3.0
Average output *per capita* growth rate	1.5	1.1	3.8	2.4
Average unemployment rate	5.7	7.3	3.1	3.3
Maximum peak to trough fall in GDP	−6.7	−13.1	+0.3	−1.7

Source: Maddison (1977).

around 25 years, often called Kondratiev cycles. Such historical phases are quite marked.

To quote a distinguished Marxist historian (Hobsbawm, 1969, p. 313):

> They appear to manifest themselves most obviously as an alternation of roughly twenty-five years of inflation and an atmosphere of business confidence, followed by a similar period of price fluctuation or deflation and an atmosphere of business malaise and social tension.

and they may be identified as:

> ... the 'upswing' from the 1780s to the end of the Napoleonic Wars, followed by the troubles of the period from then to the 1840s, the upswing of the 'golden years' of the Victorians, followed by the 'Great Depression' of 1873–96, the upswing of the Edwardian 'Indian Summer' and the First World War, followed by the inter-war depression. Since, say, 1940, we have been very obviously in an upswing. If there are Kondratiev periodicities, whatever their nature, we might well expect this era to end very soon, and the 1970s to have different, and probably less pleasing characteristics. But we do not know yet.

As a qualified prediction written in the sixties, this statement has proved singularly accurate. But the problem that it poses is the following: if such fairly regular phases are observable (and this has not gone undisputed, the 'Great Depression' of the late nineteenth century having been rendered invisible by some economic historians), how are they to be explained?

One approach, often adopted by neo-classical economists or historians, is to see these phases as the result of a series of accidents, sometimes called 'system shocks'. Thus the slump of the thirties is seen by some as the result of a failure by the US monetary authorities to prevent the fall in the money supply in the 1930–32 period; more recently the slump of the seventies is seen as the joint product of over-expansionary policy by a number of governments and the quadrupling of the price of oil initiated by the OPEC cartel in 1973.

The problem with this is that the phenomenon is left largely unexplained. While, perhaps, the *proximate* causes of booms and slumps are identified, the underlying reasons as to why they exhibit a fair degree of regularity are not exposed. Of course, if no such reasons are to hand, we must be satisfied with only limited understanding. But in our view some explanation of these underlying regularities can be attempted. Since it is writers in the Marxist tradition who have attempted this, it is to these that we must turn. The analysis is usually presented under the heading of 'theories of crisis', a term borrowed from medicine referring to the critical period in an illness where the crucial struggle between the disease and the recuperative powers of the body takes place.[1]

One group of Marxist writers tends to emphasize the role of class struggle in causing crises in capitalism. Intensified struggle over wages in periods of boom tends to reduce profitability to critical levels, leading eventually to a collapse of investment, output, and employment. The rise in unemployment tends to dampen down wage demands, particularly if sustained, thereby restoring profitability, although sometimes only at the cost of increased political instability.

Such relationships have undoubtedly been important in the post-war period. Indeed, it will be argued that a quiescent labour force was one of the conditions necessary for the post-war long boom. However, it cannot provide an explanation of earlier phases of expansion and downswing, and it is unlikely that these writers intended it so to serve. For these phases occurred when there was massive surplus labour and when most of the labour force, except for skilled sections, was not organized in trade unions.

An alternative explanation is in terms of the interrelationship between the process of accumulation of capital and the capital intensity of production (the 'organic composition of capital'). Accumulation is seen as necessarily involving increased mechanization (that is, the use of machines instead of direct labour), and this in turn is seen as raising the capital costs of production. The result, it is argued, is a fall in the rate of profit, although this decline may be offset for a while by a reduction in wage costs per unit of output. As in the previous argument, the decline in profitability eventually leads to a fall in investment and output. As a result of this crisis, major reorganizations of firms, production methods, and work practices take place. This acts to restore profitability, so that the period of crisis (which may be extended) provides the basis for a period of renewed expansion and boom.[2]

There are, however, problems with this argument. It is not made clear why firms should switch to techniques of production that entail a lower level of profitability. Why not simply carry on production on a larger scale but using the same techniques of production? Of course, capitalists, either individually or as a group, may wrongly assess the relative profitability of

---

[1] The concern here is not with the short-run trade cycle crises every five to ten years, but with the major system shocks like those in the thirties and seventies.

[2] Aficionados of Marxist debates will recognize the simplifications made in this account and what follows. For fuller accounts and controversy see Fine and Harris (1979).

alternative techniques of production, and may in certain periods switch in error to less profitable techniques. And once committed, it may be some considerable time before the mistake can be undone. But to postulate a general theory of crisis on the basis of such errors of judgement (a 'law of the tendency to make mistakes') is manifestly unsatisfactory.

In fact, capitalists as a group cannot simply expand production and total profits just by raising the level of production with existing techniques, for bottlenecks will certainly arise. One such bottleneck is the available labour force, since such extensive forms of industrialization will eventually absorb labour reserves. When this happens, wage costs will rise, squeezing profitability. It will then prove profitable to switch to more capital intensive methods of production, economizing on labour, so that the organic composition of capital will then rise. But this is a *result* not a *cause* of declining profitability. This view of crisis takes us back to the first theory, although with the rise in wages seen as a result of tightening labour market conditions. But, while it may helpfully be applied to the post-war period, it is hard to see how crises prior to that can be explained in terms of labour bottlenecks, when unemployment and underemployment were pervasive. Clearly, different bottlenecks must be identified for earlier periods.

It does seem to have been the case in the second part of the nineteenth century (when Marx was writing) that the organic composition of capital did rise, for while the use of machinery was becoming widespread, the production of machinery was still by unmechanized techniques. Thus capital costs tended to rise significantly in the 'Great Depression' of that period. But such biases have not been marked at other periods, and the post-war long boom certainly saw no such tendency. Thus while the organic composition of capital *may* rise, resulting in a fall in profitability and crisis, there is no necessity for it to do so. And it seems that the evidence does not fit this theory as a general explanation of crisis.

However, the preceding discussion does point to a more general approach to crisis, which emphasizes the variety of necessary conditions required to let expanded reproduction—growth and accumulation—proceed.

Necessary for the continued smooth expansion of the capitalist system are: adequate supplies of compliant labour; adequate markets; and an adequate balance between different sectors of production, so that no sector emerges as a constraint on the expansion of other sectors and hence of the system as a whole. Conversely, a crisis may result from labour shortages and class struggle; from a constraint on the continuous expansion of capital to new markets; or from the emergence of one or more sectors as a bottleneck; or from all simultaneously. The ultimate source of crisis is that capitalism contains no mechanisms adequate to ensure that these necessary conditions for continued expansion are maintained. Some bottleneck inevitably emerges in the course of a sustained expansion, acting to curtail profitability. As a result, the potential profitability of innovations to eliminate this bottleneck rises very sharply. But such innovation may occur only after considerable lags, dependent as it is on the particular state of knowledge and the individual capacity for enterprise. In the interval, the squeeze on profitability is likely to lead to a collapse of investment and output and a period of sustained slump.

Our view of crisis sees it, therefore, as a result of uneven development in capitalism, or of the emergence of general forms of disproportionality between labour needs, markets, or sectors in the process of accumulation. Thus, for example, the period of downswing after the Napoleonic wars may be seen as a result of a failure of development in transportation to keep pace with the growth of industrial production: the consequent narrowness of markets on one side and higher food (and hence wage) costs on the other acted to squeeze profitability. The consequent profitability of innovation in transportation led to the subsequent boom in railway construction in the UK and elsewhere, and laid the basis for the following era of rapidly expanding markets and falling costs.

But like all booms, the railway boom over-reached itself. While original investments were highly profitable, a wave of speculation led to many unprofitable lines (see Hobsbawm, 1969).

The adjustments that the system needs to remove (temporarily) the obstacles, require restructuring throughout world capitalism, which takes considerable time, hence the length of the cycle. This pattern of acceleration and then deceleration of accumulation together with expansion and contraction of commodity production arises directly out of the nature of competition and its lack of mechanism to ensure that the necessary conditions for continued expansion are maintained. But since there are many necessary conditions, different ones will play different roles at the various historical turning points. The severity and character of the crises reflect the number and nature of the conditions that fail. Therefore an analysis of the factors that laid the foundations for the long boom and that brought it to an end must examine all the main conditions for the maintenance of profitable accumulation and the expansion of commodity production. These conditions are political as well as economic, and it is to political preconditions that we first turn.

12-2 THE POLITICAL REQUIREMENTS

By its very nature, capital is international. It is directed to expanding production and profits wherever they are available. But the smooth expansion of accumulation and realization requires the provision of a variety of functions that cannot be provided by capital itself. These were discussed in Chapter 8, on the role of the state. However, a contradiction arises, since the world is divided up into nations, each with its own state, while capital—and, increasingly, individual firms—operate on a world level, relatively unrestricted by national boundaries. Thus, although capital requires a variety of state functions to be performed at an international level, there is no single international state to provide them. These functions include those of a world central bank, organizing and controlling the international credit system and acting as a lender of last resort; the guarantee of adequate and appropriate supplies of labour and raw materials; and the maintenance of the necessary international stability and legal system to enable contracts, trade, and production to proceed with security. These are analogous functions to those discussed in Chapter 8, except that they are required on an international rather than intra-national basis. As world capitalism expands and the internationalization of capital proceeds, the complexity of the system increases, as does the need for these functions. Thus, in the nineteenth century, when most production took place within nations by national capitals, the organizational requirements of the system were much simpler than they are today.

Given that there has not existed a world state, there are three main institutional ways in which these necessary functions may be performed. First, one individual nation state, which has predominant economic, political, and military power, may effectively be able to organize the system to meet the necessary requirements. Through coercion and influence, a 'hegemonic' power of this sort may be able to dominate and organize other states. Britain had this role before the First World War, acting as world banker and world policeman, while the US took up this role during the Second World War, providing the political requirements for the long boom. The length and depth of the slump of the thirties was partly the consequence of the lack of a hegemonic or organizing power, Britain being unable to take on this role and the US being unwilling. (Kindleberger, 1973, argues this case.) Likewise, the disruption of US hegemony was a major factor in the disturbances of the seventies. Of course, the requirements that had to be met by a hegemonic power in the second half of the twentieth century are much more extensive than those met by Britain in the late nineteenth century, because of the growth in complexity and extension of internationalization of capital in the intervening period. This process of internationalization is discussed later in this chapter.

The second method by which the system may be organized is through groups of states acting together to organize the system to their mutual benefit. In the seventies, when American economic dominance of the capitalist world had broken down, attempts were made to reconstruct the international economic order through agreements made at economic summits by the main powers. But it proved impossible to form and maintain a dominant coalition of states around any coherent long-term strategy for the international economy, since the short-term interests of the individual states were in conflict. Attempts to reach agreement in the thirties were equally fruitless. Joint action by groups of states to organize the system merges into the third method, the creation of supra-national organizations to which national states delegate power to regulate the system.

In the inter-war period, the League of Nations was given this role to some extent, and since the Second World War such institutions have proliferated. These include the World Bank, IMF, NATO, the EEC, and the OECD. The problems with such institutions is that they rarely have any independent power of their own, whether military, economic, or political. Their ability to organize then depends either on their status as a representative for a hegemonic power, or on their success in obtaining the support of a powerful group of nation states. One or other is required to implement their policy. In this respect most supra-national institutions can be reduced to organization by either the first or second method. However, such institutions may facilitate agreement by providing a mechanism to distinguish the formation of the 'rules of the game' from decisions on individual cases.

Historically, coalitions of states have proved unstable under the pressures of inter-imperialist rivalry, since concern to promote the interests of national capital and workers has taken precedence over the need to compromise to establish a stable international order. Supra-national institutions like the UN, IMF, and EEC have lacked the sanctions to coerce powerful states, and can only regulate the weak or dependent. Thus to the extent that the international economy has been coordinated to provide the security and order necessary for expansion and accumulation, it has been done by a hegemonic state. In the case of the long boom, it was US hegemony that provided the political preconditions for the necessary economic regulation. To see how this arose it is necessary to go a little further back in time.

The period 1914–45, between the start of the First World War and the end of the Second World War, had represented one of major and continuing crisis for international capitalism. The two major wars devastated much of Europe physically and economically. The 1917 revolution in Russia marked the start of a process of contraction of the geographic boundaries of world capitalism, which continued with the loss of much of Eastern Europe and China in the period after the Second World War, and which has proceeded up to the present day in the third world. The relative decline of Britain, plus the rivalry between France, Germany, the UK, and the US, weakened the cohesiveness of an international system, hitherto sustained by British dominance. The onset of the slump of the thirties saw a shattering of international cooperation, and the spread of competitive protection and currency depreciation, which cut world trade. The slump itself, although remembered for the mass unemployment, the poverty of ordinary working people, and the hardship suffered by the producers of primary products, also represented a disastrous period for the capitalist class. Many firms went into liquidation, a vast number of banks folded, and those capitalists who continued operation experienced depressed levels of profitability. The economic rivalry between the main imperialist powers was matched by political rivalry, most evident in the territorial ambitions of Germany and Japan, which led to war. Within Europe, the rise of fascism in Germany, Italy, and Spain associated the capitalist class of these countries with the suppression of democratic institutions and political rights.

With this legacy of instability, the major concern for the capitalist class in the post-war period was to stabilize the relations of production, exchange, and distribution. In this, the US, as the only major capitalist country not devastated or seriously weakened by the war, assumed the major role, and the post-war stabilization was based firmly on US hegemony. The basic strategy was to create a new economic unity between the capitalist states, fostering the growth of economic links primarily by means of free trade. Below, the basic elements in this strategy are briefly outlined. It should be emphasized that this is a very schematic picture; the actual history was much more complicated. Rivalry between the US and UK, and between different interests in the US, contradictions within the requirements for stability, and the lack of an articulated unified policy—all these factors made for political complexity. US policy went through what appeared as major U-turns during the period 1943–9 and it was not inevitable that the structure should have developed in the way it did.

12-3 THE ORGANIZATION OF THE SYSTEM

Planning for reconstruction began during the Second World War, and it was done by politicians and economists who had little confidence in the likelihood of sustained expansion. Their main concern was to establish an economic order that would prevent the rivalry and conflict of the inter-war period. In the bargaining over the construction of such an order, the US inevitably dominated because of its economic and military power. After the end of the war, the US was also the only source for much of the imports necessary for reconstruction. The fact that European exports were inadequate to pay for these essential imports created a dollar shortage, giving the US further leverage.

Chronologically, the first element in the reorganization was the establishment of a post-war monetary system. This was embodied in the Articles of Agreement of the International Monetary Fund (IMF), which were approved during a conference held at Bretton Woods, New Hampshire, in July 1944. This 'Bretton Woods' system was to provide the basis for international monetary arrangements until 1971. The details of the system were largely negotiated between the British, represented by Keynes, and the Americans, represented by Harry Dexter White. Given the relative economic power of the two countries, White's proposals had the most influence. Since the Bretton Woods system, embodying many of White's proposals, is widely seen as a pillar of capitalist stability and vitality in the post-war period, it is ironic that during the McCarthy period he himself was accused of being a communist agent.

There had been previous attempts to ensure that by acting together states could establish rules of the game for international monetary relations and simulate a world central bank. Britain had proposed such schemes at the Geneva International Monetary Conference of 1922 and the World Economic Conference in London in 1933, but without success. In 1944, however, the combination of a general desire to avoid the exchange rate instability and depression of the thirties, plus the influence of the US, produced a general acquiescence by the capitalist states.

The scheme involved a number of distinct elements, a major one being the exchange rate regime. Each country undertook to maintain the value of its currency within a narrow range of a par value against the dollar, the dollar being fixed against gold. Countries could only change their par values to correct a 'fundamental disequilibrium'. How rigid it was expected these exchange rates to be is a matter of debate, but during the fifties and sixties the maintenance of fixed exchange rates became the major objective of the system. The IMF articles also obliged countries to make their currencies convertible for current account transactions—i.e., freely exchangeable with other currencies; although they did not have to do this immediately. In fact, the European currencies only became fully convertible in 1958. Intervention (i.e., buying and selling currencies to maintain parities) was largely done in dollars, and the dollar became a major reserve asset, held by non-US governments along with gold. The system was supervised by the IMF, who could lend to countries in balance of payment difficulties, usually on condition that policy changes were made. The World Bank (International Bank for Reconstruction and Development) was also established to provide development loans. Along with the reform of the international monetary and payments system there was general US pressure for the liberalization of trade through the removal of import quotas and the reduction of tariffs. This was embodied in GATT (General Agreement on Tariffs and Trade).

It would not have been feasible to have developed this system of steady liberalization of monetary and trade arrangements unless the European countries could implement the changes without destroying their economies. Given the low level of their exports and the state of their economies in the immediate post-war years, they would have been unable to do this without US loans and, in particular, the aid provided under the Marshall Plan. This aid was important in starting the growth process off and was a major factor in consolidating the European states into a bloc supporting the US in its confrontation with communism. The organization that administered Marshall Aid, the OEEC, became the basis for the OECD, the main grouping of advanced capitalist states.

The US also played an important role in guaranteeing the security of the capitalist system as a whole against any potential socialist threat. At a military level, the US guaranteed security in Europe through stationing troops there, organizing NATO, and subsequently providing whatever protection was afforded by the nuclear umbrella. In the immediate post-war period, however, given the devastation and loss of life suffered during the war by the Soviet Union, the threat to the capitalist states was largely ideological. But the fear of a Soviet threat not only induced a new unity among the capitalist states; it was also used to split working class movements and reduce the political influence of the large communist parties in France and Italy.

The final major function the US performed was guaranteeing the supply of necessary primary products. Some markets it controlled anyway because it was an important producer; some it influenced through economic, military, or covert intervention and pressure on client regimes; some it dominated through the manipulation of its large strategic stockpiles which could be used to influence price. For instance the draft of the 'Economic Co-operation Act' intended as the legislative foundation of Marshall Aid and put before Congress in December 1947, required every country receiving aid to pledge, among other things, 'to stimulate the production of specific raw materials and to facilitate the procurement of such materials by the US for stockpiling'. Subsequently, in the Four Year Plan produced by the Labour government in the spring of 1949, paragraph 191 stated 'Under Article V of the Economic Co-operation Agreement the United Kingdom Government for their part intend in collaboration with the colonial governments to take all possible steps to increase the production of materials which the United States Government may require'. The plan specified the increases in colonial output of particular raw materials that were envisaged (Pritt, 1963). The US thus saw one of its major tasks as being the organization of production of basic raw materials; and one consequence of its organization was that from the Korean War to the end of the sixties, the terms of trade between primary products and industrial goods moved fairly steadily against the poor primary product producers.

Although the organization of the world capitalist system and the maintenance of its security was a necessary condition for the long boom, it was not a sufficient condition. It was the combination of organization by a hegemonic power and the necessary material preconditions that made it possible. Growth results from the expansion of the circuits of capital, and this requires not only available markets and a stable monetary and trading system but also the economic conditions for profitable production to proceed. It is to these we now turn.

12-4 THE MATERIAL PRECONDITIONS

The generation and maintenance of the long boom depended on a complex dynamic process within which there were a number of links. Although the pattern differed somewhat from country to country, the general process in most of the advanced capitalist world can be summarized as follows. The combination of a large reserve army of labour and a cooperative working class plus the great potential for the restructuring of capital and the transformation of production processes generated low unit labour costs and high productivity growth, increasing relative surplus value. Simultaneously the reorganization of the international system under US hegemony maintained raw material supplies and encouraged the internationalization of capital, while domestic state regulation of the economy allowed capitalists to realize the increased surplus value so generated as higher profits. The increase in profits not only encouraged further accumulation, which generated more growth, but also allowed higher wages to be paid. Growing real wages helped maintain the working class compliance that allowed the process to proceed.

Given that all these conditions held, a virtuous circle could be generated, but since the process depended on the conjunction of a variety of factors, the failure of any one could bring the expansion to a halt. In fact, the process could even run in reverse. Depletion of the reserve army and working class opposition could reduce profits, slow restructuring, and discourage accumulation, thus reduce the rate of growth of productivity, hitting the rate of growth of real wages and increasing class conflict. This instability in the process arose from the fact that all these conditions were necessary but none was sufficient alone. For instance, Keynesians emphasized the role of state regulation—in particular, demand management policies—in maintaining the growth process; and it is true that these policies did play an important role in allowing the process to proceed. But they would be (and subsequently were) insufficient to maintain growth in the absence of the other conditions.

Some of the elements in the process have already been mentioned; others need a little more consideration.

Labour Reserves

In the immediate post-war years, demobilization from the military provided an immediate source of industrial workers, but subsequently it was the reserve army in agriculture that proved crucial. For Japan and all European countries except the UK (where the share of labour in agriculture was already very small by 1940) the transfer of workers from agriculture to industry was a major factor in growth. This shift not only provided an elastic supply of cooperative labour to capital but also raised the average level of productivity. This happened because, although productivity was growing rapidly in agriculture, freeing the labour, the absolute level was still lower than in industry. Post-war population movements were also a major source of labour supply, particularly in West Germany, where migration from the east added substantially to the labour force. As the reserves in agriculture were depleted, immigration provided a further source—in the case of the UK and France, largely from ex-colonies. In the UK, although political pressure subsequently restricted the inflow from Asia and the West Indies, Ireland remained an important source. In Germany, the *Gastarbeiter* or guest workers, temporary immigrants, largely from mediterranean countries (Turkey in particular), were a major source of labour supply. A final source of labour force growth was increased participation by married women. Thus for most of the advanced capitalist economies up to the late sixties, firms faced an elastic labour supply, even when measured unemployment rates were quite low.

Working Class Compliance

The existence of the large potential reserve army of labour in itself reduced the bargaining strength of the working class, but this was combined with a variety of political factors. Fascism in Germany and Italy, and occupation by the Nazis in other European countries, had weakened labour movements, as had the high unemployment of the inter-war years. The Cold War ideology, Stalinism, and the consequent split between the communists and other sections of the labour movement also weakened working class solidarity. Given this, the social democratic ideology of cooperating with capitalism, while trying to remove its worst excesses from within the system, proved very powerful. To the extent that real benefits were obtained— improved social services, social security provisions, and growing real wages— this gave the system considerable legitimacy. The terms on which the working class cooperated with capitalism varied from country to country, depending on relative strength, and historical circumstances, but the pattern of compliance and the dominance of social democratic strategies among the working class was general.

Transformation of Production

The war had not only caused considerable physical destruction of plant and machinery (exactly how much is controversial), it had also disrupted many traditional forms of social relationships and reduced the power of social groups that would oppose various forms of restructuring. These groups included major capitalists in France, Germany, and Italy, who were discredited by virtue of their collaboration with the fascist regimes. This destruction of physical plant and social relations thus introduced a considerable amount of flexibility into the system, allowing change and restructuring to proceed more easily. Not surprisingly, it was in the UK where the power of traditional ruling groups was least disrupted, that the transformation was least complete. This fundamental restructuring was essential, as without it no country could establish a maintainable growth process. Given that the society was willing to adjust, there was great scope for innovation in the production processes. There was a backlog of

improvements arising from the postponement of replacement and modernization investment during the war; there were spin-offs from war-time
research and development work; and since European technology had fallen
behind that of the US, there was a range of American techniques that could
be copied. The need to re-equip and modernize produced a large demand
for new plant and equipment and an expansion in Department I industries,
which produce capital goods, thus creating further multiplier linkages.
Given the elastic labour supply, the political balance, and state regulation
of the expansion, the process became self-sustaining.

In all the advanced capitalist countries the state took an increasing role
in the regulation of capitalism, though the form and extent of its intervention
varied. A detailed indicative planning mechanism was used in France;
monetary and fiscal policy to govern demand in the US and UK; close
relations with the banks and large corporations in Germany and Japan;
and more corporatist tripartite forums of unions, companies, and state in
Scandinavia and the Netherlands. The development of new forms of state
regulation derived partly from Keynesian theory, but as much from the
success of war-time economic planning and the example of corporatist
policy under fascism.

While the immediate post-war period saw transitions to growth rates that
were higher than previously experienced and were sustained until the late
sixties, the extent to which countries shared in this boom varied. The next
section examines the growth process in a little more detail, in order to
identify some of the sources of inter-country variations.

12-5 EXPLANATIONS OF DIFFERING INTERNATIONAL GROWTH RATES

Chapter 6 drew attention to the very different post-war growth rates of the
major advanced capitalist countries, ranging from rapid growth of 10 to 11
per cent in Japan to 'stagnant' growth of 2 to 3 per cent in the UK and US.
We now turn to consider how these differences have been explained.

The neo-classical approach emphasizes the growth and allocation of
factor inputs. Growth is seen as resulting from increases in labour or capital,
and in their reallocation from low productivity sectors, such as agriculture,
to high productivity ones, such as manufacturing. Activities such as
education are seen raising the productivity of labour, thereby adding to
growth. By obtaining estimates of the magnitude of each of these influences,
differences in international growth rates are explained as the differences in
the sum of a host of rather diverse factors (see, for example, Denison, 1967).

The problem with this approach is that it leaves many of the differences
in growth performance unexplained and put down to a residual factor. This
is not particularly surprising. Much of the dynamic of expansion in the
post-war period has come from technical change, whereby production

processes are reorganized and restructured to yield greater production from similar inputs. The neo-classical approach, which takes technical change to be exogenous and places the emphasis on changes in inputs, is therefore not particularly helpful.

An alternative approach, advocated in Kaldor (1966), emphasizes the role of increasing returns to scale in manufacturing industry in explaining differences in growth rates. It is argued that a rapid expansion in manufacturing permits the rapid adoption of the most advanced methods of production, yields the full benefits of economies of scale, and thereby generates a more rapid growth in productivity. Thus productivity growth in manufacturing is positively associated with output growth. Other sectors, such as agriculture and services, are not seen as having this characteristic. Thus the manufacturing sector, and sometimes the industrial sector more broadly, is seen as the 'engine of growth' (see the thorough, if partisan, exposition of this view in Cornwall, 1977). Countries, such as Germany, Italy, and Japan, that have been able to expand their manufacturing sector have therefore experienced dynamic advantages in productivity growth. Countries, such as the UK and the US, where output growth has been slower have exhibited a weaker productivity performance, and have a relatively larger part of the production capacity in the form of older, less advanced capital equipment.

This hypothesis is usually augmented by a second, which stresses the role of technology transfer in productivity growth. Countries with more backward technology are seen as being able to adopt advanced technology pioneered in more developed countries. This transfer takes place by a variety of mechanisms, including direct investment and licensing arrangements. Since the level of technology is usually seen as correlated with income levels, this means that low income countries are able to grow faster, through a process of imitation, than high income countries, which have to develop new technology from scratch. This mechanism is seen as one of the explanations for rapid post-war growth in Japan and Germany relative to the UK and the US. As low income countries experience rapid growth, the technology gap tends to close and the gains are reduced. This in turn is seen as explaining the slow-down in growth rates of the fast growing countries, and, indeed, the post-war tendency for productivity growth trends to converge internationally.

These hypotheses contain a significant element of truth, and have their strength in emphasizing the dynamic process of accumulation and growth against the rather static conceptions of neo-classical theory. Their weakness, however, is that they are overly mechanical, failing to emphasize the necessity for a favourable balance of class forces and for an entrepreneurial class able to take advantage of production and trading opportunities. The role of class forces in providing the conditions for rapid growth can be seen most simply by considering the interrelated issues of profitability and labour supply. Abundant reserves of labour in the immediate post-war period were a general characteristic of advanced capitalist countries, with the major exception of the UK. This acted as an important check on real wages, helping to establish favourable profit levels. In those countries, such as Japan and Germany, where fascism, defeat in war, and action against workers by the occupying powers had brought with it a major weakening of labour movement organizations, the lack of militancy by workers meant a still more favourable set of conditions for growth. Not only were real wages kept depressed initially, but workers had little choice but to acquiesce in a major reorganization of industry, with associated changes in work practices. Moreover, unlike third world countries in a similar position but dominated by imperialism, these economies also possessed a developed capitalist class able to take advantage of these favourable circumstances.

These factors, together with the 'catching-up' process as war-torn economies started to restore output levels, led to generally rapid growth in manufacturing industry. The dynamic benefits from this, stressed by Kaldor (1966), meant sharp gains in productivity. Real wages could also rise quickly, although the existence of labour reserves meant that this increase generally was not large enough to threaten the high profitability on which it was based. Rapid growth in demand was ensured by the heavy demand for capital goods, the rapid expansion in consumer expenditure consequent upon large real wage increases, and the general expansion of world trade as tariff barriers and other obstacles to trade started to fall in the fifties. Those countries that were able initially to expand rapidly found that the correspondingly higher growth in productivity acted to sustain this, avoiding too rapid a depletion of labour reserves and helping to maintain their competitive position internationally (a factor that assumed particular importance in the sixties, when international competition intensified). By contrast, initially slow growing economies found themselves caught in a vicious circle of slow growth, low investment, and low productivity gains.

In the UK these unfavourable factors were particularly acute. The Second World War ended with the working class in a strong defensive position, which enforced the political commitment to full employment and high wages. With the transfer of labour from agriculture already virtually completed, the lack of an elastic labour supply created unfavourable conditions for accumulation. And with a capitalist class already largely committed to a strategy of expansion overseas rather than to domestically based growth (for details, see Chapter 6), almost all factors were adverse. Slow growth meant low productivity growth, and the UK economy got locked into a low growth spiral. From being a high wage economy at the end of the Second World War, the UK economy progressively became a low wage (but high cost) economy, with consequent exacerbation of class stalemate.

Towards the middle or end of the sixties, several factors became increasingly adverse for growth in advanced capitalist countries. First, continued expansion had substantially depleted labour reserves in most economies. While the import of foreign labour acted as a temporary buffer, with particular advantage because of the low overhead social capital associated with the typical guest worker, this could only be temporary. And an inelastic labour supply meant that former rates of expansion were unsustainable.

The argument concerning labour shortages requires some care in development. The evidence suggests that labour shortages have *not* constrained the expansion of the manufacturing sector, the growth rate of which has primarily been determined by the growth of demand. Thus Kaldor, apparently rejecting his former view that labour bottlenecks accounted for the slow growth of the UK economy, argued that lack of demand was the principal cause of lack of growth in manufacturing, and hence on the 'engine of growth' hypothesis in the economy as a whole (Kaldor, 1975).

However, the conflict is more apparent than real. It is important to distinguish between labour shortages acting on the manufacturing sector and those acting on the rest of the economy. Here it is necessary to introduce the concept of a 'dual labour market'. Since rates of pay in manufacturing (and industry more generally) are typically significantly above those in the service sector, it is arguable that manufacturing faces a relatively elastic supply of labour irrespective of the overall state of labour market conditions. Rather than relative wages acting as the signal for workers to transfer from one sector to another, as the neo-classical view emphasizes, transfer is regulated by changes in job vacancies. The implication of this is that labour constraints will bite, not on the manufacturing sector, but rather on other sectors, particularly those, such as services, that are net absorbers of labour.

Labour supply became a more general problem in most advanced capitalist countries towards the end of the sixties. This helped to fuel greater militancy on the part of workers, generating wage increases and labour unrest generally. (However, the role of labour shortages in this should not be exaggerated. The entry to a position of influence in labour movements of a generation of workers who had only experienced the prosperity and boom conditions of the post-war period must also be taken account of.) This force in itself was a major factor in bringing the period of the long boom to an end. For a while, the period of expansion was sustained by a shift to inflationary monetary and fiscal policy in most of the advanced capitalist countries. Moreover, the response in the more internationally competitive sectors (particularly manufacturing) to a slow-down of demand seems to have been an intensified attempt to raise productivity, as individual firms sought to offset the effects of slump by expanding their market share. In the event, the result was a general and sharp fall in manufacturing profitability (except in the US, where the sharp devaluation of the dollar in the 1971–3 period acted to raise international competitiveness, enabling

US domestically based firms to expand their market shares). The eventual outcome of the depletion of labour reserves was a general reduction in rates of growth and levels of investment and increases in unemployment. Paradoxical though it may seem, the appearance of labour shortages constraining the rate of growth created widespread redundancies and unemployment.

12-6 INTERNATIONALIZATION OF CAPITAL

The long post-war boom saw not only higher growth rates but a growth in the internationalization of capital and an associated tendency towards the world capitalist economy being integrated into a single market. While the expansion of capital is inherently an international phenomenon, since the search for profit is not constrained by state boundaries, the form and the extent of the international circulation of capital changes through time. It is useful to distinguish three forms in which capital becomes international, corresponding to three circuits of capital:

(a) The circulation of commodity capital through trade flows in the export and import of goods and services.
(b) The circulation of money capital through international financial markets and portfolio investment (e.g., buying shares in foreign companies).
(c) The circulation of productive capital, in which there is direct investment (setting up factories, etc.) in a number of countries and production is increasingly integrated and controlled on a world scale as within the multi-national companies (MNCs).

To an individual firm all three forms represent possible strategies that may lead to national boundaries being crossed in the completion of the circuits of capital. The proximate causes or immediate reasons for a firm's becoming involved in international trade, finance, or production are various, and some specific factors will be discussed under each heading. Ultimately, however, it is the drive to expand or maintain profitability that is the motive for internationalization, and since this drive is operating in each country in the capitalist world it leads to interpenetration of each others' markets, increased interdependence, and a tendency for the capitalist world to be increasingly integrated into a single market. Below, the internationalization of each form of capital is examined in turn.

Commodity Capital

Trade in commodities pre-dates the capitalist mode of production but industrialization and growth in the late nineteenth century, together with the improvement in transport and communications, generated a substantial increase in the volume of trade, despite the prevalence of protection. With the growth in trade came an international division of labour, with the industrial nations increasingly monopolizing manufactured exports and the non-capitalist world becoming specialized in the production of raw materials. The displacement of craft methods of manufacture disrupted these societies, while the cost advantages the industrial societies gained from their scale of operation made it difficult for them to get started on the process of industrialization. This pattern of uneven development, with its tendency to magnify the initial advantages, condemned the non-capitalist world to poverty and created major barriers to its development. The one country that broke these barriers was Japan, where after the Meiji restoration trade and development were systematically planned, and industry received various kinds of state aid ranging from subsidies to protection. The general expansion of world trade was disrupted by both world wars and further damaged by the breakdown of the international economic system and the growth of protection in the thirties. Between 1870 and 1913 the volume of exports of the 16 major capitalist powers grew by 3.7 per cent a year, between 1913 and 1950 by only 1.1 per cent, actually falling in the thirties. In contrast, between 1950 and 1970 the volume of exports grew by 8.6 per cent a year. (These figures are taken from Maddison, 1977.)

A number of factors were involved in this rapid growth in trade. From 1948 onwards, under US leadership, there was a steady liberalization of trade and the removal of protectionist controls. This was partly done on a multilateral basis through GATT (General Agreement on Tariffs and Trade) and the Kennedy and Tokyo rounds of tariff reductions, and partly on a regional basis through the creation of free trade areas such as the EEC and EFTA (European Free Trade Area). Trade can be restricted in a number of different ways and these negotiations were more effective in reducing some restrictions than others. Quantitative restrictions, by which absolute limits are placed on the total amount of goods that can be imported, became very much less common in the fifties and sixties. Tariffs, by which a customs duty is imposed on imported goods, were reduced substantially. However, countries in balance of payments difficulties still developed ways of circumventing the international agreements on restrictions. Both the UK and the US imposed import surcharges, temporary across-the-board tariffs; the UK and Italy used import deposit schemes, which imposed an interest cost on importers; and many tax and subsidy systems discriminated between importers and exporters. More difficult to deal with were what became known as 'non-tariff barriers', sets of domestic regulations that discriminated against imports. But despite the fact that substantial barriers remained, with the possible exception of Japan the absolute levels of the barriers were reduced substantially between 1948 and 1970.

The main source of trade growth in the post-war period was in manufactures and, in particular, in trade between the advanced capitalist countries. Although this is not what would be predicted by traditional international trade theory, it is not surprising, since it was among the advanced capitalist countries that removal of restrictions was carried furthest and income was, in general, growing fastest. Within the advanced capitalist countries there developed increasing diversification of both demand and supply, so that each country would become exporters and importers of very similar goods. Britain thus both imports and exports cars, which means that British consumers have a large range of models to choose from, while each producer can produce a model in sufficient volume to keep costs low. Whether the benefits of allowing consumers to choose between 50 models of car produced in different countries offsets the balance of payments and employment costs of the choice is another matter. What is clear is that the growth of trade, by making the markets for some goods international, reinforced the process of uneven development. Efficient firms and countries became stronger and the less efficient weaker. At the level of the firm this appeared as increasing concentration and centralization of capital in the hands of the largest MNCs; at the level of the nation it appeared as a growing divergence between the performance of weak and strong countries in terms of growth and balance of payments. However, to understand the conflicts that developed between those countries with a chronic deficit on balance of payments and those accumulating surpluses requires a consideration of the internationalization of financial markets.

Money Capital

Corresponding to the liberalization of trade after the war, there was a similar liberalization of international financial flows. Currencies were made convertible, various forms of exchange controls removed, and the gold market in London re-opened in 1954. The turning point in the development of the financial system was 1958. That year saw the full convertibility of a number of important currencies, the end of the dollar shortage, and the first tentative appearance of a Eurodollar market. Up to the mid fifties, the demand for imports from the US by Europe and the rest of the world exceeded by far the amount of dollars they could earn by exports. Marshall Aid, loans, and capital flows had offset this dollar shortage to some extent, but not enough to meet demand. Since most trade was done in dollars and the dollar was convertible into gold, central banks also wanted to hold part of their reserves in dollars. But by the late fifties, the end of reconstruction, the growth of European exports, capital investment by US companies in Europe, and US aid and military expenditure abroad had changed the balance of demand and supply, and the dollar shortage disappeared. What was significant was that the dollars acquired in Europe—from exports to the US, from payments by US firms, etc.—were not repatriated to the US and invested there but held in Europe. These dollar deposits held in Europe, which became known as Eurodollars, grew rapidly. The estimated size of the market was $9 billion in 1964; $16 billion in 1966; $44 billion in 1969, and over $80 billion by 1972 (Strange, 1976). By 1979 it was estimated at

$500 billion. These are, however, only estimates, since by its nature measurement and definition of the market is very difficult. Eurodollars were later joined by other Eurocurrencies (e.g., sterling held outside the UK and DM held outside Germany) but they remained the largest market.

The initial development of the market was by British overseas banks in London, but they were subsequently joined by American and then other foreign banks in London and then on a smaller scale by banks in Switzerland and other European financial centres. After 1968 there also developed an Asian Eurodollar market, starting from Singapore. Three main factors account for the growth of the market. First, the US balance of payments deficit (initially on capital account and after the late sixties also on current account) provided the large supply of dollars that allowed the market to grow. Second, the interest rate differential between the US and Europe made it more profitable to hold the dollars in Europe rather than repatriate them to the US. The differential arose partly because of US restrictions, such as Regulation Q, on the interest rates that could be offered; and partly because the spread between borrowing and lending rates of US banks was larger than in Europe, allowing the European competitors to undercut them. The third factor was that it was effectively unregulated. Domestic banking and credit systems were in every country heavily regulated, with reserve requirements, controls on transactions by banks, etc. The Eurodollar market, being offshore (the banks being involved in dealing with foreign currency), is not so regulated. But while lack of regulation means that profitable opportunities are greater, it carries a risk of lack of stability. There is no lender of last resort in the market and no guarantee of the soundness of banks' balance sheets; thus the danger arises that default on large loans could cause a bank collapse and a domino effect through the market. The market had repercussions on stability in another way. The development of a large very liquid international market for short-term funds meant that monetary managers (bankers, corporate treasuries, and the like) became more sophisticated in their portfolio management. They learned to switch funds from one currency to another in the light of interest rate movements. Since the size of the Eurocurrency market dwarfed the reserves of most central banks, these switches between currencies could make foreign exchange markets very volatile and exchange rates unstable.

Up to 1970 the demand for credit in Eurodollars came largely from the advanced capitalist world (US MNCs, for instance, being large borrowers). After 1970, however, less developed countries entered the market on a large scale. The market had a substantial impact on domestic money markets. Since it was possible to switch into the Eurodollar market in response to interest rate differentials, domestic interest rates became sensitive to international ones.

The international financial markets, of which that in Eurodollars was the largest, thus became a way in which national regulation could be avoided, a source of instability in exchange rates, and a major constraint on the operation of domestic economic policy. To regulate the markets to restore control would require international agreement. For long such agreement was not forthcoming, since at any particular time the existence of the market was of benefit to at least one major country (for instance, by recycling petrodollars earned by OPEC, in 1974–5). In 1979 both the US and West Germany came to the view that they must be regulated. The UK however, continued to oppose regulation since the free Eurocurrency market generated large earnings for banks located in London. The renewed strength of the dollar in early 1980 weakened US support for regulation.

Productive Capital

Although there had been firms that had operated and produced in a number of countries since the nineteenth century, the post-war period saw a vast growth in their size and influence. These multi-national companies are examined in detail in Hood and Young (1979).

Within the MNCs the production process is integrated on an international basis, and they have revenues as large as the GNPs of many countries. In 1976, the three largest were Exxon, General Motors, and Royal Dutch Shell, with sales of $48.6 billion, $47.2 billion and $36.1 billion respectively. By comparison, UK GNP was $219.9 billion and 11 of the 24 OECD countries had a GNP smaller than the revenues of Exxon. Again, in 1976 the major capitalist countries with large overseas production had a stock of overseas direct investment of $270 billion. Of this, $137 billion originated from the US, and the next highest amount, $32.1 billion, from the UK (figures from Hood and Young, 1979). In 1975, 74 per cent of this investment was in other advanced capitalist economies, 6 per cent in OPEC, and 20 per cent in other developing countries. Even among the developing countries investment tended to be centred in the richer ones.

There is a variety of motives for setting up production facilities in many countries. The firm may not be able to import because of local protection; wage rate or subsidy differences may encourage diversification of production; having a variety of sources of supply may provide security against industrial action or government controls; or production location may be determined by resource requirements. Initially this last reason was the most important, and the typical multi-nationals were US or European firms working in extractive industries. The large oil companies and mining companies were of this type, expanding abroad to acquire sources of raw material supply which would be shipped back to their country of origin for processing and marketing. But increasingly in the post-war period the typical multi-national became a manufacturing company. By the mid seventies, in both the US and the UK, about a quarter of the foreign investment was in extractive industries, a half in manufacturing, and a quarter in services (including banking, finance, and transport).

The internationalization of production through the growth of multi-national companies has three major implications:

(a) A large range of economic decisions and international trade become internalized within the firm, and less susceptible to government influence.
(b) The size of the companies gives them great bargaining power and influence over individual governments.
(c) Capital becomes 'denationalized', in that companies cease to be acting in the interests of national as opposed to international capital. As the proportion of profits derived from the country of origin declines, their concern at maintaining production or employment there is reduced relative to their international concerns.

To illustrate these three features, consider Ford, in 1976 the fourth largest MNC. In 1976 Ford produced 5.4 million vehicles, had sales of $28.8 billion, and after-tax profits of $983 million, manufacturing, assembling, or selling vehicles in over 100 countries. Outside the US the main production centres were West Germany, Britain, Canada, Brazil, Australia, Mexico, Argentina, South Africa, and Spain. Forty-six per cent of its assets were held, and 45 per cent of its profits earned, outside the US. In 1975, a slump year for the US car market, 71 per cent of its earnings were external. In total it employed 450 000 people in 1976. Much of its production is integrated across national boundaries, components being manufactured in one country, transported to another country to be assembled into a car, which is then sold in a third country. In the first 10 months of 1979, half the Ford cars sold in the UK had been imported from other Ford subsidiaries, making Ford the largest car importer in Britain.

When a company is integrated across national boundaries, profit-maximizing location of production becomes a complex decision, reflecting a variety of factors. Economies of scale are important in the car industry, where production costs tend to fall sharply with volume, so that it pays to concentrate production. Against this, very large plants become difficult to manage and are more prone to industrial militancy. To a certain extent this dilemma can be solved by separating production of components. One centre produces most of the engines, another transmissions, and a third assembles them. Thus the economies of scale in each component (which may be very different) can be gained, while the total size of individual plants can be kept down.

Although technical economies of scale may indicate that all of a particular component should be produced in one plant, the company would then become very vulnerable to a strike at that plant, or to action by the state in which that plant is situated. Therefore security and bargaining power are increased if there is more than one source for any crucial component. Multi-sourcing of essential components thus becomes the rule unless minimum efficient volume is very large. Otherwise, some security can be provided by holding large inventories of the component and locating the plant in a place where industrial militancy is low and the state likely to be compliant. Location decisions will also reflect transport costs, relative unit labour costs, industrial militancy, labour supply, size and likely growth of nearby markets, the political background of the country, and the subsidies and tax benefits available, etc. When a multi-national announces that it intends to build a large new plant, governments queue up to tempt it to locate in their country. Conversely, threatening to close plants gives MNCs great leverage over governments.

Within a multi-national there develops a large market, internal to the company but international to the host countries in which it operates. When Ford UK sends engine castings to Ford Spain, the prices at which they are transferred are set by Ford but determine the value of UK exports, Spanish imports, and the relative profitability of the two companies. Through its choice of these transfer prices, Ford can determine the profits made by each subsidiary and thus the tax paid by each. A subsidiary operating in a high tax country could sell components to the subsidiary in a low tax country at very low prices, thus transferring profits to the area where they are taxed least. A similar procedure can be used to transfer cash reserves from a weak currency to a strong currency when exchange controls would otherwise stop such transfers. Transfer prices gain great significance because of the importance of intra-firm transactions in total exports. Fifty per cent of US exports in 1974 and 30 per cent of UK exports in 1973 were intra-firm transactions (Hood and Young, 1979, p. 171). The balance of payments position of a country can then be very sensitive to transfer pricing practices and location decisions of an individual firm.

Most multi-nationals originated in one particular country and are often thought of as belonging to their country of origin: thus Ford in this sense is an American company. There are some—Unilever and Royal Dutch Shell, for instance, joint British–Dutch companies—that do not have a single country of origin, but these are exceptions. In 1973, of the 260 largest MNCs, 126 were of US origin, 49 UK, 21 West German, and 19 French. No other country had more than 10, although since then more of the large Japanese companies have become multi-national. Although it may be common to think of these giant companies as being corporate citizens of their country of origin, this is becoming increasingly less accurate. As foreign profits and assets account for larger proportions of the firm's total, their interests become increasingly international and may diverge from those of their country of origin. It is in this sense that the MNCs may be said to become denationalized. This is of particular significance to the UK, since it is a relatively small and slow growing market. Profitability then demands that MNCs of UK origin concentrate their concern on the rapidly growing markets where the potential for profit is greater even at the expense of domestic production or employment. To ensure that the multi-nationals, whether of UK or foreign origin, maintain production and employment in Britain requires that the government follow policies conducive to the well-being of MNCs, irrespective of domestic political objectives. In addition, the international integration of the companies makes nationalization of them more difficult. Ford plants in Britain depend on Ford plants elsewhere in Europe, both as markets for the components produced here and as a source of essential components. Without the cooperation of other Ford subsidiaries, which would be unlikely following nationalization of the UK subsidiary, operation of Ford UK by a British government would present some difficulties.

12-7 CONCLUSIONS

The internationalization of capital and the increasing integration of markets and production within the capitalist world during the post-war period had a number of important consequences:

(a) The capitalist world as a whole became much more interdependent, with the consequence that a shock or crisis in any one part was rapidly transmitted to the rest of the system.

(b) Economic processes—competition and the law of value, concentration and centralization, uneven development—operated directly on a world level, destroying weak and inefficient capitals and strengthening the powerful ones.

(c) The power of individual states relative to international capital was reduced. Exchange rate and monetary policies were dominated by international financial markets; balance of payments and employment policies by MNC decisions.

(d) The need for regulation of the anarchy and irrationality of the market on a world level grew just when the ability of any individual state to regulate it was being eroded. To a certain extent the market was being replaced by rational planning procedures within individual MNCs, but these procedures remained subordinate to competition and profit maximizing, so planning at a higher level was necessary.

These consequences of internationalization were to have important implications for the form that the crises of the seventies took. These crises are examined in the following chapter.

FURTHER READING

For general overviews of world capitalist development see Mandel (1975 and 1978) and the very important review of the first book by Rowthorn (1980).

The rapid development of capitalism as a world system is described in

Hobsbawm (1975); for a description of the slump of the thirties, see Kindleberger (1973).

Long waves in capitalist development are traced in Maddison (1977).

The post-war development of the world monetary system is well described in Block (1977) and Strange (1976). For other discussions on world monetary problems see also Williamson (1977), and Crockett (1977). The Brandt Report (1980) deals with current relations between rich and poor members of the system.

Internationalization of capital is dealt with in Hood and Young (1979), Barnet and Müller (1975), and Radice (1975).

Statistical and descriptive material on the main capitalist economies can be found in the publications of the OECD and the EEC as well as in United Nations reports.

THIRTEEN

CRISIS IN WORLD CAPITALISM

Ron Smith

13-1 THE COLLAPSE OF THE LONG BOOM

Although economists differ as to the exact date of the turning point and the cause of the change, it is generally agreed that there is a qualitative difference between the pattern of economic performance in the seventies and that characteristic of the earlier post-war years. Unemployment and inflation rates are higher and growth rates lower; exchange rates and capital movements more volatile, bankruptcies more common; the pace of accumulation slower, and policy less effective. Although the extent to which individual countries suffered varied considerably, the phenomena were general across the whole of the advanced capitalist world. In this chapter the same theoretical approach that was used in the last chapter to explain the genesis of the long boom will be used to explain the generalized crisis. The approach involves examining the conditions (economic and political) necessary for the maintenance of profitable accumulation and the expansion of commodity production. In the early post-war period these conditions were all met, but with the passage of time disproportionalities appeared, which posed threats to profitability.

The sixties saw the development of a variety of different barriers to accumulation, each arising from the failure of a necessary condition for continued expansion. The appearance of these barriers was not merely a matter of unfortunate chance; each was the outcome of the previous process of expansion itself. There were four main factors.

First, the long period of expansion had depleted the reserve army of labour in the advanced capitalist countries, in particular the surplus labour that could be transferred from agriculture was much diminished. In the short run this could be offset by drawing non-working women into the labour force, and by immigration, such as the use of short-stay migrant labour like the *Gastarbeiter* in West Germany. Given the patriarchal structure of these societies, there were limits to the increase in the female participation rates, while political and social opposition appeared to limit the large-scale use of cheap immigrant labour. Thus these only provided short-term palliatives.

Second, the potential for easy increases in relative surplus value through productivity growth and internationalization was also exhausted. The technological backlog accumulated during the war was used up, and Europe and Japan had copied and adopted the more advanced US production techniques. Furthermore, as each of these countries accumulated large capital stocks specific to particular types of process and technology, the costs of changing (in particular, the need to scrap large amounts of existing plant and equipment) grew larger, inhibiting productivity growth. Trade liberalization was completed by the sixties and, although internationalization continued, the productivity gains from international division of labour and economies of scale were much smaller.

Third, the uneven nature of the development during the expansion generated disproportionalities. These imbalances then created a major constraint on further growth. The most significant one was between the raw material and energy requirements of the advanced capitalist countries and their conditions of production in the third world. Imbalances between supply and demand for primary products (in particular oil) and erosion of capitalist control over the conditions of supply became very apparent in 1973, but the problem was of longer standing. Within the advanced capitalist countries similar disproportionalities between sectors of the economy—for instance, between manufacturing and services (including government services)—appeared. The organization and techniques of production in manufacturing had gone through repeated renovation, with consequential high productivity growth. Within services (and some other industries, like construction in the UK) conditions of production had changed much less, and productivity growth was much slower. Thus to maintain growth, a larger and larger proportion of the labour force was required to provide services, and this became a drag on the growth process in general. It also tended to reduce the rate of exploitation, since the inefficiency increased the value of labour power. Whether provided by capital or the government (like health and education), these industries provided important elements necessary for the reproduction of labour power. If their efficiency lagged behind other sectors, this increased the cost of providing these elements, raised the value of labour power, and reduced surplus value. To remedy these disproportionalities required major restructuring and transformation of production techniques, but competition and the market provided no mechanisms to make these adjustments smoothly. For the transformation to proceed required crisis and slump, so that the consequent bankruptcies and redundancies would unfreeze the structure, allowing the necessary reallocation. In the areas controlled by the state, restructuring required political implementation of the transformations. This was the basis of the major attacks on public expenditure in the late seventies in many of the advanced capitalist countries.

Fourth, the long period of growth, the depletion of the reserve army, and the disproportionality in raw material production, combined with the success of hostile political movements in both advanced and less developed countries, shifted the balance of class forces against capital. On top of the other factors (although partly as a result of them), worker militancy and anti-imperialist movement prevented capitalists increasing absolute surplus value and put further downward pressure on the rate of exploitation. In response to the developing shortage of labour and the reduced scope for increasing pure labour productivity growth, companies started to substitute capital for labour, increasing the organic composition of capital and the pressure on the rate of profit. The process was accentuated in the relatively backward countries like the UK because growing internationalization of capital increased competition, cutting away the surplus profits local firms had gained from their domestic monopolies.

In the short run these obstacles to accumulation could be circumvented and the pressure on the rate of profit reduced by the expansion of credit and inflation, and this was the route taken in the late sixties and early seventies. Inflation had a number of advantages. It reduced the growth of real wages and the cost of labour power to capital; it reduced the real cost of primary products in terms of industrial goods; and it reduced the real cost of borrowing, transferring surplus to capital through the savings of the working class. The expansion of credit and inflation thus supported profitability and allowed many firms to continue in operation that would otherwise have gone bankrupt. But inflation could only be a short-term palliative; money wages, raw material prices, and interest rates would eventually adjust to the rate of inflation, and profits could only be maintained by accelerating inflation. More seriously, inflation did nothing to remove the fundamental obstacles to accumulation or the underlying pressures on profitability. Postponing the restructuring merely meant that when the crisis did come it would be far worse.

Inflation may have been an inadequate and irrational way for the system to respond to the growing contradictions, but the changing balance of class forces made it the only way. By the end of the long boom the power of capital relative to workers in industrial countries and primary product producers was substantially reduced, as was US hegemony, the basis of post-war capitalist power relations. The relative rigidity and weakness of the political, ideological, and organizational structures by which capital regulated the system made it unable to orchestrate the vast economic transformations required. Thus unresolved, the developing contradictions expressed themselves on the one hand as inflation, and on the other as the inability of the US to continue to organize the system. Given this form of expression, the first manifestation of the contradictions as crisis was in the breakdown of the post-war monetary system and of US hegemony. The political basis of the system was thus undermined at the same time as the growing internationalization of capital increased the need for supra-national regulation. But despite the importance of political regulation, the main regulator of any capitalist system remains the rate of profit. So before examining the chronology of the crisis we must consider the movements in international profitability in more detail.

13-2 INTERNATIONAL PROFITABILITY

As has been suggested above, movements in profitability are of critical importance to the dynamic of capitalist accumulation. Since profits provide a major source of funds from which investment is to be financed, low profits represent a constraint on the possibilities of investment. At the same time, current profitability provides at least some guide, however imperfect, to future profitability. Since it acts as an indicator of whether or not conditions are favourable to accumulation, it is of considerable interest to examine international trends and differences in profitability. It was also noted that some Marxists have argued that the cause of crisis lies in a rising organic composition of capital, depressing profitability and leading to a collapse of investment, and it is of interest to see whether empirical trends afford any support to this position (although strong reservations about the use of standard national income categories to measure Marxist categories need to be kept in mind).

A decline in profitability can either result from a fall in the profit share (due, for example, to a rise in wages) or a fall in the output/capital ratio (perhaps because of inefficient investments), and these ratios are often loosely associated with the rate of exploitation and the inverse of the organic composition of capital, respectively.

There is a host of problems in obtaining reliable measures of profits and capital invested. Inflation makes the measurement of real profits hazardous. Measurements of the capital stock may be questioned theoretically on the grounds that they presuppose a rate of profit for their calculation. However, from a practical point of view, such statistics probably contain no more conceptual problems than many others that are freely used in empirical work. More critical are the inaccuracies that result from the sheer enormity of the task of measuring the capital stock at any point in time. Since it is quite impossible to assemble a complete list of existing capital equipment and then value each item, the capital stock is usually calculated from investment series by a 'perpetual inventory' approach. Given an initial value for the capital stock in a certain period, additions to the capital stock may be obtained from the investment series, and depreciation calculated by means of assumed fixed lifetimes for different types of capital equipment. The weakness of this is that the economic lifetime of capital equipment is not fixed, but is determined by considerations of profitability. Marked changes in economic circumstances, such as occurred in the slump of 1974, with sharp shifts in relative prices associated with the rise in the price of oil, may result in the early scrapping of machinery. In this case, the perpetual inventory approach would overstate the existing capital stock (and hence understate profitability) for a significant period.

Despite these difficulties the available series, if treated with care, are of interest, although because of the problems of measuring the capital stock, the data on *profit shares* are of greater reliability than those on *profit rates*. Table 13-1 provides a summary of profit statistics for a number of countries for manufacturing industry for 1975, together with figures for 1958 for comparison. The first point to note is the wide disparity of profit rate internationally. In 1975 the range was over four to one, ranging from the high profitability exhibited by the US and Japan to the depressed levels in

Table 13-1 Comparisons of international profitability in manufacturing industry

	Profit shares	(P/Y)	Output/ Capital	ratio (Y/K)	Profit rates	(P/K)
	1958	1975	1958	1975	1958	1975
Canada	34.0	33.3	47.4	40.6	16.1	13.5
US	23.6	27.0	70.0	71.9	16.5	19.4
Japan	47.1	40.3	51.6	45.2	24.3	18.2
West Germany	39.5	25.5	55.3	46.0	21.8	11.7
Italy	39.9	21.1	27.4	na	10.9	na
Sweden	32.0	30.8	39.9	37.2	12.7	11.4
UK	31.8	16.0	38.3	28.3	12.2	4.5
Australia	30.4	22.5	na	na	na	na
Denmark	43.4	34.4	na	na	na	na
Netherlands	40.3	35.8	na	na	na	na

Source: T. P. Hill (1979).

the UK. (Profitability was probably equally low in Italy: profitability in the two countries was similar in 1972 and showed a similar subsequent fall—see McCracken, 1977). While high profitability in Japan resulted from a very high profit share, that in the US resulted from high measured capital productivity. Judging from the sample, rates of return in western European countries are generally lower than in non-European OECD countries.

Discerning trends from time series data is a somewhat hazardous business. As far as the data in Table 13-1 are concerned, the end of the data series (1975) corresponds to a year of very depressed output levels, resulting in very low levels of profitability simply for this reason. It is more interesting to know whether profitability exhibits any trend movements abstracting from such changes in capacity utilization. This is done in part in Table 13–1 by choosing the earlier year also to be one of generally depressed output levels, but since the recession of 1958 was much less acute than that of 1975, this does not really deal with the problem. To get round these difficulties, it is sensible to examine profit trends up to 1973, before the international slump of 1974–5 developed. If this is done (see Hill, 1979), we find that western European countries have generally experienced a significant downward trend in manufacturing profitability, due mainly to a fall in the profit share. Figures for industry and transport (a wider definition, which includes manufacturing) also show a significant downward trend, although less significant. On the wider definition, however, the fall is attributable more or less equally to a fall in the profit share and a rise in the capital/output ratio. The evidence for non-EEC countries is much less clear. Canada, in common with European countries, experienced a significant fall in profitability. However, profitability in Japan showed a different profile for both industry and manufacturing, rising in the fifties, maintaining a plateau in the sixties, and then falling in the boom of 1971–3, both because of a falling profit share and a rising capital/output ratio. No significant linear trend throughout the period therefore emerges. The US experienced a steady rate of profit throughout the fifties and early sixties, but then a decline from about 1965–6 onwards, due more or less equally to a fall in the profit share and a rise in the capital/output ratio. What distinguishes it from other countries is the subsequent *rise* in profitability since 1974, so that no significant trend exists for the period as a whole. This rise from 1974 seems largely to be due to the earlier fall in the dollar, which restored the international competitiveness of the US domestically based manufacturing industry, which was able to recapture a larger share of world trade, largely at the expense of western European competitors. This added to the downward pressures on European profitability in the seventies.

We may summarize these results as showing a general decline in profitability for western European countries, with less clear-cut results for non-European advanced capitalist countries. Also of interest, particularly for what follows, is the fact that there were clear signs *generally* of a decline in profitability in the late sixties and early seventies, *prior* to the slump of 1974 onwards. Since the early seventies was a period of general boom, when profitability would usually be expected to rise, this is clear evidence of growing strains in the international capitalist economy well before the slump developed. Any satisfactory explanation of the 1974–5 slump must take account of this.

To what extent do these conclusions support or undermine the view that crisis results from a rising organic composition of capital? We can address this question if we are prepared to identify the capital/output ratio with the organic composition of capital, and the profit share with the rate of exploitation. The evidence then seems to show that the decline in the rate of profit is due more or less equally to a fall in the rate of exploitation and a rise in the organic composition of capital (although, if anything, the former predominates, particularly in manufacturing). Of course, the identification of the capital/output ratio with the organic composition of capital is a poor one. The measure of capital includes only fixed capital, not circulating capital, and refers only to the specific sector in question, not to an economy-wide measure. Thus capital advanced by the commercial and service sectors is entirely omitted, as is that advanced by the public sector. But then one has to deal with the problem of how to treat taxes and government expenditure (including the so-called 'social wage') in Marxist analysis. If the objection is to be sustained, it requires a thorough study to show that inclusion of these factors would change the results.

So far, we have been considering operating profits, which are generated from a process of production whereby labour and intermediate inputs are physically transformed into outputs. It is this measure of profitability that measures the return from productive activities by a firm. However, firms also derive other profits, revaluation profits, which accrue simply from holding a good that remains physically untransformed over a period of time in which its price rises. Since firms engaged in production typically hold stocks of goods, whether in raw material or finished form, they may well receive revaluation profits. However, such profits are in no way linked to production: firms engaged purely in trade or speculation equally may receive them.

Such revaluation profits have typically been quite small throughout most of the post-war period. However, in the late sixties and early seventies they assumed a major proportion. This was because firms found that, with the rise in inflation, the rate of price increase of its holdings of goods (whether in raw material or finished form) greatly exceeded the marginal cost of external borrowing. The difference between these two items represented a revaluation profit to the firm. Moreover, firms that had borrowed long term in periods of relatively low inflation found that the rise in inflation reduced significantly the real value of these liabilities, yielding revaluation profits almost irrespective of how these funds had been used.

The significance of this factor varied internationally. It is also rather complex to measure. However, a study for the UK (*Bank of England Quarterly Bulletin*, 1978) suggests that this factor may largely have offset the decline in operating profitability throughout the sixties and seventies. More generally, we can observe the general tendency internationally towards negative real short-term interest rates in the seventies. The real cost of borrowing long term (measured *ex post*) fell still more sharply. Although we are forced to speculate here, it seems likely that a rise in revaluation profits was a general factor tending to offset the fall in operating profitability that we discussed above.

The implications of this are mainly redistributive, since, as we have argued, it is operating profitability (both absolute and relative to the real cost of external finance) that governs investment. But it is important to understand this redistribution in class terms. The corporate sector as a whole has tended to be cushioned from the decline in operating profitability by increased revaluation profits. These gains were made principally at the expense of holders of long-term corporate debt, who in the main are the large pension and insurance funds. As a result of this lower return, these companies have paid benefits reduced in real terms in the form of pensions and life insurance. The gains to companies have accrued primarily from older and retired sections of the working population.

13-3   THE COLLAPSE OF US HEGEMONY

Between the end of the Second World War and the late sixties, US economic dominance of the system declined substantially, for two main reasons. First, the growth rate in the US was substantially slower than it was in most of the other advanced capitalist countries, being about the same as that in the UK. This low growth in productivity and output meant that the US became relatively less important as a market and a supplier. US firms expanded rapidly abroad, but, as was argued earlier, they tended to become denationalized and did not necessarily support the exercise of US power. The second factor was the glut of dollars on the market, which drove down the US exchange rate and undermined US policy. The net effect of these two factors can be seen in Table 13–2, which shows the GNP of the US relative to the other major advanced capitalist powers in 1953 and 1977. During the period US GNP declined from two-thirds to less than a half of the total. It remained by far the biggest, but its relative dominance diminished substantially. Corresponding to this there was a loss of relative military dominance, symbolized by the defeat in Vietnam and Soviet attainment of strategic nuclear parity.

In the monetary sphere, the decline of the dollar was of special significance because the dollar was the basis of the Bretton Woods system. Foreign central banks held a large part of their reserves in dollars; trade was

Table 13-2 GNP at market prices, US $ billion, current prices and exchange rates

	1953	%	1977	%
West Germany	35.02	6.5	516.2	13.21
France	42.97	8.0	380.7	9.74
Italy	20.52	3.8	196.1	5.02
Japan	19.56	3.6	691.2	17.69
UK	47.94	8.9	244.3	6.25
US	369.72	69.0	1878.8	48.08
Total	535.73	100	3907.3	100

Source: OECD

conducted in dollars; and intervention to maintain the fixed parity system was in dollars. This gave the US substantial advantages, since it could use dollars which would be held by others to buy assets abroad, fight foreign wars, or to finance an excess of imports over exports. The inherent contradictions of this gold exchange standard, in which gold and dollars were the main reserve assets, were noticed very shortly after the period of dollar shortage ended. The argument was put clearly by Robert Triffin in 1960. As trade grew, so the need for reserves grew, but the supply of gold grew much more slowly than the volume of trade. If the growth of trade was not to be constrained by a shortage of liquidity, then the amount of dollars held in reserves would have to grow in line with trade. To provide these dollars the US would have to run a balance of payments deficit, but in so doing would undermine confidence in the dollar. People's willingness to hold the dollar outside the US depended on the fact that it could be converted into gold at a fixed price—$35 an ounce. As externally held dollars multiplied relative to US gold holdings, the ability of the US to convert these dollars into gold must become less plausible. Since confidence was basic to the use of dollars as reserves, a loss of confidence would promote an attempt to convert dollars into gold, generating a crisis.

Two possible resolutions to this contradiction were widely canvassed. First, a new reserve asset could be created that was not the currency of any one country—for instance, it could be made up of a basket of major currencies, so as not to depend on the fortunes of any single one. Keynes had suggested such a plan during the preliminary negotiations for Bretton Woods, and the idea became the basis for the special drawing rights (SDRs) subsequently established by the IMF. Although creating a new international paper money had theoretical attractions to economists, there were many practical problems, such as ensuring that people would be willing to hold and use such 'paper gold'. The second resolution was to raise the price of gold. Even if the physical supply of gold could not be increased in line with trade, the value of the supply could if its value appreciated against paper currencies. Since the pivot of the system was the gold–dollar price, this involved steady depreciation of the dollar against gold, something the US opposed. In addition, raising the price would provide a large capital gain to the gold producers and holders, in particular to South Africa and the Soviet Union. There were few other countries that did not object to one of these two so benefiting from a reform of the system. Most economists followed Keynes and regarded it as arbitrary and irrational that the functioning of the international system should depend so intimately on the vagaries of one particular metal.

The fundamental objection to both of these solutions was that the US gained great benefits from the dollar reserve arrangement, which enabled it to finance foreign wars, investment, and balance of payments deficit at very little cost. Any effective reform would deprive the US of this special position. Thus, although the creation of SDRs as 'paper gold' was approved at the 1967 IMF meeting and allocated in 1970, their role was so limited and restricted as not to displace dollars. Despite the slow pace of reform, the volume of dollars held outside the US was growing rapidly, while willingness to hold these dollars and confidence in the ability of the US to convert them into gold declined. From 1965 De Gaulle led this attack, by converting French dollar reserves into gold. Most speculation, however, still concentrated on the subsidiary reserve currency in the system, sterling, in which there was even less confidence than in the dollar. This line of defence was breached, however, by the 1967 devaluation of the pound, and in 1968 the speculative attack on the dollar began in earnest. The US responded by ceasing to convert dollars into gold for anyone but central banks; creating a two-tier gold market: an official market in which the price nominally remained $35, and a private market in which the price was set by demand and supply and was much higher.

The palliative of a two-tier market maintained the system until 1971, when the persistence of the US deficit, together with an expansionary US monetary policy, increased speculation against the dollar and caused various central banks to start converting their dollar reserves to gold. In August 1971, losing gold rapidly, the US abandoned official convertibility of the dollar for gold, imposed a 10 per cent import surcharge, and demanded that other countries should revalue. The consequent speculative movement out of dollars into other currencies put great pressure on exchange rates, and induced most capitalist countries to float their currencies. Floating involved letting the market determine the exchange rate rather than the central bank intervening to preserve a declared parity. At the end of 1971 a new structure of fixed rates was agreed at the Smithsonian Conference in Washington, but it was not sustainable. In the face of the large speculative currency movements, more and more countries reverted to floating. The US monetary expansion had already generated inflationary pressures; but added to this most capitalist states had reflated their economies after the Smithsonian agreement, and floating rates had seemed to remove the balance of payments constraint on expansion. The consequence was a synchronized, highly inflationary expansion throughout the advanced capitalist world.

During most of the post-war period, although growth had been cyclical in all the capitalist countries, the cycles had been out of phase. Thus when the US was growing rapidly, others were slowing down, and total world output and trade grew more steadily than that of individual countries. The simultaneous boom of 1972–3 increased world output much more rapidly, and in particular more rapidly than could be matched by primary product supply. The inadequacy of primary product supply was worsened by a number of natural phenomena, such as harvest failures, and the consequence was a commodity price explosion, which accentuated inflationary pressures. By mid 1973 it was becoming obvious that the boom was not sustainable, but the inevitable collapse was made more spectacular by the Arab oil embargo following the October War of 1973 and the fourfold increase in oil price by OPEC.

13-4 GENERALIZED ECONOMIC CRISIS

For the 16 major capitalist countries examined in Maddison (1977), the average growth rate of GNP during the sixties had been 5.1 per cent. This had dropped to 3.7 per cent during 1970–71, but had risen with the post-Smithsonian reflation to 5.4 per cent in 1972 and 6.2 per cent in 1973. The OPEC price increases and the subsequent financial panic and bank failures reinforced the growing disproportionalities discussed in Section 13–1, causing the growth rate to plunge to 0.1 per cent in 1974 and −1 per cent in 1975. This was the first time that the total real GNP of these countries had fallen since 1946. Between July 1974 and April 1975 OECD industrial production fell 10 per cent, and intra-OECD trade by 13 per cent. By the second quarter of 1975 unemployment in OECD countries had risen from a low of some 8 million during the boom, to around 15 million, about $5\frac{1}{2}$ per cent of the civilian labour force (McCracken, 1977). The unemployment would have been higher but for a net return of migrant labour, and the total number of foreign workers in European countries declined by over one million. High unemployment was combined with historically high inflation. The rate of growth of the GDP deflator for all the OECD countries had averaged 4.1 per cent in the mid to late sixties; 8.1 per cent in the early seventies; and 10.9 per cent in 1974–5 (McCracken, 1977). Around this average there was, however, a large dispersion, Germany keeping inflation in single figures, and the UK and Italy shooting over 20 per cent. These large differences in inflation rates, increased exchange rate instability; unemployment and trade deficits generated pressure for protection, and much trade liberalization was reversed. The high average rates of inflation also reduced the real cost of oil (the price of which was fixed in dollars) in terms of the industrial goods produced by the advanced capitalist powers. 1975 saw a cautious re-expansion of demand, but the recovery was fragile. For the whole of the next four years unemployment and inflation rates in the OECD area remained much higher than during the long boom, and rates of growth of productivity lower. A variety of conferences was held to attempt to orchestrate a more strongly based recovery, but they achieved little, and covert protectionist measures became more common. The fragility of the recovery was shown by the effect that the further oil price increases of 1979 and the events in Iran had in pushing the system back into inflation and recession. The fundamental problems of the system that brought the long boom to an end could not be dealt with quickly.

The general need for regulation and coordination of the international capitalist system has been emphasized in the last two chapters, as have the problems that arose in this respect from the decay of American hegemony. But this feature must be kept in perspective. First, the end of the long boom and the need for greater regulation arose from the failure of fundamental material conditions for the expansion of commodity production and profitable accumulation. The decline in the reserve army of labour, the change in the balance of class forces, the disproportionality between industrial and raw material production, and the reduced potential for increasing relative surplus value—all represented major constraints on profitability and expansion. More powerful regulation may have mitigated these constraints; it could not remove them. Second, although coordination was inadequate, it was substantial, and the crisis would have been much worse without it. In contrast with 1930, when bank collapses had a domino effect throughout the capitalist world, the financial crisis of 1974–5 was contained. Although it appeared a close run thing at the time, there was no massive reduction in credit after bank defaults and consequent reduction in expenditure. Thus cooperation worked to an extent, only to be further tried in 1979, when the expulsion of the Shah of Iran, further increases in oil prices, and the US freeze on Iranian assets held in American banks once more threw the international system of trade and finance into turmoil. Although optimists had hoped that the instability of 1973–6 was an isolated occurrence, it seems more likely that the troubles will persist through the eighties.

13-5 THE FORM OF THE CRISIS

To economists the most striking characteristic of the seventies was the combination of high rates of both unemployment and inflation. This was not merely a British phenomenon, but characteristic throughout the advanced capitalist world. There were substantial differences between countries in the levels of inflation and unemployment reached, but almost everywhere there was a general tendency for both to be much higher than in the sixties. It may be helpful, therefore, to provide a little background to these two phenomena.

Unemployment

The unemployment rate u is measured as the labour force L less employment E, divided by the labour force

$$u = (L-E)/L = 1 - (E/L)$$

It is usually multiplied by 100 to express it as a percentage. It will be more convenient here to use the employment rate $e = (E/L)$, and to identify the factors influencing that. The unemployment rate can be calculated from the

188 INTERNATIONAL CAPITALISM

employment rate as $u=1-e$. The number employed can be derived from the level of output or demand Q, divided by the level of productivity q

$$E=Q/q$$

This is merely a definition or identity, since productivity is measured by output per worker (Q/E). The labour force L depends on the eligible population N (say, the number of people aged between 15 and 65) and the participation rate n (the proportion of those people in the labour force)

$$L=nN$$

Putting these two definitions together, the employment rate can be expressed in terms of the level of demand, the level of productivity, the participation rate, and the eligible population

$$e=E/L=\frac{Q/q}{nN}=Q/qnN$$

This equation can be rewritten in terms of the growth rates of each of the variables, denoted by a dot over the variable as

$$\dot{e}=\dot{Q}-\dot{q}-\dot{n}-\dot{N}$$

In this equation $\dot{Q}$ is the rate of growth of output (i.e., $\Delta Q/Q$) and likewise for the other variables. Thus, looking at these proximate or immediate determinants, the equation indicates that a decrease in the employment rate (a rise in the rate of unemployment) may be associated with either (a) a slower growth of output, (b) a faster growth of productivity, (c) an increase in the participation rate, or (d) an increase in the available population of working age.

The first thing that should be noted about this relationship is that it does not constitute a theory, but an *ex post* identity, a relationship that is true by definition but says nothing about causality. The way the equation is written seems to imply that the employment rate is determined by the right-hand side variables, but in fact the reverse is more probable. The need of capital for a reserve army of labour of a certain size to maintain a balance of class forces may require an increase in the unemployment rate. Then the system operates to produce a crisis which reduces the rate of growth of demand and leads to the restructuring of capital, increasing productivity. Both of these forces then re-create the necessary reserve army. Further, the expansion of capital itself, by displacing pre-capitalist modes of production, extends the potential workforce. Thus in analysing the rise in unemployment it is necessary to consider what the forces were that required an increase in the reserve army of labour and what the mechanism was by which it was expanded.

The second point about the relationship is that there is a variety of interconnections between the variables. For instance, an increase in the rate of growth of productivity may not lead to an increase in the unemployment rate (reduction in the employment rate) if it leads to changes in the other variables. For instance, the higher productivity may lead to reduced prices and an increase in the rate of growth of demand that offsets the labour shedding effects of productivity growth. The effective participation rate may also adjust as. people take the benefit of the higher productivity in longer education, earlier retirement, or a shorter working week. Thus it is wrong to assume that higher productivity arising from technological innovations, such as microprocessors, must necessarily increase unemployment. But while the effect of such a transformation does depend primarily on how the system adjusts to it, the most profitable adjustment may be higher unemployment. Technological innovation thus becomes one method by which the reserve army is expanded.

Inflation

One common orthodox approach to inflation is to treat prices as the sum of four components. These are (a) unit labour costs (wages, salaries, etc., per unit output); (b) unit cost of imports from abroad; (c) indirect taxes per unit output; and (d) overhead costs (profit, rent, interest, etc.) per unit output. The overall rate of inflation is then the sum of the rates of increase of these components, each weighted by their share in total costs. This is a purely accounting framework, which defines prices as the sum of costs and treats profits as a cost. Although it implies no theory about the determination of inflation, this framework is often used in cost push type theories. These argue that in modern capitalist economies the monopolistic power of firms and trade unions is such that they are not constrained by competition, market forces, or the pressure of demand. Firm price on the basis of 'full costs' (i.e., average costs plus a mark-up for profit), and if unions obtained a money wage increase, the firm would merely pass it on in higher prices, generating further wage demands to restore living standards, and thus an inflationary spiral. Since this spiral was the consequence of the social irrationality of individual decisions, there was a need for the state to intervene to impose social consistency on capitalists and workers through a prices and incomes policy, which short circuited the price–wage–price spiral.

Cost push explanations of this type are contrasted with demand pull formulations, in which excess demand is the stimulus for rising prices. Demand pull theories, however, come in monetarist and Keynesian versions. The monetarist version can be derived from the identity $MV = PY$, where M is the quantity of money, V the velocity of circulation (a measure of the speed at which money changes hands), P a general price index, and Y real national income. As it stands, the equation is true by definition; it merely says that V is measured as the ratio of PY to M. To make it a theory of the price level requires that (a) V is constant, or at least stable and predictable; (b) Y is fixed independently by non-monetary forces (it is often assumed that market forces will set it at the level corresponding to full employment of available resources); and (c) the supply of money is fixed independently of demand, either by the quantity of gold available or by the state. Then with V and Y fixed independently, exogenous changes in M determine movements in P, and thus the rate of inflation.

This quantity theory can be traced back to at least the sixteenth century but in its current monetarist resurrection it is largely based on the work of Milton Friedman. The monetarist argument is that if the rate of growth of the money supply exceeds the natural rate of growth of real output, excess demand pressures will be generated, unemployment will be reduced below its natural rate, money wage increases will exceed the rate of growth of productivity, and inflation inevitably results.

In the sixties both cost push and demand pull theorists could agree on one element in the process by which inflation was transmitted: the Phillips curve. This was an empirical relationship that showed a negative association between the rate of growth of money wages and the rate of inflation. There remained, however, a dispute about the theoretical interpretation of this relationship. By the seventies, however, the relationship seemed to have broken down, since unemployment and inflation were both rising. In addition, during the seventies theories of inflation had to allow for the role of exchange rate variation. During the earlier period of fairly fixed exchange rates, if the prices of traded goods in a particular country rose faster than the world average, then that country's exports would fall and imports would be sucked in. This would lead to a deterioration in the balance of payments and a loss of reserves, and provoke deflationary action by the state to bring the rate of increase of those prices into line with competitors. Thus free trade and fixed exchange rates provided a discipline that inhibited large differences in rates of inflation for traded goods. With the collapse of the Bretton Woods system this discipline was removed.

It is important to notice that under fixed exchange rates the discipline applied to the prices of traded goods (e.g., manufactures), and was consistent with significant differences in total rates of inflation. For instance, during the fifties Japan combined steady export prices with what were by OECD standards comparatively high rates of domestic inflation. Under fixed exchange rates the factor that dominated inflation rates was uneven development within the structure of production. Manufacturing tended to have higher rates of growth of productivity and to be forced by international competition to keep prices fairly steady. Money wages in manufacturing tended to grow at about the rate of manufacturing productivity, and set the going rate for wage increases that had to be paid by other sectors. This did not mean that the wage levels were equalized, merely that the relativities remained stable. However, the rate of growth of productivity in the other sectors tended to be lower, and capitalists in these sectors had to raise their prices to cover costs and maintain profitability. The rate of inflation in these other sectors was then equal to the difference between their rate of growth of productivity and the rate of growth of wages, which itself was equal to the rate of growth of productivity in manufacturing. Thus the average rate of inflation depended on the dispersion or differences in productivity across sectors, and the relative shares of the sectors in output—i.e., the extent of uneven development.

This model, which is discussed in detail in Jackson, Turner, and Wilkinson (1975), explains international differences in inflation during the fifties and sixties quite well. The sectors other than manufacturing are dominated by services, which tends to have a measured productivity growth close to zero, and does not differ much between countries. The main variation comes from the rate of growth of productivity in manufacturing. A country like Japan that had a high rate of growth of productivity in manufacturing, had a high domestic rate of inflation, since the rate of growth of money wages in manufacturing set the pattern for the rest of the economy. But although it had a high general rate of inflation, the rate of inflation of the export price index (dominated by manufactures) was close to zero. A country like the UK, on the other hand, with a low rate of growth of productivity in manufacturing, had a rate of inflation below the world average over this period. In addition, across countries there was a positive association between the rate of growth and the rate of inflation, because a country's rate of growth was strongly influenced by its rate of growth of manufacturing productivity. But in the late sixties and early seventies this positive relationship was replaced by a negative relationship, as uneven development was replaced by conflict as the motive force behind inflation.

In the simple model used above it was assumed that exchange rates were fixed and there was no distributional conflict. The lack of distributional conflict is implied, since capitalists did not try to increase their profit margins and workers accepted the consequent rate of growth of real wages, while the fixed exchange rates caused rates of inflation for traded goods to be equalized. Neither of these assumptions held for the UK and other advanced capitalist countries during the seventies. The high rates of inflation characteristic of that period were the product of major conflict over the distribution of the product, which capitalist states accommodated by monetary and exchange rate policies. The negative relation between growth and inflation rates that was observed across countries arose because the rapidly growing economies could afford the resources to meet the conflicting claims of the various groups much more easily than slow growing economies, and thus were able to buy off the conflict and moderate inflationary pressures.

The mechanics of the process by which distributional conflict gives rise to inflation are set out in Rowthorn (1980), but in essence the process is straightforward. The conflict arises because total claims on output by workers, capitalists, the state, and raw material producers are greater than the available output. In these circumstances firms put up their prices to maintain their target level of profitability, workers press for money wage increases to restore their real incomes, the state increases taxes to finance its target expenditure, and raw material producers raise the price of primary products to maintain the purchasing power of their revenue. The conflict of inconsistency between the target or aspiration levels of each of these groups thus manifests itself as inflation. The extent of the inflationary consequences depends, of course, on the power of each group to implement its claims. The seventies saw not only the growth of these claims—in particular, the expansion of state expenditure—but also the failure of the disciplinary mechanisms that had enforced consistency for most of the post-war period. The exhaustion of the labour surplus and the improvement in social security benefits reduced the coercive effect of unemployment on the working class. The breakdown of US hegemony and its failure in Vietnam reduced imperialist dominance of primary product producers, in particular OPEC. The collapse of the fixed exchange rates removed a major constraint on the domestic monetary policies of individual states.

To maintain target levels of profit required (a) an increase in unemployment to reduce the working class claims on output; (b) a reduction in public expenditure to free resources for profits; and (c) a reduction in the real costs of primary products, initially through increases in the prices of the manufactured goods produced by the advanced capitalist countries. The exact pattern of these adjustments differed between countries, depending on the combination of exchange rate and monetary policies followed, but the general pattern was for both inflation and unemployment to increase. Because of the structural weakness of the British economy the policy adjustments to the crisis produced large increases in both inflation and unemployment, as was discussed in Chapter 7. But those policy adjustments were conditioned by the extent of the integration of British capital into world capital. The extent to which capital has become international, both at an economic level (through trade, financial flows, and multi-national production) and at a political level (through supra-national institutions like the IMF and EEC), means that it is impossible to examine national economic policy or performance in isolation. The form in which British capital is integrated into world capitalism is examined in the next chapter.

FURTHER READING

Many of the reading references given for Chapter 12 will be useful for Chapter 13 as well and we do not repeat them. In addition, see Kaldor (1966), and for detailed essays on the economic crisis in the US see URPE (1978), Magdoff (1969), and Sherman (1976).

An orthodox and optimistic account of the crisis can be found in McCracken (1977); on international profitability see Hill (1979).

FOURTEEN

INTERNATIONAL ASPECTS OF UK CAPITAL

Sam Aaronovitch

14-1 INTRODUCTION

In the last two chapters we have considered the general development of the international capitalist system in the post-war period. The purpose of this chapter is to focus on UK capital in its international operations. We have already noted that a heavy international orientation has been a long-standing feature of British capitalism, an orientation that goes back to the initial stages of the Industrial Revolution in the eighteenth century, or even before, when giant London-based trading companies such as the East India Company dominated trade in many parts of the world, providing the basis for the subsequent annexation of territory to form the British Empire.

We have argued that while this expansion overseas secured a dominant position for UK capital that has persisted to the present day, it has also brought with it the relative industrial decline of the UK. This apparent paradox is not difficult to explain. In the late nineteenth and early twentieth century, about one half of investment went overseas in pursuit of higher profits, taking advantage of the monopoly trading position afforded by the Empire. In that period, major competitors, such as Germany, the US, and France, were investing domestically, developing new industries behind extensive tariff walls that secured domestic markets against British competition. (In the case of the US, much of its investment came from the UK itself.) With the focus of interest for the most dynamic sections of British capital being overseas, and with such large investment funds being exported, it is not surprising that this period saw the first signs of failure of British domestically based industry to innovate, restructure production, and respond aggressively to the newly developing international competition. Once these trends of low domestic investment, defensive reactions to competition, lack of innovation, and slow growth became entrenched, the problems of reversing them proved too great, requiring a major shift in economic, social, and political behaviour, which in the event was not forthcoming. In consequence, the trends of relative decline have continued to the present day, and recurrently reached the point where they triggered major social and economic conflict.

The failure of domestically based industry to respond to the challenge of overseas competition may itself be traced back to the early international orientation of British capital. Elsewhere—notably in Germany, France, and Japan—the links between domestic industry and financial capital have been very close, with the banks taking a major role in financing, supervising, and even initiating new investment projects in industry. This position has enabled the banks and other financial institutions to foster innovation, and even to force it on reluctant industrial firms. This has never been a feature of the UK, where the financial institutions based in the City of London have at times taken pride in their ignorance of industry, arguing that their business is money. The roots of this division may be in the origins of the City, which developed primarily around the international activities of the large trading companies. From this beginning, its activities have remained international in orientation. Finance of the beginnings of the Industrial Revolution came not from this source but from the accumulated wealth of small merchants and rich farmers. And this division has persisted, with the dominant sections of finance capital linked closely to international UK industrial capital, and a relative lack of involvement with domestic industry.

An equally important effect has been political. The high international involvement of UK capital has meant that the most powerful and dynamic sections of British capital have had no great commitment to nor concern about the development of the domestic economy. Such an effect should not be exaggerated: with significant interests in the domestic market, concern was clearly there. But with eggs in many baskets, the internationally oriented sections of British capital were more concerned to protect their overseas investments and were not compelled to react vigorously to the relative decline of the UK economy. And without this response, the political will required to take action to reverse these trends was absent.

With this background, we proceed to examine the main characteristics of British capital and of overseas involvement in the UK. In Section 14-2 we explain balance of payments accounts, and consider their significance. In Section 14-3, we proceed to look at the major trends in UK trade with the rest of the world, corresponding to the way the internationalization of commodity capital has impinged on the UK. We then proceed to Section 14-4 to examine investment overseas by UK firms, together with foreign investment in the UK. Although our primary focus in this section will be with direct investment (i.e., the internationalization of productive capital), we shall also describe associated trends in portfolio investment (i.e., financial capital). However, financial capital is the main focus of Section 14-5, where we examine the role of the City of London and its involvement internationally. Finally, Section 14-6 deals with the cost to the UK of membership of the EEC.

14-2 BALANCE OF PAYMENTS ACCOUNTS

Throughout this book we are concerned to emphasize that the development of the international economy, and of particular economies within this, is best understood in terms of the relations between rival blocs of capital. While these sections of capital are likely to retain allegiances and ties with particular nation states, the process of internationalization as described in Chapter 12 has made these allegiances increasingly weaker through time. Thus, for example, although Ford is a US controlled multi-national company, the international spread of its activities forces it to recognize responsibilities to other nation states on the one hand, and to make corresponding claims. Similarly, the allegiance of the major oil companies to their countries of origin showed major cracks when they acted to enforce the OPEC price increase and embargo in the late part of 1973.

In examining the international operations of particular sections of capital, it is therefore vital to keep these complexities firmly in mind. But we start by discussing the conventional way in which international economic relations are recorded and discussed: in terms of balance of payments accounts. These present a description for a given period of time of the transactions between the residents of a nation state (in our case, the UK) and residents of the rest of the world. Since British and foreign firms may operate both domestically and overseas, these accounts do not represent transactions between British capital and foreign capital. Thus, entries may represent transactions between the domestic and foreign branches of two firms (or even the same one).

It is usual to divide balance of payments accounts (like corporate accounts) into current and capital items. The current account represents items arising from income and expenditure flows across national boundaries in the period under consideration. The capital account shows new investment flows between the domestic economy and the overseas economy: these take place in order to yield returns in the form of future income that, if it materializes, will appear in future current accounts.

Items in the account are divided between credit and debit items. Table 14-1 presents the UK balance of payments account for 1977 and 1978. Credits in the current account comprise exports of goods; exports of services, such as transport, tourism, insurance, banking and other invisibles; interest, profits and dividends earned on direct or portfolio investment overseas by UK nationals; and transfers to the UK. Correspondingly items appear on the debit side. All except the last item are self-explanatory; transfers represent the value of goods, services, and financial assets passing between UK residents and overseas residents without any corresponding payment or exchange. These may be divided between official transfers and private transfers. Private transfers consist of gifts, transfers of money to dependents, and transfer of assets resulting from migration. Official transfers on the credit side are in the form of receipts arising from the operation of the EEC Common Agricultural Policy, while on the debit side they comprise payments to the EEC, aid contributions, contributions to international agencies such as the UN, overseas military expenditure, and UK state benefits to overseas residents.

Netting out the credit and debit items, several balances may be calculated, and are shown in Fig. 14-1. The trade balance records the net balance between the export and import of goods. This data is quickly available from customs returns, and so this is the figure reported monthly in the

Table 14-1 The UK current account (£ million)

	1977		1978	
Credits				
(1) Exports of goods		32 148		35 532
(2) Exports of services	11 587		12 204	
(3) Interest, profits and dividends	3 964		5 047	
(4) Transfers	862		1 084	
(5) Total invisibles $(2+3+4)$		16 435		18 335
(6) Total credits		48 583		53 767
Debits				
(7) Imports of goods		33 892		36 607
(8) Imports of services	8 596		8 915	
(9) Interest, profit and dividends	3 651		4 211	
(10) Transfers	2 023		3 002	
(11) Total invisibles		14 270		16 128
(12) Total debits		48 162		52 735
Net transactions				
(13) Trade balance $(1-7)$		−1744		−1075
(14) Invisible balance $(5-11)$		+2165		+2207
(15) Current balance $(13+14)$		+421		+1132

Source: Central Statistical Office, *United Kingdom Balance of Payments* (1979).

press. The UK persistently runs a trade deficit, and in only a handful of years over the past two centuries has the trade account shown a surplus. By contrast, the balance on invisible transactions (which includes services, interest, profit and dividends, and transfers) always shows a surplus, although it fell sharply between 1978 and 1979. The sum of the two, called the current balance, has been in sharp deficit since 1973, although it showed a small surplus in 1977 and 1978, swinging into deficit again in 1979. Over the post-war period up to 1973 the current account on average balanced or showed a slight surplus.

It is important to note that the transactions recorded in the current account (and, as we shall see, in the capital account) do not necessarily correspond to flows of money. Thus, for example, exports may be sold on credit: the sale of goods enters the current account, while the extension of credit appears as a debit item on the capital account. Although these appear as two separate but cancelling items, in reality no currency flows take place. A more important example is the transactions recorded under interest, profit, and dividends. About 70 per cent of profits earned by overseas subsidiaries of UK firms are retained overseas and reinvested in those subsidiaries, and just over 60 per cent of UK private investment overseas is financed from this source. Nonetheless, unremitted profits are included

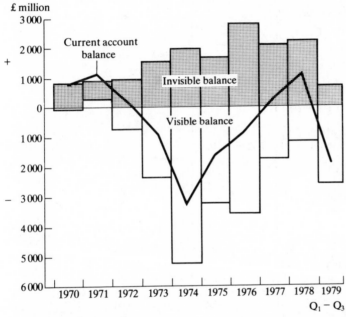

Fig. 14-1 Current account 1970–8. (*Source:* Central Statistical Office, *United Kingdom Balance of Payments* (1979).

in the current account, and a corresponding debit item entered on the capital account, despite the fact that no corresponding money flows take place.

The capital account, presented in Table 14-2, shows the lending and borrowing of new money capital between the UK and overseas economies. Negative items show an outflow of capital (increased lending or repayment of borrowing by the UK), so that they represent an increase in UK assets (or a reduction in liabilities) held overseas. Positive items represent an inflow of capital (increase of borrowing or receipt by the UK of repayment of loans), thereby reducing UK net assets held overseas. Items are recorded net: that is, a negative item might include a substantial level of borrowing

Table 14-2 The capital account (£ million)

	1977	1978
(1) Official long-term capital	−319	−348
(2) Overseas investment in UK public sector	+2182	−81
(3) Overseas investment in UK private sector:		
Direct	+1257	+1373
Portfolio	+821	+705
Oil	+989	+692
Total	+3067	+2770
(4) UK private investment overseas:		
Direct	−1790	−2178
Portfolio	+5	−1063
Oil	−437	−846
Total	−2222	−4087
(5) Net overseas currency borrowing by UK banks of which:		
To finance UK overseas investment	+520	+835
Other	−136	−1354
Total	+384	−519
(6) Import credit	+351	+243
(7) Export credit	−613	−685
(8) Exchange reserves in sterling	−19	−119
(9) Other external sterling liabilities	+1481	+301
(10) Other short-term transactions	+114	−406
(11) Balance on capital transactions	+4406	−2931

Source: Central Statistical Office, *United Kingdom Balance of Payments* (1979).

outweighed by a larger volume of lending. The main items in the account are overseas investment in the UK, UK investment overseas, import and export credit, and exchange reserves in sterling (which show net purchases by overseas central banks of UK government and banking liabilities in sterling, bought by central banks as a convenient form of holding reserves). Since the UK sells a larger proportion of its exports on credit than it buys imports on credit, the extension of export credit always exceeds new import credits by a large amount: the interest on this credit appears as a positive item in the current account. Overseas investment in the UK and UK investment overseas is classified into direct (that is, in factories and machinery) and portfolio (that is, in financial assets). An exception is made in the case of investment by oil companies, which is classified separately since technical problems make a division into direct and portfolio impossible.

Overseas investment in the UK more than balanced UK investment overseas in 1977 (although there was a deficit on direct investment), and contrary to much mythology, the UK has received slightly more investment funds from overseas over the past 10 years than it has invested overseas, although, again, this was reversed in 1978, as shown in Table 14-2. Moreover, the balance of payments benefits strongly from overseas investment, because almost all investment is financed from unremitted profits earned overseas or from overseas borrowing and because the current account benefits from that portion of overseas earnings that are remitted to the UK. On the other side of the account, the balance of payments is helped by overseas investment in the UK, since much of this is financed overseas and therefore represents a genuine capital inflow. Thus criticisms of the export of capital based on the resulting balance of payments costs are largely misplaced, since the net export of money capital from the UK is largely non-existent; in effect, UK investment overseas is financed from surplus generated overseas, whether directly in the subsidiary concerned or borrowed from other sources. This may have been the result of the existing controls on capital movement that were in force in the UK up to 1979.

While criticisms of overseas investment based on balance of payments costs may be misplaced, an alternative argument has much greater force. The UK has persistently engaged in more direct investment overseas than overseas direct investment in the UK. Although, as we have seen, this has no balance of payments costs, it has important implications for growth and employment prospects in the UK. If UK companies have persistently invested in overseas subsidiaries as a substitute for investment in the UK, this is one factor behind the relatively weak development of the productive forces in the UK. (At the same time, it must also be seen as a result of this weak development.) This is a question to which we return.

In 1977 the capital account of the balance of payments showed a large surplus of more than 4 per cent of GDP at market prices and went into deficit again in 1978. Prior to that, the capital account showed a persistent deficit in the decade 1957–66, being in surplus in only one year, but for the decade 1967–76 the capital account was in surplus for exactly half the years, showing a small cumulative deficit for the decade as a whole.

The overall surplus or deficit in the balance of payments—that is, the sum of the balances on current and capital account—has to be financed by the monetary authorities. This may be done either by borrowing from (or lending to) overseas central banks, by public sector borrowing in foreign currencies in overseas markets, or by drawing on, or adding to, official reserves. These items are shown in Table 14-3. However, in practice, the balance for official financing is not identically equal to the sum of the balance on current and capital account, since certain transactions go unrecorded. The balancing item that enters Table 14-3 is simply the identified statistical error in drawing up the accounts, and is the amount required to make the accounts balance.

In making the usual orthodox distinction between items in the current and capital accounts that are seen as contributing towards the overall balance of payments and that therefore need to be financed, and those items that appear as official financing of the resulting payments position, some arbitrariness is involved. Essentially the distinction is between relatively autonomous items and items that respond passively to the other components in the account. However, the distinction is not clear cut: for example, official transfers, which enter the current account, may well be curtailed

Table 14-3 Official financing (£ million)

	1977	1978
(1) Current balance	+293	+1032
(2) Balance on capital transactions	+4406	−2931
(3) Balancing item	+2662	+773
(4) Balance for official financing (1+2+3)	+7361	−1645
Official financing		
(5) Net transactions with overseas monetary authorities	+1113	−1016
(6) Foreign currency borrowing by UK public sector	+1114	−187
(7) Drawings on official reserves	−9588	+2329
	+7361	−1126

Source: Central Statistical Office, *United Kingdom Balance of Payments*, (1979).

because of balance of payments problems. And while, under a fixed exchange rate system, official financing may be entirely passive, under a floating exchange rate system where the authorities do not intervene in the foreign exchange market, the overall balance of payments must of necessity balance. In this case, the components of the current and capital account must necessarily interact, and no clear distinction can be drawn between autonomous and passive items.

From a Marxist perspective, the balance of payments accounts are in several respects unhelpful. Because of the increasing international spread of large firms, a growing proportion of transactions recorded in the balance of payments simply represent intra-firm transactions between branches of the same multi-national company, so that a record of transactions across national boundaries becomes, for many purposes, increasingly meaningless. (We have already noted above that the accounts are misleading concerning geographical flows, particularly with regard to capital flow and associated profit streams.) At the same time, a record of transactions between nations is inappropriate for an economic analysis of transactions between classes.

Nonetheless, this does not mean that the balance of payments is unimportant. The nation state continues to represent the basic unit that ensures the reproduction of capitalist relations of production. National governments have to take political responsibility for the level of employment, improvements in living standards, etc. The ability of the state to fulfil this role depends, *inter alia*, on the international trading position of domestically based capital, which determines, for example, the ability of the state to sustain the value of its currency internationally.

14-3 TRENDS IN UK EXTERNAL TRADE

This section is concerned with summarizing the main trends in UK trade with the rest of the world, corresponding to the process of internationalization of commodity capital. Within this we include not only trade in goods but also trade in services (sometimes called invisibles).

The degree of integration of UK trade with the rest of the world has risen steadily in the period following the Second World War. This trend is common to all the advanced capitalist countries, and is in marked contrast with the inter-war period, when international trade collapsed with the Depression. Table 14-4 shows the share of exports and imports of goods in GDP, together with total current account credits and debits, for selected years. All the measures rise steadily through time—if anything, rising more rapidly in the seventies.

This trend has been accompanied by a steady decline in the share of UK exports in world trade, illustrated in Table 14-5 and Fig. 14-2. The loss in world market share of manufactures has been fairly steady throughout the period. By 1976 it had fallen to 44 per cent of the 1955 share, (though the sharp fall in sterling in 1975 helped to increase the price competitiveness of British goods, thereby checking the trend somewhat. Similar declines,

Table 14-4 Share of imports and exports

	Ratio of manufacturing imports to manufacturing sales	Ratio of manufacturing exports to manufacturing sales
1955	0.06	0.15
1960	0.08	0.15
1965	0.09	0.15
1970	0.13	0.18
1975	0.18	0.23
1976	0.21	0.25

Source: Brown and Sherriff in Blackaby (1979a).

Table 14-5 The United Kingdom share in world trade in manufactures, invisible and private services (%)

	Manufactures[a]	Invisibles[b]	Private services[c]
1955	19.8	24.9[a]	26.3[d]
1960	16.5	20.9	22.3
1965	13.9	17.9	17.2
1970	10.8	15.9	17.2
1973	9.4	15.3	16.0
1974	8.8	13.4	15.6
1975	9.3	13.4	15.7
1976	8.8	12.5	15.0
1976–1955	0.44	0.50	0.57

[a] Arms excluded; re-exports included from 1960; figures adjusted for under-recording from 1965.

[b] 'Services' (see note c) *plus* 'investment income' and 'government credits' in IMF 'Standard presentation' (see also IMF, *Balance of Payments Yearbook*).

[c] 'Freight', 'merchandise insurance', 'other transportation' and 'other services' (see also IMF, *Balance of Payments Yearbook*). Negligible amounts of non-monetary gold included for 1955 and 1960.

[d] These figures not strictly comparable with subsequent years, see CSO, *Economic Trends*, March 1961.

Source: Taken from Brown and Sherriff in Blackaby (1979a).

though less steep, are observable in the UK's share of world invisible trade and trade in private services.

These two trends—the rise in import penetration and the loss of international markets—represent the two most evident symptoms of the post-war relative decline of UK economic power. Since a country has, by and large, to balance its external trading position,[1] these trends provide a constraint on the rate of growth of domestic income and output. This rate of growth of output permitted by the balance of payments is given by the rate of growth of exports divided by the income elasticity of the demand for imports. This permissible rate of growth is reduced by either a low rate of growth of exports or a high import elasticity. A country like the UK, where both factors are unfavourable, experiences low growth; by contrast, countries like Japan, where both factors are favourable, are able to expand their economies much more rapidly.

Such simple relationships are sometimes elevated to the level of explanations of poor economic growth in the UK, which has resulted in the decline of importance of the UK as an industrial power illustrated in Table

[1] Countries may benefit from capital inflows over extended periods if investment opportunities domestically are particularly profitable, and so may run a current account deficit. This was not the case for the UK nor for most advanced capitalist countries in this period; the UK current account has broadly balanced over the long run in the post-war period.

14-6. Thus the decline in UK share of world markets is 'explained' in terms of a low measured income elasticity of demand for UK exports. In fact, this is not an explanation, but rather a restatement of the problem, for the measured elasticity simply reflects the low rate of growth of exports relative to the growth of world income. Similarly, the high measured income elasticity of import demand merely reflects high recorded import penetration.

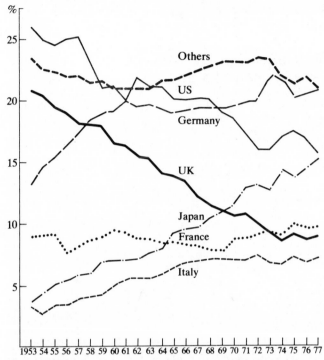

Fig. 14-2 Various countries' shares in the value of 'world' exports of manufactures, 1953–77.
(*Source:* Taken from Blackaby, 1979a)

To restate the problem in this way in terms of elasticities advances us not at all, for these elasticities in turn require explanation.

The decline in the UK's trading position cannot be attributed to a loss of relative price competitiveness. Price competitiveness may be measured in several ways: in terms of relative export prices, in terms of relative wholesale prices, or in terms of relative unit labour costs. Each of these is depicted in Fig. 14-3. Perhaps the most reliable indication is given by the last of these, since it provides a measure of underlying relative cost conditions, which are likely to govern trade performance in the longer run. This shows a cyclical movement (exhibited by all three series), but with a clear downward trend over the period since 1969, during which period the

UK's trading position has continued to decline. The other series show less obvious trends, since exporters took advantage of low unit labour costs to raise profit margins; but none of the series exhibit the upward trend necessary to explain the deteriorating UK trading position. It is clear that before the recent rise in the exchange value of the pound, other factors have dominated trade performance, and that even if price competitiveness has exerted an influence, it has been swamped by adverse trends elsewhere. Of course, these adverse trends have been amplified by the recent rise in the value of the pound.

Table 14-6 The United Kingdom share in OECD manufacturing output and world GDP, 1960–75 (%)

	OECD manufacturing output[a]	'World' GDP[b]
1960	9.6	8.2
1963	8.4	7.9
1966	7.3	7.6
1969	6.4	6.3
1972	5.9	6.4
1973	5.8	6.0
1974	5.7	5.9
1975	5.8	6.3

[a] At constant prices, based on 1963 weights for 1960 and 1963, and on 1970 weights for 1972 onwards. Figures interpolated for 1966 and 1969.

[b] At current prices and exchange rates.

Source: Taken from Brown and Sherriff in Blackaby (1979a).

It is not possible to explain poor UK trade performance in terms of an adverse composition of trade, either in terms of commodities or geographical markets. It is certainly the case that the protection of the thirties and the reliance by the UK on markets in the Empire meant that in the immediate post-war period UK trade was somewhat concentrated on slow growing markets in the colonies, and not oriented towards the fast growing markets in Europe. However, the geographical structure of trade has shifted away from the Commonwealth and the US towards Europe, and has therefore become increasingly favourable. The UK's geographical composition of trade is in fact rather similar to that of Germany, whose trading performance has been very strong. A similar finding applies to the commodity composition of trade. Thus UK performance tends to be systematically worse in *every* commodity and in *every* geographical market, so that the explanation of poor performances must be sought elsewhere, in terms of underlying forces affecting general performance.

It has been suggested that showing that the commodity composition of UK trade is not unfavourable, say, with respect to that of Germany, reflects a failure to disaggregate to a sufficiently low level. This is probably so. Thus there is considerable evidence that British exports tend to be rather more downmarket in terms of quality than those of competitors. For example, the price/weight ratio of British exports of machinery is roughly half that of Germany's, probably reflecting a concentration on low quality, high

Fig. 14-3 Recent trends in alternative indices of competitiveness (1970 = 100). (*Source:* Taken from Blackaby, 1979a)

weight products. A sufficiently fine disaggregation (into detailed classifications of products) should pick up these differences; if it is then found that the demand for poorer quality products rises less quickly than that for more upmarket products, this may then be identified as an 'explanation' of the UK's poor trading position. In fact, it is no such thing, but rather yet another symptom. An inability to compete adequately in overseas markets, perhaps because of lack of innovation, may well leave exporters selling relatively obsolete products. But this is an *effect* not a *cause* of the UK's failure to compete. Once again, the explanation must be sought elsewhere.

At this point a further word should be added on the effect of North Sea oil. By the end of 1979 the UK had become almost self-sufficient in mineral oils and it was widely believed that this would lead to a large UK surplus on current account, whereas in fact there was a deficit of the order of £2600 million on the visible current account in the first three-quarters of 1979. Had North Sea oil not saved the UK economy over £4000 million in oil imports the deficit could have been of the order of £6000–7000 millions 'other things being equal'. Import penetration of finished manufactures

Table 14-7 The geographical distribution of UK trade (as of GDP)

	1966	1976	1978
Exports			
EEC	4.1	8.4	9.68
Other Western Europe	2.6	3.7	3.21
North American	2.6	2.9	2.94
Other developed countries	2.2	1.8	1.64
Oil-exporting countries	0.9	3.0	3.28
Rest of world	3.6	3.9	4.33
Total	16.0	23.7	25.08
Imports			
EEC	4.2	10.4	11.27
Other Western Europe	2.0	3.7	3.59
North American	3.3	3.6	3.49
Other developed countries	1.8	1.8	1.81
Oil-exporting countries	1.3	3.6	2.16
Rest of world	3.5	3.9	3.58
Total	16.1	27.0	25.90
Visible balance			
EEC	−0.1	−2.0	−1.59
Other Western Europe	+0.6	−0.0	−0.38
North American	−0.7	−0.7	−0.55
Other developed countries	+0.4	+0.0	−0.17
Oil-exporting countries	−0.4	−0.6	+1.12
Rest of world	+0.1	+0.0	+0.75
Total	−0.1	−3.3	−0.82

Source: Central Statistical Office, *United Kingdom Balance of Payments* (1979).

continued to rise through 1979, while exports of manufactures did not increase. Not surprisingly, by the beginning of the eighties control of imports had become a live issue.

Looking once again at UK external visible trade, in Table 14-7 we can see that the importance of total trade in the UK economy has greatly increased since 1966 and that the most significant shifts in UK trade have been towards the EEC and Western Europe and with the oil-exporting countries.

In the previous section on the balance of payments we saw from Fig. 14-1 that the balance on 'invisibles' has also declined since 1976, falling very sharply in 1979. The main causes have been (a) the rise of about £1 billion in foreign oil companies' earnings in the UK; (b) the growth of UK government expenditure abroad on defence and aid and especially its budgetary contribution to the EEC; (c) increased interest payments to overseas holders of sterling as interest rates have risen and more sterling is being held by overseas holders; (d) a reduction in net earnings from UK banks' foreign exchange activities; and (e) more tourist spending abroad. North Sea oil has made in fact negative contributions to the invisible balance and this rise in foreign oil companies' UK profits will increase further with time and with the rising price of oil.

14-4 FOREIGN DIRECT INVESTMENT AND THE UK

The previous section considered the trading relations of the UK with the rest of the world. In this section we shift the focus to the inward and outward investment activities of UK and foreign firms; we are concerned primarily with the internationalization of 'productive' capital, and in particular with UK capital operating internationally. The evidence shows that UK capital in its totality represents a major block within the international capitalist system. In Section 14-2 foreign investment was classified into direct (i.e., in factories and machinery) and portfolio (i.e., in financial assets).

The 'agents' of direct investment (inward or outward) are the multi-national companies (MNCs). Large-scale direct investment abroad and the formation of large multi-national companies is not, of course, a recent development for the UK. On the contrary, British capital has pioneered the MNC, although it was overtaken by the US after 1945. However, in more recent times a substantial revival of direct overseas investment from the UK has taken place. We can judge the scale and significance of this overseas investment in a number of different ways. One way is to look at the proportion of overseas production as a percentage of exports and of overseas production as a percentage of GDP. Both are shown in Table 14-8, which compares the UK with a number of other countries.

The UK shows the highest ratio of overseas production to domestic production with the exception of Switzerland, which for geographical and historical reasons has always invested heavily overseas. Other major European countries have at most one half of this level of overseas production in relation to domestic production. A similar pattern is shown by the ratio of overseas production to exports, except that the US moves to the top of the list because of a very low average share of exports in GDP (only around five per cent in 1971).

When we look at estimates of the stock of direct foreign investment by the main exporters of capital the UK falls into second place behind the US, while France, West Germany, Switzerland, Canada, and Japan, in that order, follow well behind.

In addition, and as we might expect, the major part of foreign direct investment (FDI) is carried out by a small number of large firms; at a rough estimate 80 per cent of FDI from the UK is accounted for by 165 firms. Furthermore, the ratio of FDI in manufacturing from the UK to net

208 INTERNATIONAL CAPITALISM

domestic investment in manufacturing rose from 0.28 in 1967–9 to 0.79 in 1973–5.

The international role of British capital is in large part a legacy of the dominant industrial position of the UK in the nineteenth century and of the British Empire. However, it would be wrong to think of it simply in these terms, rather as though the UK were simply living off a large but dwindling inheritance from the past. For while it is the case that sections of UK international capital rely on traditional markets and products that are subject to erosion by competitors, nonetheless, other sections are highly

Table 14-8 Overseas production of the major capitalist countries

	Overseas production as % of exports in 1971	Overseas production as % of GDP in 1971
US	396	22
UK	215	50
France	94	16
West Germany	37	8
West Germany	37	8
Switzerland	236	73
Canada	68	15
Japan	37	4
Netherlands	52	25
Sweden	92	23
Italy	44	9
Belgium	52	23

Source: United Nations (1978).

dynamic, adapting to changes and opportunities in the international market, and therefore continually regenerating themselves.

Signs of this adaptation may be seen in the changing geographical distribution of UK capital overseas, shown in Table 14-9. Concentrated heavily in North America and Commonwealth countries (included in the categories of 'other developed countries' and 'rest of the world') in the immediate post-war period, the direction of new investment soon shifted to the more rapidly expanding markets of Western Europe. Thus over the fourteen years from 1962 to 1976 the share of total investment in Western Europe more than doubled, largely at the expense of investment in the third world. In this respect, the overseas investment trends of the UK, Germany, and Japan have tended to converge: for Germany has always invested primarily in Europe, although the share going to North America has risen with the increased profitability of US production after the fall in the dollar in the seventies; while Japanese overseas investment has shifted from its main orientation to developing countries towards Europe and North America.

Table 14-9 Distribution of UK outward and inward direct capital stake

	Western Europe	North America	Other developed countries	Rest of world	Total value (£m)
	Percentage shares				
Outward investment					
1962	13.4	23.1	27.1	36.5	3 405.0
1965	15.4	21.8	29.9	32.9	4 210.0
1968	17.6	23.0	30.8	28.5	5 585.3
1971	21.9	20.0	29.8	26.3	6 666.9
1974	27.5	22.0	29.3	21.3	10 117.8
1976	27.5	23.2	27.5	21.8	13 320.3
Inward investment					
1962	20.9	75.9	2.3	0.9	1 429.7
1965	19.9	77.3	1.0	1.8	1 999.9
1968	21.8	75.3	1.8	1.1	2 728.0
1971	23.4	71.2	4.1	1.3	3 817.0
1974	28.1	62.1	4.6	5.2	6 585.3
1976	28.3	60.9	5.0	5.7	7 821.2

Note: Capital stake is defined as the book value of fixed assets (net of depreciation) plus current assets (net of debt) less current liabilities (net of amount owed to investing companies) less long-term liabilities of overseas subsidiaries and branches.

Source: Dunning (1979), Table 2.

The meaning of the internationalization of capital was discussed in detail in Chapter 12. In the case of the UK a powerful stimulus has undoubtedly been the fact that markets were growing faster outside the UK, especially in Western Europe, and also the need to meet the rivalry from MNCs operating from US and other bases.

In the early seventies, British firms were investing in Western Europe at three times the rate at which Western Europeans were investing in the UK; and in 1975 there was more UK manufacturing investment in North America than there was North American investment in the UK. The ratio of outward investment to inward investment in manufacturing has risen substantially from the early sixties to the middle seventies. At this point we turn to look at inward investment into the UK.

Foreign investment in the UK has traditionally been mainly from the US, which accounted for over three-quarters of the total in the early sixties. But as Table 14-9 shows, this has tended to fall, particularly in the seventies, when inward new investment from Europe and Japan rose sharply.

US firms have remained the dominant investors in manufacturing and also in North Sea oil. But some developing countries have built up sizeable

UK investments in property, management and development, distribution, and finance. A very high proportion of foreign direct investment in the UK is in the technologically more advanced industries (chemicals, mechanical and electrical engineering, electrical engineering, vehicles, and rubber).

The overall picture that emerges is that British capital has greatly expanded its overseas productive operations relative to its domestic investment in manufacturing. Against this, foreign firms have preferred to export to the UK rather than set up new production units here.

Note to Section 14-4

The data in this section excludes investment inwards or outwards by oil companies and by banks and insurance companies. In the case of oil, Dunning (1979) gives estimates of the oil companies' stake (in £ million) as follows:

	Inward	Outward
1965	850	1500
1977	3700	5300

14-5 THE ROLE OF THE CITY OF LONDON AND ITS INTERNATIONAL INVOLVEMENT

In the case of the UK, loans and credit abroad became significant after the Napoleonic wars. The world-wide operations of UK financial capital therefore developed along with the development of UK international commodity trade, the expansion of the operations of commercial capital, and the overseas investment of productive capital. When we talk about the City of London we are considering a very complex set of institutions and relationships involving all kinds of capital operating on a world scale but which are especially linked to the circuits of financial and commercial capital. The characteristics of the City of London have grown out of the overseas orientation of the UK's financial system and the key role of Britain as the base for major trading and raw materials producing corporations.

Although the City of London is no longer the dominant financial centre of the capitalist world, it nevertheless remains one of the major world centres. But since 1945 it has undergone a number of important changes.

First, there has been a further 'internationalization' of financial and commercial capital. In part this is because the enormous growth of multinational companies has required a corresponding adaptation by financial and trading organizations, and partly because the technological revolution in communications has brought every part of the world into immediate contact.

Second, the role of financial institutions in the domestic economy has become more important and in particular has acquired a crucial role in financing the public sector deficit.

Third, as a result of expansionist strategies and competition, the boundaries between financial institutions have tended to break down and given way to the formation of giant financial conglomerates.

In the course of time, many sections of financial and commercial capital that had their headquarters in the UK moved to other countries, such as South Africa, Hong Kong, Canada, Australia, etc. But often the connections these companies have with the City of London remain very close and they can for some purposes often be regarded as part of the same complex. The difficulties in defining the precise boundary should not lead us to ignore the specially close interdependence. Examples might be the Anglo-American Corporation of South Africa (the Oppenheimer empire), whose Diamond Corporation has its HQ in London, and the Hong Kong and Shanghai Banking Corporation with its HQ in Hong Kong.

It is widely agreed that the City of London exercises a great deal of influence on government policy and on economic and financial policy-making institutions. There are two very obvious reasons for this. One is that the City of London stands at the heart of financial flows in and out of the UK. Its attitude can sometimes determine and always influence whether there is a balance of payments crisis by withdrawing support from sterling. In addition the 'invisible' earnings of city financial institutions are a very important part of the surplus on the current balance of payments whereas the visible balance has generally been in deficit. For these reasons alone the City of London plays an extremely important part in decision making by governments and institutions like the Bank of England.

But in addition, the City of London has traditionally close links with the Conservative Party as well as with state institutions such as the Treasury and the Bank of England (the latter only 'nationalized' after the war). The leadership of the Tory Party was traditionally drawn from City circles. And, as we already pointed out, the City is a vital element in state and local authority financing. It also 'creates' avenues for making profit in non-manufacturing investment which have become increasingly important.

Clearly, there is a powerful basis for the City of London's influence but what is also important is that the City of London has been left very largely to regulate its own affairs. Powers that do exist in broad terms are exercised informally; and for the rest, the institutions police themselves. A whole series of scandals has begun to create a widely held view that such self-regulation in areas that affect the economy so profoundly must give way to effective public accountability.

The intention of this section is to review some of the most important of the institutions of the City of London in the light of the growing tendency, already referred to, to diversify and increase their international connections.

The Banking System

The first major component is the clearing banks, where the 'big four' dominate domestic banking with a widespread network of branches. Since the late sixties the clearing banks diversified into credit finance and other kinds of finance companies and joint ventures in leasing and factoring services. Responding to the growth of competition from foreign banks, the increased activities of the MNCs and the dramatic rise of the Eurocurrency market, the major clearing banks expanded their international operations. Barclays, for instance, which already is in a strong position in former colonial territories, South Africa, etc., has established itself in the US and other major centres. Lloyds merged with the British Bank of London and South America in 1971 and also expanded into the US. The Midland Bank sought to internationalize via consortiums with overseas bankers but then changed its strategy to establishing or acquiring overseas operations.

To the clearing banks we must add the British overseas banks, the largest of which is the Standard Chartered, with extensive operations in South Africa, West Africa, the Far East, South East Asia, the Middle East and the Mediterranean.

The second component is the merchant banks. These have traditionally operated on an international scale. Their main activities have been in the market for corporate finance, financing international trade, lending to foreign governments, financing overseas government bills, foreign exchange dealings, and, increasingly important, the management of pension and investment funds. They have become active in property development and have greatly expanded their overseas branches and subsidiaries.

The third component is the credit finance companies. Companies like UDT and Mercantile Credit sought to expand into banking, as did the First National Credit Corporation, becoming important parts of the so-called 'secondary banking system'. They involved themselves in the Eurocurrency market and in property, borrowing short through certificates of deposit (part of the wholesale parallel inter-bank market) and lending long, in property for instance. This group, however, received a severe mauling as a result of the collapse of the property boom in 1974–5. A massive rescue operation ('the lifeboat') was mounted by the Bank of England, which saved some; others were taken over by big banks and insurance companies.

The Money and Foreign Exchange Markets

The institutions directly concerned here are to a large degree the same bodies we have already looked at under banking. Apart from the overseas banks we need add only the discount houses, who make their money in two ways: first, by borrowing from the clearing banks and investing in Treasury bills, short-dated government stocks, etc.; and second, by providing a market in commercial bills.

The areas of activity involving overseas operations are foreign exchange and currency deposits, including the Eurocurrency market—which involves complex chains of operations between banks internationally—and the gold market—which comprises five authorized dealers (three of these are banks and two are bank subsidiaries). London and Zurich are the two main world gold centres.

The Securities Market

This mainly involves the sale of stocks and shares by the personal sector and their purchase by the financial, industrial, commercial, and overseas sectors. It is mainly a secondary market—i.e., it deals in existing financial claims. Here again, a major process of internationalization has taken place because of the importance of London as a world financial centre. The London stock exchange has the largest listing of foreign securities in the world and its turnover is bigger than all the other European exchanges combined. The international bond market is regulated by the Association of International Bond Dealers, one of the number of such international organizations that operate in the City of London.

Insurance

Insurance constitutes a major part of the City of London and is very much an international operation. In 1978 British Insurance Association members received £6.9 billion in premiums from worldwide general business (fire, accident, motor), £528 million from marine aviation and transport, and £5 billion in premium income on life insurance. Overseas business accounted for 55 per cent, 60 per cent, and 15 per cent, respectively, of the earnings in these areas.

In addition, Lloyds (the world's most famous insurance market) accounted for a third of total net earnings of UK insurance institutions and for over 15 per cent of the total net overseas earnings of the City of London.

Together with pension funds, the insurance companies have become the major institutional holders of company equity (for detailed discussion see Chapter 17), large-scale property investors, and significant buyers of government and local authority bonds.

Trading Companies and Commodity Markets

These form another important part of the City of London. The major trading companies are the survivors of British colonialism. Some of them still operate from London but others are now based elsewhere (like Jardine Matheson and the Hong Kong and Shanghai Banking Corporation, now centred in Hong Kong). The trading firms (like Lonhro, Booker McConnell, Dalgety) have diversified to become conglomerates, operating on a world scale in merchanting, insurance broking, plantations, property, etc.

To the trading companies we should add the major shipping companies (like P & O) who are diversified financial and service conglomerates (or part of such conglomerates). In London also the Baltic Exchange undertakes over half the world shipping freight movements. London shares with New York as world trading centre for 'soft' commodities (sugar, coffee, cocoa, wool, etc.) and metals (copper, lead, zinc, and silver).

The Bank of England

The Bank plays a critical role in international exchange operations and policy and also acts as supervisor and coordinator of the operations of the City of London. It constitutes, with the Treasury, the main source of continuous economic policy and has been the most consistent defender of reducing and abolishing controls on capital and currency movements. It pressed for the total abolition of exchange controls that took place in 1979, even though this necessarily weakened its regulatory and supervisory powers. Perhaps we could think of its advocacy of the abolition of all controls as part of its bid to preserve the importance of the City of London as a world financial centre. It acts as the linchpin in a series of committees that bring together City institutions (such as the City Liaison Committee, the City Capital Markets Committee, the City EEC Committee, etc.). The Bank also has direct relationships with other government departments, such as the Department of Trade. And, of course, it also maintains very close connections with the major central and other banks in the main capitalist countries and with the IMF and the Bank of International Settlements.

We can get some overall view of the scale of overseas earnings by City financial institutions from Table 14 10.

Although we have described these component parts of the City of London as distinct institutions, in fact they are closely interconnected by financial

Table 14-10 Overseas earnings of City financial institutions (£ million)

	Insurance	Banking	Commodity trading	Baltic Exchange	Total
1970	294	90	87	47	602
1971	345	71	100	25	622
1972	370	122	125	35	745
1973	347	159	165	53	831
1974	375	181	209	103	998
1975	437	202	286	146	1221
1976	790	382	309	147	1797
1977	893	318	230	155	1790
1978	970	652	295	154	2307

Note: All figures net of debits due abroad

Source: Central Statistical Office, *United Kingdom Balance of Payments*, (1979).

links and interlocking directorates (which are more intense within the financial sector than among industrial and commercial companies). Not only has the distinction between domestic and international operations broken down, but the City institutions have gone through a process of diversification to become multi-service conglomerates.

Whatever the competition may be from other financial centres, the City of London remains a massive power-house of economic and financial leverage. Its interests lie in abolishing all constraints on movement of capital and resources.

14-6 BRITAIN AND THE EEC

How does the formation and development of the EEC fit into the picture presented in earlier chapters? The formation of the EEC lies in the conjuncture of a number of powerful forces. The first was the desire of Western European states together with the US to create a unified political and military front against the Soviet 'threat' and against the dangers of revolutionary change within Western Europe itself, especially within France and Italy. Simultaneously the need was felt for some international framework within which the power of a reconstructed West Germany could be contained. These concerns created the Marshall Plan and a series of organizations and initiatives that led up to the EEC itself.

With the reconstruction of the West German and French economies, the importance of an alliance grew. First, it would permit West Germany not only to exert its growing economic influence but even more to establish the political respectability and leadership that was a counterpart of its economic strength. Second, it would allow France, which already exercise world political influence as one of the victorious allies, to push forward its economic revival without fear of a Franco-German conflict and also prevent Germany from becoming an instrument of the United States. And then third, there were, as described in Chapter 12, the growing forces of internationalization of capital and the MNCs, which saw economic advantage in breaking down barriers to both trade and capital movement (the philosophy embodied in the Treaty of Rome).

The formation of the EEC in 1959 was essentially a block around a Franco-German alliance. It was formed in a period of economic expansion that accelerated during the sixties and in which the West German, French, and Italian economies fully participated. It also involved the creation of the Common Agricultural Policy, which was essentially part of the deal struck by France with Germany that allowed the EEC to come into being. German access to French markets (which potentially threatened less competitive French capital) was traded for heavy protection of agriculture, greatly benefiting the large and efficient French farmers, while sustaining the peasant farmers of both countries. The political importance of the farming lobby in certain key areas has meant that the creaking and increasingly expensive machinery has been largely maintained, despite certain reforms.

The Attitude of the UK

As might be expected in the light of the main thesis presented in this book, British capital did not wish at that stage to join the EEC precisely because it saw its role as a world power with major connections—economic, financial, political, military—with the non-EEC world. Various alternative proposals were floated and a European Free Trade Association involving the UK, the Scandinavian countries, Austria, Switzerland, and Portugal was established. As a counterpart or bargaining weapon EFTA had only limited significance. The Franco-German alliance and the states that had grouped round it had clearly created a new force in world politics and economy. The main groups of British capital, who were facing major political changes in the Commonwealth, recognized the need for a new approach and new alliances but in approaching the EEC were rebuffed by De Gaulle, who regarded the UK as the agent of the US and as creating the possibilities of an Anglo-German alliance that might weaken France's position. The situation changed after the death of De Gaulle, and the continued economic growth in Europe created optimism for the future. The UK was admitted (with Ireland and Denmark) on terms more severe than might have been the case had the UK been one of the original partners. The real severity of the terms of entry only became clear when the international economic and political climate changed as it began to do with the world economic crisis, the Israeli–Arab war, and the dramatic rise in oil prices. Political changes were also taking place in France and in the UK. In 1974 the newly elected Labour government renegotiated the terms of entry (completed in 1975) and in that year organized a referendum, which confirmed EEC membership. The renegotiated terms of entry nevertheless reflected the weaker international position of the UK domestic economy. The argument, however, was presented in optimistic terms, with the emphasis on the long-run dynamic effects, which, it was said, would outweigh the short-run costs.

The dynamic effects expected were those that were said to arise from increased competition and economies of scale.[2] As the 1970 White Paper *Britain and the European Community* (HMSO, 1970) puts it:

> The creation of an enlarged and integrated European market would provide in effect a much larger and much faster growing 'home market' for British industry. It would provide the stimuli of much greater opportunities—and competition—than exists at present or would otherwise exist in the future. There would be substantial advantage for British Industry from membership of this new Common Market, stemming primarily from the

[2] This section owes much to articles in the *Cambridge Journal of Economics* (1979), CEPR. 1979, MAFF Working Paper No. 27 (1979).

opportunities for greater economies of scale, increased specialisation, a sharper competitive climate and faster growth. These may be described as the 'dynamic effects' of membership on British Industry and trade.

This is the concluding section:

> This would open up to our industrial producers substantial opportunities for increasing export sales, while at the same time exposing them more fully to the competition of European industries. . . . The acceleration in the rate of growth of industrial exports could then outpace any increase in the rate of growth of imports with corresponding benefits to the balance of payments. Moreover, with such a response, the growth of industrial productivity would be accelerated as a result of increased competition and the advantages derived from specialisation and larger scale production.

The Costs to the UK: the Record since 1973

In discussing the economic effects of British membership of the EEC, it is useful to distinguish between direct and indirect costs. By direct costs is meant the costs arising from the formal structure of the EEC, such as payments into and out of the EEC budget arising from the Common Agricultural Policy (CAP), regional and social funds, and the administration costs of the EEC bureaucracy. These costs may be estimated relatively easily from the accounts of the EEC itself. By indirect costs is meant those effects on prices, industrial balance of payments, expansion, employment prospects, and living standards resulting from CAP and the EEC policy of removing tariffs, promoting competition, and generally freeing market forces. These costs are much more difficult to assess, partly because they are not captured in the formal EEC accounts and also because it is hard to distinguish them from the effects of other spontaneous market forces. Thus, for example, in examining employment changes in a specific industry, it is difficult to separate the part that is attributable specifically to EEC policy from the part that would have occurred anyway.

The Budgetary and Agricultural Costs

Three-quarters of the EEC budget is used to finance the CAP and the rest goes to maintain the EEC apparatus and to finance regional and social funds, etc. The budget itself is financed by levies on imports of food covered by CAP, tariffs on industrial goods, and a share of the value added tax collected in each member country. Estimates suggest that in 1979 the UK contributed 17.6 per cent of the budget, rising, unless other action is taken, to about 20.5 per cent. The UK share of the budget is much higher than the UK share in European GDP because: (a) the UK imports more from outside the EEC and therefore pays more in customs duties—in particular, being a smaller agricultural producer, the UK imports more food and to the degree that it imports more of this from non-EEC countries, it has to pay levies to the EEC budget; and (b) because VAT is levied on consumption, and consumption is a higher proportion of GNP in the UK than in some other EEC countries, it contributes disproportionately. The UK fares no less badly in its share of EEC spending, because it gains little from CAP and the amounts received from the regional and social funds are relatively small by comparison with CAP expenditures.

Both the social and regional funds have rather limited roles. The former is able to support retraining and resettlement of workers switching from one industry to another, and has been used extensively to reduce the agricultural workforce within the EEC. The regional fund has the responsibility of coordinating the policies of member states towards the deep-seated regional inequalities within the EEC (which have partly been exacerbated by the operations of the EEC itself). Such coordination is seen as necessary to avoid the danger that member states may compete in offering increasingly advantageous incentives to international capital to locate in their less developed regions. However, it is important to note that the regional fund has generally been operated so that each country receives benefits roughly in line with its contributions. This means that the fund is limited to the role of harmonizing between countries' policies, to reduce inequalities within member countries, and can do little to offset economic and social inequalities arising between member countries. Since, as is argued later, the EEC has promoted a strengthening of the stronger central regions of the EEC at the expense of the poorer peripheral areas, pressures have arisen to extend the regional fund to deal with inequalities at the European level as a whole, and so to help mitigate inequalities between countries. Not surprisingly, this has been firmly resisted by the stronger states, who would lose by it. Thus the UK, one of the poor countries in the EEC if measured in terms of *per capita* income, received only £60 million from the regional fund in 1977.

In addition to the budgetary costs there are also the costs that arise because the UK imports food from the rest of the EEC at higher prices than it would otherwise have to pay. Some countries gain because they export food to the rest of the EEC at prices higher than they could get on world markets. When these two costs are combined, Table 14-11 shows the picture in 1978.

The system of support to agriculture that operated in the UK prior to entry was one of allowing imports of agricultural produce, largely without tariff, and subsidizing home production to the extent required to maintain some domestic agricultural sector for strategic and other reasons. Since the transfer of surplus labour from agriculture to industry was largely completed early in the nineteenth century, British agriculture was highly efficient. Relatively small subsidies were therefore required to maintain production at around 40 to 50 per cent of requirements, and the system offered the advantage of cheap food imports to meet the residual. Consumers enjoyed low food prices, and the subsidies to producers, financed through taxation, did not place too great a burden on the state.

In continental Europe such a system would have been unworkable. With large numbers of inefficient producers, the costs of subsidies would have represented an enormous burden. This was exacerbated by the much higher degree of self-sufficiency in European agriculture. For these reasons the opposite system was adopted. The consumer was charged the high price of domestic production, and an elaborate system of tariffs was used to ensure that cheaper imports did not undercut domestic producers. This system had the added advantage of providing the state with additional revenues from imports, obviating the need to find funds for subsidies.

The cost to the UK of switching from the old system of agricultural support to the CAP have been substantial, involving a phased but significant increase in food prices over the five years following entry. As a consequence of the CAP tariff on imported food from outside the EEC, the prices of a

Table 14-11 Net receipts and payments between EEC members

	Total net receipts (£ m)	Total net receipts *per capita* (£ per year *per capita*)	National income *per capita* (% of unweighted mean)
UK	− 1046	− 19	69
Italy	− 1002	− 19	55
West Germany	− 326	− 5	130
Belgium–Luxembourg	+ 100	+ 10	129
Ireland	+ 566	+ 139	48
Netherlands	+ 595	+ 43	120
France	+ 599	+ 11	113
Denmark	+ 712	+ 143	136

Source: Cambridge Economic Policy Group, *Economic Policy Review* (1979).

number of key agricultural commodities were in 1978 some 20 or 30 per cent above world prices, with a still wider margin for certain commodities, such as butter. In the earlier years of British entry, the disparity between world and EEC agricultural prices was still greater. The argument put forward by EEC proponents, that cheap world supplies of food now no longer exist, is simply not true. When allowance is made for the fact that not all food imports are subject to tariff, the CAP is estimated to have raised the retail price of food in the UK by a little over 12 per cent in 1978. The effect of this fell particularly on the poorer groups in the community, who spend proportionately more of their income on food. It is also important to note that the average price increases resulting from the CAP vary between member countries because of differences in the composition of agricultural imports. In this respect, the economically weaker countries—Italy and the UK—suffer most, while the price increases in France and Germany have been estimated to be very much less.

The political importance of the farmers' lobby in certain key areas of

France and Germany has meant that agricultural support prices (the prices guaranteed to farmers) have been set at consistently high levels. The result has been a persistent tendency for production of a number of agricultural products to outstrip consumption, so that the EEC has had to buy up the surplus. Over time this has led to the much publicized 'lakes' and 'mountains' of stored surplus produce. Measures to reform the system have tended to be limited to incentives to persuade the small, inefficient farmers to leave the land; but this has often resulted in the consolidation of smaller farms into larger, more efficient ones, exacerbating the problem of surpluses. Unpublished forecasts by the EEC Commission suggest that on present trends surpluses are likely to emerge for all the main commodities to which the support system applies. The absurd waste involved in this is evident: not only are consumers prevented from buying cheap food from outside the EEC, but also prices are set so high that consumers also have to pay (through taxes going to the EEC) for excess production. The effects on countries outside the EEC, particularly third world countries, are less obvious but no less real: as the EEC becomes increasingly self-sufficient in agriculture, markets for the rest of the world become closed; and periodic sales on world markets by the EEC of surplus agricultural produce depress world prices. Both effects reduce foreign exchange earnings of third world countries, harming development prospects.

Not surprisingly in these circumstances, pressure for reform has been building up. The principle of a common price for agricultural produce throughout the EEC has already been abandoned. This occurred with the shift towards floating exchange rates: devaluing countries were reluctant to allow food prices paid by consumers to rise by the full effect of the devaluation; while revaluing countries, notably Germany, were unwilling to see the prices received by their farmers fall. Accordingly, a separate set of accounting exchanges was adopted, leading to the so-called 'green pound', which governs the price of agricultural produce in the UK. The effect of this was to shield the British consumer from the full extent of the high prices in the EEC. Thus it has been estimated that the retail price of food would have been some eight per cent higher in the early part of 1978 had the 'green pound' been devalued in line with the real exchange rate (although this discrepancy fluctuates, depending on the strength of the pound). But it should be emphasized that this small mitigation of the costs of entry was not a result of the CAP itself, but rather an outcome of the hostility shown to it by the Labour government, responding to the strong anti-EEC feeling in the UK. Whether significant reforms in the CAP can be obtained by further hard negotiation remains to be seen.

Taking the CAP, regional and social funds, and other formal aspects of the EEC together, the total annual direct cost of British membership in terms of the balance of payments has been estimated at around £1100 million, or around one per cent of total national income. This estimate is very close (in real terms) to the estimate provided by the 1971 White Paper, which was concerned to assess the effects of membership prior to entry.

It would seem, therefore, that the direct costs of entry were well anticipated. However, it has been strongly argued that this estimate understates the true cost. For in the UK depressed output levels and high unemployment have been enforced by the failure of British capital to compete internationally, expressed in the weak state of the balance of payments. An additional burden of £1000 million on the balance of payments required a cutback of imports by a similar amount, at least in the longer run, since the UK could not persistently run large external deficits. This cut in imports occurred through contractionary policies, cutting domestic output and incomes and therefore reducing the demand for imports. A cut in imports of £1000 million required a cut in output of roughly three times as much, or £3000 million, and an associated fall in employment. Thus the real direct costs were some three times the estimated balance of payments costs. These additional costs, in terms of forgone output and higher unemployment, were not anticipated. Part of these additional costs may have been avoided through the fall in the exchange rate (coupled with incomes policies) cutting real wage costs, for this would have had the effect of raising exports and lowering imports, via increased international competitiveness, without changes in the level of domestic output. But it seems doubtful whether more than a part of the costs were met in this way, so that the direct costs of entry probably amounted to two to three per cent of national income. Either way, the burden of entry was shouldered by ordinary working people whether in lower real wages or in higher unemployment.

The indirect costs of entry

As discussed above, the effects of dismantling the obstacles to trade in the form of tariffs and other non-price barriers, between the UK and the EEC is particularly hard to assess. Proponents of entry have always argued that these effects would be beneficial; that increased competition would force British industry to modernize and become more productive, therefore providing considerable dynamic benefits in the UK in the form of increased growth. It was these benefits that were seen in the 1971 White Paper as outweighing the costs arising from the CAP. In the event, of course, the British growth rate since entry has slumped disastrously, with national income rising by only one per cent a year between 1973 and 1978.

The theoretical debate was summed up very well as follows (Fetherston, Moore, and Rhodes, 1979):

> There are two diametrically opposed views on the effects of increased trade arising from economic integration. The standard static neoclassical argument is that increased trade will improve the efficiency of resource utilisation and so, given the assumption of

continuous full employment, will increase output and welfare. A contrasting view is that of a relatively weak industrial country such as the UK, where the level of output is constrained not by the supply of factors of production but by the need to maintain satisfactory balance of payments position, the dynamic effects of joining a common market in manufacturing products in which other members are relatively strong may well be adverse. This will be the case if increased integration has a greater effect on imports than on exports, so that economies of scale may actually be lost by the resultant reasons. This factor would reinforce for the weak country the process of cumulative decline identified by Myrdal (1957).

The collapse of growth in the UK cannot be attributed directly to EEC entry. The relative decline of the UK economy has been a long-standing trend, dating back to the end of the nineteenth century, and the loss of international markets has proceeded steadily since the Second World War, as Table 14-12 shows. Superimposed on this trend has been the effect of the recent international capitalist crisis, which has lowered growth rates generally in the capitalist world since 1973. Clearly, then, any assessment of the effects of entry cannot rest on a simple comparison of the state of the economy prior to and after entry.

Table 14-12 Share of world markets in manufacturing goods

	1950	1960	1965	1970	1975	1978
UK	25.5	16.5	13.9	10.8	9.3	9.5
France	9.9	9.6	8.8	8.7	10.2	9.8
West Germany	7.3	19.3	19.1	19.8	20.3	20.7

Note: The table indicates manufactured exports as a proportion of total defined to be the major OECD countries).

Source: National Institute Economic Review, recent issues.

Moreover it is important to realize that tariff barriers between the UK and the EEC were really rather low by the time of British entry. This was because the EEC and the UK were party to a series of internationally negotiated tariff reductions under the auspices of GATT, starting in the fifties and continuing right up to entry. Thus when entry came, the necessary reduction in tariff barriers was fairly small, so that although some increased import penetration resulted from entry, it was probably not very substantial. Entry also had some harmful impact on UK exports to third world countries, when the termination of the Commonwealth Preference Agreement (and its partial replacement by the Lome Agreement) ended the UK's preferential trading position. These effects, together with the direct costs discussed above, undoubtedly imposed a significant burden on the balance of payments, leading to depressed levels of output and increased unemployment.

Nonetheless, the deterioration in the UK's external trading position was undoubtedly due to trends established well before entry to the EEC. The dismantling of tariff barriers in the post-war period meant that the British home market was already suffering the depredations of overseas competition, the signs of which appeared very rapidly. Import penetration proceeded steadily in the sixties, and accelerated from 1970 onwards, prior to entry. Much of this increased competition came from EEC countries particularly West Germany, and the UK's net trading position in industrial products with the EEC has deteriorated sharply. The impact of this has been very great indeed, as Fetherston, Moore and Rhodes (1979) indicated:

> The estimated annual average cost to real national income over the period 1973 to 1977 of the adverse shift in manufacturing trade is about 6%. These estimates suggest, however, that in 1977 national income was almost 12% less than it might have been had no deterioration occurred. Taking the EEC budget, the CAP arrangements and estimated manufacturing trade shifts together it seems that, far from there being any evidence of net gains accruing from EEC membership, the total cost to real national income in 1977/78 could have been as high as 15%. If EEC membership has had harmful effects on the UK's manufacturing trade performance and industrial growth prospects, then even the crude 'membership fee' argument breaks down, as far as purely economic factors are concerned. Instead the divergent influence of the system of transfers merely reinforces the process of cumulative divergence between richer and poorer areas already encouraged by free trade in manufactures.

At root, the problem arises from uneven development between the main EEC countries and more generally in the advanced capitalist world. Economies like West Germany, with strong domestically based capital, have been able to secure rapid rates of domestic expansion through penetration of markets of other countries. The expansion of demand permits gains from economies of scale in production, facilitating more rapid productivity growth and therefore underwriting the expansion of demand. The obverse of this is that other countries, such as the UK, experience the opposite process: a declining share of world markets, coupled with increased import penetration, depresses output and investment, generating a spiral of stagnation. Within the EEC this concentration of economic power has also assumed a geographical form, with increasing concentration of industry in central regions and a relative weakening of peripheral countries.

These effects are reinforced by EEC policy itself, which places at the forefront the unleashing of market forces, except in agriculture. At the same time, EEC emphasis on harmonization between member countries increasingly places constraints on the ability of member states to respond to the particular problems of their economies by specific national policy measures. Thus EEC measures increasingly limit the ability of particular states to take measures to aid depressed industries. The recent European Monetary System—although motivated, perhaps, by the objective of establishing a rival (under West German hegemony) to the US domination of the international monetary system—places similar constraints on the ability of nation states to pursue independent macro-economic policies. For the maintenance of relatively fixed exchange rates between member countries will require coordination and harmonization of policy, despite the widely differing circumstances of the particular economies. The EEC, in almost all its activities, acts to foster rather than restrain the concentration of industrial power.

In 1980 the Conservative government succeeded in getting the agreement of the EEC to a rebate of £717 mn on it's budgetary contribution. However, the bulk of that rebate is to take the form of new projects to be agreed by the EEC. In the meantime, the growing costs of the EEC (and of CAP in particular) will raise the budgetary contribution to new heights; and the accession of new members will cut the share which Britain could expect to receive from the EEC's regional fund. Those sections of capital that are focussed on the domestic market are ill-equipped to withstand the pressures from the rest of the EEC. Not surprisingly, opposition to Britain's membership has continued to grow.

FURTHER READING

For comprehensive statistical series see the annual Pink Book, *United Kingdom Balance of Payments*, produced by the central statistical office. Useful essays on foreign trade, etc., can be found in Morris (1979), Prest and Coppock (1978), Major (1979), and the exceptionally useful collection of essays in Blackaby (1979a).

On UK foreign investment see Dunning (1979); on multi-national companies see Hood and Young (1979); on the City of London and the banking and service sectors see Channon (1977 and 1978).

For more general discussion see Barratt-Brown (1972 and 1974) and Radice (1975).

On the third world see Griffin (1978) and Owen and Sutcliffe (1972). For a description of the EEC see Swann (1978), and for analysis of the costs to the UK see Morris (1980) and *Cambridge Economic Policy Review*, April 1979 and April 1980.

FOUR

CAPITAL

The sections on the state and international capitalism have described the arena in which class conflict is staged. We are now ready to examine the classes themselves in more detail. Chapter 15 describes the structure of capital in the UK and its distribution between sectors and between finance and industry. This analysis of the structure is at the level of aggregate social capital, but the characteristics of capital in general are derived from the fact that it is composed of many competing blocks of capital organized into firms. Chapter 16 continues the analysis at this level, the level of the firm. The force of competition also leads to the continual restructuring of capital into larger and larger blocks through the process of concentration and centralization, and Chapter 17 examines the operation of this process in the UK. The final chapter in the section examines what is the whole point of the process for capital, the generation of profit and the expansion of accumulation, and reviews the 'crisis of profitability'.

FIFTEEN

COMPOSITION OF CAPITAL AND CHANGES IN ITS DISTRIBUTION

Sam Aaronovitch

15-1 INTRODUCTION

We have frequently used the term 'capital' in an aggregative sense but in fact it is made up of heterogeneous blocks of capital that also combine in different ways. One kind of distinction, already referred to, is between capitals operating in different circuits (such as industrial, commercial, and financial capital). A good deal of specialization emerged between such capitals, but this in turn has given way to a new phase, where such capitals combine to form conglomerate groupings whose surpluses are launched on different circuits by the same controlling groups. Capitals, in another dimension, can be seen as competing blocks, but to function at all they must involve themselves in particular activities, requiring given stocks of fixed capital and employing given types of labour and so constituting an economic structure with a complex division of labour and interrelationships between the various parts.

The composition of capital—the sectors between which it is distributed—is subject to changes according to the operation of market forces (national and international), the way in which growth and decline are handled, and many other forces. Both the distribution of capital and shifts in that distribution are important for the system and for the people because of their impact on economic growth, employment, regional differences, etc. The relative decline of the UK economy has made all these major issues of public concern.

We can look at capital distribution in different ways. One aspect of the concentration and centralization of capital—i.e., shifts in ownership and control—is dealt with at length in Chapter 17. This chapter, which is largely descriptive, concerns itself with two other aspects: first, the functioning of capital in terms of output, employment, and profit between sectors of the economy (what is conventionally discussed as the structure of the economy); and second, the role played by capital operating in the financial field and its relationship to the rest of the corporate sector.

Two additional points are worth making at this stage. One is that the fact that capitals operating in different sectors receive different rates of return throws some light on shifts in capital distribution and the attempts to restructure it. The second point is that distributions of output between sectors will not correspond to those for capital stock and employment. Capital intensive industries will show larger capital stocks and lower employment relative to outputs and, of course, output can be rising with rising, static, or falling employment.

As we have stressed throughout this book, capitalism is in a continuous process of change, which is itself the result of many different forces. Advanced capitalist economies show broadly comparable trends in the distribution of capital even though the differences between them and in the utilization of capital are important. How are we to classify the reasons for given distributions of capital and the changes that have taken place? Very often the explanation is given mainly in terms of changes in the structure and pattern of final demand, with consequent impact on the structure and pattern of intermediate demand, jointly with changes in technology. This approach, however, needs to be seen within a framework that places more emphasis on class and intra-class relationships. Without putting them in order of importance, perhaps the following four factors are among the most powerful.

First, there is the impact of rivalry between blocks of capital on the expansion and contraction of capital stocks, which affects not only individual industries but the overall structure of economies. These shifts express success and failure in inter-capitalist competition at the national and international level.

The second factor is the outcome of class and democratic struggles in conjunction with rising incomes. This is shown in (a) the major expansion of services provided by the state or in other collective forms; (b) the overall growth of other services as compared with the growth in demand for the products of manufacturing and agriculture; (c) the shifts in employment that result because services are more labour intensive than manufacturing; and (d) shifts within the manufacturing sector, because changes in the differing income elasticities of demand (as incomes rise) favour one sector as against another. These changes combine in turn to shift the composition of capital in industries supplying intermediate goods.

Third, there is the impact of technological change, with its effects on technical coefficients of production. As a result, the distribution of capital stock, output, and employment tend to diverge, as we noted earlier. The rate of technological change also differs between industries as well as between countries.

Fourth and last comes the process of urbanization, which in the UK has gone further than in any other comparable economy. Seventy-five per cent of the UK population lives in a fairly well defined group of urban conglomerations. This urbanization in turn has led to changed patterns of demand among those who live and work in cities and to competition for space, which has concentrated high profit activities in city centres and enlarged the share of rent in total capitalist income.

15-2 SECTORAL CHANGES

In general, the information we present is for the period since the mid fifties, i.e., for fairly recent changes.

A very broad picture of the distribution of output as between 1956–7 and 1977–8, together with the percentage change over that period, and of the changed importance of the sectors over that period, can be constructed from Table 15-1.

Table 15-1 Main economic sectors

	Output[a] Per cent change				Weight		
	1956–7	1977–8	21 years	*p.a.*	1956–7	1975	1977–8
Agriculture, forestry, fishing	70.5	113.5	61.0	2.3	28	27	29
Industry	67.2	107.8	60.4	2.3	406	391	398
Transport and communications	59.0	101.5	72.0	2.6	77	85	81
Distributive trades	66.0	101.5	53.8	2.1	98	97	93
Insurance, banking, finance, business services	42.0	106.5	153.6	4.5	44	70	70
Ownership of dwellings	65.5	104.5	59.5	2.2	60	59	58
Professional and scientific services	55.0	105.5	91.8	3.2	105	124	124
Miscellaneous services	70.5	108.0	53.2	2.1	76	70	72
Public administration, defence	90.0	103.0	14.4	0.6	106	77	75
GDP (output)	64.6	106.2	64.4	2.4	1000	1000	1000

[a] 1975 = 100.

Source: NIER, August 1979, p. 40.

From this Table we can see that the sectors that have performed above average are: banking, finance, and insurance; professional and scientific services; and transport and communications. Industry and agriculture perform only slightly below the average, with distributive trades and miscellaneous services very close behind. Lagging far more is public administration and defence (but the measurement of output in the case of services raises many questions and at this stage the figures given must be used as trend indicators alone). In describing shifts in economic structures, economists often use a threefold division of primary (extractive industries and agriculture), secondary (industry), and tertiary (services). In broad terms, as we have suggested, the same kind of shift towards the tertiary sector is seen in all advanced capitalist economies. It finds its reflection in the shift in the balance of overall investment from manufacturing to distribution and services and, even more strikingly, in the shift in the distribution of employment (see Chapter 20).

Under the general heading of 'de-industrialization' there has been a good deal of discussion on the shift away from manufacturing, but before we look at that more closely we propose to see what changes have taken place within the industrial sector itself (which overall contributed, at 1975 prices, about 40 per cent of GDP in 1978). That picture is given in Table 15-2, which first takes the main categories within industry and then looks more closely at the major branches of manufacturing.

Table 15-2 Main industrial categories

	Output[a] Per cent change				Weight		
	1956–7	1977–8	21 years	p.a.	1956–7	1975	1977–8
Mining and quarrying	162.8	210.3	29.2	1.2	97	41	80
Manufacturing	64.2	103.2	60.7	2.3	651	697	667
Construction	76.1	101.8	33.8	1.4	202	182	172
Gas, electricity, water	43.0	108.4	152.1	4.5	50	80	81
All industries	67.2	107.8	60.4	2.3	1000	1000	1000
Manufacturing:							
Food, drink, tobacco	66.1	104.8	58.5	2.2	73	77	75
Chemicals, etc.	39.5	114.9	190.9	5.2	39	68	73
Metals	106.4	101.4	−4.7	−0.2	72	47	44
Engineering and allied	61.6	99.0	60.7	2.3	264	298	274
Textiles, clothing	84.4	101.4	20.1	0.9	81	67	63
Other manufacturing industries[b]	59.6	107.0	79.5	2.8	122	140	139

[a] 1975=100.
[b] Includes the brick, cement, pottery, glass, timber, furniture, paper, printing, and other manufacturing industries.
Source: NIER, August 1979, p. 41.

If we look at the broad categories in the first part of the Table, the fall in mining and quarrying by half was later offset by the rapid growth of North Sea oil production, which is included under that heading. The major expansion in gas, electricity, and water (critical services to industry as a whole) is shown in their increased share; manufacturing share rose until 1975 and then fell away again, and construction declined. The steady share of manufacturing appears to contradict the fears of de-industrialization, but the situation is put more into perspective by Table 15-3, which compares the share of manufacturing output in GDP at constant and current prices and looks at the share of manufacturing employment as percentage of total civilian employment.

Table 15-3 Manufacturing and employment shares

	1956–7	1975	% change
Manufacturing output as % of GDP:			
At 1963 prices	29.7	28.9	−2.7
At current prices	35.7	28.9	−19.0
Manufacturing employment as % of			
total civilian employment	35.8	30.9	−13.7

Source: Brown and Sheriff (1979).

Another way of looking at the distribution of capital is in terms of capital employed (based on company balance sheets) and it is noticeable that between 1960 and 1975 the sector within manufacturing showing the greatest increase was food, drink, and tobacco, bringing its total very close to the share of capital employed in the engineering industry.

In looking at shifts in the distribution of capital we have focused on what has happened within the UK itself. But the reader needs to put together the other important changes described in other chapters—in particular, the increases in overseas investment and production by the largest firms.

When we look at profitability we can observe a major change in the ratio of gross trading profits in the manufacturing sector to that in the financial sector, from the order of 19 in the early sixties, to about 10 in the early seventies, to nearer 4 by 1976. The share of profit and the rate of profit, as we shall see in Chapter 18, has held up better in non-manufacturing than in manufacturing and has been associated with the shift in the balance of investment from manufacturing to services and shipping.

15-3 DE-INDUSTRIALIZATION?

For reasons already given, the UK economy has not simply reflected the broad structural changes taking place in all advanced capitalist countries. It also shows characteristics that come from its peculiar history and from its decline relative to other rival economies. Although in constant prices the share of manufacturing in GDP has been maintained in the UK from the early fifties, it has not held up as well as in countries like West Germany and Italy. The share of manufacturing employment in total employment has fallen by more in the UK than in other advanced countries. Within the manufacturing sector, although there has been a shift towards chemical and oil products and electrical engineering, this has not been so marked in the UK as in other advanced countries. The view has therefore gained ground that a serious weakening of the UK productive base is taking place.

We can summarize the concern by saying, first, that UK industry is increasingly unable to compete with its overseas rivals as shown by rising import penetration of manufactured goods; this in turn leads to major losses in income and employment (since the income and employment are generated in the exporting countries); and, second, that the UK is increasingly unable to finance the imports regarded as necessary for full employment levels of output and to meet the changing needs of the people. Manufacturing is the major source of export earnings of foreign currency, important for the flow of advanced technology, and a major employer of labour.

An attempt to define de-industrialization that has attracted much interest was made by Ajit Singh (1977):

> To the extent that manufacturing may constitute the major source of foreign exchange earnings for a country, an 'efficient' manufacturing sector must also be able to provide (*currently and potentially*) sufficient net exports to meet the country's overall import requirements at socially acceptable levels of output, employment and exchange rate. It is in this important sense that the UK manufacturing sector is becoming increasingly inefficient. The evidence suggests a structural disequilibrium, whereby the trading position of the manufacturing sector in the world economy continues to deteriorate in spite of increasing cost and price competitiveness. Deindustrialisation is a symptom or consequence of this 'inefficiency' or of disequilibrium, rather than its cause....

Since those words were written, the rise in the value of the pound on the world exchanges has substantially increased the UK's cost and reduced price competitiveness.

The debate has been complicated by the thesis presented by Bacon and Eltis (1978), which focused on the growth of the *non-marketed* sector in the UK economy and argued (a) that the market sector must finance the resources, especially the imports, needed for the non-market sector, and is increasingly unable to do so; (b) this is caused by the market sector (broadly identified with the private sector) being starved of labour and funds ('crowded out') by the expansion of state services and the non-market sector generally; and (c) that the effect of expanding state services, together with working class demands on the resources available, squeezed net of tax profitability and hence reduced investment. These causes have been heavily criticized on the grounds that the growth of service employment has accompanied or even followed the decline in the market sector; that the greater part of the labour so employed has been female, part-time labour, not the kind of labour favoured by the private sector, especially in manufacturing; and finally, that there is little evidence that investment has been low because of shortage of finance.

Bacon and Eltis do not, however, present a directly de-industrialization view, since the market sector includes marketed services. It is certainly true that UK marketed services have grown in importance relative to manufacturing in terms of output, net balance of trade, and in share of world export of services, but the actual values involved show clearly that marketed services cannot compensate for the severe weakening of the manufacturing base of the UK (*CEPR*, 1978).

There is the more general argument that the UK is simply sharing in a process of de-industrialization characteristic of all advanced economies and that it must adapt to inevitable changes in the world division of labour. The UK, however, is not engaged in a planned adaptation to world change but in an uncontrolled process of relative decay. Nor is it the outcome of changed expectations, unless it is believed that British capitalism's relative decline is the result of such changes in popular expectations. Singh's definition, however, needs to be developed not so much in terms of necessary import requirements but of other important reasons for a dynamic manufacturing sector in the UK economy (a matter to which we shall return in our concluding chapter).

Now it is time to give some attention to the financial sector, which, as Table 15-1 showed, has grown faster than any other sector of the economy.

15-4 FINANCIAL CAPITAL AND THE FINANCE OF THE CORPORATE SECTOR

One of the most important changes in modern capitalism has been the growth of the credit and financial system and therefore of financial capital. Moreover, it is the area where the role of the state has been especially influential. First, it is a major mobilizer of funds for use as capital in all sectors and abroad as well as in the UK; second, it plays an important part in the way those funds are distributed between sectors and different groups of capital, influencing the development of some firms and sectors rather than others and playing a role in the restructuring of capital; third, it accounts for the massive expansion of credit for personal consumption; and fourth, it stands in a very complex relationship with the funds generated by firms operating in the industrial and commercial sectors. The importance of financial intermediaries has been exceptionally high in the UK as measured in the ratio of financial claims to real net worth. Estimates for the UK for 1958–60 showed the highest ratio (1.65) for all countries analysed (Revell, 1973) and that ratio has probably increased since.

As already suggested, the financial and credit system should not be seen simply as a reflection of a 'real' process going on somewhere else in the economy; its influence is real enough, but its development will in the 'last instance' depend upon the creation of surpluses available for distribution and reinvestment.

In terms of mobilizing money resources, 'scattered over the surface of society' as Marx commented, we can think of savings flow (a) from wage and salaried employees (who also receive interest), and (b) from capitalists and firms who have funds not required for immediate use, either for personal consumption or investment. The other side of the process is that workers also borrow and pay interest and the capitalists and firms also borrow or raise new issues to increase the money capital needed for the expansion of their activities.[1]

[1] On the matters raised in this and the following paragraphs, see especially Harris (1976).

Today the great majority of the adult population are deeply involved in various kinds of saving: contractual saving (through insurance and pension funds) and other forms of saving, (bank deposits, friendly societies, unit trusts, etc.); and in various kinds of borrowing: contractual (mortgages especially) and consumer credit. From a class standpoint, the interest received by workers on their savings is to be regarded as a portion of their wage revenue, since their need to save for pensions and insurance, etc., is a necessary part of reproduction of labour power (interest paid by capitalists to workers is, correspondingly, part of variable capital). And interest paid by workers for consumer credit is part of the profit on commercial (merchants') capital.

In addition to the mobilization of funds, the banks are in a position to create credit, which occurs by way of the credit multiplier. This was explained by Black (1980) as follows:

> If a bank has more reserve assets or till money than it needs for its minimum requirements, it can buy securities or make loans to its customers. The people selling the securities or receiving the loans will presumably spend most of the money they receive. If the people who supply the goods, services or securities that are bought with the borrowed money, hold accounts with the original bank, it will once again have excess reserves and will be able to lend some more. If the recipients of the expenditure hold accounts with other banks, the other banks will find that their reserves and deposits have gone up equally, so their reserves-to-deposits ratio will have risen. These other banks will now have excess reserves, and in turn can afford to buy securities or make loans. The process of making loans and buying securities. so that total bank deposits rise, can go on until some bank needs to hold the available quantity of reserve assets and till money. This process is known as the 'credit multiplier'.
>
> Conversely, if a bank feels short of reserves assets or till money it can get hold of more by selling securities or by reducing its loans. If it is in a great hurry it can call in existing loans, but this is not regarded as a sensible policy; the kind of customer whose credit elsewhere is good enough for him to be able to pay off a loan at short notice is the sort a banker would rather not lose, while the less desirable customers could not pay up quickly if called on. If the bank has more time, it can let its total loans go down by not making new ones as fast as the old ones are paid off. The reduction in loans or sale of securities lowers deposits, with the original bank or with other banks; the process of shrinkage of deposits must go on until the banks as a whole are satisfied with the ratio between their deposits and the amount of reserve assets and till money that they are holding.

The great bulk of personal saving is channelled through the financial institutions (including pension funds), who in turn act as investors; and the major part of borrowing by wage and salaried employees is in the form of mortgages, i.e., investment of those savings by the building societies in property.

Official statistics do not, of course, analyse matters from a class standpoint and we are obliged to fall back on conventional categories. With this 'warning', we can illustrate the structure of UK financial markets through the diagram in Fig. 15-1.

We can simplify this picture by seeing it as a flow between households

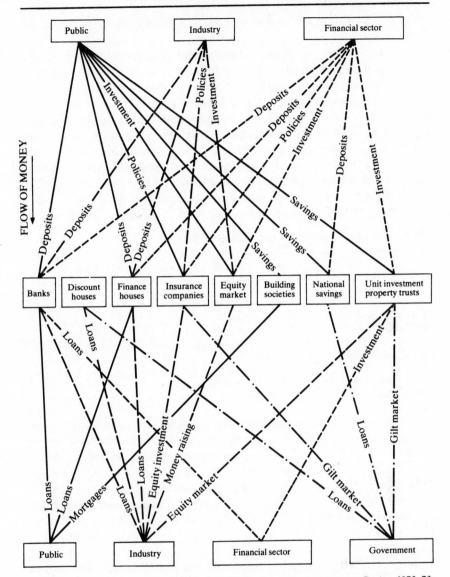

Fig. 15-1 The structure of UK financial markets. (*Source: Financial Services Review 1972–73*, Gower Economic Publications, Gower Press, 1972)

(the personal sector), companies (other than financial), financial institutions, and the government.

It is possible to set out the transactions within these sectors (including also an overseas sector) and show the net balances between the sectors. Since one sector's surplus must mean another sector's deficit, the sum of the sector's deficits and surpluses must cancel each other out (apart from errors of calculation). If we do that for the years 1974 to 1978, we get Table 15-4.

What Table 15-4 suggests is that the substantial deficit in the public sector and that of industrial and commercial companies have been financed through the surpluses of the personal sector as well as through borrowing from the financial sector. A very large part of personal savings, as we have already indicated, is channelled through the insurance companies, pension funds, bank deposits, building societies, etc., who, in buying government bonds as well as shares and lending to companies, finance both the government and the industrial and commercial sector. The rise in savings of the personal sector (personal disposable income not spent on consumption) has been one of the most striking developments of the seventies, rising from an average of 7.3 per cent for 1966–9 to 15.7 per cent for 1978–9.

Table 15-4 Sector surpluses and deficits (£ billion)

Year	Public sector	Overseas sector	Personal sector	Industrial and commercial companies	Financial institutions
1974	−4.8	+3.7	+4.9	−4.4	−0.7
1975	−7.9	+1.8	+6.9	−0.4	−1.0
1976	−8.3	+1.1	+7.9	−1.0	−0.8
1977	−5.6	−0.3	+8.0	−1.8	−1.2
1978	−7.3	−0.3	+9.8	−2.3	−1.2

Source: Bank of England Quarterly Bulletin, recent issues.

The rise in personal savings, however, is not just the result of the spread of pension schemes, etc., but also the result of the effect of inflation. As inflation reduces the purchasing power of money assets, people feel obliged to save more in order to preserve the real value of those assets. If we look at the flow of funds not in nominal terms but taking inflation into account, a rather different picture begins to emerge. The personal sector holds monetary assets which decline in value with inflation. The public sector debt is held in the form of fixed interest securities, and the real burden of interest charges falls with inflation. The corporate sector holds its debt in various forms, including fixed interest debt, which it has used to buy physical assets, which rise in value with inflation.

We cannot say that the financial *institutions* that channel private savings lose; on the whole, their rate of return (as we suggest later) has held up well. The most likely outcome is that it is the premium payers and policy holders—i.e., the bulk of small savers—who lose out in terms of real benefits and pensions received. In that sense a transfer of resources takes place.[2]

[2] For an attempt to adjust the flow of funds for inflation see Taylor and Threadgold (1979).

While the financial institutions have grown in importance in the economy, there has also been a redistribution of capital between them, to which we now turn.

15-5 CHANGES IN THE DISTRIBUTION OF CAPITAL BETWEEN FINANCIAL INSTITUTIONS

A picture of the interconnections between the financial and other sectors of the economy was given in Fig. 15-1. In a broad sense, financial institutions can be divided into two: the banking sector (of which the clearing banks are the most important), and the other financial institutions, of which the insurance companies, pension funds, and building societies are the major components.

For historical reasons the UK has long had a very well developed capital market but there has been a further important growth in the financial and credit system. The following two changes stand out as important. First, financial intermediaries have become far more important as the main channel for the funds of the personal sector. Second, insurance companies, pension funds, and building societies have become more important for personal savings relative to the banks. On average for the years 1972–6, 90 per cent of all personal savings in the UK were in the form of investment in housing, pension funds, and life assurance. Deposits with building societies have risen to become the biggest single outlet (£3580 million in 1976), whereas the share of bank deposits has declined. The cash flow of life companies and pension funds increased from 3.5 per cent of GDP in 1966 to 5.1 per cent in 1977 (when it reached £6.3 billion).

Two important reasons for the growth in these forms of saving are the tax advantages that such institutions have, and the tax relief on mortgage payments.[3]

One result has been conflict between sections of capital engaged in finance—in particular, between the banks and the building societies. Just such a conflict contributed to the credit and competition policy of 1971, which removed many of the restrictions on competition for deposits. In the circumstances at the time, the main banks as well as the 'fringe banks' lent heavily to property companies (who could claim tax relief on their borrowing, which therefore increased their rate of return). Following their lead, the insurance companies and industrial and commercial firms plunged in. With

[3] Owner occupiers receive tax relief on their mortgage payments (unlike other kinds of personal borrowing) and are exempt from capital gains tax on their principal residence. In the case of life assurance, half of all premiums paid can be deducted from taxable income, amounting at 1978 rates to a 17 per cent subsidy on the premiums. The funds of insurance companies are treated in a favourable way for tax purposes and little tax in fact is actually paid. And in the the case of pension funds, contributions are exempted from taxable income, and no tax is levied on the investment income of such funds. For all this, see Kay and King (1978).

the onset of the economic crisis in 1973, credit restrictions were imposed and interest rates rose sharply. Property companies began to find it hard to renew deposits in the money market, and in November 1973 London and County Securities was in danger of collapse. Confidence began to weaken, a series of companies, including such then prestigious names as Slater Walker, were in danger. But even more striking than the danger of collapse was the massive support operation mounted by the Bank of England and the clearing banks. The so-called 'lifeboat' support at its peak reached a figure of nearly £1200 million. With powerful memories of 1929–31, when the bank failures triggered off the world economic crisis, the main public and private financial organizations acted decisively. It was a demonstration of how much had changed since the inter-war years. The outcome of that financial crisis was a series of rationalizations and acquisitions that 're-concentrated' financial capital by eliminating a number of independent financial institutions that had collapsed or were in danger.

The third major change, stimulated by competition not only between UK financial institutions but from foreign financial institutions, has been the renewed move by the major financial firms to diversify into other sectors of finance and to form financial conglomerates (see further Chapters 14 and 17).

It is when we look at the investment policies of the financial institutions that we see the fourth main change. Collectively they have become the owners of 50 per cent or more of UK-listed ordinary shares. In 1977 estimates suggested that insurance companies and pension funds accounted for 36 per cent of UK-listed ordinary shares, divided almost equally between insurance companies and pension funds. The financial institutions have bought shares from individuals and they are the biggest single buyers of new share issues. This in turn has raised major questions as to the relationship between institutional investors and the active direction of the companies in which they have shareholdings. In general this has been of an 'arms-length' character, but as institutional investment in shares has become more important both for the institutions and for the companies whose shares are held, and as difficulties have increased for UK companies, so the conventions have begun to break down. Previous organizational forms have proved inadequate and led to new attempts to form a coherent block of institutional investors. More generally, the Bank of England has sponsored a City Liaison Committee, composed of representatives of the main associations from the City, which meets quarterly and has a series of subcommittees dealing with capital markets, the EEC, taxation, and other areas (not so far named).

However, the financial institutions are also major holders of government securities and property as well as other miscellaneous investments, and Table 15-5 gives some idea of the distribution and magnitude of the holdings by only one part of the financial sector over the years 1975–8.

Table 15-5 Insurance companies and pension funds: breakdowns of investments (% of total investments at end-year market values)

	Short-term assets	British group security	Company security	Property	Other investments	Total (£b)
1975	7	16	47	18	12	40.6
1976	6	21	44	18	11	46.3
1977	5	24	45	18	7	65.2
1978	5	24	43	18	10	76.3

Source: Posner (1979).

So far we have discussed the growth in the importance of financial capital and, though we have noted their rise as investors in ordinary shares, we have not examined the financing of industrial and commercial companies, to which we now turn.

15-6   THE FINANCING OF INDUSTRIAL AND COMMERCIAL COMPANIES

Firms that wish to enlarge the scale of their operations can use money capital derived from three main sources: their own retained earnings, loans (short and long term), and new issues of shares. For historical reasons (see Chapter 6) the company sector has tried to meet the greater part of its financial requirements from its own earnings. The advantages to firms of doing so are that the company then has no obligation to third parties; its availability is more certain than short- or medium-term finance (which, for instance, can be made difficult by a credit squeeze or a sudden shift in interest rates): and there are no cash costs in servicing it, whereas the movement of interest rates cannot be predicted.

A more comprehensive picture can be given by looking at Fig. 15-2, which shows the sources and uses of funds of industrial and commercial companies.

For a number of reasons the degree of dependence on retained earnings was reduced after 1965. The 1965 company tax reform, introducing corporation tax, made interest on borrowing tax deductible and so created powerful advantages in increasing the debt element in the company's resources. Preference shares were virtually killed off as a result. A more specific and contingent cause was the falling rate of return in some sectors, especially manufacturing, which combined with sharply rising prices of energy and materials created a liquidity crisis in 1974. Bank borrowing rose sharply over the period; the ratio of debt (net of cash) to equity for

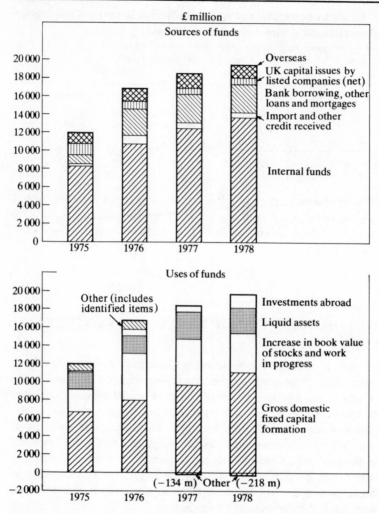

£ million

Sources of funds

Overseas
UK capital issues by
listed companies (net)
Bank borrowing, other
loans and mortgages
Import and other
credit received

Internal funds

1975 1976 1977 1978

Uses of funds

Other (includes
identified items)

Investments abroad

Liquid assets

Increase in book value
of stocks and work
in progress

Gross domestic
fixed capital
formation

(−134 m) Other (−218 m)

1975 1976 1977 1978

Fig. 15-2 Sources and uses of capital funds of industrial and commercial companies. (*Source: Economic Trends,* January 1980)

manufacturing and distribution companies increased from 18.2 per cent in 1966 to 50.3 per cent in 1975.[4]

Industrial and commercial companies evidently felt, however, that they had increased their debt to an undesirable degree, and the revival in new issues on the stock exchange in 1975 was partly in order to repay debt with

---

[4] Tax relief and situations where profits rise sharply over the rate of interest naturally increase the advantages of borrowing. On the other hand, a company that runs into difficulties in a situation where it is burdened with heavy fixed interest commitments faces bankruptcy or loss of control.

equity shares, which did not require fixed interest payments to be made. In 1979–80 there were once again signs of a gathering liquidity crisis.

As we have shown, there has been a revival of new issues, partly to reduce the high gearing that arose from increased bank lending. In general, however, new issues form a very small part of companies' financial sources. The costs of new issues are substantial, and are cheaper the larger the issue; large companies, therefore, are favoured as against smaller ones.

With respect to sources of funds, two deserve to be specially listed. One is the large amounts made available by governments in various forms as shown in Chapter 10; the other is the large inflow from foreign-based multi-nationals to their UK subsidiaries, although the greater part of this has to do with US and other firms involved in North Sea oil. That balance is changing as profits rise relative to North Sea oil investment and are repatriated. That inflow does not directly improve the productive power of UK manufacturing.

When we examine the uses of funds then, apart from investment in fixed capital formation (which we deal with directly in Chapter 18), there are again two important features. One is the large outflow for investment abroad, much of which is taking the form of acquisitions in Western Europe, the US, and other parts of the world. As a percentage of total capital expenditure by industrial and commercial companies, long-term investment overseas averaged 13.3 per cent 1963–7; 14.6 per cent 1968–72; and 15.8 per cent 1973–7. Undoubtedly this is part of the strategy of large companies to achieve higher rates of return than achieved or expected in the UK as well as a reflection of their need to be able to challenge competitors on a world scale.[5]

The second feature is the large (although annually fluctuating, amounts that companies have spent on buying firms, as against investment in new productive capacity, and in fact much of the finance raised through new issues has been used for acquisitions. Expenditure on acquiring subsidiaries by quoted firms in manufacturing averaged (as a percentage of expenditure on fixed assets) 21.7 per cent for 1959–63; 35.8 per cent 1964–8; and 24 per cent 1969–75. Some companies have also built up large cash accumulations and holdings of government bonds, etc., partly by borrowing and partly by running down investment (the most striking case being that of GEC, with cash resources of over £700 million in 1979–80, much of it earmarked for an acquisition programme).

---

[5] 'That the desire to derive a larger proportion of profits overseas has been sharpened by the deterioration in the economic and financial climate in this country is very probable.' Evidence by the Accepting Houses Committee to the Wilson Committee. Vol. 5, p. 39. HMSO, March 1978.

15-7 CONCLUSION

This chapter reinforces the view of an economy with a highly developed financial sector that has grown in importance, and an industrial sector that appears to be losing ground within the UK faster than its rivals in other countries and that has turned towards a restructuring of ownership and overseas expansion rather than the major programmes of modernization needed.

FURTHER READING

For statistical series on economic sectors see the *Annual Abstract of Statistics*, and the Blue Books on *National Income and Expenditure*.

For an analysis of sectoral changes see Ray (1979) and Blackaby (1979a and 1979b); there are also valuable series in Bacon and Eltis (1978).

On the growth in the financial sector see Revell (1973); on changes within the financial sector see the books already referred to by Channon (1977 and 1978).

For a survey of sources and uses of funds by companies see series in the Central Statistical Office's *Economic Trends* (monthly and also an annual survey) and *Financial Statistics*.

For a discussion of the relationship between industry and finance see Thompson (1977). On land ownership see Massey and Catalano (1979); and on capital and the urban economy see Castells (1978), Holland (1975), and Broadbent (1977).

SIXTEEN

THE FIRM

Sam Aaronovitch

16-1 'CAPITAL' AND FIRMS

In this chapter we propose to look more closely at the firm itself, its ownership and control, and at the pricing and investment decisions firms must make.

Resources that function as capital serve to produce surplus value, either directly or indirectly by providing conditions necessary for the surplus to be realized. Whereas production, distribution, and exchange become ever more social in character through an expanding, complex division of labour, the appropriation of the surplus in its various forms is based on private ownership of the means of production, distribution, and exchange. In this scheme, as we presented it in earlier chapters, capitalists are constituted as such by reason of their ownership of functioning capital; they are in that sense the representatives of capital. The structure of the system imposes certain requirements on capital but it is not the inanimate elements of capital (whether money, equipment, raw materials) that plan, produce and accumulate. The capitalist is therefore more than a representative of the category 'capital', just as the worker is more than a 'hand' in the production process. But it is his place in the set of property relationships that defines the capitalist.

We have also made the point that capitalist economies are composed of blocks of capital that appear in various legal forms as firms or combinations of firms.

The fact that blocks of capital may be acquired by the state or built up by the state (as, for instance, rail transport and nuclear energy in the UK) partly expresses the fact that the increasingly social character of production and distribution may require resources that go beyond those available to private capital (see our discussion on the varied reasons for state ownership in Chapter 10). In democratic societies, the state owned enterprises become arenas of conflict between those who wish them to help maintain the dominant system of private ownership and those who wish them to become levers of change in the interests of the majority.

There is no more familiar story than the evolution of the firm: from the entrepreneur who owned and directly controlled the enterprise, through various forms of partnership and associations, to the full development of the modern joint stock company, which has become the dominant form of the organization of capital in all advanced capitalist economies.

The rise of joint stock companies came about first because the growing scale of operations required the mobilization of resources that went beyond the fortunes of the individual entrepreneurs. Second, the development of the credit and financial system opened up the possibility of such an extension of scale. Third, the creation of a secondary market in shares made it easier to mobilize financial resources. Finally, legal protection of investors had become an important issue. With the growth and dominance of joint stock companies, the *functions* of capital (ensuring that the circuit of capital is successfully carried out) become separated from the *ownership* of capital, a theme to which we shall shortly return.

In a much quoted paragraph, Marx (1978, p. 427) wrote:

> The capital which in itself rests on a social mode of production and presupposes a social concentration of means of production and labour-power is here directly endowed with the form of social capital of directly associated individuals as distinct from private capital, and its undertakings assume the form of social undertakings as distinct from private undertakings. It is the abolition of capital and private property within the framework of capitalist production.

Capital can only function through units of activity, whether it be a plant, a warehouse, or an office, but the starting point in our analysis is the ownership of capital blocks—the entities that may acquire units, construct new ones, recombine, and diversify in innumerable ways. In so far as firms represent distinct blocks of capital, we can analyse them as critical centres for the ownership, organization, and direction of capital. Different kinds of firms may represent, to some degree, different kinds of capital (as we saw in the preceding chapter) as well as a division of labour between capitalist groups within the same sphere.

In examining the objectives of firms, we are inevitably brought back to our discussion on the nature of capital as based on accumulation—i.e., on a process of expansion. But the development of large joint stock companies whose legal owners are the holders of ordinary shares has raised important questions of analysis.

16-2 OWNERSHIP VERSUS CONTROL?

The growth of firms that operate on a massive scale, often across continents, has meant that their operations are more and more directed and executed by salaried employees at the highest level. Firms have become bigger and increasingly diversified by products and countries. High levels of specialization in every field of the firm's activities (scientific and technical, production, distribution, management, finance, marketing, etc.) become vital. A large administrative and managerial group has come into being which, as indicated earlier, is directly responsible for ensuring that the functions of capital are successfully carried through, but as a result these functions become separated from the ownership of capital.

The other major aspect of joint stock companies is that they are owned by the owners of the ordinary shares in those companies and that these shares can be (in the case of the UK, and especially for large companies) freely traded on the stock exchange. A body of shareholders has arisen, the vast majority of whom are not (nor need be) involved in the functioning of any given firm.

These two developments have given rise to the debate on the separation of ownership from control that underlies the greater part of the discussion among economists on the theory of the firm and its objectives. Essentially, the argument runs as follows: shareholders are primarily interested in maximizing profit, which can be interpreted as maximizing the present value of their shares (which, in turn, depends on some optimal combination of flow of dividends and capital gains); managers, on the other hand, are concerned with some combination of growth and size that confers the advantages that most interest them, such as status, high salary levels, etc.

The theories of Marris (1964) and Williamson (1970), which assume the dominance of managers, are of this kind but, because firms are still owned by shareholders, build in constraints on managerial objectives. Of course, depending upon what objectives managers may be said to pursue, such theories need not be of the profit maximizing type but may assume pursuit of a 'reasonable' or 'satisfactory' rate of return. These theories, we shall suggest, are 'misplaced' but it was an important advance to develop a theory of the large firm that explicitly recognized the significance of firms as joint stock companies with freely traded shares.

We can approach the issues raised in the following ways:

(a) We can ask whether in a capitalist economy firms have critical imperatives imposed on them by the way the system functions which are independent of the balance between shareholders/managerial control.
(b) We can examine the roles of shareholders and managers to look for likely sources of convergence and divergence.
(c) We can review the evidence for and against the main thesis in terms of who the controllers are and the performance of firms.

Our thesis has been that the drive to accumulate is built into the structure of capital and that this leads to rivalry between blocks of capital. This rivalry in turn imposes on firms (as blocks of capital) the need to seek the highest possible profits or risk extinction or subordination. This is because, over time, profits are the necessary source of increased economic strength. The 'highest possible profit' is not, however, an unambiguous term.

Perhaps the bigger problem is that it makes sense only in terms of long-term strategies. The conventional short-run profit maximizing thesis requires knowledge, over the short run, of a firm's marginal cost and marginal revenue, which, in turn, implies knowledge of the demand curve facing the firm. Such knowledge is even less likely over longer time horizons, and the apparent 'determinateness' of the theory has been undermined by the fact that most industries in most advanced capitalist economies are dominated by small numbers of firms, a situation that produces conditions of interdependence and uncertainty.

Firms are required to adopt relatively long-run strategies in pursuit of the highest possible profit also because of their relationships with each other. Goodwill and contractual agreements are often important (and trade between firms makes up a large part of total economic exchange). Further, the building up of powerful market positions as a result of technological development, acquisitions, etc., may take time and involve a large number of 'sub-strategies', such as subsidizing loss makers, pursuing rapid growth even if rates of return are temporarily depressed as a result, and phases of consolidation (as after making substantial acquisitions). These sub-strategies are constant once adopted but alternate over time.

The need for the greatest possible profit over time, however loosely formulated, assumes that the forces of rivalry in the end assert themselves and the monopoly positions and complete dominance are actually unstable or potentially unstable so that they require continuous effort to keep them intact.

To the degree, however, that firms singly or by collusion weaken rivalry, other objectives held by the firm's controllers may have greater play, and it would be absurd not to recognize this. In the circumstances, therefore, firms are seen to adopt many different sub-strategies and, according to the degree of long-run dominance, even different longer-run strategies.

The drive to accumulate in conditions of rivalry also provides the context in which the objectives singled out by the 'managerialists' are most easily explained: the need for growth and for large size, both absolute and relative, and more is said about this in the next chapter. Of course, some firms are more able than others to formulate and carry through appropriate sub-strategies; and many forces act on firms (apparently at random) to weaken or improve their growth rates, profit rates, and chances of survival. But this is the case without regard to the distribution of control between shareholders and controllers. This leads us directly to our second point.

Before looking at the roles of shareholders and managers separately, we should note why the share market is an important factor in the calculation of firms. Collectively, shareholders hold the key to legal control. Because shares are marketable, company control is itself a marketable commodity, and this is especially important for those who are employed in companies. But the role of the credit and financial system also makes the share market an important factor in the calculations of firms. The valuation put up by the share market on a company's shares affects its 'standing' in the market for funds (both borrowing and equity share issues). It affects the ease with which a company can make acquisitions or defend itself against a takeover threat. If, for instance, a firm with a high price/earnings ratio, on the basis of a share exchange as valued on the market, takes over a firm whose shares are priced lower but whose earnings are the same, the acquiring firm will immediately increase its earnings per share. A firm whose share price climbs relative to others can, on this basis, buy assets more cheaply. A firm whose share price falls relative to the value of its assets may become a bargain to an acquirer. Of course, earnings per share will not continue to improve if the acquired firm is not made more profitable.

The centralization of money so that it can perform a role as capital has the effect of dispersing the holdings of shares among a much larger group of people. This dispersal is accomplished as large blocks of shares are broken up through legacies, mergers reshuffle owners, and the operations of the share market take their effect. The larger firms become arenas in which relatively small blocks of holdings become instrumental in the struggle for control of the total committed capital.

At any one moment we can place shareholders in the following categories:

(i) Small shareholders (the bulk of shareholders)—i.e., those whose *total* shareholdings produce an income small relative to their total income from employment, and who are, in effect, long-term lenders to companies. They play no part in the companies' activities, they are concerned only with regular and preferably rising dividends, and they are undoubtedly separated from control. Nor are capital gains their main concern, because buying and selling shares involves costs of brokerage, etc., that are out of proportion to their likely gains (unless handled through unit trusts, for instance).

(ii) Large shareholders who have diversified portfolios and who are essentially rentiers, uninvolved in the companies whose shares they hold at any given moment.

(iii) Large shareholders who are in a controlling position in one or more companies in which they hold substantial blocks of shares, even though they may have diversified portfolios. They are 'insiders' with respect to the firms in which they exercise control and 'outsiders' with respect to their other holdings.

Categories (ii) and (iii) will vary in their attitude to dividends as against retained earnings (with the prospect of capital gains), depending on their attitudes to risk and their varying tax situations.

Such large shareholders may be thought of as individuals and/or as companies who construct pyramids of control—as, for instance, an individual holding a controlling block of shares in Company A, which in turn holds a controlling interest in Company B, which in turn holds a controlling interest in Company C, etc.

(iv) We should now add the category of financial institutions as shareholders who have traditionally been concerned with security and transferability. But as the size of their share stake has grown and the problems of British capitalism affected many large firms, their interest in control has grown and must be expected to intensify.

For non-financial companies who hold shares in other companies, the crucial factor is likely to be control, but sometimes they may hold shares in rival companies as a hedge against losing ground to them (e.g. Imperial Tobacco's secret holdings in Gallaghers, which they were obliged to dispose of). If this classification is accurate, it is a mistake to lump shareholders together in a single category with interests that can be expressed in a single immediate objective.

When we turn to managers it is even more important to recognize that we are concerned not with the managerial staff as a whole but with a relatively small group of top executives who are in controlling positions, a group that may overlap with certain categories of shareholders. Controllers may be substantial shareholders with diversified holdings and/or with significant holdings in the firms in which they operate. Their salaries may include not only the 'going rate' for the job, together with dividends, but a way of extracting profits before they are recorded as available for dividends and new investment—what we might call 'the profits of control'. Controllers may have only minor or limited shareholdings but be able to extract profits of control on top of 'normal' salaries from the rentiers who are the legal owners of the firm's equity. It seems to be the case that controllers wish to cut in on shareholding and may be offered favourable terms on which to do so.

In all these senses, the controllers are nearer to the imperatives that the system imposes on the firm than the large number of small shareholders. Successful pursuit over time (with appropriate sub-strategies) of the highest possible profit is the necessary condition for meeting all those objectives, commonly described as managerial, such as desire for power, status, perks which increase with size, job security, etc. The coincidence of interest and frequently of role (see Nyman and Silberston, 1978) of large shareholders and controllers justifies their inclusion as the key element in the class of capitalists. The nature of the divergence between non-shareholder controllers and shareholders is not therefore of the character that conventional theory describes.

In everyday life, controllers who are not buttressed by share control face problems of security. And as firms grow in size, the possibilities of conflict between top executives over policy and perspectives can become typical. As a result, given the 'mixed' nature of the controllers, differences between them may be as significant as the alleged differences between the categories of controllers and shareholders.

Our third approach is to review the evidence for the existence or extent of so-called managerially controlled firms and the tests of performance. And here the first point to be made is that the separation of ownership from control is primarily an Anglo–American thesis. It is *not* valid in general for Japan, West Germany, France, or Belgium, to name those countries where studies have been made. It is therefore *not* valid for the most important sectors of capitalism outside the US. Theories of the firm, therefore, based on these countries have no particular validity for firms based in other countries.[1] The second point, however, is that the evidence of such separation in the case of both the US and the UK has been taken too much for granted. We shall report only on the most recent work on the UK, that by Nyman and Silberston (1978), based on a study of the top 250 firms, of which 20 were studied intensively.

Their study, they say, 'does suggest that the position taken by Galbraith, Marris, and others—that most large corporations are controlled by managements with little proprietary interest in their companies—is not warranted by the evidence' (p. 80). They accepted as their definition of control that put by Zeitlin (1974):

> When the concrete structure of ownership and of intercorporate relationships makes it probable that an identifiable group of proprietary interests will be able to realise their corporate objectives over time, despite resistance, then we may say that they have 'control' of the corporation.

Nyman and Silberston were led by their studies to believe that of the top 250 firms, 56.25 per cent can be classified as 'owner-controlled' according to one of the factors considered important.[2]

Nyman and Silberston looked at the percentage of votes held by a known individual, institution, or cohesive group: the percentage of votes owned by the board of directors and their families; the identity of the chairman and managing director, and their relationship to the firm's founder and his family. Potential control was assumed to be present with a shareholding of five per cent. This is an underestimate of the extent of ownership-control because there are many giant private firms big enough to be in the top 250 that are excluded, such as Littlewoods and the Vestey Organization, and much is also concealed by nominee holdings.

Their research therefore suggests that the 'managerialists' are wrong with

---

[1] For West Germany, France, and Belgium, see Jacquemin and De Jong (1977). Other critical reviews may be found in Burch (1972), Chevallier (1969), Fitch and Oppenheimer (1970), Zeitlin (1974).

[2] From their research it appears that ownership-control is predominant in food, electrical engineering, construction, retailing, merchanting, and miscellaneous services; management control predominates in chemicals, metal goods (not elsewhere specified), building materials.

respect to the UK; and it appears also to be the case that managerial control is not increasing; nor is there evidence that the larger firms are, the more likely they are to be managerially controlled.

Analysis of the ownership-control question takes the form of setting up the hypothesis that managerially controlled firms will pursue growth at the expense of profitability, whereas owner-controlled firms will pursue profitability rather than growth. Owner-controlled firms should have higher rates of return and lower growth rates than managerially controlled firms. If we look at a whole series of studies (summarized in Nyman and Silberston, 1978) there is *some* support for the proposition that owner-controlled firms have higher rates of return than managerially controlled firms, but not significantly so.

On the view that we have presented, the character of control should have little impact in differentiating the behaviour of large oligopolistic firms whose sub-strategies are shifting over time, and the evidence does not seriously contradict this. But, of course, the empirical evidence itself is extremely shaky.

In pursuing their objectives, there are two vital areas of decision making for firms: the pricing decision and the investment decision, which are dealt with in the next two sections.

16-3 THE PRICING PROCESS

Within our framework of analysis pricing has two functions. The first is as a method of distributing the surplus produced in society, within the class of owners of capital and between capital and labour, and also a means of *redistributing* the surplus—as, for instance, by the exercise of monopoly power. But in addition it is the means of realizing the surplus embodied in the product or service; buyers must be available to buy the commodities at the price that allows the circuit of capital to continue its course. Although this is to look at pricing at a very high level of abstraction, the two functions continue to operate at all levels.

Here, again, our starting point is capital and its movement, not the product and the product market. In neo-classical theory, prices are set by the interaction of supply and demand; prices move from competitive prices under conditions of perfect competition to monopoly prices, along a continuum that encompasses monopolistic competition and oligopoly. In our framework, firms are engaged in enlarging their share of the economic surplus produced or expected; their pricing behaviour is part of this objective. The growth of the firm means enlarging the capital circuit and the attempts to grow involves competitive struggle. This competition to grow is by way of investment, innovation, and acquisition of other firms.

As concentration and centralization of capital grow, the giant firms attempt increasingly to mould the market structures that they favour; they are engaged in a continuous process of restructuring markets and products. Capital mobility, which has grown in importance with the development of capitalism (as the advance of the multi-nationals testifies) leads to massive efforts to break down barriers between industries, markets, and economies, so acting as a force towards equalizing profit rates. Increasingly giant firms are compared with each other independently of the industries or markets in which they are currently engaged.

Essentially, in this approach, *all* firms are price setters and *in general* prices are not determined by fluctuations in supply and demand, even in a short-term sense. This is not the same as saying that prices do not fluctuate or change. But it is more fruitful to think of pricing behaviour as deriving from the *character* of the conflict between firms for the economic surplus (and that will differ between different situations and conditions) and also from the degree of dominance that firms may have established singly or in collusion. With the emergence of giant firms, each with the capacity to influence the position of their rivals, the forces for price collusion become powerful and the dangers of price warfare are viewed typically more as threats to secure agreement rather than as desired strategies. The preference for non-price competition—e.g., promotion, advertising, product development and differentiation—is, of course, a matter of everyday observation.

We have already made the point earlier in the chapter that the drive for profitable accumulation cannot be understood in a short-run maximizing sense and, for the same reasons, pricing rules are not set by firms on that basis either.[3] More specifically, the reasons for this include the following:

(a) The necessity for long-term strategies (as discussed in the previous section).
(b) Varying attitudes to risk between firms, which also affect the character of their strategies.
(c) Interdependence between firms in conditions of oligopoly and the threat of entry.

[3] In general, if profit π equals total revenue TR minus total cost TC, and these are functions of output Q, then to maximize π we need

$$\frac{d\pi}{dQ} = \frac{dR}{dQ} - \frac{dC}{dQ} = 0 \qquad \text{i.e. } \frac{dR}{dQ} = \frac{dC}{dQ} \qquad \text{i.e. } MR = MC$$

But second order conditions have also to be met:

$$\frac{d^2\pi}{dQ^2} < 0 \quad \text{ or } \quad \frac{d^2\pi}{dQ^2} = \frac{d^2R}{dQ^2} - \frac{d^2C}{dQ^2} < 0$$

In conditions of monopoly, a firm pursuing profit maximization would set a price where $MC = MR$, which would be below average cost, and therefore monopoly profits would be earned. The monopoly firm, however, need not maximize profits but has an area of discretion. Firms are assumed to gain in discretion as market structures move away from perfect competition towards monopoly.

(d) The specific characteristics of the markets in which firms are involved.
(e) The continuously changing environment.

There is general agreement on this and that the various pricing strategies firms are observed to use do not yield short-run profit maximizing results. Given that this is so, we can briefly review a number of important pricing strategies. There is no reason to think that a firm is committed to one strategy for ever: according to circumstances, it may go through a whole range of strategies.

First, surveys have suggested that many large firms attempt to practise a pricing policy based on a target rate of return. A classic and much quoted example is provided by General Motors, who pioneered this pricing strategy. General Motors set itself the objective of earning, on average over time, a 15 per cent post-tax return on total invested capital. As summarized by Scherer (1980, p. 185):

> Since it does not know how many autos will be sold in a forthcoming year, and hence what the average cost per unit (including prorogated fixed costs) will be, it calculates costs on the assumption of *standard volume*—i.e. operation at 80 per cent of conservatively rated capacity. A *standard price* is next calculated by adding to average cost per unit at standard volume a sufficient profit margin to yield the desired 15 percent after-tax return on capital. A top level price policy committee then uses the standard price as the initial basis of its price decision, making adjustments upward or downward to take into account actual and potential competition, business conditions, long-run strategic goals, and other factors.

Scherer notes that the realized return on invested capital has in fact averaged well over the 15 per cent target rate because sales have exceeded standard volume in most years.

To be able to hold to such a strategy, of course, is much more likely to be feasible for a market leader. The target rate of return will also be influenced by the financing requirements for the planned growth of the firm and the degree to which it proposes to depend on internal as against external sources of funds. Companies in monopoly positions can clearly compel their customers, through monopoly pricing, to finance the entire weight of the future expansion of the firm. This would be another case of pricing as an instrument for redistributing the surplus between firms.

In general the tendency has been for changes in demand to affect output more strongly than price, but we may guess that where changes in demand are substantial and persistent, firms will adopt different strategies, just as we would expect accelerating inflation to alter their behaviour.

A second strategy is that typified in *price leadership*, where, within a group of firms (commonly unequal in size, but this is not a necessary condition), one firm acts as price leader. This implies that other firms will follow and this is more likely to happen if either the price leader is a low cost producer in a powerful market position or price leadership is simply a device among a group of powerful firms to operate an informal price agreement that escapes the provisions of the law. In the first instance, price leadership may be a temporary phase in the strategy of a dominant firm and it may be threatened by entry from a powerful potential competitor. If the firm is not a low cost producer, then potential entry or an aggressive rival within the group may undermine its position.

Price leadership shades very easily into various kinds of average cost pricing of the sort that trade associations, when legal, commonly used. In these cases, the costs of a certain number of firms were averaged and a fixed mark-up applied, resulting in a common price for all firms. Where firms were anxious to avoid price warfare, price changes would be made when cost changes occurred that were common to all.

Another strategy is specifically connected with the threat of entry. As firms grow in size they are increasingly able to enter territory occupied by others, and in attempting to limit such entry the existing firms construct barriers of various kinds. Among such barriers pricing strategies may play a role.

Entry barriers are those that would make it harder for an entrant to compete with already established firms. Such barriers include cost advantages (specialized technology not generally available), consumer/customer preferences established through product development and advertising, some kind of contractual or monopoly ownership of vital materials, etc.

In order to examine the pricing strategies open to established firms we have to consider the scale of entry in relation to total demand and the elasticity of demand where new output comes onto the market. But there are two important assumptions that must be examined. The first assumption is that the potential entrant believes the established firms will *not* contract output but will, on the contrary, maintain it and allow prices to fall (dependent upon the elasticity of demand). The second is that the potential entrant believes the existing firms will expand output. In the first case the established firms seek to determine a 'limit price' that is higher than the competitive price to the extent that, with a given elasticity of demand, their costs are lower than the new entrant would actually face. In the second case the assumption that existing firms will simply maintain their output level is removed. Here existing firms build excess capacity as a deterrent to entry so that their ability to expand output is apparent. The building of excess capacity as a deterrent in conditions of oligopoly is a point we shall return to; but if the potential entrant understands this, then he might see little point in entry if the outcome may not only be below the existing level of profits, but even a loss. And if the existing firms believe the point has been taken, they can charge prices higher than would otherwise be possible. Excess capacity, of course, has a cost, and therefore the calculations on pricing can become very complex and the strategy misfire. We should note that the building of excess capacity is also used by oligopolists to threaten each other within the same sector or to deter overseas firms from building up new capacity.

Finally, we should mention predatory pricing, where a firm deliberately attempts to knock its rivals out of the market by cuts in price that competitors cannot match. Obviously this is a strategy available only to firms with large resources relative to their competitors. When the rivals have been eliminated or severely weakened and brought to heel, a different pricing level is established.

16-4   THE FIRM'S INVESTMENT DECISION

Within the framework of the capitalist economy as a whole, we have treated investment as the use of produced resources to continue and expand the process of capital accumulation. For each individual block of capital (which, for practical purposes at this level of discussion, we will simply identify with the firm), the investment decisions are decisions about its growth and the position relative to its rivals. The consequences for competition and monopoly are discussed in Chapter 17, and the levels, rate, and 'productivity' of investment are discussed in Chapter 18. Our aim in this section is much more limited: to look at the issues involved in financing the investment decision and to discuss these further in the context of methods used by firms to 'appraise' investment proposals.

For an individual firm, growth not only means investing in new capacity but acquiring other going concerns (although for firms collectively, acquiring other firms is essentially a redistribution of the control of capital as compared with investment, which adds to the stock of capital equipment). The financial and credit system, however, functions in such a way that for any individual firm, acquisition may be more than the simple combination of two firms. The financial structure of the two companies may be such that a merger makes it possible to increase borrowing for further expansion. Again, if a firm's earnings per share rises as a result of the acquisition, its ability to raise funds on the market for further expansion may also increase.

Financing the Investment Decision

For any firm, investment must be financed either from internal or from external funds. Following Wood (1975), if we assume that firms seek a rate of return that would finance their growth strategies (something also considered by us in Section 16-3) the following financial ratios become relevant:

(a) The ratio of internal funds (retained earnings and provision for depreciation) to profits, to be called r.
(b) The ratio of external funds (new borrowing and share issues) to investment, to be called x.

(c) The ratio of the acquisition of financial assets, (cash, marketable securities, etc.) to investment, to be called f.

If P is the profit level and I the level of investment, then the company's capital spending is $(1+f)I$—i.e., the sum of its investment and its acquisitions of financial assets. The amount of external finance used is xI. The remainder must be financed internally—that is, $(1+f-x)I$, which must therefore be equal to the amount of internal finance rP. Therefore $rP=(1+f-x)I$ and $P=[(I+f-x)I]/r$. This is the equation firms must solve to determine the level of profits needed to finance any given level of investment.[4] However, in practice, firms cannot decide what their growth rate will be with certainty and all the elements of the equation will be estimated (and adjusted) in the light of the expected conditions confronting the firm. The solution therefore takes the form more of a series of iterations.

In selecting from among alternative investment projects, they have to consider the time pattern of expenditure and receipts as well as how the investment decision is to be financed. In the financing decision, the firm clearly has both short-term and long-term aspects to consider. In the short term it will have to have some regard to liquidity, given that the short-run cash flows are not fully predictable; but we can presume that firms will in general wish to keep their liquid funds at a minimum. Part of the firm's borrowing will be short term, normally in the form of bank borrowing. Longer-term borrowing typically involves debentures and loan stock. But borrowing raises questions of risk for both lenders and borrowers (in the latter case it raises the crucial issue of control). The gearing ratio for the firm is therefore itself an important decision.

As we discussed in an earlier section, the relatively low gearing ratio in the UK compared with firms in West Germany and Japan, among others, arises from the different relationship between financial and industrial capital. For the UK, whatever the gearing limit set by the firm on the basis of its expectations about future profitability and of the rate of interest, it would seek to reach those limits, since interest on debt is allowable against tax and the benefit of increased profitability will go to the firm and its shareholders. The scale of growth proposed and its financing are clearly interrelated

---

[4] Wood points out that these ratios correspond very closely with common accounting conventions used by firms.

The appropriation account:
> Profits + non-trading income − interest payments − taxation − dividends
> = Internal finance

The sources of funds account:
> Internal finance + proceeds of new share issues + net new borrowing
> = Total sources of funds

The uses of funds account:
> Investment + acquisition of financial assets
> = Total uses of funds

decisions and they necessarily involve the pricing decisions of the firms. For instance pursuing market share by price competition may produce a lower price–cost margin than would otherwise be desired, yet at the same time this may lower the preferred gearing ratio and call for a higher rate of return on the planned investment.

The problem that arises for the firm has been put very concisely by Wood (1975, pp. 99–100):

> ... the firm must know its growth rate before it can know its target rate of return, and, strictly speaking, it cannot know gk (the real rate of growth of the firm's stock of physical assets, net of depreciation) until it knows P (the minimum average profit rate which the firm considers it must exceed) since growth rate depends on what investment projects the firm decides to undertake.

One possible consequence of the limited relationship between industrial and financial capital and the heavy dependence on retained earnings by UK firms is to raise the yield necessary on a project. The tendency, therefore, will be to reduce the scope of investment more than would otherwise be the case. And it is obvious that, where substantial innovative risks are involved, as in areas of technology, this will make such investments less likely, unless firms believe they have little alternative.

Appraising the Investment Decision

Among large firms, a number of methods of appraising investment proposals have been developed and we are discussing them, partly because they represent attempts at a 'rational' method of choice (adopted also by nationalized industries), and partly because they offer the opportunity to bring out some of the constraints that firms have to face in making decisions. In making an investment decision, firms need to calculate the change in the firm's profits expected from the investment in relation to the costs of making it. If firms, for instance, have a target rate of return, then they need to calculate whether the proposed investment (or which of a number of investment proposals) will yield them that rate of return. Among the most widespread calculations used by firms are the so-called 'payback' method on the one side, and those grouped under the general heading of 'discounted cash flow' analysis (DCF) on the other. The assumptions involved in the latter are that money now is worth more than the same amount of money later; and that cash flows from an investment as they arise can be reinvested at the expected rate of return. The calculations are closely linked, therefore, to the concept of the rate of interest. At this stage we are concerned not with the theoretical debate as to what gives rise to interest and what determines its rate(s), but with the form in which matters appear to the firm. If a firm uses resources in one way rather than in another, the yield it would have got from the investment it chose *not* to follow is the opportunity cost of the investment it does make.

In the case of the payback method, the rule is to choose the investment that will repay the capital sum invested in the shortest possible time. Many companies (and this has been put forward by Unilever and others) prefer investments that can be recouped in five years or less. They prefer to finance investment out of retained earnings and they do not want these tied up for very long periods, since the future is uncertain. They wish to write off the outlay as quickly as possible. The criticism of this approach is that the firm does not consider the real gains from the investment that continue after the payback period; that it treats the time pattern of cash flows as equal, ignoring their variation over the period; and that uncertainty can be estimated by other and less crude means. Implicit in this approach is the requirement of a high rate of return (or, as we put it below, they are discounting at high rates of interest).

The two most popular types of discounted cash flow methods calculations are net present value (NPV) and the internal rate of return (IRR).

In the case of compound interest, an investment P_0 now would be worth $P(i+r)^n$ in n years time. Discounting is to do the opposite. It asks, if we expect a sum P_n at some time in the future, what would be its present value P_0 where P_n is discounted by the rate of interest?

We can express this in *net* terms—i.e., in each year consider revenue minus outlay to give net revenue and deduct the initial cost of the investment

$$\text{NPV}=\left[\frac{R_1}{(1+i)^1}+\frac{R_2}{(1+i)^2}+\dots+\frac{R_n}{(1+i)^n}\right]-C$$

$$=\sum_{t=1}^{n}\frac{R_t}{(1+i)^t}-C$$

where R is net cash flows, i the rate of interest, C the initial cost of the project, and n the project's expected life.

If NPV is negative, the project would be rejected. If, in comparing two projects A and B, the NPV of A was greater than that for B, A should be preferred. Account has been taken of the time pattern of cash flows. We shall come back to the question of the discount rate.

The internal rate of return is that rate of discount that would make the present value of expected future cash flows or receipts equal to the initial outlay. This can be expressed as

$$\sum_{t=1}^{n}\frac{R_t}{(1+d)^t}-C=0$$

where d is the discount rate that has to be found and that will equate

$$\sum_{t=1}^{n}\frac{R_t}{(1+d)^t}=C$$

In other words, d is the IRR. If that discount rate is equal to or greater than the cost of capital to the firm, then the project will be preferred, and similarly this can be used also to rank projects. There are technical problems involved in IRR, which relate to the ranking of projects and the possibility of multiple solutions to IRR, but we do not propose to pursue these and they can be followed in texts on managerial finance. In general, economists prefer NPV (modified in various ways) as offering the best approach.

The NPV calculations raise a series of important questions. The first relates to the objectives the firm sets itself. If the firm at one stage prefers projects that will expand sales even at the cost of depressing the expected rate of return, it may accept a lower or even non-existent gap between net revenue and the cost of capital. But, as we suggested, its strategies may change over time or vary in each of the markets in which it is involved. The choice of the discount rate raises problems of varying objectives. Similarly, because of oligopolistic interdependence, firms may pursue projects that rank lower than other projects available because these particular ones are needed to match the actions of rivals or preempt a market in a foreign country, etc. The second question concerns uncertainty rather than risk—the possibility that the environment may shift in a way that cannot be assigned any probabilities. Fear of this, of course, leads to very conservative strategies, of which the payback method is the most obvious. Third, there can be interdependence between the scale of the project and the rate of interest, so that the calculation becomes circular; moreover, the cost of capital may vary over time in a way that cannot be predicted. There is, fourth, the unreal assumption that the supply of capital is unlimited at the going rate. Firms will have varying attitudes towards the amount of debt they are prepared to incur; the capital market will discriminate between firms; new equity will cost the firm more than its existing shares.

As a concluding point these approaches, however modified, propose that projects be pursued if they meet, at the minimum, the cost of finance as determined by the market. And this is the recommendation successive governments have made to the nationalized industries.

FURTHER READING

For explicitly Marxist discussions see Baran and Sweezy (1968), O'Connor (1974), and Scott (1979).

For more general textbook reviews see Devine et al. (1979), Hay and Morris (1979), and Sawyer (1979). Books that have had a major influence have been Galbraith (1967), Penrose (1959), and Marris (1964).

For a review of evidence on ownership and control see Nyman and Silberston (1978).

Discussions and evidence on pricing can be found in the textbooks by Devine et al. (1979) and Hay and Morris (1979) referred to above. See also Coutts, Godley, and Nordhaus (1978), Sylos-Labini (1979), and Sawyer, Samson, and Aaronovitch (1979).

SEVENTEEN

THE REORGANIZING OF CAPITAL: CONCENTRATION AND CENTRALIZATION

Sam Aaronovitch

17-1 COMPETITION AND CONCENTRATION

Having defined capital as, in essence, a social relation, the restructuring of capital involves changes in the relationship not only of capital to labour, but of blocks of capital and of individual capitalists to each other. This chapter is mainly concerned with the second aspect, the restructuring of the relations between capitals.

The history of capitalism is a history of continuous and dynamic restructuring in a number of different ways and it has a variety of sources. One is the consequence of pursuing accumulation in conditions of rivalry. Within that context we can examine the processes of concentration and centralization, the role of technical change, and the tension between rivalry and monopoly.

A second source arises from periodic crises that give rise to capital reorganizations, weeding out weaker capitalist firms and re-creating the conditions for profitable accumulation. Schemes of rationalization are carried through in order to get rid of unprofitable sectors or 'over capacity' so that the remaining sectors can become more profitable. In this chapter we concern ourselves mainly with the most striking and important restructuring process: that which has given rise to high levels of concentration and centralization, and the growth of giant firms that are multi-product and that operate more and more on a world scale.

Although our focus is on the UK, the trend is inherent in all capitalist economies. It does not proceed at an even rate—we can see *waves* of restructuring—nor is it tied to the business cycle. In both conventional and Marxist economics, concentration and centralization are considered in relation to their impact on competition and monopoly and the spectrum between, but there are important differences in approach, which we shall deal with first. We then review the trends in concentration and centralization in the UK, and finally examine the main mechanisms that have acted to bring about the major post-war changes.

Conventional theory, which is strongly focused on products and the markets for them, begins typically with an examination of two polar cases: perfect competition at one end and pure monopoly at the other. Between them, along a continuum, lies a series of market structures that represent various mixtures of competition and monopoly. Perfect competition is defined as a situation of small firms producing for a given homogeneous product market, each firm too negligible to influence the price for its output. There are no barriers to firms' entering or leaving an industry: resources are perfectly mobile; factor markets are perfect and undifferentiated; economies of scale are trivial; and firms maximize their profits. If positive profits are being made, firms enter the industry and ensure that in the long term, firms produce that output at which production costs are at their minimum. This model is also important because its properties are often used to establish the benchmark for good performance in terms of productive efficiency, market efficiency, and the optimal allocation of resources.[1] It is assumed that any change that moves away from an atomistic structure will represent a move from competition towards monopoly.

Conventional theory does not occupy itself with the historical process by which perfect competition gives way to monopoly. Essentially, it has set up a series of market structures lying along the spectrum and has attempted to define the properties of these structures in terms of what determines the level of prices in equilibrium and to compare these structures.

The model of perfect competition was amended and developed into a theory of imperfect competition because of dilemmas in the theory itself as well as through observation of the practices of firms. If long-period average costs fall as output expands, because of economies of scale, marginal cost is less than average cost; and if competition means that each producer can sell as much as he pleases at the going market price, then to maximize profits he will expand output so long as marginal cost is less than price. In this case there is no position of long-period equilibrium until one firm has established a monopoly.

Moving up the spectrum towards monopoly, we encounter oligopoly, where there are few firms, each large enough to affect output and price for all the others, thus creating a combination of interdependence and rivalry. But what determines whether the size distribution of firms approaches monopoly? In neo-classical theory this is largely the relationship between, on the one hand, technology, which determines the cost conditions, and on the other hand, the slope and position of the demand curve facing industry and the firms composing it. The aspect of technology that is specially important in this approach is that of returns to scale. If all inputs are increased in fixed proportions then, if output increases more than proportionately, increasing returns to scale exist; constant returns exist if output increases in proportion; and diminishing returns if it increases less than

[1] A full account of perfect competition will be found in every textbook on micro-economics and industrial economics.

proportionately. With increasing returns to scale, given certain assumptions about the state of demand, there will be a tendency for the number of firms occupying a market to decrease in number. But whatever the reasons (and we shall say more about these presently), market structures 'depart from' the model of perfect competition, the price to be paid is, in neo-classical theory, a loss of welfare. Perfect competition is thus regarded as expressing the essence of competition. But it is, in fact, a completely false view of what constitutes competition in capitalist economies, on a number of counts.

The meaning of competition is given by the assumed condition of free entry and exit. But firms engaged in any kind of production process (as distinct from someone buying and selling) must invest in fixed capital. That fixed capital locks up resources, which are only gradually released as the commodities are produced and sold. Such firms, especially if they are small, must compete by improving their efficiency, which is likely to mean reinvesting in their own enterprise. Their freedom to enter and exit is very much less than that of large firms. Not surprisingly, we find that as firms grow in size they become more diversified and less specialized; they are more able to enter the territory of others and thus compete.[2] The reality of capitalism stands the model of perfect competition on its head. But if this is the case, what becomes of the supposed continuum between perfect competition and monopoly? Certainly, the growth in the importance of large firms cannot be equated with the decline of competition. A different approach is needed.

Our own approach is implicit in the discussion of capital and accumulation in Chapter 3. Capital exists in discrete 'lumps' (blocks of capital), owned and controlled by different groups. Their expansion involves them in rivalry with other blocks of capital, seeking to grow and occupy the available economic space. The battle to occupy space and enlarge the arena itself is the competitive process and is waged by a wide range of economic, political, ideological, and legal measures, which include technology, communications control, managerial skills, etc. Capital accumulation is not the consequence of competition. In a system of private ownership, competition is the form in which each capital's drive for accumulation impinges on other blocks of capital. Given initial differences in the rate of profit in each sector, competition of capitals leads to a tendency to equalize the rate of profit and the process of diversification of firms can be seen in that light also.

For the process of accumulation to go on, firms (which are the legal entities within which the blocks of capital function) must seek control of three important areas. One is the labour process within its own sphere, since this cannot be taken for granted and is vital for control of costs and use of new technology. The second is the market for the product it produces. The third is the finance and credit necessary for expansion.

In competition, cost reduction for both price and non-price competition

[2]See Aaronovitch and Sawyer (1975b) and Clifton (1977).

can be a powerful weapon and will tend to enlarge the necessary plant size. The rise in plant size, it is true, is only one element necessary for the process of capital accumulation; technical change, however, is hardly a matter that firms can simply sidestep. Once introduced by one firm, competitors will need to copy or improve or else find their survival in danger through bankruptcy or takeover. Firms are therefore assumed to be normally producing a surplus, part of which will be used for accumulation. As blocks of capital, they are the loci of the production process. Capital is not particularly interested in production as such, but in the possibilities of accumulation. Which market to be in is a tactical question.

For success in rivalry, the weight and impact of the contestants is important. The need to become large in relative terms—that is, to exert dominance through share of the market—is continuously pressing. Given initial size, the size that firm can achieve in a given span of years will depend on the rate of growth of its own capital or on its ability to amalgamate its capital with that of others.

What we call the concentration of capital arises from the process of accumulation, the use of the surplus generated by the circuit of capital commanded by the firm or appropriate entity. It corresponds with the notion of 'internal growth' and is therefore linked to the concentration of output. This is not identical, however, with the centralization of capital, which is the process by which existing blocks of capital are amalgamated into larger agglomerations. Centralization is about the distribution of blocks of capital, their agglomeration and dispersion. A major form of centralization is the merger—the process often referred to as 'external growth', contrasted with the 'internal growth' already mentioned.[3]

As firms grow, they build up, through their investment strategies, networks both on a national and international level (the multinationals, for instance) which allow them to transfer funds across sectors and countries without recourse to the capital market. Capital therefore can be made very mobile and go to areas where the rate of return might be higher or where the rate of return would be higher than the marginal rate of return that would be earned if the funds were reinvested in the firm's own line of activity. Or for that matter, it can go where rivals might preempt important markets even if the expected rate of return might be lower than in other sectors.

The ability of firms to enter each other's territory as they grow in size and where the costs of entry are not critical, because of accumulated resources plus borrowing power, makes the conventional notions of barriers to entry and of limit pricing less important. Barriers to entry may exist more by virtue of a tacit or explicit bargain struck between large firms.

This kind of capital mobility open to firms as they grow is epitomized in the growth of holding companies, now very common, that concern

---

[3] These distinctions are not without their conceptual difficulties because the mobilization of money capital to be used as capital can itself be described as a process of centralization.

themselves precisely with flows of funds and major investment decisions rather than with the problems of production and supervision of production. Many of the main channels, therefore, for direction of money capital are outside the financial and money markets themselves. We referred earlier to the significance of technical change as a weapon in the competitive process contributing to cost reduction and/or product differentiation. The growth of firms is not, however, explained by economies of scale. Undoubtedly the average size of plants has grown but the growth of firms is not dependent on or closely correlated with the growth in the size of plants. Between the thirties and 1968 the hundred largest firms increased their share of net output from about 23 to 41 per cent, but the proportion of output accounted for by the 100 largest plants (11 per cent) was still the same. What has happened is that as firms grow they become increasingly multi-plant firms and, in the UK at least, those plants are of medium size.

Technical change and scale economies are nevertheless major instruments of rivalry and means of establishing dominant positions. The ability of IBM, for instance, to devote massive resources to research and development helps to secure its continuing dominance. Scale economies in industries like vehicles, petrochemicals, and steel make it possible for only a small number of giant firms to survive. Scale economies also mean that in many industries a plant of optimal size can supply all or a very large share of the market; any firm considering entry would need to enter at suboptimal scale (and therefore have higher costs) or create substantial excess capacity, with resulting pressure on prices and profit margins. Of course, if firms believe a market is growing rapidly, they may decide to do this, although the result may be severe losses should the growth rate slow down, as it did in branches of the chemical and vehicle industry.

An important effect of technological change has been the revolution in transport and communications that has enabled large multi-plant and multi-national firms to carry out complex operations across vast distances. But again, the needs of giant firms have themselves contributed to the technical changes that make it easier for them to operate.

The thrust of our argument is that the drive for accumulation by discrete and competing blocks of capital (between firms or clusters of firms) gives rise to the tendency for concentration to increase. Economists have discussed the role of 'random forces' in increasing concentration. It can be shown that if firms differ in their rates of growth, then over time, on certain assumptions, the dispersion of firms' sizes will increase. Clearly, there are many reasons why some firms will do better than others in any given period of time, and the degree of success or failure of any one firm relative to others is the product of all these factors; it is in this sense that we can speak of 'random forces'. As dominant firms emerge, however, they are able to use economic and non-economic levers to reinforce their dominance (through the state, for instance) and the ability to carry through numerous and/or large-scale acquisitions. The probability of being acquired also falls with increasing size. The rise in concentration is therefore the combined outcome of both systematic forces and the action of many different factors (including 'luck') which appear to be random in their impact on the population of firms.

To accumulate and compete successfully, size and market power are both sought. Size is important in four ways: absolute size, where some threshold of costs or resources exist; size relative to the economy (or number of economies) in which the firm operates, enabling it to compete at the level of the economy and become built into the economic and social structure, often not only in one country but in a number; size in relation to the relevant factor markets (as buyers of labour power and of inputs); size relevant to the product market (the importance, that is, of market share, to which attention has increasingly been paid in industrial economics).

The pursuit of the advantages of size is carried on at an international level. Advantages established may be threatened by rivals operating at home or internationally. There may be no final victories—the path turns out to be a treadmill, sometimes even for the largest. The result is a continuous reciprocal movement between competition and monopoly, whereby competition is extinguished at one level (as when firms in the same line of business merge) and enlarged at another. The growing concentration (partly through mergers) of the motor car industry accompanied by severe competition, is a good example.

As giant multi-plant, multi-product firms arise, competition develops, not in individual product markets so much as at the level of the system or of entire dimensions of the economy (such as competition to monopolize the leisure spending of the population).

Because *concentration* is the word used throughout the literature to describe both concentration and centralization, we will use it from now on for simplicity's sake, using the term centralization where we think it is especially important to separate it out. As we shall see, the process of concentration is far advanced in the UK and in all developed capitalist economies. It is the outcome of competition and at the same time it provokes new levels of rivalry at higher levels of concentration. In this framework, concentration expresses the increase in the collective dominance of a relatively small group of giant firms at the level of the economy and of specific sectors. It is *not* a statement about the degree of competition in the system and in itself it cannot be assumed that a rise in concentration expresses some equivalent decline in competition.

Economists brought up on conventional theories will debate whether this state of collective dominance matters, if there is competition in product markets. Does it matter, for instance, if trade in groceries becomes monopolized by a smaller number of giant supermarkets if these then compete among themselves?

The point here, surely, is not whether the composition of firms within the dominant group changes but the existence of such a dominant group. We can also see that the increase in concentration applied not to employment but chiefly to assets and share of output, so that concentration measures based on employment will show less significant rises, or may even show a fall.

We could begin to analyse this under two headings: the costs of collective dominance and the costs of rivalry.

The costs of collective dominance If, for instance, five firms account for 75 per cent of the output of a given product, or the largest hundred firms account for over 40 per cent of the total net manufacturing output, then that degree of dominance may impose costs on the rest of society (including other firms). These costs arise, for instance, from the fact that the interdependence of the firms leads to a shift from price competition to non-price competition. A dominant group, even if in rivalry in some areas, will also possess economic, social, and political 'muscle'—e.g., in seeking state aid here and abroad, or in lobbying for changes in government policy—will be a sole or main employer in labour and materials markets, and will possess control of the mass media etc.

The costs of rivalry These are costs that firms impose on each other by their rivalry as well as on the rest of society. For each firm, intensification of rivalry implies a loss of market power; it tends to increase the amount of product differentiation (with the consequent research and development costs), increases the costs of promotion, and involves systematic maintenance of excess capacity in order to be able to increase market share.

Some of these costs appear to be simply transfers from one firm to another, but this is itself too simple a picture. For society as a whole, the cost of rivalry may mean lower real output, with more resources spent on advertising and other forms of promotion as well as wasteful investment through the need to maintain reserve capacity. But the transfer of resources to those more successful in rivalry from those less successful may show itself in insecurity and unemployment and give rise to considerable social costs. Success in rivalry, given the variety of methods used, cannot be *identified* with superior efficiency, even though rivalry may also stimulate innovation and cost reduction. The struggle for market power is one aspect of the fight to reduce uncertainty and overcome rivalry, thus reducing the cost that increasing rivalry imposes. In this way rivalry continuously generates a movement towards monopoly power. But in turn the growth strategies of firms threaten the positions established by others.

17-2   TRENDS IN CONCENTRATION IN THE UK

In this section we attempt to give some picture of the changes in concentration in the UK economy and the most recent information on its level. But before we do so, there is one vital point to emphasize. Our starting point is the concentration of capital irrespective of the industries in which it may operate. We therefore begin by looking at what is often called 'aggregate' or 'business' concentration, as against concentration in given industries (often referred to as 'industrial' concentration). We use absolute concentration ratios (CR), which measure the proportion, for instance, total sales or output accounted for by the largest firms, ranking them from the largest firms downward. CR100 = 41 per cent of output means that the 100 largest firms account for 41 per cent of total output.[4]

We spoke earlier of collective dominance. The increase in the degree of control of domestic output (or sales or employment) by, for instance, the largest 100 firms in manufacturing is some measure of the increase in dominance. Such an increase in aggregate concentration need not mean that concentration is increasing in each product market—although in fact these two processes (rising aggregate concentration and rising product concentration) have tended to move together.

When we present aggregate concentration for, e.g., the manufacturing sector, we are, it should be clear, considerably understating the degree of dominance in the economic system as a whole. This is because the statistical analysis does not take account of the interrelationships between firms of a minority or informal kind (common shareholders, interlocking directorates, joint ventures). We can illustrate one part of this by making the point that if 100 firms account for, say, 41 per cent of net manufacturing output in the UK, *and* the financial sector is highly concentrated, *and* financial institutions hold about 58 per cent of shares in the quoted company sector (especially in the large firms), then a full picture of concentration would require all these aspects to be put together (along with other kinds of connections). Regrettably, the work necessary for such an analysis is a long way from being done. However, we turn first to the trend in aggregate concentration in manufacturing.

Concentration in UK Net Manufacturing and in the quoted Commercial and Industrial Sector

The rise in the share of the 100 largest firms in the UK net manufacturing output has been quite remarkable, as Table 17-1 shows, increasing from 16 per cent in 1909 to 41 per cent in 1972 (industries that have become nationalized have been excluded from the analysis for the entire period). A rather stronger picture emerges if we look at all *quoted* industrial and commercial companies, which by definition, therefore, are all large companies. The figures calculated by George show a rise from 46.5 in 1948 to 63.7 in 1968

---

[4] Such a measure focuses on what we might call collective dominance; inequality of firms' size will also affect the behaviour of firms and there are 'relative' concentration measures (e.g., Gini coefficients) that try to capture this. There are also attempts to capture the combined effect, of which the Herfindahl index is the best known and most widely used.

in the share of net assets of the 100 largest firms. There are, of course, some very large non-quoted companies and it is not possible to be sure how the proportion would change if they were included, but the trend is unlikely to be different.

Estimates made by the BSO of the 1500 largest companies for 1976 showed that the top 20 companies accounted for a third of the capital employed and the largest 100 accounted for 60 per cent.

The 100 largest firms do not, of course, occupy the same positions of power in each industry. In 1972 the 100 largest UK firms in manufacturing accounted for nearly two-thirds of the net output of vehicles, about

Table 17-1 Aggregate concentration in the UK

	Share of the largest 100 enterprises in net manufacturing output	Share of 100 largest manufacturing establishments in net output	Share of 100 largest commercial and industrial companies in net assets of all quoted industrial and commercial companies
1909	16	10.8 (1930) 11.2	
1935	24	9.0 (1948)	46.5 (1948)[a]
1949	22	10.5	50.7 (1957)[a]
1958	32		
1968[c]	41	10.8	63.7 (1968)[a]
1972[c]	41*		77.6[b]
1975	42		78.3[b]
1976			79.4[b]

[a] George.
[b] Listed companies asset concentration, Business Monitor 013 (Sawyer, 1979).
[c] Break in series from 1970 makes comparability between 1968 and 1972 difficult.

Sources: Prais (1976) up to 1968; Sawyer (1979) for 1972 and 1975.

half the net output of food, drink, and tobacco, and of chemicals; and around a third of the net output of engineering and electrical goods, of textiles, of bricks, etc., of paper, printing, and publishing, and of other manufacturing.

Unfortunately, changes in the share of the largest 100 in the different sectors for any long period of time are available only for employment and this is not the best index of changes in concentration; but the period 1958–72 shows very striking increases in food, drink, and tobacco; chemicals and engineering; textiles; and paper, printing and publishing. It is likely that the changes would be more striking if measured in terms of output.

International comparisons are difficult to make, but there is some evidence that the UK manufacturing sector is more concentrated than that of the US or West Germany. And UK companies in 1976 accounted for a third of all Western European industrial companies with a turnover exceeding £350 million. We have already made the point in an earlier section that firm growth is not to be explained by growth in plant size. If we refer back to Table 17-1 we can see that output accounted for by the 100 largest *establishments* has changed little between 1930 and 1968.

Nevertheless, when we compare the levels of concentration between industries, there is a common pattern in most advanced industrial countries suggesting that underlying technology has an influence (determining the lower bound, as it were) on the level of concentration. This is clearly the case with capital intensive industries, but this is not to argue that the growth in giant firms is technologically determined, a point already made.

It is worth noting that just as the UK leads the field in giant firm concentration, so it seems true that the small firm plays a less important part in the UK than in several major industrial countries.[5]

Concentrations at the Level of Industries

Although we are following the census of production's definition of industries these data have serious limitations. Dominance within industries is not necessarily coincident with the *market* for a given product or group of products (e.g., the market for bags is served by paper and plastics manufacturers who are in two distinct census industries). Concentration ratios also do not take account of imports, which may be a powerful competitive force but one that is difficult to estimate when so much trade across national boundaries is between the subsidiaries of multi-national companies. Nevertheless, concentration ratios based on domestic output, sales, or employment and assets still have relevance if the focus of interest is on control of domestic labour and manufacturing resources and the consequential economic, social, and political influence.

Concentration ratios will understate dominance because at the industry and product level they will not reveal the degree of vertical integration. It is also the case that, in general, the closer we get to the *product*, the higher

---

[5] *Proportion of manufacturing employment in smaller establishments in countries with comparable data*

		%
UK	1963	31
US	1963	39
West Germany	1963	34
Canada	1968	47
Sweden	1965	53
Norway	1967	64

Source: Bolton Committee on Small Firms (1971).

Bolton further concluded that the decline of the small firm has been more apparent in the UK than elsewhere.

the degree of concentration is likely to be. In the chemical industry, for instance, there are many producers. But for a whole range of major products there may be only one or two producers. If we are able to take into account regional markets, again, the degree of concentration would rise.

Figures, unadjusted for imports, show that 73 industries (46 per cent of the total) had a CR equal to or greater than 50 per cent. In addition, the average level of industry concentration rose quickly between 1935 and 1968. The figures below, taken from Aaronovitch and Sawyer (1974), show how five UK manufacturing firms' concentration ratios changed between 1935–68.

	Concentration ratio (%)
1935	52.0
1951	55.8
1958	58.7
1963	63.5
1968	69.0

Output concentration ratios continued to increase after 1968 but at a slower rate.

Concentration in Non-Manufacturing

As the giant firms grow, they diversify. They not only invade each other's territory but they move back into their supplying field and forward into their fields of distribution and sales. Since there are special risks of economic warfare involved in invading the territory of other oligopolists, and because once oligopoly is established there will be limits to the profitable reinvestment of funds in that sector, entry often takes place into territory previously occupied by small or medium firms.

This process of diversification combined with the emergence of large firms within non-manufacturing sectors results in the restructuring of such sectors as retail trade. The position has been well summarized in HMSO (1978):

> In 1971 multiple retail chains accounted for more than half the turnover sold through organisations other than co-operative societies in the cases of dairymen; off-licences; footwear shops; men's and boys' wear shops; women's and girls' wear; household textiles and general clothing shops; radio and TV hire shops; and variety and general household stores. Multiples accounted for nearly half of the turnover sold through bakers, chemists and photographic dealers, and department stores. It is interesting to note that several of these trades involve a substantial degree of vertical integration, e.g. off-licences, footwear shops, radio and TV hire shops, bakers and chemists.

Concentration in the Financial and Credit System

The same process of concentration described above in manufacturing has also been taking place in the financial and credit system. Of the current and deposit accounts of the private London clearers, four (Barclays, Lloyds, Midlands and National Westminster) account for 90 per cent. Six firms account for one half of HP business (and three of these firms are controlled by the big four banks above). Of the 25 largest companies in the UK life assurance industry, 47 per cent of life funds are in the hands of the largest four (headed by the Prudential); of the 25 largest non-life insurance companies, the four largest account for 60 per cent of premium income; twelve companies are among the top 25 in both types of insurance.

The number of firms engaged in discounting bills, in jobbing, and in broking has been sharply reduced. At the same time as concentration within the UK owned sector has grown, so too has competition from overseas based financial institutions, and this is part of the reason for the increased merger activity in the field of finance and credit. This pressure was reinforced by the property boom collapse of 1973, which led to a full-scale crisis in the 'secondary banking system'. The liquidations and mergers that followed increased concentration further in the financial sector.

There is, in fact, an astonishing disproportion between the degree of concentration in the financial sector and that in the industrial and commercial sector, which serves to reinforce the leverage that the former enjoys in economic policy making and strategy.

17-3 MAJOR FORCES IN THE RISING CONCENTRATION IN THE UK

We have discussed the general process by which accumulation in conditions of rivalry leads to increased concentration and centralization of capital. Three major instruments or mechanisms have operated to bring about and to accelerate the process since the fifties. These are the merger movement, the financial and credit system, and the activities of the state itself. The last is dealt with separately in Chapter 10. The first two we review below.

The Merger Movement

Since the mid fifties the massive merger movement that has taken place has made the biggest single contribution to changing the structure of many sections of British industry, trade, and finance. Firms have acted to change their environment. Estimating the precise contribution that mergers make to concentration is not easy, but Table 17-2 gives a range of estimates.

As the Green Paper itself comments:

> ... it would seem safe to conclude, that in the later 1950's and early 1960's mergers

accounted for about one half of the growth in concentration and probably for most of the increase between 1963 and 1968.

The reasons for mergers are many and complex, but there are certain key explanatory factors.

First, mergers, when involving firms in the same line of business, are major ways of attempting to eliminate rivalry and uncertainty. By definition, horizontal mergers reduce competition at that point in time. If rivalry increases, the pressure to merge will also increase, since takeovers both eliminate a rival and avoid adding to overall productive capacity.

Second, rationalization and modernization, where the objective is to avoid increasing capacity or to scrap some portion of existing plant, often require mergers. The mechanism of bankruptcy by which firms would be driven out of business may not be effective, especially where large multi-product and multi-national firms are involved. Mergers are important for rationalization because they confer complete legal control over assets.

Table 17-2 Estimates of the contribution of mergers to the growth of concentration

Study	Hart, Utton, and Walshe (1973)	Utton (1971)	Aaronovitch and Sawyer (1975a)	Hannah and Kay (1977)		Prais (1976)
Time period	1958–63	1954–65	1958–67	1957–69	1969–73	1958–70
Percentage of the change in concentration attributable to mergers	33	43	62	116[a]	95	50

[a] So concentration would have fallen in the absence of mergers.

Source: HMSO (1978).

Third, large size (absolute and relative to market) is important for survival. Dominant market shares contribute to market power and profitability. There can be no swifter way to grow than by mergers, which can double the size of the firms by the stroke of a pen.

Fourth, profitable investment may not be possible in the sector in which the funds arise or finance may be available that cannot profitably be used in a given sector. Diversification is generally more safely carried out by acquiring firms already in the field than by 'green fields' development.

Fifth, mergers can offer swift financial gain to investors where companies with high price/earnings ratios take over those with lower ones. The resulting increase in earnings per share, together with stock market optimism about growth, can further its ability to buy other firms even more cheaply. This has been an important part of the financial conglomerates' spectacular rise in the sixties and early seventies.[6]

Sixth and last, the tax system also provides benefits from mergers. Acquiring unused capital allowances and stock relief together with post-merger losses of the acquired company can be offset against the acquiring company's profits, so reducing tax liabilities.

Even if the pressure to merge increases because rivalry increases, certain conditions need to be met if the actual merger process is to expand. These conditions lie mainly in the share market itself and in the prospects of expansion that fuel share market hopes of profitability. A buoyant share market is specially important because the most important way of financing mergers is by exchange of shares; because, in such conditions, the acquiring firm's shares appear worth having and the shares of the acquired firms seem not to be undervalued in the eyes of their shareholders.

Merger activity is, however, a lumpy and discontinuous process. Its incidence has not only shifted over time but between industries and between sectors of the economy. One of the most noticeable changes has been the shift towards mergers in finance and non-manufacturing rather than in the manufacturing sector. For a large part of the post-war period there has been a systematic tendency for the larger firms to grow faster than the smaller ones; and it is noticeable that it is the very large firms that account for the bulk of acquisitions in terms of value—and it is these in turn who are more likely to avoid takeover themselves because of their size.

The Role of the Financial and Credit System in the Centralizing Process

The centralization of money resources to be used as capital has taken place through two main channels. One is through the joint stock company with shares quoted on the stock exchange. The share system itself is an instrument for bringing money together for use as capital and making the expansion of capital swifter. Accelerating the pace of accumulation has facilitated the concentration of capital. The rise of shareholdings depends on an adequate market in shares through the stock exchange. But this in its turn has its consequences for centralization. First, shares are bought for regular income and capital gains. If these are not combined as individual shareholders wish, they want to be able to sell their shares. However, the larger the firm, the more tradeable the shares because the market will consider that larger firms present

---

[6] There has been increasing discussion and research on the degree to which mergers are successful. On one level, the discussion is misplaced. The search for market power, for overcoming and reducing the costs of rivalry, is inherent in the conflict of capitals, but for various reasons, the achievements may be temporary or illusory. Nevertheless, there is interest in the growing body of evidence not only that firms involved in mergers do less well when unified than their separate entities had done previously, but that they performed less well than the average in their sector. There is evidence that mergers create new problems (especially of integration) and provide fresh rivalries; firms are, as it were, on a treadmill. (See Green Paper, 1978.)

fewer risks. Individual shareholders will favour the larger as against the smaller firms. The growth of financial institutions with contractual and other savings flowing to them in increasing amounts means an enormous expansion in the funds they need to invest. In sofar as they invest in the private sector, their concern must be with risk minimization, especially in the case of insurance companies and pension funds. There is evidence showing that in the first place they have preferred to invest in firms quoted on the stock exchange rather than in the non-quoted sector, and second, they have preferred larger as against smaller companies, even within the quoted sector (Prais, 1976).

Another aspect of the centralization process is the extent to which shares formerly held by individuals and new issues of shares have been acquired by financial institutions. The scale of this transfer is brought out in the following estimates of the percentage of market value of shareholdings held by financial companies and institutions; the figures for 1957–65 are taken from Erritt and Alexander (1977), and those for 1979 from Phillips and Drew (1979).

1957	18
1963	30
1969	36
1975	48
1979	58

In turn, concentration of funds among financial companies and institutions has itself grown and together these changes represent a marked increase in the centralization of share ownership.

The banking system too will be risk averse and prefer to lend to large firms. The cost of capital will, in general, be less for larger than for smaller firms, notably when it comes to new issues. Moreover, the financial system has played a crucial role in providing funds for the merger movement. This is because a large proportion of all new issues has been for use in acquiring other companies.

Because the stock market favours large firms, their price/earnings ratios tend to be higher (and price/earnings ratios will be higher if they are also growing faster) and this in turn makes it easier for them to take over smaller ones. The combined effect of the share market and the growth of financial institutions has also created a dynamic, which has fostered the amalgamation movement. As joint stock companies became large (and they became large also partly because they are joint stock companies), controlling shareholdings will often be a minority of shares. It is possible for an outsider, sometimes in collusion with others, to buy shares so as to launch a takeover bid against the controlling group. If successful, this generally means a merger, creating a larger firm. But this may open the way to a later but similar act by another group, leading to a further merger, so further enlarging the size of the firm.

The struggle of competing blocks of mobile money capital increases the process of centralization.

The state itself is one of the most important forces in the centralizing process, but a more detailed discussion is to be found in Chapters 8 and 10.

At the beginning of this chapter we pointed out that the restructuring of capital also involved restructuring the relation between labour and capital. The vast movement of concentration and centralization has had significant consequences for labour. First, it has involved the growing socialization of the labour process, creating large concentrations of labour power. Even more, however, it represents a concentration of economic power and potential political and social power. And finally, in the form of the multi-national companies (industrial, commercial, and financial), it represents a limiting force on the democratic processes within Britain.

FURTHER READING

Marx's own approach has been brought together in a number of books on Marxist economics, including King and Howard (1975) and Sweezy (1968). Lenin's *Imperialism* and R. Hilferding's *Finanz kapital* have exercised very great influence (although no English translation of the latter yet exists).

For comprehensive reviews of concentration in the UK see Aaronovitch and Sawyer (1975b), Hannah and Kay (1977), Hannah (1976), and Prais (1976). Earlier studies for the UK can be found in Aaronovitch (1955 and 1961).

The role of mergers is also treated in the previous four works, but additional material can be found in Singh (1971 and 1975). Cowling *et al.* (1980), Meeks (1977), and HMSO (1978).

Several of the titles listed as further reading for Chapter 16, e.g., Scott (1979) and O'Connor (1974), are also relevant.

EIGHTEEN

ACCUMULATION AND PROFITABILITY

Sam Aaronovitch

18-1 INTRODUCTION

The purpose of this chapter is first, to discuss the relationship between accumulation and profitability; second, to describe what has happened to investment (i.e., capital accumulation) in the UK since the war and its contribution to the relative decline of the UK industrial base; and third, to examine the nature and significance of the highly publicized 'profit squeeze'.

We have already proposed that the major objective of each block of capital (which, with qualifications we can identify as firms) is profitable accumulation. Positive profits over some time period provide the resources and the incentive for re-launching the circuit of capital on an enlarged scale, enabling more equipment, materials, and labour power to be set in motion.[1]

The relationships between accumulation, growth, and profitability are important in both theory and practice. If overall economic growth is taking place, profitable accumulation is likely for the firms in the system. If it is not, then rivalry will tend to be sharper and one firm may grow only at the expense of others.

For each individual firm, growth depends on reinvestment from its own profits and its ability to mobilize money capital (through share issues or loans) to enlarge its capital circuit. But the profitability of the firm is critical in the sense that it not only provides the resources for growth but (as actual or expected profits) determines the firm's ability to raise external resources. Growth in turn increases the possibility of expanding profit. Put differently, the sum of the investment decisions taken by firms is vital for overall growth and for future profitability and, reciprocally, growth and expected profitability are necessary for investment to take place.

Investment is also important in another sense, for the economy as a whole, since it is a very volatile component of aggregate demand. Some kind of systematic relationship between investment, growth, and profitability at the level of the system as well as at the level of the firm has held in the long run, but it is in fact a contradictory process. Within the capitalist system, accumulation itself produces barriers to further accumulation, which express

[1] In that sense, accumulation also represents a reproduction of the capital–labour relationship.

themselves in crises: interruptions in growth and the restoration of conditions for a further wave of profitable accumulation.

As we have seen, the UK economy is one that, *relative* to other advanced capitalist economies, has shown lower rates of growth, lower rates of investment, and possibly (although that is less clear) a greater fall in the rate of return. The investment–growth–profitability relationships cannot, for the reasons given in Chapter 3, be abstracted from the specific historical conditions in which class and institutional relations are important. But the conventional treatment of these relationships helps to bring out the cumulative causation that has contributed to this relative decline. Figure 18–1 sets out some of these connections.

One way of looking at the argument Fig. 18–1 presents is that investment is potentially important for sustained increases in productivity and therefore for lower unit costs. This in turn can increase profitability. Increased profits,

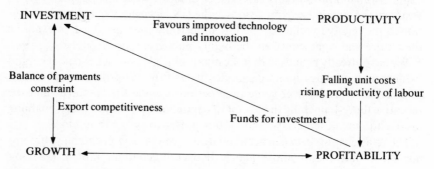

Fig. 18-1 Cycle of causation

in turn, can mean more retained profits available for reinvestment if there is confidence in future growth. Such rising investment would be a stimulus to overall growth. Investment will also, through these mechanisms, improve competitiveness on the domestic and world markets. It can therefore reduce competitive imports over the level at which they would otherwise be and provide exports enough to finance the imports of non-competing goods and desired competing goods. This in turn reduces the balance of payments constraint on expansionary policies and improves output and earnings at home.

If overall economic growth and investment go together, firms are readier to improve technology, to take a longer-term view of investment, and to be more flexible and innovative in meeting changing demand and influencing demand.[2]

What this account clearly obscures is the conflicts that give rise to periodic crises irrespective of whether economies invest more or less, grow faster or slower, etc. But it remains useful in terms of the *relative* positions of capitalist economies.

[2] For a discussion of this approach see Stout in Morris (1979).

We have identified profitable accumulation as the key objective of firms as blocks of capital. But this objective is not itself precise, nor is it easy to make it so. In the discussion that follows, we assume that our concern is with both the *rate* of profit (i.e., the profit made in relation to the capital employed) and with the *mass* of profit (i.e., its absolute size or, more accurately, its size relative to the perspectives of the firm).

Is there some minimum acceptable level of profit rate that will sustain the process of accumulation? We can list two elements: (a) that level necessary for the survival of the firm in the sense that it would otherwise not even maintain its position relative to competitors and would risk extinction; (b) the level below which alternative uses of money capital would be more attractive both to the firm and to those who might finance it (put differently, the cost of capital would exceed the rate of return).

It follows that there is no sacred and fixed rate of profit below which investment will not be undertaken. But investment is for *future* gains, and therefore expectations of profitability and the expected risks of investment, actual or expected, become important. In a broad sense, the rate of return acts as a signal of success or of the need to change the conditions under which accumulation takes place.

Given that capital is organized in competing blocks (as independent firms or groups of firms, for instance), rivalry between firms impels them to seek the highest possible profit. Even though we can present this only as a tendency, there are strong reasons why it operates. The outcome of rivalry depends on the resources available and how they are deployed. If one could visualize the system as a network of colluding firms, each helping the other whatever the consequences, then we would have no reason to postulate such a tendency. But in conditions of rivalry, the greater the profit, the greater the resources for expansion and the firm's attraction for external funds. Collusion may modify the rivalry; it does not eliminate it. Of course, the aggregate outcome of actions by firms may be quite different from the outcomes desired by each individual firm and the actual outcome will in turn influence expectations and actions.

But such an objective as the 'highest possible profit' has normally to be understood in a long-run sense. One reason is that firms pursue different strategies at different times. A firm at one stage of its history may sacrifice current profits to swift expansion, heavy sales promotion, etc. Another reason is that firms do not just trade with individual final consumers but with each other; they are in regular and often contractual relationships with other firms, where goodwill is important and profit snatching by ruthlessly exploiting shortages may invite retaliation, and so not be in the long-term interests of the firm.

Presenting the objectives in this way lacks the precision of models based on short-run profit maximizing firms but, textbooks aside, economists do not concern themselves with such short-run models. However, once the idea of long-run profit maximization is admitted, then, especially in conditions of oligopoly, the concept cannot be rigorously defined and it is difficult to distinguish profit maximizing firms from those allegedly pursuing strategies of growth or sales maximization. We can think of maximizing growth or sales as arising from the conditions under which profitable accumulation is being pursued.

From the objective of seeking the greatest possible profits, even in this loose sense, it follows that resources will tend to flow where profitability is greatest, and it is this mobility of capital that leads to a tendency for the rate of profit to equalize. Capital mobility, however, is itself a contradictory process for the following reasons.

In the first place, the circuit of capital involves expenditure on fixed capital (capital equipment and structures), which tends to be specific and localized; there are consequently substantial costs of exit. As against this, as firms become large the *mass* of profit available to them relative to that available to smaller firms increases their potential and actual mobility (the growth of multinational and diversified firms). Again, large firms become involved in a process of constructing barriers to entry so as to protect their market power and at the same time try to surmount such barriers in fields that are not their own. This gives rise to costs of rivalry and costs of trying to overcome it.

So far we have avoided any attempt to define more exactly the profit being sought. The Marxist concept of the rate of profit is the surplus produced in relation to the capital advanced (both constant and variable). But measuring that in its various forms at aggregate or at the level of the firm, is far more tricky, as is the measurement of capital stock. At the aggregate level, we would need to consider *all* forms of property income (rent, interest, and profit) since these are different forms in which surplus value is distributed. At the level of the firm the figure of profit and the ratios considered relevant depend upon different interests and are affected by accounting conventions and tax considerations.

This brief theoretical sketch is intended as a background to the problems of investment and profitability in the UK economy. We have already explained the significance of investment but now we look at the factual record, comparing the UK with other advanced capitalist economies in a rather more detailed way than in previous chapters.

18-2   THE INVESTMENT RECORD

Investment as a Proportion of GDP

In general since 1960, both in current and constant prices, investment in the UK as a proportion to GDP has been well below that of other countries as Table 18-1 shows.

Table 18-1 Gross fixed capital formation as a percentage of gross domestic product by country for selected years (1970 prices)

	1960	1965	1970	1975
Canada	21.6	22.6	20.8	22.8
US	17.2	19.1	17.3	15.3
Japan	24.1	28.3	35.0	32.1
Belgium	20.6	22.8	22.4	21.4
France	18.6	21.7	23.4	23.2
West Germany	24.6	26.7	26.4	23.0
Italy	22.5	20.0	21.3	18.3
Netherlands	21.6	24.2	25.7	21.4
Sweden	20.9	22.6	22.3	20.8
UK	15.0	17.5	18.7	17.8

Source: OECD National Accounts 1975, quoted from Brown and Sherriff (1979).

Table 18-2 Gross fixed capital formation per head of employed labour force in manufacturing[a] in various countries, 1960–75 ($) (current prices and exchange rates)

	1960	1965	1970	1973	1974	1975
UK	334	460	604	741	920	1006
Belgium	468	772	1226	1740	2357	2389
France[a]	. .	905	1439	2182	2288	2682
West Germany[b]	. .	. .	. .	1638	1707	. .
Italy[a]	332	367	751	1224	1469	. .
Netherlands[a]	. .	779	1633	2252	2743	3108
Japan	492	460	1317	2147	2141	1768
Sweden	669[d]	767	1207	2007	2443	2934
US[c]	. .	1675	2145	2551	2785	2947

[a] Figures refer to manufacturing plus other industrial sectors.

[b] Total investment per employee in production industries excluding quarrying and construction from *Statistisches Jahrbuch für die Bundes Republik Deutschland*, p. 139.

[c] Manufacturing employment estimated as industry employment multiplied by the proportion of manufacturing wage earners and salaried employees in industry wage earners and salaried employees.

[d] For 1961.

Sources: OECD: Manpower Statistics, Labour Force Statistics, and National Accounts of OECD Countries, Table 5.

Since GDP in the UK has been growing more slowly than in other countries, this lower share of investment reinforces a dismal picture.

Investment Per Head of Labour Force in Manufacturing

Manufacturing investment plays an important role because it is crucial to the expansion of productive capacity and is the way in which technical progress is embodied and made available. Investment per head in manufacturing (see Table 18-2) offers a useful comparison. The gap between the UK and other advanced economies in this respect is clearly very considerable.

Significance for Productivity

Increasing productivity is one of the most important mechanisms in increasing the surplus available for expansion and accumulation and for overcoming rivalry. Measuring productivity is not simple, however. Where there is more than one input into a production process (labour, capital equipment, scale, organization, etc.) it is difficult to measure the contribution of each. The most familiar attempts to measure productivity are by using the production function approach.

A straightforward indicator is to measure output per person employed O/L, or its rate of change form $\Delta(O/L) \div (O/L)$. When this is estimated we

Table 18-3 Selected growth rates in productivity in industrial countries, selected periods

	1950–73 (%)	1960–73 (%)	1973–9[a] (%)
Real GDP per employed civilian			
US	2.1	2.1	0.1
Canada	2.6	2.4	0.5
Japan	7.8	8.8	3.3
France	4.6	4.6	2.7
West Germany	5.0	4.4	3.1
Italy	5.3	5.8	1.5
UK	2.5	2.6	0.5
Output per hour in manufacturing			1973–8
US	2.7	3.2	1.7
Canada	4.2	4.6	2.5
Japan	9.7	10.0	3.5
France	5.3	5.7	4.8
West Germany	5.8	5.5	5.1
Italy	6.6	7.2	2.6
UK	3.1	3.9	0.2

[a] OECD forecast value for 1979.

Source: Survey of Current Business, August 1979, part II. OECD, *Economic Outlook*, July 1979. (Taken from *NIESR*, November 1979).

see that the level in the UK is relatively low; and even improvements in the rate of increase in productivity have still left us well below the main rivals.

Table 18-3 sets out the annual average rates of change in output per employed person in manufacturing for selected countries.

Obviously there are many factors that can account for differences in productivity: the age of the capital stock; its amount and quality; the technology used; the quality of the labour force and of management, etc. A very clear picture of the fall in the rate of increase in the gross capital stock of manufacturing in the UK is given in Fig. 18-2.

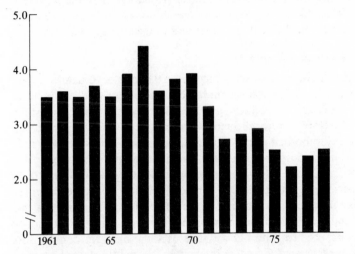

Fig. 18-2 The rate of increase in the gross capital stock of manufacturing industry, 1961–78. Per cent changes: figures at 1975 replacement cost. (*Source: National Income and Expenditure*, various issues)

Some evidence has also been produced to suggest that the increase in output per unit of investment has been lower in the UK than in other advanced countries (often measured as a rise in the capital/output ratio). A comparison based on measuring the change in GDP over total investment (Carrington and Edwards, 1979) indicated that the UK lagged in average 'productivity' of investment for 1960–76:

UK	0.134
US	0.169
France	0.200
Japan	0.227
West Germany	0.318

The reasons for this lag are undoubtedly complex. Apart from the scale, utilization and quality of investment, it has been argued that the capital–

labour conflict has played an important part in lowering the 'productivity of capital'. This would imply that the British trade union movement was either stronger in resisting the efficient use of new equipment or had different objectives from the trades unions of other countries. That discussion remains inconclusive but it is likely that a slow growing economy will in fact create a climate less favourable for exploiting technological change and stimulating management. The contribution investment can make may be reduced by an unfavourable distribution between industries. A study conducted by NEDO for 1975 and 1976 suggested that UK manufacturing investment was more heavily weighted towards traditional industries such as textiles and iron and steel, whereas West German investment was more concentrated in such growth industries as mechanical engineering and electrical machinery.

Technical Progress and R and D

Research and development represents the material and intellectual resources used in advancing scientific and technological knowledge and applying it to improvements in existing products, greater efficiency in producing existing output, and to developing new products. To a large degree advances in technology tend to be embodied in new equipment, and this provides the link with our previous discussion, especially on 'innovative' investment. We would expect R and D to be a significant factor in the growth and competitive power of industries and economies. In comparing industries and economies we have to take into account that in some sectors the *absolute* size of the R and D is crucial, but in comparing industries the proportion of the industries' resources devoted to R and D will give us some basis for comparison (using, that is, measures of R and D intensity). We should note, however, that industries or economies can license and/or copy the results of R and D in other countries and can therefore grow fast without a corresponding *direct* investment in R and D.

But while embodied technology is important, a great deal of technical progress is embodied not in machines but in people. Very important industries, such as the computer industry, are highly labour intensive and require enormous R and D.

The picture presented by the UK is, on the surface, paradoxical. Britain was a leading nation in the size of its R and D through the fifties and early sixties, and yet the expected growth did not materialize. The position has since changed: in the seventies the share of industry financed R and D was 14.6 per cent in the UK as against 25.1 per cent in West Germany and 35.4 per cent in Japan.

First, although the UK devoted greater resources to R and D compared with West Germany and Japan in that earlier period, the R and D was concentrated predominantly in the aircraft industry by comparison with West Germany and Japan; and reinforcing this, a large part of R and D was financed by the government and directed at military technology and aerospace, with a correspondingly lower proportion devoted to areas like machinery. The Japanese and West German situation was the reverse. But in these areas, such as aerospace, the UK was attempting to compete with the US, which had enormous advantages of scale over the UK. Second, in the key sector of engineering (and especially in mechanical engineering) the UK effort fell seriously behind that of our competitors. This reflected itself in the low value/weight ratio of UK engineering exports compared with those of West Germany, for instance. And it connected with the backwardness of UK higher and technological education especially for the 16–19 age group. In 1974, as an illustration, the proportion of qualified engineers and scientists in the total workforce of the metal working industries was 6.6 in Sweden, 5.7 in Germany, 5.3 in France, and 1.8 in the UK.

The situation has been summed up as follows (Freeman, 1979, p. 70):

> The peculiar paradox of the post war period was thus one of a completely inappropriate allocation of government and industrial R & D resources at a time when the total British R & D effort was temporarily greater than that of any of our major competitors except the US. Whereas the US at least derived substantial trade advantages from its world dominance in military-related technologies, British Trade and industrial performance gained little from the heavy UK investment in these areas and may indeed have been weakened by it. Even the considerable British R & D work in military electronics did not provide the basis for exploitation of civil electronic markets to any great extent, although the potential here was and remains enormous.
>
> In product groups which were decisive for world trade in the 1950's and 1960's British technical effort was relatively poor in comparison with Germany and several other countries. Whereas machinery, vehicles, metals and metal products accounted for about half of world exports of manufactures in this period, aircraft exports accounted for only about 4% and nuclear reactors for even less. The quality and number of engineers was woefully inadequate for the needs of British industry in the 1950's, and despite various reforms the quality remains inadequate.

It is hard to understand the causes of this misallocation without referring back to the attempt to maintain a world role and the relative neglect of the UK productive basis that flowed both from this attempt and from the preoccupation of the dominant groups of British capital and governing circles with their international operations.

Significance of Rate of Investment and Capital Stock

In general we would expect that the higher the rate of gross investment in proportion to gross output, the greater the net addition to total capital stock. This would mean a higher proportion of capital stock would be younger than if the investment rate were lower. It would follow that a smaller proportion of total investment expenditure would be on replacement of capital stock worn out and obsolescent. Conversely, the lower the investment rate, the older the capital stock and the greater the proportion of investment that would be spent on replacement.[3]

[3] Replacement of obsolescent or used up equipment is unlikely to be of identical units but will embody improvements.

A distinction may also be drawn between 'heritage' replacement and 'innovative' replacement. In a country with a large but ageing capital stock and where there is some stagnation in investment, replacement is more likely to be of piecemeal additions ('heritage' replacement) rather than of major replacements ('innovative' replacement). International estimates also suggest that the UK, as would be predicted from the earlier argument, spent a higher proportion of fixed capital formation on depreciation (except for the US). Looking at UK figures alone, the ratio of replacement to net investment began to rise through the sixties and became, as one would expect, very high as the 1975 depression got under way.[4]

So far we have concentrated on international comparisons. In terms of our own history, the rate of accumulation of capital accelerated from the fifties through to the beginning of the seventies. But the rate of growth of output per labour hour did not rise as fast. The result was a rise in the capital/output ratio (or declining trend in the average 'productivity of capital').

We can see that, although the relative position of the UK in terms of investment has declined, there has been a high rate of growth in investment in terms of our own history. The grounds for this lie in the fact that, again by our own historical standard, the post-war years have been ones of faster growth. This accelerated capital investment up to the end of the sixties was aided by a fall in the cost of capital, to which large-scale government aid contributed. We shall say more about this when we discuss profitability in the next section. However, this increased rate of investment should not obscure the continuing relative decline.

What is also clear is that, as discussed in Chapter 15, British capital has increased its investment overseas. Many firms have preferred to produce in more swiftly growing markets, where their operations tend also to be more profitable; they see the advantages of supplying the UK from their overseas plants; they desire to meet the rivalry from multi-national companies based in other countries; and they wish to take advantage of profitable opportunities in the less developed but rapidly industrializing countries.

18-3 THE 'PROFIT SQUEEZE'—MYTH OR REALITY?

We have already discussed the role of profit as of critical importance to the dynamic of capitalist accumulation. In this section we propose to look at the evidence for the UK economy and to do this involves problems of measurement. To measure profitability we need to have appropriate measures of profit P and capital advanced K, so that the profit rate is

---

[4] The way the figures are constructed means that they do not show the degree to which depreciation reflects the rate of scrapping caused by economic and technical factors.

measured as the ratio P/K. If we also have measures of output Y, then we can write

$$P/K = (P/Y) \cdot (Y/K)$$

so that we can express the rate of profit as the product of the profit share (P/Y) and the productivity with which capital is utilized (Y/K), which we refer to as the output/capital ratio. A fall in profitability can either result from a fall in the profit share (due, e.g., to a rise in wages) or a fall in the output/capital ratio (perhaps because of inefficient investments or reduced utilization of capacity). And these ratios can very loosely be associated with, respectively, the rate of exploitation and the inverse of the organic composition of capital (noting that the problems of measurement of capital stock and of profit are very great).

In practice, no single profit figure or ratio is 'the true' profit, not only because of the problems of measurement but also because the kind of ratios calculated depend upon the interests of those who are calculating them. If we are looking at the distribution aspect, then the profit/wage ratio represents the distribution between the two main classes; but there is also the distribution between sections of capitalist class, as between for instance, equity holders and lenders of money capital (although these two groups will also overlap). Another obvious kind of distribution is that carried through by the state through company taxation and government allowances and subsidies.

As we have argued in an earlier chapter, the real rate of return *to a firm* will not equal the total surplus value realized because the overall surplus produced is distributed between firms and groups of capitalists through the market for inputs and outputs as well as through the borrowing and lending of money capital, etc. The way profits are calculated will reflect these concerns. In addition, the problems of measurement have been made still more complicated by the attempts to take into account the effects of inflation.

We start with a summary of what seems to have happened to profitability in the UK.

UK Profitability: a Summary

(a) The share of corporate profits in GNP has fallen from its relatively high level in the fifties, when it averaged about 18 per cent, to about 11.5 per cent in the seventies.

(b) There has been a rise in the capital/output ratio, although the reliability of such estimates must be suspect.

(c) The rate of return on capital employed has fallen from the fifties, and particularly so during the economic crisis that began in 1973. In general, the rate of profit fell more severely in manufacturing than in the distribution and financial sectors.

(d) For most of the time since the beginning of the sixties the cost of capital has fallen in line with the fall in the rate of profit—i.e., the fall in the return on investment has been accompanied by a fall in the real cost of raising funds for investment.

(e) Because of inflation, the corporate sector which is a net borrower, has benefited at the expense of the lenders, so that a redistribution of the surplus has partially taken place. The net worth of the company sector has increased to the disadvantage of the people who pay premiums and save in insurance societies, pension funds, and the like.

(f) For the large multi-nationals, the rate of return on their overseas operations is higher than on their domestic activities; and a small group of oil companies has had substantial improvements in profitability from their North Sea oil interests.

(g) Governments have taken action to make investment cheaper and to reduce the weight of corporate taxation.

The fall in the rate of return in manufacturing operations has undoubtedly discouraged manufacturing investment in the UK and encouraged the use of funds in the non-manufacturing sector and outside the UK.

The fall in the UK rate of profit has been the subject of intense debate but much of it has been in terms of the impact of inflation in obscuring the 'actual' profitability of firms. Before we can present the record we must say something about the issues involved.

The two that have most sharply affected the estimates of profitability have been the treatment of capital consumption (capital stock used up in the process of production) and stock appreciation (the rise in the price of stock of materials held by firms).

Capital consumption

In Marxist terminology, equipment used up in the course of production *transfers* its value to the commodities being produced. The replacement of equipment thus used up is not part of the surplus product. The replacement cost of such equipment should therefore not be included in profits (in accounting terms they are included in gross profits, and then depreciation is deducted to give net profits). If we are examining the capacity of the firms in the system to maintain a rhythm of expanded reproduction, the maintenance of their productive capacity is the minimum that is needed. If firms do not set aside sufficient for depreciation (or do not spend enough to replace their capital stock at current prices) then the productive capacity of the firm deteriorates. Since firms calculate depreciation at historic costs (the cost at which the equipment was bought) the sums set aside for depreciation (and the amounts actually spent) may well signify a run-down of capital stock. If, as a result of inflation, the price of capital goods rises, then the replacement cost of a firm's capital stock will also rise and 'true' depreciation would need to be based on replacement cost prices. If firms do not take account of the replacement cost when the prices of capital goods are rising rapidly then their conventional estimates based on historic cost will seriously overstate their net profits. If *all* prices are rising in line then the cost of replacement in 'real' terms will not change in relation to other costs and incomes. But if capital goods' prices rise faster than all other prices, the 'market value' of a firm's capital assets will rise faster than those of other goods, and firms will register capital gains (although if they should all try to realize those capital gains by selling their capital stocks, they would necessarily fail). It is therefore appropriate to deduct some estimated figure for capital consumption at replacement prices from the gross profits of firms. The importance of this can be seen from estimates that capital consumption at replacement cost as a proportion of gross trading profits and rent, rose from 20 per cent in the early sixties to 35 per cent in 1977.

Another way of looking at this is in terms of the circuit of industrial capital. That circuit must be endangered if the replacement of productive capital is inadequate.

Stock Appreciation

As with equipment used up in the course of a firm's activities, so also materials used up in the production process *transfer* their value (in Marxist terms) to the product. In the same way, this transferred value is not part of the surplus. But firms also hold stocks of materials. If as a result of inflation, the prices of materials rise faster than other inputs or outputs, the stocks held by firms will increase in their market price. In conventional accounting this will show itself as a rise in nominal profits. Until 1974, this profit rise would then be taxable.

But since the firm must use the materials to engage in its productive activity, it finds itself both needing more money to finance the same amount of materials, which now cost more to buy, and also, until 1974, finding itself taxed on the nominal profits that arise from holding the stocks. The exceptionally rapid rise in the prices of materials created a severe liquidity crisis for many firms. Between 1972 and 1974 stock appreciation as a percentage of gross trading profits and companies' rents rose from 12 per cent to 40 per cent. Bank borrowing rose sharply and the pressure on government was such that it granted, temporarily, tax relief on stock appreciation.

The holding of stocks as such may be thought of as the firm exercising the functions of commercial capital (M–C–M' in the notation used in Chapter 3). The gains that arise from this may be thought of as holding gains. This stockholding activity can be financed by borrowing, repaid when the materials are sold or embodied in products that are priced to cover the increased cost of materials. But although firms were obliged to do this, the pressure arose from an acute shortage of liquidity; and the debts they incurred, were they not repaid, could raise problems of higher fixed charges on their income and endanger their independence.

At this stage, let us make two points. The impact of rising prices for capital goods and for materials will vary greatly between industries. Further, accounting gains can be made which, for any individual firm, will enhance the market value of the company (provided all do not try to realize these gains at the same time).

Profit figures adjusted for replacement at current costs and adjusted for stock appreciation will show a fall compared with conventional profit figures (which are in terms of historic costs—i.e., in terms of prices actually paid) and in general will reduce the firm's taxable income.

But there is a third adjustment which is also significant in terms of measuring profitability and also from the standpoint of distribution.

Adjusting Monetary Liabilities for Inflation

With inflation, the monetary liabilities of firms are reduced in real terms. If firms are net borrowers, the shareholders therefore experience a capital gain. Without this adjustment, profit figures adjusted only for capital consumption and stock appreciation will substantially *understate* the profitability of firms, as we shall see in a moment. On the one side, the revaluation gain to shareholders due to a reduction in the real value of company liabilities is omitted, and on the other, the rise in interest rates due to the inflation premium is included in the costs. Such revaluation gains increase the net worth of the shareholder but obviously do not provide cash gains for distribution to the shareholders. Nor, of course, do they represent increased profit on manufacturing operations. The increase in the net worth of a manufacturing firm, for instance, will be realized only if the firm is itself sold.

Profits: some estimates[5]

Profit Share The figures set out in Table 18-4 for the shares of industrial and commercial companies (excluding North Sea oil) profits in national income 1920–77 show that, even when deduction is made for stock appreciation and capital consumption at replacement cost, the resulting 'real profits' share remained fairly stable for most of the inter-war years; rose from the late thirties and maintained a fairly high, stable level through to the early sixties; fell back to the inter-war level in the late sixties; and then declined sharply with the impact of combined inflation and economic crisis from 1974–7. These are pre-tax figures and the share of corporation tax in GDP was reduced substantially in the seventies.

If we take a wider view of profits to include the trading surpluses of public corporations and an estimated profit element of income from self-employment, then from the twenties to the fifties the share ranged between 20–22 per cent, fell to $17\frac{1}{2}$ per cent in the sixties, but fell severely to 12 per

[5] In what follows we have been obliged to use the best calculations available and sometimes this means providing alternative calculations.

Table 18-4 Shares of industrial and commercial companies' profits in domestic income 1920–77[a]

	Historic cost profits (%)	Profits, net of stock appreciation (%)	Real profits[b] (%)
1920–24	13	$14\frac{1}{2}$	12
1925–29	$13\frac{1}{2}$	14	$12\frac{1}{2}$
1930–34	12	13	11
1935–39	$16\frac{1}{2}$	$15\frac{1}{2}$	14
1940–44	$18\frac{1}{2}$	$17\frac{1}{2}$	$15\frac{1}{2}$
1945–49	18	17	15
1950–54	$18\frac{1}{2}$	$17\frac{1}{2}$	$15\frac{1}{2}$
1955–59	$17\frac{1}{2}$	17	15
1960–64	$16\frac{1}{2}$	$16\frac{1}{2}$	14
1965–69	$15\frac{1}{2}$	15	$12\frac{1}{2}$
1970–73	15	$13\frac{1}{2}$	$10\frac{1}{2}$
1974–77	13	9	$5\frac{1}{2}$

[a] Excluding North Sea activities.

[b] Profits (i.e. gross trading profits plus rent net of stock appreciation and capital consumption at replacement cost) as a percentage of net domestic income (total domestic income net of stock appreciation and capital consumption at replacement cost).

Source: Bank of England Quarterly Bulletin, December 1978.

cent in the period 1970–77. On this evidence the share of domestically generated profits in domestic output (incomes) has shown a tendency to fall from the sixties even when measured on historic costs. (It should be noted that from 1976, company profits from North Sea oil were rising rapidly and in 1977 totalled over 10 per cent of the gross trading profits of industrial and commercial companies.) In the case of profit shares in national income, the figures are obviously affected by changes in capacity utilization, especially through the trade cycle and also by cost changes, which may squeeze profit margins and relatively improve the non-profit share. It is also clear that the most important factor in pre-tax profit share in the seventies has been stock appreciation. In 1974 the government acted to relieve companies of tax on changes in the book values of their stocks.

Companies, however, contribute a declining proportion to net domestic income. If real profits are shown only as a proportion of companies' value added, the decline up to 1975 is less marked (the profit share began to rise after that).

Rate of Return on Capital This measure concerns itself with the extent to which the profit made is proportionate to the capital stock involved and the extent to which firms would find other kinds of investment more profitable. It therefore acts as an indicator of the incentive to invest in different spheres. It is, of course, possible for the share of profit in national income to rise while the rate of return on capital falls, as a result of a rise in the capital–output ratio.

Table 18-5 presents calculations made by the Bank of England for 1963–79.[6]

Table 18-5 Rates of return on trading assets of industrial and commercial companies[a]

	Pre-tax historic cost (%)	Pre-tax historic cost, net of stock appreciation (%)	Pre-tax real[b] (%)	Post-tax real[c] (%)	Pre-tax real rate of return of equity[d] 'Natural' gearing adjustment (%)	Real interest rate[e] (%)
	(i)	(ii)	(iii)	(iv)	(v)	(vi)
1963	16.1	15.6	11.6	6.5	11.8	5.6
1964	16.9	16.1	12.1	6.8	13.1	2.7
1965	16.0	15.2	11.4	6.3	12.6	3.3
1966	14.3	13.5	10.1	4.3	11.4	4.0
1967	13.7	13.5	10.2	4.6	11.1	5.5
1968	15.0	13.5	10.3	5.0	11.8	2.7
1969	15.0	13.4	10.0	5.2	11.1	4.5
1970	14.5	12.2	8.7	4.4	10.3	1.3
1971	15.3	13.3	8.9	5.1	10.7	− 0.3
1972	16.8	14.5	9.3	4.9	10.4	0.8
1973	19.6	15.0	8.8	6.1	9.6	0.8
1974	19.1	10.9	5.2	4.3	6.9	− 6.5
1975	17.7	11.2	4.7	3.6	7.2	− 13.1
1976	19.6	12.8	5.1	3.8	5.6	− 2.5
1977	18.8	14.4	5.8	4.2	6.1	− 0.7
1978	18.0	14.9	5.9	4.5	5.6	− 3.3
1979	17.8	11.6	4.1	3.5	4.0	− 1.5

[a] Excluding their North Sea activities.

[b] Gross trading profits, plus rent, net of stock appreciation and capital consumption at replacement cost, as a % of capital employed at replacement cost.

[c] Taking account of investment allowances in force when capital stock installed.

[d] Crediting to profits the decline in the real value of debt at a time of inflation.

[e] Derived from the implied nominal rate of interest on industrial and commercial companies' gross debt.

Source: *Bank of England Quarterly Bulletin*, June 1980

We pointed out earlier that, with inflation, the holder of monetary liabilities gains and the lender loses. Some attempt to show the effect of allowing for this on equity interest has been made (*Bank of England Quarterly Bulletin*, June 1980) by crediting to profits the decline in the real value of debt at a

[6] The article in the *Bank of England Quarterly Bulletin* that contains this Table asks the reader to treat with caution the inference in the post-tax columns that the tax burden on companies has increased in the last two years.

time of inflation. These results showed higher rates of return as compared with profits adjusted for stock appreciation and capital consumption only but, once again, manufacturing improves less than firms in the non-manufacturing sector. Column (v) of Table 18-5 shows that on this basis the rate of return to equity assets showed little trend between 1963 and 1972; the main fall came with the economic crisis from 1973.

The impact of the business cycle on profitability is clearly important and has to be separated from longer-term trends. We would expect that the rate of return would tend to fall in depressions and to improve with the recovery.

Fall in the Cost of Capital Estimates of the cost of capital, published by the Bank of England, suggest that for most of the sixties (no calculations are available earlier) the real cost of capital fell but began to rise again from the end of the sixties. If we look at the ratio between the real rate of return to the cost of capital as an incentive to invest, then that ratio tended to fall right through the sixties until about 1974, and then started to rise again. The decline in the rate of return has therefore to be considered not only in absolute terms but in terms of the cost of raising finance for investment. Taken at its face value, this suggests that the disincentive for companies to invest is weaker than the fall in the rate of profit might suggest. However, the fall in the cost of capital was probably itself a reflection of declining profitability and cannot be taken as an independent factor. The reader should keep in mind that the Tables in this section generally exclude both North Sea oil profits and companies trading mainly overseas, including the UK activities of such companies. This means that many of the very largest companies have been excluded.

Effects of Tax Policy

So far, we have been examining the way to approach a relevant estimate of profits based on the ability of firms to sustain their productive activity and finance the process of accumulation. What firms have available for accumulation is influenced by the state, both in terms of direct assistance given by the state to firms and by way of actual taxes firms pay.

Chapter 10 dealt with government subsidies to firms, while the general position on corporation tax has been summed up by Kay and King (1978, p. 198):

> As we have seen, the corporation tax which exists in the UK today is far removed from a tax on company profits. A company earns profits on its productive assets but before paying tax it may deduct interest payments on loans taken out to finance the purchase of some of its fixed and working capital, and also any expenditure on investment on a wide range of assets (by taking advantage of free depreciation).

With regard to investment in plant and machinery, the government already provides virtual replacement cost depreciation. On top of this, stock relief mitigates the taxation of stock appreciation. The effect of these allowances is to reduce the size of taxable profits, thus lowering the burden of corporation tax. In fact the situation has been reached where for the 'average' industrial company mainstream corporation tax has effectively been abolished.[7] Retailers benefited enormously from the government's stock appreciation relief, as was shown by a study made of the accounts of six leading food retailers. Between 1974–8 these companies claimed £88.5 million in stock relief, but their stocks were financed by trade creditors, and in any case part of the increase in stocks was not due to inflation but to expansion in the stock volumes. In this sense, the taxpayer has been funding the expansion plans of the retailing giants under the guise of protecting them from the effects of inflation.

Many firms have negative taxable profits while still being in a position to pay dividends, and are building up unrelieved tax losses which they will carry forward to offset future years' tax. This reality is often obscured by

Table 18-6 Mainstream corporation tax paid by the 20 leading UK industrial companies, 1977[a] (£ million)

Company	Profits 1976[b]	Tax payment 1977
British Petroleum	1784	nil
ICI	540	23
BAT Industries	374	2
Rio Tinto-Zinc	279	nil
Esso	69	nil
Imperial Group	130	9
Courtaulds	43	nil
Grand Metropolitan	57	nil
P & O Steam Navigation	31	nil
Guest Keen and Nettlefolds	98	nil
General Electric Co.	207	42
Dunlop	73	nil
Reed International	75	nil
Bowater	78	nil
Distillers Co.	91	7
Bass Charrington	69	24
Allied Breweries	63	9
British Leyland	56[c]	nil
Ford Motor Co.	122	nil
Marks and Spencer	84	29
Totals	4323	145

[a] Companies are largest 20 by capital employed from *The Times* 1000 (1976–7), excluding Shell, Unilever, Burmah, Rank/Rank Xerox.
[b] Profits are latest full year figures at 30 April 77.
[c] Annual rate.
Source: Kay and King (1978).

[7] Mainstream corporation tax is distinguished from advance corporation tax, which companies pay as a deduction at source, on dividends at the standard rate of tax.

the accounting practices of firms, whereby their profit and loss accounts show tax charges that do not take into account accelerated depreciation or stock relief. Kay and King made their own estimates of the actual position of the largest 20 companies by capital employed listed in *The Times* 1000, and Table 18-6 shows their findings.

Obviously, financial institutions whose assets are monetary can hardly claim tax relief on stock appreciation. Not surprisingly, they take a different view of the appropriate accounting procedures, since they too would like to reduce their tax burdens. The debate over accounting conventions thus partly reflects the conflicting interests of the financial and non-financial sectors.

18-4 CONCLUSIONS

We began the chapter arguing that profitable accumulation was capital's major objective. The evidence suggests that in UK manufacturing industry profitability has sharply declined. Because this has been so, and because the expectations of change are low, investment in manufacturing has been affected, and the fact that it may still have risen as a percentage of GDP is hardly relevant given that it did not improve the slow growth of GDP.

To some degree the fall in investment that would be expected from the decline in profitability has been offset by government tax relief and allowances, by the fall in the cost of capital, and by some transfer of resources from lenders to borrowers as a result of inflation. But these counter forces are either subject to policy changes by government or themselves show the importance of placing funds elsewhere so as to earn a higher rate of profit.

Within manufacturing, some sectors, such as chemicals and allied industries, have shown greater ability to sustain 'real' profitability, partly because there are industries whose leading firms possess greater market power and the ability, therefore, to achieve higher price–cost margins than those with lesser market power.

We have noted that some sectors have not done as badly—distribution and finance institutions, for instance, and, of course, the oil companies. The profitability gap between the manufacturing and financial sectors has become much wider.

We have suggested that in a very broad sense the result of inflation has been a redistribution of resources, in that the corporate sector as a whole has tended to be cushioned from the decline in operating profitability by increased revaluation profits. The holders of long-term debt (the large pension and insurance funds) have lost to the corporate sector and as a result have paid benefits reduced in real terms in the form of pensions and life assurance. The gains to companies have therefore accrued primarily from older and retired sections of the working population and have contributed to the rise in the personal sectors' savings ratios, as the latter try to preserve the 'real' value of their savings. Such gains, however, are not typically available for new investment in manufacturing.

A number of explanations have been put forward to explain the 'crisis' in profitability in the UK, and we shall review these very briefly.

The first, advanced by some Marxists (but not all or even most), goes back to the Marxian notion of the tendency of the rate of profit to fall, which comes about because of the rising organic composition of capital. The argument runs as follows. Through competition, firms are obliged to apply and develop technology in order to increase productivity and lower unit costs. This increases the technical composition of capital—i.e., the mass of materials and means of production acted on by a given number of workers. The result is a tendency for the total value of the product (in Marxist terms— i.e., constant capital used up *plus* variable capital advanced *plus* surplus value produced) to come in greater proportion from used up means of production and less from living labour. The ratio of dead to living labour rises, and in value terms this means a tendency for the rate of profit to fall *unless* either the rate of exploitation rises faster than the rise in real wages or productivity increases lower the value of the constant capital (or some combination of both). Attempts to see whether in practice the organic composition of capital has risen have run into difficulties. The most likely approximation is the ratio of capital to net output (or value added). Evidence suggests that there may be a *long-run* tendency for the capital/output ratio to fall, or at least not to rise. In the more recent period such a rise can be noted in the UK, but the calculation of these ratios is dependent on valuing the capital stock and these estimates have high margins of error. The rise in capital/output ratios could arise from a combination of increased capital investment, which did not achieve the desired rise in output due to the economic crisis, and stagflation.

The second explanation is that labour has grown in strength and has been able to increase its share in national income. This could arise from pressure on governments to pursue full employment policies and the subsequent 'taut' labour markets that are favourable to trade union bargaining; it could arise from a high degree of trade union organization and militancy which, whatever the state of the labour market, increases the workers' share more than the growth in productivity and faster than prices. This explanation is necessarily linked with a third one: increasing competitive pressures which, as Glyn and Sutcliffe (1972) have argued, prevent capitalists from raising prices sufficiently to offset the rise in labour costs. British capitalism, in this argument, has been squeezed between working class pressure for higher wages and international competition. There is evidence, as we have seen, for the rising share of labour (even if we look at the company sector alone), and there is little doubt as to the growth of competitive pressures. Trade union resistance to a fall in real wages has been considerable, wage restraint tending to be followed by a swift catching-up process in money wages. A different outcome could be that prices rise faster than wages with inflationary results;

but in so far as UK inflation is more rapid than that of its competitors, UK companies are threatened with defeat in both national and international markets.

A fourth explanation derives from the 'crowding out' argument, that rising state expenditure starves the private sector of investment funds, which in turn reduces its competitive power and so also its profitability. We have dismissed this argument elsewhere (page 232) as invalid.

A fifth explanation is to see the movement in profits as basically cyclical, arising from the upswings and downswings in the economy. There is certainly a cyclical element, as we can see from the figures, but in terms of the rate of return on manufacturing investment there is clearly also a more powerful downward trend.

The second and third explanation in tandem seem to be more strongly supported, and there is also some support for this in US experience (Weisskopf, 1979).

We have suggested that expected profitability of investment and long-term growth are interrelated. If confidence in such long-term growth is not established, then even when profits rise, investment may not rise correspondingly. Furthermore, if the rate of return is higher in such sectors as finance, property, etc., then the tendency for manufacturing investment to slacken or stagnate will become very powerful. The stimulus to invest overseas if the marginal rate of return is higher will also be strong. To the extent that happens, then because of the importance of manufacturing in the economy and to exports, the basis for profitability in the non-manufacturing sectors will be undermined in time.

So far we have assumed that the impact of falls in the rate of return or in profit shares falls equally throughout the corporate sector. We know, however, that firms with strong market power can protect their profit margins better than those more exposed to competitive pressures. Because of accounting conventions, especially where firms are multi-national, it is difficult to measure the existence of monopoly profit, although from time to time investigations reveal the tip of the iceberg.

FURTHER READING

For statistical series on profitability, see especially the various articles in the *Bank of England Quarterly Bulletin* published in various issues since 1976; additional series can be found in *Economic Trends* and *Financial Statistics*, and more detailed analysis of company accounts in *Business Monitor*. The same sources are useful for series on investment.

For discussion of the issues see Blackaby (1979a). An important discussion on profitability can be found in Glyn and Sutcliffe (1972). For discussions on inflation accounting see Kennedy (1978) and G. Thompson (1977). The debate, however, is a continuing one.

FIVE

LABOUR

The focus of the last chapter was the surplus value that is realized as profit and that provides the engine of accumulation. This surplus value is produced by workers within a specific labour process. To understand the production of surplus value therefore requires an analysis of the labour process, and this is the task of Chapter 19. The labour process is not only the source of surplus value: it also establishes the class relations and class struggle which form the bourgeoisie and working class. The formation of the British working class and the development of the labour movement are the subject of Chapter 20. A major determinant of the strength of the working class is the condition of the labour market and in particular the size of the reserve army of labour. These are dealt with in Chapter 21. Chapter 22 concerns class struggle, the outcome of the antagonism between labour and capital. The chapter also examines one of the major consequences of the conflict, inflation, and the role of state intervention and regulation in the inflationary process.

NINETEEN

THE LABOUR PROCESS

Jean Gardiner

19-1 MEANING AND SCOPE

The labour process in its most general sense refers to all the activities by which people transform their natural environment in order to reproduce the social formation in which they live. It embraces the whole range of practices considered as work – material production and services, manual and non-manual labour – and some activities misleadingly often treated as 'leisure' because they are not paid a wage or salary – housewifery, childcare, do-it-yourself. All labour processes can be categorized in two ways: according to the useful content of the labour (its component tasks and end product), and according to the social relationships within which the labour is performed (how it is organized and controlled). While the catering worker has in common with the housewife the content of her labour, the social relationships within which they work and the organization of the labour process itself are quite distinct. In the latter sense the catering worker has more in common with the bank clerk because they both work within capitalist relations of production. This chapter focuses on labour processes performed under capitalist relations of production because of their dominant position in an economy in which the accumulation of capital provides the major impetus for development of the productive forces. Thus we shall be primarily concerned with those labour processes where the means of production are owned by a private enterprise, where labour is performed by workers who receive a wage for selling their labour power to the enterprise, and where the work process itself is determined and controlled by the enterprise and the products of that process are its property.

However, before examining the capitalist labour process in greater detail a brief discussion of other labour processes is required. Categorizing labour processes in terms of distinct social relationships is quite alien to orthodox economics, which regards the money payment corresponding to work as the only measure of its economic significance. Thus labour that receives no money payment, like housework, is invisible and is not considered to be contributing to social production. Marxism, on the contrary, provides a framework for looking beyond market relations and money flows at the real social relations of production and at the processes by which the labour of some is appropriated by others.

Marx himself and most subsequent Marxists have been preoccupied with capitalist relations of production, because of their dominant position, to the exclusion of all other coexisting production relations. Greater attention has begun to be given to some other production relations—e.g., domestic labour (the reproduction and maintenance of the household and its members), homework (paid work for a capitalist enterprise performed within the home), and public sector employment. Others have received very little attention—e.g., self-employment and family work (work within the family for a family business). Within each separate set of production relations, the organization of the labour process and forces making for changes within it are distinct and need separate analysis. However, all non-capitalist labour processes are subordinate to the dominant capitalist mode of production. To illustrate let us turn to the analysis of domestic labour.

19-2 DOMESTIC LABOUR

With the development of the women's movement in recent years considerable attention has been given to analysing the domestic relations of production within which housework and childcare are performed, and to specifying the relationship between domestic labour and the capitalist mode of production. There have been broadly three different approaches to this question. The first is to view the family as a separate pre-capitalist mode of production, a remnant from previous social orders which has gradually been undermined by the development of the capitalist mode of production as first men and then women have been drawn into wage labour. The second approach, identified with the demand for wages for housework, sees domestic labour as an essential part of the capitalist mode of production and equivalent to wage labour except for the fact that it receives no wage. Thus if houseworkers were paid a wage, the social relations within which they worked would be those of wage workers. The third and most satisfactory approach is to view domestic labour as an integral and necessary part of the capitalist mode of production but with social relationships that are quite distinct from those of wage labour in ways other than the non-payment of wages. Thus capitalism has developed in a way that depends on the domestic labour process for the daily maintenance and generational reproduction of labour power. However, unlike wage labour, domestic labour is not performed because workers are forced to sell their labour power to the capitalist class, nor is the domestic labour process itself subject directly to capitalist control. In order to identify the distinct social relationships within which domestic labour is performed it can be separated into three elements. The first involves the biological processes of pregnancy, childbearing, and feeding. The second relates to the social processes of childcare and education. The third concerns the daily care and maintenance of the household and its adult members.

While it is biology, subject to varying degrees of control over fertility, that ties women to the first element of domestic labour, it is the social and economic dependence of children on women and mothers on men that ties women as housewives to the other two elements of domestic labour. Because the development of the capitalist mode of production has required the elimination of the family as a self-sufficient economic unit, an alternative economic structure for parenthood involving maternal economic dependence and a specifically capitalist form of domestic labour has evolved. On the one hand, women are tied to the domestic care of children and men, and on the other, men's dependence on the sale of their own labour power is reinforced by the need to provide for a family.

These social relationships within which domestic labour is performed are maintained by a whole range of factors—e.g., the low level of women's wages, the absence of socially supported childcare facilities, state financial and legal reinforcement of marriage, and powerful ideological forces. However, it would be wrong to suggest that the relationships described here are purely the result of pressure from the capitalist class and state. They also evolved from a pre-capitalist sexual division of labour, which may have been less economically inegalitarian than its modern form but none-theless reflected a patriarchal family and society. Moreover, defence of the economic structure of the family has been a goal of working class struggle, as evidenced by the demand of male workers for a family wage, even though the extent to which this represented a meaningful demand for the working class as a whole as opposed to a male labour aristocracy is the subject of debate. In fact the model of the working class family discussed here—supported by the wage of the man and the domestic labour of the woman—has failed to correspond with the actual experience of major sections of the working class throughout the history of capitalism. Many married women and mothers have always been forced to do paid work in addition to domestic labour in order to provide for their families, often on a highly exploited and casual basis. This has happened where there has been no husband to provide support, or where husbands have been unemployed, disabled, on very low wages, or on wages that have not been equitably shared within the family. This indicates also how the capitalist labour process impinges on domestic labour through the demand it generates for women as wage labourers.

19-3   THE CAPITALIST LABOUR PROCESS

The emphasis within Marxist political economy on the processes that go on within production itself is one of the features that most distinguish it from orthodox economics. Orthodox economists have been preoccupied either with the market transactions that precede and follow the production process—i.e., markets for labour, raw materials, products—or with the distribution of output as a whole. The production process itself has been regarded as a technical and not a social process, with technology always viewed as an exogenous variable. There have been some studies of labour organization and management structure but these are generally explained in terms of technical or market conditions. Hierarchical patterns of authority and control tend to be regarded as the product of natural laws.

Marx made it clear that the capitalist labour process, far from being a technical matter, was at the very heart of the antagonistic social relationships of capitalist society. Capitalism is a dynamic system in which each capitalist is driven to increase to the maximum the productivity of the labour power purchased relative to the capital laid out in wages. To understand the fundamental source of profit in the capitalist mode of production one has to look not for unequal exchange in the market for labour power but at capitalist domination in the sphere of production. Here the conflict of interest between labour and capital is clear. The capitalist purchases labour power in order to get as large a surplus product over the wage as possible; the workers sell their labour power to get a living, and it is their wage and working conditions, not their output, that matter to them.

The essentially social as opposed to technical nature of the production process is obvious if one looks at concepts like a 'fair day's work'. Taylor, the originator of scientific management, defined it as all the work a worker can do without injury to health at a pace that can be sustained throughout a working lifetime. (In practice his definition led to work standards that could only be maintained by a few 'model' workers.) Alternatively the socialist concept of a fair day's work would involve only the work necessary to produce sufficient to pay the worker a wage and whatever surplus was regarded as socially necessary. It is clear that this concept is open to a whole range of ideological interpretations and in no way technically given.

The conflict of interest between labour and capital within production is illustrated by Marx's use of the concept 'variable capital'. Labour power purchased represents capital that is capable of performing a variable quantity of labour and producing a variable quantity of output, depending on a range of factors. Its capacity cannot be technically specified in the way of a machine (constant capital in Marx's conceptual framework). The variability of labour power can be seen to have two aspects. On the one hand, individual workers are intelligent human beings guided by subjective states. On the other hand, workers are alienated from the labour process and actively build organizations to resist managerial authority. Through the different stages of capitalist development, managers have attempted to extend their control, both reducing the unpredictability inherent in the first aspect and counteracting the risk attached to the second aspect. Scientific management was not concerned with finding the best way to do work in general but with how best to control labour power that is bought and sold according to capitalist relations of production. It was founded on the premise that as long as workers have any control over the labour process itself they will thwart efforts to realize the full potential inherent in labour power.

The level of productivity of workers in the production process is as crucial to profitability as, and often more crucial than, the level of wages paid. In fact, an offer of higher wages may be used by management as an attempt to raise both productivity and the rate of exploitation of the workforce. Thus in 1914 in the US during the implementation of scientific management, Ford used higher wages to reduce labour turnover and avoid unionization of the labour force, which had both been provoked by intensification of labour. Subsequently Ford wrote in his autobiography: 'The payment of five dollars a day for an eight hour day was one of the first cost-cutting moves we ever made' (Braverman, 1974). This is why trade unions need to concern themselves with employment levels and the organization of the labour process itself and not just with wage levels.

Despite the key importance of the labour process in workplace class struggle and the recognition given to this by Marx, there has only relatively recently been a resurgence of interest amongst Marxists in this area of study. Although most of the research this interest has generated has continued to focus primarily on manual production workers, some has also taken account of those changes within the labour process that have led to an expansion of clerical and technical work. Orthodox labour economists and industrial relations experts have been preoccupied almost exclusively with manual engineering workers, as was evident in the report of the Donovan Commission. This preoccupation is related both to the strategic position of the engineering industry within the economy as a whole and to the related bargaining power of manual engineering workers. It necessarily provides a highly misleading picture of labour processes in general and of the industrial relations surrounding them. It is unfortunately impossible to avoid this bias altogether in what follows, although attempts will be made to relate the analysis to other industries and occupational groups.

Amongst Marxists and radical economists concerned with the labour process, debate has concentrated on the following questions. What have been the historic tendencies within the capitalist labour process on the questions of control, skill, bargaining power, and fragmentation of labour? What are the major forces bringing about change in the labour process? What economic and political effects have those changes had?

To examine these debates we will look first at the concept of control, which has been interpreted in a number of different ways, in order to clarify what is meant here by the term. Then we will discuss the major theoretical arguments. Finally, we will turn to the industry in Britain that has received the most attention from researchers in this area: the motor car industry.

19-4   THE CONCEPT OF CONTROL

Disputes over control at work and the frontier between the rights of management on the one side and those of the workers on the other have been a major battlefield of the class struggle in Britain during this century. These disputes have ranged from conflicts over work effort and payment, to a questioning of the nature, purpose, and control of production itself. The vast majority of control disputes that have occurred have been at the level of job control and have often involved only small groups or particular sections of workers. The more far-reaching initiatives that have questioned capitalist economics and control as a whole—e.g., the Lucas Aerospace Alternative Corporate Plan—have impinged on wider sections of workers but have been relatively rare and isolated in the absence of a generalized political shift in the direction of socialism.

Job control and workers' control struggles have distinctive political implications. Workers' control struggles may be seen as a part of a revolutionary process and as a step towards the achievement of working class political power. They arise from a process of developing class consciousness. On the other hand, job control struggles are concerned with the defensive devices built up by workers through years of struggle at the point of production. The workers' ability to 'control' what takes place in the factory in no way necessarily leads to working class political power, as was pointed out in Goodrich (1920):

> The demand for personal freedom in industry is not identical with the demand for political power within industry; the one begins as a desire for no government, the other is a desire for a share in self-government.

Whereas varying degrees of job control by workers have been compatible with capitalism, workers' control could only become a reality in the transition to socialism. It is therefore on the struggle over job control that we shall concentrate here.

The different meanings attached to control exerted by workers within production are necessarily mirrored in discussions of capitalist control. There is a distinction between the absolute control exercised by capitalists as legal owners and managers and the relative control that capitalists may exercise to varying degrees over work itself—e.g., pace and methods of work. Variations in relative control as between capital and labour must always be seen in the context of the ultimate power capitalists have to close a plant or divert investment elsewhere.

The potential for workers to establish job controls also varies enormously across industries and occupational groups, depending on the nature of labour processes themselves and the degree of skill and bargaining power of the workforce. Continuous flow production, as in chemicals, is harder for workers to control than mass or batch production, as in engineering. Skilled workers can generally exert more controls than the unskilled.

Workers with very great power to disrupt may in practice have least scope for controlling output where to do so involves health and safety hazards—e.g., health workers or workers in water or power supply. Generalizations on the subject of control at work are therefore very difficult to make, and this should be borne in mind in what follows.

19-5 TENDENCIES WITHIN CAPITALIST DEVELOPMENT

From his analysis of changes taking place in the capitalist labour process in Britain during the nineteenth century, Marx concluded that the working class would be unable to resist the deskilling and homogenization of labour. Thus craftsmen would be replaced increasingly by young and female unskilled labour. These changes were the result both of competition's forcing the adoption of the cheapest techniques of production on each capitalist enterprise, and of capitalist determination to destroy the resistance of workers to the establishment of full managerial control of the labour process. In his analysis of twentieth century US capitalism, Braverman documented the same tendencies at work (Braverman, 1974). This approach, while providing important insights into the internal workings of the capitalist labour process, fails to take sufficient account of other offsetting factors—e.g., the role of worker resistance and the maintenance of divisions in the workforce for purposes of hierarchical control.

The way in which capitalism established itself as the dominant mode of production, first through concentration of ownership of the instruments of production and subsequently through control of the labour process itself, can be analysed in a number of stages and elements. The first stage, involving the imposition of discipline and supervision, corresponds to what Marx referred to as the expansion of absolute surplus value—i.e., increasing the length and intensity of the working day and week. By centralizing employment in factories, without necessarily changing production methods themselves, employers were able to enforce work discipline (e.g., rules against talking or breaks), and to impose regular and long hours. This was made possible initially by direct coercion—i.e., the use of unfree labour from prisons, workhouses, and orphanages—and because of the capitalists' ownership of the means of production and the workers' lack of any alternative source of income. However, the expansion of absolute surplus value meets with definite limits imposed by resistance from developing workers' organizations (e.g., the nineteenth-century struggle over the 10-hour day).

Subsequent stages correspond to the expansion of relative surplus value—i.e., increasing the productivity of labour. This is achieved in the case of craft labour first through the subdivision of each productive speciality into limited operations and the creation of detail workers, none of whom will thereafter be capable of carrying through any complete production process. This is intended to have three effects. Concentration on a single operation makes the worker more productive. Tasks requiring skill are separated from tasks that do not, and it therefore becomes possible for the capitalist to purchase only the precise quantity of skill necessary for each process. Finally, management begins to assume technical and not just disciplinary control, because workers cease to have an overall technical knowledge of the labour process. Subdivision therefore leads to a decline in the overall level of skill in the workforce.

Managerial assumption of technical control of the work process, which subdivision makes possible, has been elaborated most clearly in the theory of scientific management, which began to influence capitalist development internationally from the eighteen-nineties. It involves the gathering together of knowledge of the work process, its systematization into rules and formulae, and its dissociation from the production worker. This knowledge is then applied to control each step of the labour process and the payment for it.

Finally, the imposition of capitalist control of the labour process involves a scientific–technical revolution, the transformation of technology and development of machinery. In the last two decades of the nineteenth century, science began to be used to plan the progress of technology and product design. Previously it had lagged behind the spontaneous technological developments brought about by working mechanics. For example, the steam engine, the central working mechanism of the Industrial Revolution, developed in advance of the prevailing scientific theory of heat, which had little to say on the properties of steam. On the contrary, an entire branch of physics, thermo-dynamics, developed in part as a result of empirical observations of engineering methods and performance. The form taken by successive stages of mechanization and the uses to which it has been put have reflected the capitalist search for great control as well as improved labour productivity. As Braverman (1974, p. 195) wrote:

> Machinery offers to management the opportunity to do by wholly mechanical means that which it had previously attempted to do by organisational and disciplinary means. The fact that many machines may be paced and controlled according to centralised decisions, and that these controls may thus be in the hands of management, removed from the site of production to the office—these technical possibilities are of just as great interest to management as the fact that the machine multiplies the productivity of labour.

Moreover, technological developments do not themselves determine what will be the appropriate division of labour. This can be illustrated by examining the use of numerically controlled machine tools to cut metal automatically for the production of machines. These are machine tools whose movements are controlled not manually by a skilled machinist but automatically by means of a programme punched on to a tape. They could be used to improve the performance of the skilled worker without under-mining his control or skill. Since knowledge of metal-cutting practices required for programming is part of the craftsman's skill, he could continue to carry out the conceptualization required by the process while being relieved of the need to control the machine and make calculations while cutting is in progress. Yet under capitalist relations the process offers opportunities for the destruction of craft and cheapening of the resulting pieces of labour into which it is broken. The design that will enable the operation to be broken down among cheaper operators is the design sought by managers.

The processes described above—the imposition of work discipline, the subdivision of labour, the control of work methods through monopolization of knowledge, and mechanization—represent the means by which the capitalist class has sought to control labour in such a way as to extract from it the maximum surplus labour. However, the extent to which and manner in which these processes have actually occurred have varied enormously between industries, economies, and historical periods. Three sets of relationships influence the way in which the labour process develops in practice. These are the relations between capital and labour, the relations among capitalists, and the relations among groups of workers.

The effect of relations between capitalists appears considerably more complex than Marx envisaged. Intense competition in product markets, instead of forcing capitalists to adopt the most advanced techniques of production, may act as a constraint on this process by weakening the hand of capital *vis-à-vis* labour, especially strategic groups of workers within the labour process. Thus in the first quarter of the twentieth century the highly competitive nature of the British newspaper industry and its uniquely perishable product enabled skilled printworkers to secure control over new composing machines as they were introduced, at wage rates that made them into the best-paid manual workers in the country. Equally, the fragmented structure of the British steel industry and its relatively weak competitive position in the latter part of the nineteenth century appear to have wedded employers to a strategy of industrial peace. By contrast, the larger and stronger US steel firms were able to undermine craft unionism through industrial confrontation and technological change.

In practice there is a continual process of conflict, compromise, and cooperation between capitalists and workers over the form and content of components of technical change, mechanization, the division of labour, and the intensity of work. The actual outcome of this process in any particular situation will depend, leaving aside the impact of competitive forces, on the strength of worker organization, conditions in the labour market, the degree to which workers are united, and the extent to which capitalists continue to depend on hierarchical patterns of control within the workforce. Whether or not changes in the labour process lead to deskilling and homogenization of the labour force will also depend on these factors. Thus the skilled printworkers in the newspaper industry already referred to were assisted in maintaining their dominant position in the labour process by the unity between skilled and unskilled workers in the movement for a 50-hour week. On the other hand, in cotton textiles in the second half of the nineteenth century the skilled male mule spinners maintained control of the labour process despite mechanization in part because they provided the close supervision of younger and unskilled workers that the employers required. Thus the skilled men's interest in preventing cheap, unskilled, and female labour from operating new machines coincided with the employers' need to maintain a hierarchy of control within the workplace.

This highlights the divisive way in which control struggles may develop, since control over the labour process by craft workers—or, more recently, technicians—may also entail control over other workers. It is also clear that capitalists may be more concerned to increase control over unskilled or semi-skilled labour than over skilled labour, particularly where the proportion of skilled workers is very small. However, divisions thus created may in time be turned against skilled workers when their interests cease to coincide with those of their employers.

19-6   THE MOTOR INDUSTRY

'After almost three hundred years of performing mundane, menial tasks our people have had enough. There are people in my factory who perform the same operation day in, day out, 600 times an hour. A stoppage of work is the only way to break the hellish boredom. Until you have worked in a car factory you have no idea the excitement a spider can cause, just by crawling up a wall.' (British Leyland toolmaker, *Sunday Times*, 19 March 1978.)

In contrast to the mainstream of Marxist writers on the labour process, who have emphasized the tendencies towards maintenance and extension of capitalist control, orthodox economists have repeatedly argued that the degree of workers' bargaining power and the use to which it has been put in the UK have been key factors bringing about slower economic growth and lower productivity in the UK. Nowhere has this case been put more strongly than in the motor car industry. As was pointed out at the beginning of Section 19-3, conclusions drawn from evidence on specific occupational groups within one industry, even if correct, cannot be generalized to the economy as a whole. However, there are two reasons for looking specifically at this part of the capitalist labour process. One is the central and strategic role played by car production in the long boom of the postwar capitalist world. The other is that if we wish to criticize the conclusions drawn by economists about the role of labour militancy in Britain's economic decline, the most effective way of doing that is by reference to the industry and occupational groups where they consider evidence for their hypothesis is strongest.

In the space of only two years, 1974–6, no less than four official reports on the motor car industry were produced. Of these, the Think Tank's report (Central Policy Review Staff, 1975), in particular the conclusion quoted below, has received the widest publicity.

> With the same power at his elbow and doing the same job as his continental counterpart a British car assembly worker produces only half as much output per shift.

The view that low relative productivity in the UK (a fact that nobody disputes) is the responsibility of workers themselves has become a common argument. According to this view, a combination of laziness, strike-proneness, insistence on excessive manning, and inter-union demarcation (particularly in the area of maintenance), have produced high labour costs, low growth, and declining market shares of UK based producers.

However, even among the official reports on the industry, different interpretations of the UK car industry's problems have been given. For example the Ryder Report on British Leyland reached other conclusions (Ryder, 1975).

> We do not subscribe to the view that all the ills of British Leyland can be laid at the door of a strike-prone and work-shy labour force. While BL has suffered seriously from interruptions to production, these have often been the result of factors outside the control of BL's workforce—breakdowns in plant and equipment, faulty scheduling, shortages of materials and components, and external industrial disputes ... similarly one of the main reasons why BL workers produce less than workers at Fiat or Volkswagen is that so much less has been spent by BL on plant and machinery.

In order to disentangle the arguments and the evidence it is necessary to examine historically the constraints and external pressures operating on UK capital in this sector, the development of job control by workers, and the limits of that control, the implications of changes in the labour process for different sections of workers and for their bargaining power, and the evolution of union and workplace organization.

Motor vehicle production did not develop in Britain until after 1896, when the rule that required a man with a red flag to walk in front of a motor car was replaced by a 14 mph speed limit. Unlike other industries, therefore, the British motor vehicle industry developed later than those in the US, France, and Germany. However, from 1915 its home market was effectively shielded from international competition by a high tariff imposed on all imported cars, which remained in operation until 1956. Throughout this period the major motor firms enjoyed more or less uninterrupted economic prosperity and expanding markets, which encouraged them to adopt a relatively conciliatory stand *vis-à-vis* labour. For example, some of the big motor manufacturers were unhappy with the strategy of the Engineering Employers' Federation in the twenties to oppose union involvement in joint consultation on any issue. Some left the EEF after the 1922 lock-out because they feared the strategy would lead to another serious lock-out, at a time when the market for vehicles was recovering quickly.

The nature of trade unionism in the motor industry also reflects the historical context in which the industry developed. The labour force for the expanding new industry, centred in the Midlands, was drawn from unemployed and semi-skilled or unskilled workers from declining industries (e.g., watch-making and bicycle-making). Thus the skilled Engineers Union, which elsewhere was fighting to retain control of the new semi-automatic machines, failed to gain a major foothold; instead a new and militant organization of semi-skilled workers, the Workers Union, was established. These workers were concerned to use their strong bargaining position to improve wages and conditions rather than to defend their skill against the threat of dilution. Struggles over control of production have been primarily concerned with payment systems, as the following examples show.

Managers have persistently fought for the notion that individual workers be paid for the output they actually produce rather than for the skills they have. Thus after the 1898 engineering lock-out, the principle of mutuality, whereby 'the prices to be paid for piece work shall be fixed by mutual arrangement between the employer and the workman or workmen', replaced payment based on union negotiated time rates. The employers favoured the individual piece-rate system because it enabled them to pay low rates to workers in relatively weak bargaining positions without having to pay these rates generally. The individual piece-rate system depended on work measurement by 'experts', rate-fixers, who specified how much work ought to be done and how much should be produced. Under this system workers are paid bonus earnings over the basic rate in relation to time saved against time allowed. It is based on Taylorian principles of scientific management, where the aim is to control the worker's actual methods of work and earnings by careful setting of piece rates. The system is designed to reduce comparability of one worker's earnings with another. However, because shop stewards emerged to negotiate over piece rates and gained bargaining power in the process, they were able to change the terms of the bargaining process from the time 'scientifically' required for particular tasks to the level of earnings considered necessary by workers. Through their role as negotiators, shop stewards gained knowledge of earnings throughout a factory and were therefore able to bargain more effectively for individual workers.

There are other problems for management, arising from this system of time piece-work negotiated on an individual basis. Where demand for the product is high, the labour market tight or the technology changing, then production can be paralysed by the negotiating process. This led to the development of the gang system based on money piece-work in many sectors of engineering, including motor cars, from the late thirties onward.

Under money piece-work, production workers are paid at a price per piece directly proportionate to output. Under the gang system, the gang leader negotiates a 'contract' with top managers to produce a given output. He then keeps track of work and money and tries to ensure that each gang member keeps up his workload. The ganger is generally elected by the gang and responsible to it (unlike the nineteenth-century subcontracting system that operated in industries like cotton textiles). The gang payment system is generally more favourable from the workers' point of view than most individual piece-work systems. Wages are calculated from a base rate that allows a 'decent' wage, with incentive bonuses available for output above the contracted amount. However, the gang system also represented a solution to employers' need for an extremely flexible and 'responsible' labour force, when new materials and new tasks had to be incorporated quickly into productive activity. In order to resolve the problem of incentive in a period of boom, management acquiesced in a system that increased workers' job control, job security, and security against other forms of disciplinary action (since individual workers could not be penalized).

The operation of money piece-work in all UK car firms except Ford facilitated high production levels and the introduction of new technology in the late forties and fifties. For example, between 1948 and 1959 all the major car firms introduced transfer automation for machining, turning, grinding, and boring operations, pressing, and assembly. Output increased by 180 per cent as a result, while employment in the industry rose by only 18 per cent over the same period. Their ability to control earnings at a relatively high level was an important factor in winning the acquiescence of the workforce in these technological changes, in an industry characterized by insecurity of employment even in a boom period.

However, piece-work systems that give groups of workers a measure of autonomy and job control create problems for employers when demand for the product slackens or there is a need to discharge workers. Thus Standard Triumph, which had a record of almost 10 strike-free years from the Second World War as a result of the smooth operation of the gang system, became one of the most strike-prone car firms from the late fifties, when lay-offs were introduced as a result of sharpening international competition. The bargaining power and collective solidarity built up during the previous period with the acquiescence of employers now presented an obstacle to the implementation of capitalist strategy in the changed market conditions. Employers were now under pressure to regain control both of earnings and of work methods in order to increase labour productivity.

During the late sixties and early seventies measured day work was seen as a method of reimposing greater managerial control over the labour process, enabling intensification of work and reducing differentials disputes within and between factories. With measured day work, pay rates per day are negotiated factory-wide. Work tasks are measured closely and the shopfloor struggle shifts to how much time specific tasks should take rather than how much workers ought to be paid for the job. Managers try to claim, in the Taylorian tradition, that the former is a scientific matter to be decided by 'experts'.

The implementation of measured day work does not, however, necessarily provide a method of increasing managerial control over production where shopfloor organization is strong and shop stewards are active. At Ford Halewood, where day rates had always been in operation, stewards in the trim and final assembly departments had managed by the late sixties to establish considerable control in a number of sections over work allocations and job timings. A number of stewards had become more knowledgeable about work study than their respective supervisors. Thus 'if an operator complained that he was being asked to do too much work, the steward was able to base a case upon the efficacy of the job timings, which often served to drive a wedge between the supervisor and the work study department' (Beynon, 1973).

The problem for management is that no system of payment, work study, or any other technique intended to assert greater control over the actions of the workforce can override human ingenuity. The irony of an economic system that is forced to stifle people's creativity in order to increase their productive potential has been pointed out by a Ford senior steward (Passingham and Connor, 1977, p. 18).

> They've got the most sophisticated techniques, Fords, for timing a bloke with a watch, and they know where he can go, and how long it takes him to get from that point down to there, and they time it to the last iota. But it doesn't matter how well they do it, the bloke will always make himself two or three minutes. It doesn't matter how clever they are, he'll always try and find something to beat them on. I believe we should be releasing all that. That's why the discussion about industrial democracy is so stimulating to me, that's something we ought to get involved in.

One conclusion that emerges from this evidence is that in the UK motor vehicle industry each successive wave of managerial techniques aimed at increasing the productive potential of the workforce relative to its cost has run up against problems when shopfloor workers in key sections have had time to learn how to reassert their own control or changing conditions have allowed them to do so.

A number of further questions are raised by this conclusion. To what extent is the UK unique in this respect relative to foreign motor industry competitors? What have been the limits of worker job control in the UK motor vehicle industry, given the ultimate power of capital to decide its investment strategy? To what extent will the continued intensification of international competition for the UK industry undermine the bargaining power labour developed because of unique historical factors?

It is clear that, given the inherent conflict of interest between capital and labour within the production process, managerial strategy can never concern itself solely with economic criteria narrowly defined. Thus the decision for multi-national car firms to adopt component multi-sourcing policies from the late sixties had the political purpose of increasing managerial bargaining power *vis-à-vis* the workforce of different countries (and, incidentally, *vis-à-vis* national governments). That this policy contravened economic criteria is indicated by Ford's decision to end multi-sourcing component policies with the Fiesta in order to cut costs.

It is also the case that labour in any country represents a potential threat to capitalist profitability, although the degree to which an actual threat exists depends on factors such as the vulnerability of the workforce, its degree of unity and organization, general conditions in the labour market, historical traditions, etc. In fact the Western European vehicle industry outside the UK has depended for its expansion largely on labour that has been vulnerable and lacking in trade union traditions and experience. It could be argued that if workers in continental car plants work twice as hard as those in British car plants, this would indicate an excessive exploitation of a weak labour force consisting largely of 'guest workers' from other countries.

In practice, pressure has been exerted on British car workers to speed up rather than on managers to slow down the pace of work on the continent, except in so far as continental workers have begun to develop their own organization and controls. Thus in recent years there have been moves in the UK motor industry to reduce or eliminate tea breaks and washing, cleaning up, and waiting times. The move to measured day work discussed above and the associated increase in the ratio of supervisors to production workers from about $1:40$ to $1:25$ is another part of this strategy of labour intensification in the UK (Institute for Workers Control, 1977).

What, therefore, have been the limits on worker job control in the UK motor industry? These limits are set, on the one hand, by the power capitalists ultimately have to shift investment elsewhere or make investment that reduces their dependence on labour, and, on the other, by obstacles to the development of trade union and political strength of labour at a national and international level.

While the trade union strength of labour at a national UK and at an international level has increased in the course of the motor car industry's history, the mobility and concentration of capital and competitive pressures upon it have also grown. When a number of the engineering firms that pioneered motor car production located their plant in the Midlands, they were able to tap reserves of unskilled and semi-skilled labour lacking in the craft union traditions of the northern engineering centres and vulnerable because of high levels of unemployment. The second phase of geographical shifts that took place within the UK in the sixties, when all the major car firms set up new factories or large factory extensions in areas of high unemployment (primarily around Liverpool and in Scotland), was less effective from a capitalist viewpoint. This was partly because the new centres were this time also old centres of working class militancy. Despite high levels of unemployment, this tradition had not been lost. It was also because the car workers in the south-east and Midlands centres recognized the need for organization to be extended to the new centres. For example, when Ford built the Halewood plant, it was Dagenham workers who stopped work to make sure the Halewood plant received the same rates of pay as them. Thus a significant development in trade union strength and unity had taken place compared with the period when the semi-skilled engineering workers of Coventry fought to become organized without the support of the skilled workers in Sheffield and Glasgow.

However, it is important not to exaggerate the degree of interplant trade union organization and solidarity now existing in the UK. And whatever may exist within the UK itself, such organization has only just begun to develop internationally in response to the internationalization of capitalist production. Consequently car firms have been able to undermine the bargaining power of UK workers through international shifts in production and the threat of further shifts. A strike at Ford Halewood in 1969 resulted in a threat that production would be shifted to Europe. Dies for several of the models being made at Halewood were moved from the plants. Subsequently some national and international cooperation was achieved between the various shop stewards' committees, which prevented dies from being moved beyond Dagenham and into Europe. However, since duplicate dies can be made, the Halewood stewards established contact with their counterparts in Genk, Belgium, and Cologne, West Germany. They came to broad agreement that work should not be moved between plants. But the necessary follow-up organization was not established and duplicate dies were made, enabling Ford to shift work from Halewood. From the late sixties it has been Ford's German operations rather than those in Britain that have increasingly become the centre for Ford Europe. The ability of capitalist firms to shift production in this way indicates the very limited nature of job controls that workers, however highly organized within the workplace, can develop, particularly in the context of a shrinking and highly competitive international market like that for cars in the seventies.

Developments in the UK motor car industry illustrate both the limits and vulnerabilities of job control from labour's viewpoint and the factors influencing shifts in the frontier of control. These factors include conditions in product and labour markets as well as the pattern and degree of technical change. Another important factor, which will be dealt with more fully in Chapter 20, is the nature and strength of workplace organization itself, which does not develop merely as a reflection of market conditions and capitalist strategies. For example, the period of the fifties and sixties, which was a peak period for shopfloor bargaining power in the car factories of Coventry, was a period when the shop stewards' movement in Ford UK struggled to survive at all. In 1957 and 1963 key stewards were successfully dismissed by Ford and it was not until 1969 that Ford was forced to negotiate for the first time with shopfloor representatives.

The essentially defensive and reactive nature of job control struggles is borne out by the evidence available from the motor industry, although the potential for a developing political consciousness is also occasionally present. The growing concern among shop stewards in the seventies to influence the investment strategies of their employers arises because jobs are increasingly under threat, but this concern extends beyond traditional job control struggles to a questioning of capitalist economics. However, this will only take place if the mass of workers develop a wider political consciousness alongside their trade union consciousness, at the same time as the bargaining power underlying the organization that has been built up is being undermined by market forces. That this process was not yet occurring by the end of the seventies in the British motor industry is indicated by the widespread acceptance of redundancies, closures, and dismissal in 1979 of a senior steward at British Leyland.

FURTHER READING

For analysis of the capital labour process and its historical development see Karl Marx's *Capital* (1976), Braverman (1974), and Elbaum *et al* (1979). Two major studies of the motor car industry are Beynon (1973) and Freidman (1977). See also Nichols and Armstrong (1976) and Terkel (1977).

TWENTY

THE DEVELOPMENT OF
THE BRITISH WORKING CLASS

Jean Gardiner

20-1 INTRODUCTION

The concept of class and the definition of the working class were discussed in Chapter 4. In the last chapter we looked at one set of influences shaping the composition of the labour force working for capital, namely changes in the labour process. In this chapter the implications of these changes for class structure are explored, together with the impact of the supply of labour and sources of recruitment for the labour force. The discussion of class structure leads on to analysis of the economic, political, and ideological composition of the working class and its various sections and of the historical development of the British labour movement in comparison with those of other major capitalist countries. The relationship between skill and bargaining power and the nature of divisions within the trade union movement are examined. The specific strengths and weakness of the British labour movement are explored.

20-2 THE COMPOSITION OF THE BRITISH WORKING CLASS

The working class is constantly in process of formation, both in terms of its overall size relative to other classes and in terms of its composition. As capitalism has developed, the wage labour force has grown to incorporate sections of the population previously engaged in non-capitalist production relations (e.g., peasants, the self-employed, family workers, and housewives). At the same time its internal composition has drastically altered, industrially and occupationally, in line with the development of old labour processes and the emergence of new ones.

An examination of the composition of the adult population shows that between 1961 and 1977 there was no significant change in the proportion who were economically 'active', roughly 60 per cent, and economically 'inactive', about 40 per cent (see Table 20–1). The economically active population includes all those in, or officially available for, paid work. Thus the registered unemployed are considered economically active, while full-time housewives are regarded as inactive. Among those in employment, the proportion of employees relative to employers and self-employed also remained constant over this period. However, among employees there was an increase in the proportion of women, and particularly of part-time workers, as well as a rise in the unemployed. The most striking changes were within the economically 'inactive' group. On the one hand, there was a sharp decline in the proportion of full-time housewives. On the other, the major increase was among retired people.

Table 20-1 Economic activity of population of Great Britain, 1961–77

	Percentage of population	
	1961	1977
Economically active		
Self-employed and employers	4.3	4.4
Employees in employment	54.6	54.4
Part-time workers (included above)	5.2	10.4
Male workers (included above)	36.3	32.4
Female workers (included above)	18.3	22.0
Unemployed	1.0	3.4
Total economically active	59.9	62.2
Economically inactive		
Students	2.5	3.0
Retired	6.2	11.7
Housewives and other persons	31.4	23.1
Total economically inactive	40.1	37.8
Total adult population (thousands)	39 569	41 353

Source: Social Trends, (1974), *General Household Survey* (1977), *Annual Abstract* (1979).

The overall constancy of economic activity rates means that the rise in activity rates for women have been only just sufficient to offset the decline for men. Table 20-2 provides a breakdown of activity rates. Very sharp rises in activity rates for married women of all age groups (from 8.7 per cent in 1921 to 49.0 per cent in 1976) together with rises for non-married women in middle age groups have offset declines in rates for the youngest and oldest groups of men and non-married women. The large increase in the proportion of the population in the retirement age group has also lowered the overall activity rate.

This chapter is mostly concerned with that section of the population that are sellers of labour power. While making up over 90 per cent of the

Table 20-2 Economic activity rates for Great Britain, 1921–76

	1921	1951	1976
Males	87.1	87.6	80.6
Married females	8.7	21.7	49.0
Non-married females	53.8	55.0	41.6

Source: British Labour Statistics Yearbook (1974), Table 106; *Social Trends* (1977), Table 5.3.

employed population, it is important to remember they are only just over half of the adult population as a whole. About 40 per cent of adults have no direct relationship with production (if we do not count domestic production) and are dependent either on families or on the state. However, the great majority of this 40 per cent are part of the working class because of their dependence on the sale of labour, both their own at other stages of their life and that of their families. The dependent population is, of course, even larger than this figure suggests because children have been excluded.

Turning now to the employed population, significant changes have occurred over time in sectoral distribution associated with both cyclical and secular patterns. As can be seen from Table 20-3, the proportion of total employment in the primary sector of agriculture, forestry, and fishing has declined steadily throughout the last half century. The proportion of labour in manufacturing was roughly the same in 1976 as in 1921, although considerable changes occurred in the intervening period—a reduction in the slump of the thirties followed by an increase in the war boom of the forties

Table 20–3 Industrial structure of employment for Great Britain 1921–76

	Percentage of:						
	Total civilian employment			Total employees in employment			
	1921	1931	1941	1951	1961	1971	1976
Agriculture, forestry, fishing	8.8	7.4	5.5	3.7	3.2	1.9	1.7
Manufacturing	33.3[a]	31.4[a]	41.7	41.6	38.4	36.4	32.2
Other production industries	11.5	11.1	11.7	12.3	11.6	9.1	8.9
Services	46.5	50.4	41.1	42.4	46.7	52.4	57.2

[a] Figures for manufacturing in 1921 and 1931 include some workers from other production industries.

Source: British Labour Statistics Historical Abstract, Tables 103, 116, 135; *Social Trends* (1975), Table 3.1; *Department of Employment Gazette*, November 1977.

and a steady decline from the fifties during both boom and slump. Other production industries (i.e., mining, construction, gas electricity, water) have also shed labour steadily from the fifties. Service sector employment has expanded to offset both cyclical and secular declines in employment elsewhere. In the thirties this took the form mostly of an expansion in personal service work, while from the fifties there has been growth in a wide range of service industries.

Dividing the period from the Second World War into three phases, 1948–64, 1964–70 and 1970–77, one can see different patterns of expansion and decline in different industries. Between 1948 and 1964 labour was shed from two newly nationalized industries (railways and coal mining), from national government employment after its war-time peak, and from a narrow range of traditional manufacturing industries (i.e., clothing and textiles). Among other services, the only area of declining employment was hotels and catering, which experienced industrial and technological changes during the period. Expansion of employment was highest in a range of service industries, especially education, insurance, finance, and other professional services, followed by manufacturing, public utilities, and construction.

From 1964 to 1970 distribution, public utilities, and construction joined the declining industries of the fifties and early sixties in shedding labour. The growth in manufacturing employment slowed down. The highest levels of expansion continued to be in the dominant service areas of the previous period, notably insurance and finance.

The subsequent seven-year period 1970–77 reveals a drastically different picture, with systematic reductions in employment in every manufacturing and production industry. Meanwhile growth in employment continued in all the service industries, but was insufficient completely to offset decline elsewhere. There was therefore a small decline in overall employment. The decline in the number of full-time worker equivalents was rather higher as a result of the rise in the proportion of part-time workers.

Public sector employment has grown slightly relative to private sector employment in the last 25 years, standing at about 37 per cent of the total in 1976 as compared with 34 per cent in 1951 (see Table 20-4). The growth has occurred from the sixties, more than offsetting a decline in the fifties. The major growth area has been in local authority employment, with declines taking place in the public corporations and armed forces. However, since 1976 there has been a decline in the local authority labour force as a result of cuts in public expenditure.

Finally, there are changes in the occupational structure of employment. The most striking long-term change in the occupational composition of the working class has been the expansion of non-manual relative to manual work. This development reflects, on the one hand, the changes in the industrial distribution of employment that have been discussed above. On the other hand, it reflects changes in the labour processes of production

Table 20-4 Employment in public and private sectors for the UK, 1951-76

	Percentage of total		
	1951[a]	1961	1976
Military	3.6	1.9	1.2
Civil central government	4.9	5.3	8.1
Local authority	6.1	7.6	12.1
Public corporations	12.1	9.0	8.1
Total public	26.7	23.8	29.5
Private	73.2	76.1	70.5

[a] Great Britain only.

Sources: Social Trends (1979); *British Labour Statistics Historical Abstract* (1979).

industries (see Chapter 19). The proportion of non-manual employment in manufacturing industries increased from 8 per cent in 1907 to 28 per cent in 1975.

The distinction between non-manual and manual occupations is itself often misleading and often based on social, economic, and technical characteristics of jobs that are anachronistic. For example, most clerical work today involves machine operation of a highly manual nature and yet it continues to be categorized in accordance with the social and economic status it had 100 years ago. Equally revolutionary changes have occurred

Table 20-5 The occupied population of Great Britain by major occupational groups, 1911–66

Occupational groups	As a percentage of total occupied populations	
	1911	1966
Employers and proprietors	6.7	3.4
Non-manual workers	18.7	38.3
Managers and administrators	3.4	6.1
Higher professionals	1.0	3.4
Lower professionals and technicians	3.1	6.5
Foremen and inspectors	1.3	3.0
Clerks	4.5	13.2
Salesmen and shop assistants	5.4	6.1
Manual workers	74.6	58.3
Skilled	30.5	23.7
Semi-skilled	34.4	26.1
Unskilled	9.6	8.5
Total occupied population	100.0	100.0

Source: Bain and Price (1972).

THE DEVELOPMENT OF THE BRITISH WORKING CLASS 321

within shop work. Nonetheless, major differences do exist in the work experiences and conditions and trade union organization of manual and non-manual workers, making the different categories worthy of study.

From Table 20-5 it can be seen that between 1911 and 1966 the proportion of non-manual workers in the economically active population doubled from 19 per cent to 38 per cent. The largest increase was among clerical workers, who increased their share from 5 per cent to 13 per cent. The proportion of manual workers declined correspondingly, from 75 per cent to 58 per cent. Among manual workers there was a greater reduction among skilled and semi-skilled workers than among unskilled workers.

Table 20-6 Changes in occupational structure by sex for Great Britain, 1966–76

	Occupied men		Occupied women	
	1966	1976	1966	1976
Non-manual	33	38	53	56
Managerial/higher professional	15	20	5	5
Lower professional/ junior non-manual	18	18	48	51
Manual	67	62	48	44
Skilled	40	42	11	8
Semi-skilled/unskilled/ Personal service	27	20	37	36

Sources: Westergaard and Resler (1975); *Social Trends* (1977).

Sharp differences in occupational structure related to sex are shown in Table 20-6. The trend growth in non-manual occupations has continued since 1966 for both sexes, although slightly more rapidly for men than for women. Within non-manual groups most of the growth for men has been within the managerial and higher professional groups, while for women it has been concentrated in the lower professional and junior non-manual groups. Among manual workers, skilled men have slightly improved their relative position while the proportion of skilled women has declined. On the other hand, among semi-skilled and unskilled groups there has been a decline for male workers while the proportion of female workers has remained static.

These tendencies within the occupational structure have very serious implications for women in particular. Nearly three-quarters of employed women are presently in jobs of a low-level non-manual or manual type. These are the jobs in both the manufacturing and service sectors of the economy that will be most vulnerable, given the technological changes that are in process (see Chapter 21).

Considerably more study of changes in the labour process of specific industries in the UK is needed in order to analyse the implications for occupational structure. Even within manufacturing there is a wide diversity. The proportion of non-manual labour varies, from as high as 40 per cent in chemicals, where capitalism has carried through the most far-reaching changes in the labour process, to as low as 13 per cent in clothing and footwear, where mechanization is still at a rudimentary level. Moreover, growth in non-manual employment as a whole does not safeguard the position of specific non-manual groups. For example, in the vehicles industry, which was discussed in Chapter 19, managers, draughtsmen, and clerical workers all experienced a decline in their share of employment between 1965 and 1975 as a result of rationalization and changing non-manual labour processes. The share of craftsmen also fell, confirming a deskilling of manual work in this particular industry.

20-3 THE HISTORICAL DEVELOPMENT OF THE BRITISH LABOUR MOVEMENT

A number of unique features of the British labour movement's history will be examined in this section. These are the context of British capitalism's early and imperialistic development, the craft and general structure of British unions, the strength of trade unions, particularly at workplace level, and the nature and political role of the Labour Party. The relationships between these separate features will be explored.

The industrial development of British capitalism depended on pre-capitalist craft labour to a much greater extent than that elsewhere. This was because the Industrial Revolution pre-dated the application of science to technology and the early machines coexisted with a vast number of hand tools. New machines never suddenly eliminated all the skilled work necessary for the processes they performed. Machines had to be set up and maintained and work often needed to be rectified by hand to reach the necessary specifications. The technical dependence of British capitalists on craft workers, particularly in the engineering trades, during the peak period of British industrial dominance in the eighteen-fifties and sixties greatly enhanced the bargaining power of this section of the working class. Craft unionism, embodied in New Model unions such as the Amalgamated Society of Engineers (ASE), formed in 1851, was consolidated in the eighteen-fifties and sixties. The development of technology that the application of these workers' skills made possible was the basis for later industrialization elsewhere, less dependent on craft labour.

Craft unions played the central role in the formative years of the British trade union movement over a hundred years ago. The influence they exerted on its ideas and institutions requires brief examination, despite the transformation that has subsequently taken place in the composition of the trade union movement. Stable trade unionism developed in Britain first around the skilled trades, not just because of their key position in the industrial labour processes but also because of the economic and political weakness of the working class as a whole. The mass of labouring people led a highly insecure semi-proletarian existence, and outside a few centres a fully developed factory system did not develop until the end of the nineteenth century. Political parties of the working class had not begun to develop. The urban male artisan section of the working class had to wait until 1867 to get the vote, and other male manual workers until 1884. Women did not get the vote on equal terms with men until 1928. Trade unionism was therefore established in Britain before socialist and Marxist ideas had begun to exert a significant political influence on the working class. The dominant ideology among the skilled tradesmen was rather that of radicalism and liberalism, appropriate to a labour aristocracy cushioned by British capitalism's world monopoly position.

The principle of craft exclusivity that the New Model unions fought to establish reflected the two aims these earliest unions had: trade protection and welfare. Trade protection and enhanced economic bargaining power were achieved through controlling entry into the trade. Limiting union membership to the skilled and hence actuarially sound worker reduced the cost of sickness and unemployment benefits paid out of union funds.

The dominance of craft unions in the early history of the British trade union movement has influenced its subsequent development in a number of ways. Most obviously it meant that when unskilled and semi-skilled workers began to get organized with the militant political industrial upsurges of 1889 and 1911, general unions were set up in the major industries rather than industrial unions encompassing skilled as well as unskilled workers. Even among skilled workers, the need for unity within industries was not always established. Thus the Boilermakers Union resisted amalgamation with the Engineers in 1851 and 1920 and were still independent in the nineteen-seventies.

This heritage has meant both strengths and weaknesses for the British labour movement. The early craft unions established not only a series of institutions that have provided a firm base for the movement as a whole—trades councils, the TUC, efficient ways of running union business, strategy and tactics of short-term campaigning—but also 'solidarity and class consciousness, a belief that so long as a man worked for wages, his interests were exclusively determined by that fact' (Hobsbawm, 1964). Rather later, during the First World War and its aftermath, the shop stewards' movement emerged from the active and most left-wing sections of the skilled trades unions and subsequently spread across the trade union movement as a whole. In addition, the sectional struggles of skilled workers have at times clearly strengthened the economic bargaining power of workers as a whole. This has occurred most strikingly when labour markets as a whole have been tight, as during the two world wars—for example, skilled workers have sometimes succeeded in establishing payment of skilled rates to dilutees.

On the negative side there is both the archaism and economic vulnerability of craft unionism and the political weaknesses it has given rise to. The essentially pre-capitalist nature of craft labour and the uniqueness of its role in British capitalism have already been discussed. The extent of its survival beyond the decline of British world domination in the eighteen-seventies resulted from the adoption of imperialist rather than industrial regeneration policies on the part of the British ruling class. Between 1875 and 1918 the growth of monopoly capitalism, involving industrial concentration and mass production, was very slow in Britain by comparison with Germany and the US, while that of the imperialist state apparatus was fast. Craft unions did exist, in fact, in other capitalist countries like the US, but their position elsewhere was undermined by the transformation of the industrial structure that took place with the rise of monopoly capitalism. The slowness of technical change in Britain meant that where there was a nucleus of well organized skilled workers it was less likely that employers would swamp it in a flood of cheap labour.

The vulnerability of bargaining power based on skill was attenuated temporarily but not eliminated by imperialism. In fact, imperialism probably served to make the costs of restructuring the labour process more sudden and severe when competitive pressures finally exerted themselves—as they did, for example, in the thirties and seventies. Thus the relative archaism of British industrial structure has served to strengthen trade union bargaining power and create militant defensive organizations, which have then resisted fiercely (but usually unsuccessfully) abrupt and costly restructuring of industry.

From the eighteen-nineties there was both a growing recognition among skilled workers of their economic vulnerability and a developing political consciousness. Both developments pushed skilled workers in the direction of industrial unionism, but the pace was very slow and fierce battles were fought in the process. Thus in 1907 a Delegate Meeting of the ASE established a machinists' section for semi-skilled male workers, but a majority of branches were hostile. It was not until 1922, after a national lockout and defeat for the union, that most semi-skilled male workers were admitted to what had now become the Amalgamated Engineering Union (AEU). Unskilled men had to wait until 1926 and women until 1942. Not surprisingly, by the time industrial unionism was finally accepted, most non-skilled engineering workers, who by the twenties began to outnumber skilled engineering workers, had joined rival general or white collar unions. Thus the slowness with which the majority of male skilled workers came to recognize the need to unite with semi-skilled and unskilled men and women, linked as we have seen with the industrially archaic and imperialistic nature of British capitalism, led to an institutionalization of divisions within the working class. Sectionalism within the trade union movement was not, however, confined to those industries characterized by craft and general unionism. Horizontal rather than vertical divisions existed in certain industries like iron and steel, where unions representing different levels of skill amalgamated to form the Iron and Steel Trades Confederation in 1917. Here the monopolistic world position of the British industry enabled plants of widely varying productivity to coexist. Local bargaining meant that workers in the most productive plants were able to secure for themselves a portion of the surplus, and wage differentials therefore varied considerably more between plants than between different levels of skill within plants. Thus pressure was never brought to bear on the union leadership to develop policies for the industry as a whole.

It appears that the British labour aristocracy, deriving its position from strong trade union organization and the dominant world position of British capitalism, from the eighteen-eighties ceased to consist solely of skilled male workers. Workers of different levels of skill who were in a strong economic bargaining position in highly profitable industries and firms were able to extract relatively high wages. In another sense, the British working class as a whole became a labour aristocracy in international terms. The standard of living of the poorest was raised from the end of the nineteenth century by the fruits of imperialist policies in the form of cheap food and raw materials for the developing mass consumption industries. Wage differentials themselves therefore ceased to have quite such a sharp significance in terms of standard of living. Social differentiation became more pronounced relative to economic differentiation within the working class as the growing ranks of clerical and shop workers were encouraged to dissociate themselves from manual workers even when they were economically worse off.

Finally, let us turn to the political development of the British labour movement. The consolidation of trade unionism in Britain before the development of socialist consciousness on a significant scale and before the establishment of working class suffrage has already been referred to. The major impetus for setting up a working class political party—the Labour Party—between 1898 and 1906 was not a commitment to socialist ideology but rather the need to defend trade unions from attacks on their legal status. Sections of the most reactionary employers, backed up by ultra-conservative lawyers, led an offensive in the eighteen-nineties aimed particularly at new and weak unions of unskilled workers. The attack developed by a series of legal decisions—culminating in the Taff Vale decision of 1901, which jeopardized the right to strike—into one threatening the entire labour movement, including the skilled and most moderate sections. The trade unions thus came together to support setting up a united political organization that would represent their collective interests.

It was not until 1918 that the Labour Party formally declared itself to be a socialist party. The political development of the British labour movement was considerably behind that of continental movements, while its trade union organization was significantly more advanced. The British labour movement was committing itself to socialism for the first time at the stage when elsewhere in Europe labour movements were splitting into Marxist and social democratic wings in the wake of the October Revolution in Russia in 1917. The slowness of the political development of the British working class was linked to both the economic protection afforded by the world role of British capitalism and the political sophistication of the state, which accepted trade unionism by the eighteen-sixties, before the working class as a whole had become a strong political force. On this subject see Hobsbawm (1964, pp. 336–7):

> From that moment no systematic attempt to suppress the labour movement has been made in Britain, except by particular sections of business, never entirely backed by even the most conservative of governments.... At moments of fear and hysteria attempts to attack labour all along the line may still be made; but the rulers of a country 90 per cent of whose citizens live by earning wages and two-thirds of which are manual workers, have been far too wise to indulge in them, even in the 1930s, when European fascism made the defeat of labour look tempting and possible.

Among the most politically conscious sections of the British labour movement, syndicalism took a stronger hold than Marxism in the first few decades of the twentieth century. For example, the most active skilled engineers, quickly disillusioned with the ineffectual role of the Labour Party, turned their attention from parliamentary representation to direct action and industrial unionism in the years preceding the First World War. Syndicalist ideas were influential in the shop stewards' movement, which grew out of the First World War. Antipathy to leaders is illustrated by the constitution of the National Shop Stewards' and Workers' Committee Movement, formed in 1916, which laid down that 'no committee shall have executive power, all questions of policy and action being referred back to the rank and file'. Syndicalism reinforced the hostility to politics already present in the trade union movement. The British Communist Party, formed in 1920, drawing into its ranks many workers from the shop stewards' movement, was also influenced by syndicalist ideas and was noted in the early twenties for its ultra-leftist approach to parliament.

The growth of working class political influence and the establishment of the Labour Party were probably more significant for the unskilled and semi-skilled workers and for the general unions, which shifted to the right after their early association with revolutionary socialist ideas. These workers, because of their relatively weak economic bargaining position, were more dependent on active state support than the skilled—e.g., the development of a state social security system from 1906 directly benefited unskilled workers whose unions could not afford to carry out this function for their members. The shift to the right in the general unions was also related to the fragmented nature of their membership, which was spread over numerous diverse industries. This made it difficult for any group of workers to mobilize support for questioning the policies of the leadership. The obverse to this was that where workers within general unions were in strong bargaining positions, particularly from the Second World War on, they were also often able to pursue policies independent from the union leadership. Thus TGWU shop stewards in sections of the motor industry became powerful partly because the union was incapable of maintaining a detailed grasp of developments in what was only one of many industries in which it was active.

To sum up what has been a very brief survey of important tendencies in the history of the British labour movement, we can see that there are a number of factors that helped to produce the strengths and weaknesses of the movement. The strength of the British labour movement has undoubtedly been its ability to consolidate itself around nuclei of substantial economic bargaining power grounded in the workplace. The strength of workplace bargaining power in Britain has resulted from the archaic industrial structure, the key role of craft unions, the relative independence of sections of semi-skilled and unskilled workers in general unions, syndicalist ideology with its emphasis on rank-and-filism, and the world dominance of British capitalism, which cushioned firms and enabled some employers to buy industrial peace by paying out a portion of their monopoly profits to their workers. The political weakness of the British labour movement, on the other hand, is related both to the sectional divisions within it and to the fact that trade unionism was legalized and accepted by the British ruling class without the need for a political battle and long before socialist ideas became influential within the working class. The Labour Party was set up initially to defend trade unions, not to fight for a different society. The confidence derived by the most strongly organized workers from their workplace bargaining strength meant that many of the most politically conscious workers were drawn to industrial action and syndicalism rather than political action and Marxism.

20-4   INTERNATIONAL COMPARISONS

The UK occupies a middle position in the ranking of industrial capitalist countries by proportion of employees unionized. The UK has 50 per cent of employees unionized, compared with over 70 per cent in Belgium and Denmark and under 30 per cent in France, Switzerland, and the US. Of course, union membership may have quite different significance in different countries and is certainly not necessarily a measure of trade union strength or class consciousness. These figures in fact challenge the popular assumption that the strength of British unions lies in a higher unionization rate than elsewhere.

Comparison of the British trade union movements with others in Western Europe highlights three main features that have distinguished the British movement in the last 30 years or so. These are the significant union presence in the workplace and workplace bargaining, the relative independence of unions from the state, and the lack of political and ideological divisions.

The predominant institutional pattern of worker–management relations in manufacturing firms on the continent has been the works council, independent of the union and with only consultative powers. Collective bargaining in countries like France, Italy, West Germany and Scandinavia has generally taken place at a national or regional level only, with employers free to interpret agreements in the light of their own circumstances. However, in all these countries pressure has been mounting from the late sixties for greater union recognition and power at workplace level. For example, in Italy, after the 'hot autumn' of 1969, factory councils resembling British shop stewards' committees began to be set up to challenge and replace works councils. In subsequent years Italian shop stewards have become established in certain sectors of industry and exerted controls over wages, manning, overtime, health and safety, and investment planning. In addition they have developed broader political objectives than is the case in Britain, taking part in organizing non-unionized plants and in community action on such issues as education, health, and transport. Elsewhere in Europe, however, workplace organization is still at a very elementary level.

The independence of the British trade unions from the state has been marked, by comparison, particularly, with unions in Scandinavia and West Germany (leaving out of account Spain and Portugal where fascist regimes have until recently outlawed independent trade union activity altogether). In Scandinavia collective bargaining has been highly centralized and unions have been integrated into the state. In Sweden during the 44 years of uninterrupted social democratic government, which lasted until 1976, a 'social compact' developed between the government and the Swedish Confederation of Trade Unions. The government committed itself to a policy of social and economic reform in return for a union commitment to developing harmonious industrial relations. In West Germany all collective agreements are legally binding and industrial action illegal while agreements last. Legal strike action requires a 75 per cent vote by secret ballot of the membership in a majority of unions.

In France and Italy independent trade union activity has a considerably shorter history than in Britain. In Italy fascism destroyed the newly formed independent industrial and political organizations of the working class during the period of its reign from 1922 to 1943. In France collective bargaining remained under government control until 1950, and subsequently the govern-

ment retained a central role, especially in the public sector, where wage determination remained the responsibility of government until 1969, when wage
negotiations were introduced for the first time.

Finally, the political unity of the British trade unions and their allegiance
to one centre, the TUC, contrasts sharply with the position in France and
Italy and also the Benelux countries. In France there are five national confederations, often competing with each other to represent the same workers.
They have emerged out of the movement's history of splits between communists, anti-communists, christians, and socialists. All the major confederations have increasingly cooperated in strike activity and in common political
actions, particularly against the government, although the movement
remains divided at the national level. Closer cooperation developed in particular between the communist CGT and socialist CFDT with the Common
Programme of the French Communist and Socialist Parties.

In Italy there are four trade union confederations: CGIL (communist, left
social democrat), CISL (christian democrat), UIL (social democrat),
CISNAL (neo-fascist, monarchist). Here the unions have gone further towards unity, with communist, christian, and socialist unions forming united
federations in engineering, chemicals, printing, and building as a step towards
amalgamation. Pressure for amalgamation has come from united rank and
file activity around the factory councils movement. Some of the major political divisions in the Italian and French trade union movements occurred in
the post-war period of heightening Cold War tensions and were encouraged
by American interference. Italy and France were the two Western European
countries where communist political popularity was very high after the
Second World War and the Americans were anxious to minimize communist
influence in the trade unions. While the divisions succeeded in weakening
the trade union movements, the communist-led confederations in each
country continue to retain their dominant positions (Italy 54 per cent, France
58 per cent, estimated membership in the mid seventies).

It is difficult to form generalizations concerning the relative position of
the British trade union movement because of the wide diversity of trade union
movements elsewhere, even within the confines of Western Europe. The
points discussed above indicate a number of relative strengths of the
British movement. However, as far as the political aspect of the labour
movement is concerned, there are clear weaknesses in Britain as compared
with specific countries like France and Italy, where trade unions have engaged
in action for political ends more readily. This is related in both countries
to the much greater influence of Marxism as evidenced by the size and
strength of communist parties. In France, where action has tended to take
the form of the general strike and mass factory occupations, the strong syndicalist tradition has also played an important role.

In countries like Britain, where there is no mass Marxist party to constantly
reinforce socialist ideas, trade unions tend spontaneously to acquiesce by

their day-to-day actions in the *status quo*. To the extent that socialism is accepted it remains a distant utopian goal, in the absence of a conscious strategy showing how the labour movement gets from its immediate struggles to its long-term objectives.

However, the political structure of the labour movement in Britain together with the comparatively democratic nature of the trade unions indicates very great political potential for the British labour movement, given the necessary development of socialist consciousness. The possibilities of the Labour Party, because of its roots in the trade union movement, becoming a genuine voice for the labour movement are much greater than in other countries (e.g., Sweden, West Germany) where trade unions are allied to social democratic parties.

20-5 RECENT TRENDS IN THE BRITISH TRADE UNION MOVEMENT

Trade union membership as a proportion of employees in Britain remained static or declined slightly in the fifties and sixties after the rapid growth that took place in the forties. From Table 20-7 it can be seen that the proportion declined from 45.2 per cent in 1948 to 42.4 per cent in 1968. However, this has been followed by a new period of growth, with the proportion rising to 51.8 per cent in 1976.

The stagnation in union membership in the fifties and sixties was linked with declining employment in a number of the older industrial sectors, including several that had been highly unionized (e.g., coal mining and railways). During this period the rise in the proportion of non-manual relative to manual workers had a negative effect on unionization rates because of the historically low levels of union membership in non-manual occupations, especially in the private sector. While the decline in manual work accelerated in the late sixties and seventies, becoming an absolute and not just a relative decline, a new burst in unionization of non-manual workers was sufficient to reverse the trend in overall unionization rates. The new growth in unionization of non-manual workers was probably partly a result of increasing awareness among these sections, due to growing economic insecurity, of their position as wage workers. It was also partly a result of recognition by a number of unions of the need, if they wished to grow, to diversify into new areas. Whereas non-manual workers represented only about a fifth of union membership in 1948 their share rose to nearly a third by 1970 and this trend continued in the seventies.

Unionization of non-manual workers in the public sector grew substantially in the late sixties, with NALGO expanding its membership by 29 per cent between 1966 and 1971 and CPSA growing by 24 per cent in the same period. The scope for future growth in the public sector is limited by the high level of unionization there among non-manual workers, estimated at

Table 20-7 Total trade union membership and density in the UK: Selected years, 1892–1976

Year	Employees (thousands)	Total union membership (thousands)	Density of union membership (%)
1892	14 126	1 576	11.2
1901	16 101	2 025	12.6
1911	17 762	3 139	17.7
1913	17 920	4 135	23.1
1917	18 234	5 499	30.2
1920	18 469	8 348	45.2
1923	17 965	5 429	30.2
1933	19 422	4 392	22.6
1938	19 829	6 053	30.5
1945	20 400	7 875	38.6
1948	20 732	9 362	45.2
1950	21 055	9 289	44.1
1960	22 817	9 835	43.1
1968	23 667	10 036	42.4
1970	23 446	11 000	46.9
1976	23 871	12 376	51.8

Sources: Bain and Price (1972); *Department of Employment Gazette*, November 1977 and December 1977.

about 75 per cent. On the other hand, unionization among private sector non-manual workers was estimated in 1969 to be only between 12 and 15 per cent. In the light of this it is not surprising that the membership of four private sector non-manual unions (ASTMS, APEX, AUEW (TASS), NUBE), taken together doubled between 1966 and 1971. Unionization rates among different occupational groups remain sharply diverse, as is shown by the figures below (taken from the Government Social Survey, 1975):

Table 20-8 Percentage unionized by occupation

Occupational group	% unionized
Managers, higher professional and technical	21
Lower professional and technical	60
Clerical and allied	33
Skilled	79
Semi-skilled	73
Unskilled	62

The other most striking trend in the composition of trade union membership is the rise in the proportion of women. The trend increase in the proportion of women, from 18 per cent in 1948 to 25 per cent in 1970, has continued in the subsequent period, reaching 29 per cent in 1976. The growth in women trade unionists is due less to the expansion in female employment than to rising unionization rates. In the sixties women's trade union member-ship rose by over a third (from 1.9 million to 2.6 million), while female employment increased by only 10 per cent, and the whole of this increased employment was accounted for by part-time work where unionization rates are very low. The proportion of women workers in unions rose from 24 per cent in 1960 to just over 30 per cent in 1970. Among full-time workers, the degree of unionization appears to be about two-thirds for men and two-fifths for women.

In assessing the influence of trade unionism on the working class it is also worth noting that many non-unionists have previous experience of union membership. A government survey in 1967 found that of the 46 per cent of full-time workers not in trade unions, nearly half had been trade union members in the past. Most had lapsed because of job changes; only one in six gave dissatisfaction as a reason for having left.

The significance of women in union membership is not reflected in union activity or leadership. A government survey in 1973 found only 13 per cent of stewards and 6 per cent of senior stewards were women. At the 1975 TUC Congress a few months before the Sex Discrimination Act came in, only 7 per cent of trade union delegates were women. In the same year the TUC conducted a survey of women's involvement in unions. In the trade unions that replied, a third of the members were female yet only 3 per cent of union full-time officials were women. Women were under-represented at virtually every level of voluntary and full-time office throughout the trade union move-ment (TUC, 1976).

The position of workers of West Indian and Asian origin in the trade union movement has also come under increasing scrutiny. A survey conducted in 1973–4 found that, contrary to common belief, the level of unionization amongst Asian and West Indian workers was as high as, if not higher than, white workers, with the exception of Moslem working women (only 18 per cent unionization). This finding is not apparently due merely to occupational distribution of white and racial minorities, as indicated in D. J. Smith (1977, p. 191):

> The job-level analysis shows that among non-manual and skilled manual workers member-ship levels are about the same for the whites and the minorities, but among semi-skilled and unskilled manual workers membership is distinctly higher for Asians and West Indians than for whites. While the minorities do tend to work in unionized industries, this accounts for only a small part of the differences between the minorities and whites.

While there are substantial numbers of shop stewards from the racial minorities in many unions, they are far from being represented proportion-ally to their share of membership. Moreover they have hardly penetrated the full-time staff of unions at all. In 1972 the TGWU took on the first full-time official in the country who was not white. The survey comments: 'Such a situation could hardly exist without some racial discrimination on the part of the unions at a high level.'

Despite a policy of combating racial discrimination, few positive initiatives have been taken by the trade unions, and even when discrimination is known to occur action has not always been taken.

In fact, the growth and changing composition of the organized working class faces the trade union movement with the challenge of greater heterogeneity and potential divisions than was the case in the past, especially in the days when trade unionism was dominated by the craft unions. Increasingly class struggle entails the active cooperation of skilled and unskilled, non-manual and manual workers, public and private sector unions, women and men, black and white workers, trade unions and community organizations. Active cooperation still fails to materialize in many cases, as the trade union movement slowly comes to terms with its own history of sexism, racism, and sectionalism. The eighties may see a reversal of this slow process, as ideological and material attacks on women, black people, and the public sector reinforce existing divisions. Alternatively, progress towards unity may accelerate, encouraged by the confrontationist policies of the government and employers towards the working class as a whole.

FURTHER READING

Some of the literature on the definition of class has already been referred to in Chapter 4. Additional discussion relevant to this chapter can be found in Hunt (1977) and Braverman (1974). Major historical studies are E. P. Thompson (1968) and Hobsbawm (1964 and 1969). See also Kendall (1975) and D. J. Smith (1977).

For information on recent trends in the working class and trade unions, useful sources are *Social Trends* and *Department of Employment Gazette*.

TWENTY-ONE
THE DEMAND FOR LABOUR

Jean Gardiner

21-1 INTERNATIONAL COMPARISONS OF LABOUR SUPPLY

The role of changing labour supply conditions in industrialized capitalist countries in the long boom of the fifties and early sixties and the deceleration of capitalist accumulation in the seventies have been discussed in Chapters 12 and 13. In the UK throughout the period the growth in the labour supply has been slower than elsewhere. Some economists have argued that labour supply constraints in the UK have been a major cause of low economic growth rates. Before considering these arguments let us examine the comparative evidence on labour supply.

Table 21-1 gives figures for growth rates in the non-agricultural labour force of the major countries. It can be seen that the growth of the UK workforce was lower than that of all other countries. The West German growth rate, which is only slightly higher than that of the UK, is based only on the period from 1960. It therefore excludes the rapid growth period of the fifties,

Table 21-1 Increase (%) in non-agricultural civilian labour force, from date given to 1973

		Average annual increase	Change in population of working age	Change in participation rates	Net migration from other countries	Net migration from agriculture
				Percentage points attributable to		
France	(1954)	1.7	0.5	−0.3	0.6	0.9
West Germany	(1960)	0.7	−0.3	−0.3	0.8	0.5
Italy	(1954)	1.8	1.4	−0.8	−0.4	1.6
Japan	(1953)	3.3	2.4	−0.5	—	1.4
Netherlands	(1950)	1.6	1.5	−0.3	—	0.4
Sweden	(1950)	1.7	0.5	0.5	0.3	0.4
UK	(1950)	0.6	0.4	0.2	−0.1	0.1
US	(1960)	2.3	1.6	0.2	0.2	0.3

Source: McCracken (1977).

when there was a large inflow of refugees. Between 1950 and 1960, West Germany's population increased by an average of 1 per cent a year against 0.4 per cent for the UK.

The Table also indicates the sources of growth in non-agricultural labour supply. There was an increase in participation rates in the UK as high as or higher than other countries, with the exception of Sweden. However, growth in the population of working age was lower than elsewhere except for West Germany. Moreover the UK experienced net emigration over the period. A slow rate of growth of the non-agricultural labour force is likely to reflect demand for labour as well as supply. The fact that emigration exceeded immigration in the UK suggests that labour supply was responding to a slow growth in job opportunities.

The third and most significant factor depressing the growth of non-agricultural labour supply in the UK was the very low net migration from the agricultural sector. As can be seen in Table 21-2 only a very small proportion

Table 21–2 Industrial distribution of the labour force (%), 1950–74

	Agriculture			Industry			Services		
	1950	1974	Change	1950	1974	Change	1950	1974	Change
France	31.7	11.6	−20.1	35.4	39.2	3.8	32.8	49.2	16.4
West Germany	24.7	7.3	−17.4	42.9	47.6	4.7	32.4	45.1	12.7
Italy	41.7	16.6	−25.1	31.7	44.1	12.4	26.5	39.3	12.8
Japan	41.3	12.9	−28.4	24.5	37.0	12.5	34.2	50.1	15.9
UK	5.6	2.4	−3.2	47.7	42.3	−5.4	46.7	54.9	8.2
US	13.5	4.1	−9.4	34.1	31.0	−3.1	52.4	64.9	12.5

Source: McCracken (1977).

of the labour force in Britain remained in agriculture by 1950, leaving little scope for transfers of labour either to industry or services. All the other major capitalist countries except for the US had large reserves of labour in agriculture available for transfer to expanding sectors. Even now the proportion of the labour force in agriculture remains much smaller in Britain than elsewhere.

In all countries, participation rates have tended to be reduced by the extension of years spent in education and by the reduction in retirement age. On the other hand, they have been increased by a rise in the proportion of women in the labour force. Participation rates are somewhat higher in the UK than in most other EEC countries. The rate for working-age females was 55.5 per cent in the UK in 1975 compared with 44.1 per cent in the EEC as a whole, while for males it was 86.2 per cent compared with 81.0 per cent (*Social Trends*, 1977).

The growth in labour supply in the UK accounted for by rising labour

Table 21-3 Participation rates of females aged 25–64 (%)

	1960–61	1970	1974–75
Denmark	35.2	50.4	63.0
France	42.0	47.0	—
West Germany	43.7	45.9	—
Netherlands	16.1	17.9	18.9
Sweden	34.7	59.4	68.4
UK	41.5	49.3	52.5
US	40.4	48.0	58.6

Source: McCracken (1977).

force participation of women has been partly limited by the spread of part-time employment. Since the beginning of the sixties the bulk of increased female employment has been in part-time jobs (i.e., 30 hours or less a week). Part-time work has grown more rapidly in the UK than elsewhere. Thus, while the UK labour force has a relatively high proportion of women, UK women work on average rather fewer hours than elsewhere in the EEC. The age structure of the female labour force in the UK also differs from those in other West European countries in having a much higher proportion of older women.

The age structure of the female labour force in the UK and preponderance of part-time work are linked with the low social priority given here to child-care provision catering for the needs of full-time women workers, compared with other countries that depend heavily on female labour. Childcare provision is more extensive in the rest of the EEC, with the exception of the Netherlands where female participation rates are exceptionally low, as can be seen from Table 21-3. The Table also indicates that there are a number of countries (e.g., Denmark, Sweden, the US) where female participation rates have risen more rapidly and to higher levels than in the UK.

Comparison of unemployment rates provides another basis for examining the relationship between labour demand and supply, and Table 21-4 gives data that have been standardized to international definitions. The broad pat-

Table 21-4 Unemployment rates (%)

	1960	1965	1970	1975	1977
US	5.5	4.5	4.9	4.9	7.0
France	2.6	2.3	2.6	2.7	5.2
West Germany	0.7	0.3	0.8	0.8	3.6
UK	2.4	2.1	3.1	3.2	6.9
Italy	4.3	4.0	3.1	3.4	3.3
Japan	1.4	1.0	1.2	1.3	2.0

Source: Statistical Abstract of the US (1979).

tern was that the reserve of unemployed labour was below average in the UK in the fifties but by the late sixties and seventies had risen to equal or exceed unemployment rates elsewhere.

To conclude this section, it is clear that the growth of labour supply has been lower in the UK than elsewhere and that abundant cheap and freely available labour reserves have been smaller in the UK than in most Western European countries and Japan, especially in the fifties. However, it seems likely that labour supply could have expanded more rapidly if demand conditions had required it, either through positive net immigration or higher female participation rates.

21-2 LABOUR SUPPLY AS A CONSTRAINT ON GROWTH

The issue of labour supply receives little attention in the context of economic stagnation and high levels of unemployment. In the sixties this was not the case and there was considerable concern about the implications of deficient labour supply in terms of physical bottlenecks to expansion, wage inflation, and a general increase in the bargaining power of labour.

In Western Europe and Japan an important factor in the rapid growth rates of the fifties and early sixties was the huge internal reserves of cheap labour at the beginning of the period, which enabled rapid industrial expansion to take place while wages were held down. However, already by the late fifties and early sixties, labour shortages were beginning to appear as the rate of transfer from agriculture slowed down. One factor working against a continued rapid decline in the agricultural labour force in Western Europe was the political dependence of conservative regimes on the peasantry, which gave rise, for example, to the EEC Common Agricultural Policy, with its state subsidies to low productivity agriculture. Thus a number of countries resorted increasingly to imported labour from Mediterranean countries and, in Britain's case, from the Black Commonwealth. But the rate of immigration was limited by the hostility of local populations, inadequate recruiting systems, cultural barriers, costs of absorption, and lack of skills.

The increasing tightness of most labour markets in the late sixties was one of the factors leading to increased worker militancy and rapid wage rises in the major industrial capitalist countries more or less simultaneously. This occurred in the US in 1967–8, in Japan, France, Belgium, and the Netherlands in 1968–9, and in West Germany, Italy, Switzerland, and the UK in 1969–70. Other contributory factors were also at work—e.g., the decline in growth rates of real wages which workers in most countries had experienced from the mid sixties.

The bargaining power of labour in a tight labour market situation derives not just from absence of the threat of unemployment but also from a reduction in the proportion of 'green' labour lacking experience of wage work and trade unionism. For these reasons, Marx stressed the importance for capitalism of permanently re-creating for itself a reserve army of labour. This is achieved partly through capitalism's ability to encroach upon and undermine non-capitalist production relations (e.g., peasant-based agriculture), hence releasing new reserves of wage labour. It is also achieved through periodic crises of accumulation in which the most archaic and labour intensive, and least profitable, capitalist enterprises are written off and even the most profitable sectors shed labour so that a reserve of unemployed labour is created.

The argument that labour supply has acted as a constraint on economic growth has been adopted to explain both the slow-down of economic growth in the capitalist world from the mid-sixties and the relatively slow growth of the UK economy from the fifties. Here we shall examine the arguments concerning the UK specifically. These fall into two groups. First, there is the argument concerned with general labour shortage, which has focused on the sectoral distribution of the labour force in the UK. Second, there is the concern about shortage of skilled labour specifically.

The theory that labour shortage, arising from the relative economic 'maturity' of the UK, was a major cause of slow growth is no longer accepted even by its major exponent. Kaldor (1966) had argued that the UK had reached a level of development where real income per head was at broadly the same level in the different sectors of the economy, i.e., industry, agriculture, and services. Surplus labour therefore no longer existed and further growth with unlimited supplies of labour was not feasible.

Kaldor stressed the key role of industry, and in particular of the manufacturing sector, in the growth of output and productivity as a whole. Specifically, he pointed to the operation of dynamic economies of scale in manufacturing. He claimed there was evidence in the fifties and early sixties to suggest that within the manufacturing sector of major capitalist countries there were increasing returns to scale—i.e., productivity growth varied with the growth of output. This relationship is known as Verdoorn's Law. Subsequent empirical tests, however, demonstrated that for the period after 1965 Verdoorn's Law no longer operated. In fact its validity has also been questioned for the previous period.

While Verdoorn's Law itself is in doubt, the critical role of manufacturing in the growth process is generally accepted. Even in the absence of dynamic economies of scale, the rate of growth of industry and rate of transfer of labour to industry from the agricultural and service sectors may be major determinants of productivity growth. This is not just because the level of productivity and rate of productivity growth in industry is higher than elsewhere. More significant is the fact that growth in industrial output represents a net addition to the effective use of resources provided that (a) the capital required for industrial production is largely or wholly self-generated, and (b) the labour engaged in industry has no true opportunity cost outside industry on account of disguised unemployment in agriculture and services. There is thus a close relationship between growth of GDP and growth of manufacturing. A dynamic manufacturing base may also play a crucial role in preventing balance of payments constraints on economic growth.

However, the view that it was a shortage of labour that limited the growth of the UK manufacturing sector can be rejected on methodological and empirical grounds. Kaldor's original hypothesis over-simplified the relationships between demand, productivity, and employment in manufacturing. It took the growth of demand to be the independent and causal factor determining changes in productivity and employment. However, demand is in turn conditioned by productivity, growth and labour supply. Thus a growth of productivity may boost demand through falling relative prices and increased export markets and also possibly via higher profitability stimulating investment. In addition, if labour supply is limited, as it began to be for Japan and Western European countries from the late fifties, this will influence the rate of growth of demand that governments will allow. Given the complexity of the causal relationships involved, simple regression analysis of the kind Kaldor based his hypothesis on will not necessarily uncover the relationship between productivity, employment, and output. An approach that takes account of interaction and simultaneity in the economic processes is therefore necessary.

There is empirical evidence to support the view that the slow growth of manufacturing employment in the UK in the fifties and sixties was mainly due to demand rather than supply constraints. Economic maturity on Kaldor's definition does not seem to have been reached in the UK by the late sixties. On the contrary, it appears from an analysis of inter-industry labour flows that the service sector, and particularly specific service areas like distribution, acted as a labour reserve for manufacturing before the imposition of SET and the resultant sharp increase in productivity in these areas. Since the reduction in employment in services resulting from SET was reversed when it was abolished, it is probable that services continue to act as a surplus labour area.

In addition, evidence on industrial wage dispersion in the UK in the fifties and early sixties also casts doubt on the labour shortage hypothesis, since one might expect excess demand for labour to be associated with a narrowing of industry differentials. Instead, the dispersion of wages across manufacturing industries actually widened in the UK if successive cyclical peaks during the fifties and sixties are compared.

Another theory attributing the slow growth of the British economy to the sectoral distribution of employment associates deindustrialization in the UK with a rapid growth of employment in the non-industrial sector of the economy, and particularly in public services (Bacon and Eltis, 1978). Rapid expansion of the public sector is said to have 'crowded out' manufacturing by depriving it of labour as well as by reducing the finance available for manufacturing investment and taking a disproportionate share of profits in taxation. Here we will look at the argument concerning labour supply.

Labour in the public sector may have acted less effectively as a reserve for manufacturing than certain private service industries like distribution, both because of the relative security of employment and also because of improvement in relative pay, at least until the mid seventies. However, there is little evidence that a labour supply constraint has been a significant problem for the manufacturing sector or that it has become more so in recent years than in the fifties. In fact, from 1966 UK manufacturers have been releasing labour almost continuously. It seems probable, moreover, that where shortages have occurred in the manufacturing sector they have been predominantly for skilled labour of a kind that the public sector attracts only to a limited degree. The many relatively unskilled workers who have entered public sector employment would probably otherwise have remained unemployed or only found work in the private service sector.

Moreover, the growth of public sector employment was not particularly rapid for the period as a whole. As was pointed out in Chapter 20, the proportion of the labour force in the public sector only rose from 27 per cent in 1951 to 30 per cent in 1976. During the fifties when the problem of labour shortage was probably most significant, the proportion actually fell, reaching 24 per cent in 1961. In addition, if we compare the growth of the UK service sector as a whole with that elsewhere (see Table 21-2) it can be seen that employment in services grew considerably more slowly in the UK than in the other major capitalist countries, including the US where the level of service employment is considerably higher (at 65 per cent of the labour force compared with 55 per cent in the UK).

The evidence suggests that shortage of labour was not a direct constraint on growth in the UK and that, had demand by the manufacturing sector been sufficiently strong, supply would have been forthcoming. There are two qualifications that must be made to this argument. First, even if supply was forthcoming, it might not have been of appropriate type or skill. This question is examined in the next section. Second, the argument above was concerned with the direct physical constraint, but even if this was not binding, it may well have been that the labour market was tighter because the reserve army was smaller relative to other countries. In consequence, the balance of class forces moved against capital, and this had adverse effects on capitalist demand for labour. This is a separate argument, which was discussed in the international context in Chapters 12 and 13.

21-3 SKILLED LABOUR SHORTAGE

According to the CBI quarterly survey of business opinion, in a period of peak demand at the end of 1973 a half of all firms specified a scarcity of skilled labour as a factor limiting production. Even when demand was at its lowest (early 1976), nine per cent still reported such a scarcity (Berthoud, 1978).

The problem of shortages of skilled labour is not a new one. A study of the manpower situation in 1961 (*Ministry of Labour Gazette*, February 1962) found that there had been a shortage of workers in most skilled occupations since the end of the war. For example, in 1956, a not untypical year in the fifties in terms of overall demand for labour, the ratio of unemployed men in the main skilled occupations to vacancies in this group was 1 : 5. The degree of labour shortage is understated by this figure, both because official statistics for vacancies understate the level of demand and because of the problem of regional imbalance.

While a rise in unemployment creates a reserve of labour to offset any overall labour supply constraint, it tends to exacerbate shortages of skilled labour by reducing employers' incentive to provide apprenticeships and encouraging skilled workers who lose their jobs to switch to other occupations. Only where the state intervenes, as in the Swedish contra-cyclical training scheme, will this tendency be reversed. In Britain, for example, the number of skilled engineering workers coming on to the market in 1977 was only about two-thirds of the level in 1972. Shortages of skilled labour in engineering are therefore likely to continue despite the persistence of mass unemployment.

A number of reasons have been advanced to explain the persistence of skilled labour shortages. Fluctuations in the growth of demand throughout the period associated with the balance of payments constraint have restricted expenditure on training in the same way as expenditure on plant and machinery. Thus skill shortages have predominantly been met by overtime working. To offset adverse demand factors one might have expected a proportionately higher state involvement in training than in other countries. In fact the reverse is the case. Until 1962, when the government produced a White Paper on industrial training, total reliance had been placed on the self-regulating ability of the labour market and the voluntary system of training within industry itself. Before then government training centres (GTCs) had a social rather than economic function, providing training for disabled and other unemployed workers with special resettlement problems. Training at GTCs, which had been significant during the Second World War and immediately afterwards, was greatly reduced, from 24 000 places in 1946 to 3000 or less in the early sixties.

The 1964 Industrial Training Act embodied a recognition of the need for the state to take greater responsibility for industrial training. Output of GTCs rose as a result and GTC trainees became eligible for craft level qualifications. By 1968 GTCs provided places for over 13 000 trainees. In addition the industrial training boards (ITBs), which were set up as a result of the Act, contributed to an increase in training. The number of employees receiving training in manufacturing rose by 15 per cent between 1964 and 1968.

However, the ITBs have contributed little towards the main objective of the Industrial Training Act, which was a reduction in shortages of skilled manpower. Instead they have focused on improving standards in the craft based skilled trades. The fact that a significant proportion of resources for training is channelled through ITBs in the UK has perpetuated the relative autonomy specific industries have in this field. It has also limited the provision of training for redeployment, since ITBs do not provide training for redundant workers. In addition, British governments have not provided adequate incentives for workers to train. The ratio of training allowances to earnings has tended, if anything, to be lower in the very years the government has sought to increase the level of training (Mukherjee, 1976).

It has been argued that attempts by the state to increase the supply of skilled workers have been thwarted by opposition from trade unions representing skilled workers anxious to retain control over entry to their trade. The role of trade unions is considerably more complex than that, since it is in the interest of skilled workers both to maintain their earnings and to expand their own numbers. As a result there are a number of nationally agreed 'dilution' or 'relaxation' agreements allowing GTC trainees to be accepted as skilled workers on certain conditions that protect the interests of craftsmen. In some cases unions do resist the hiring of non-apprentice trainees—e.g., the Boilermakers, who accept no dilutees. However, survey evidence suggests that union opposition is at most localized in particular firms and has had only a partial effect on trainees' employment prospects (Berthoud, 1978).

Finally, it is argued that declining relative pay, conditions, and job satisfaction have led to a reduction in the willingness of young people to enter skilled trades and an increase in wastage rates of skilled labour. These factors may have exacerbated the problem in localities with tight labour markets. However, they cannot explain the shortage of skilled labour in the fifties, when skill differentials increased relative to their low level in the Second World War.

21-4 THE IMPACT OF UNEMPLOYMENT

Dramatic changes in labour market conditions in the late sixties and seventies shifted concern away from labour supply constraints to unemployment. There has been a rising trend of unemployment in all OECD countries except for Italy since 1966 (see Table 21-4). In the UK, registered unemployment rose by over one million between 1966 and 1977, as can be seen from Table 21-5. Unregistered unemployment was estimated to have risen by 800 000.

Table 21-5 suggests that the growth in unemployment occurred because an increase in labour supply was not matched by a sufficient growth in employment opportunities. In the sixties and early seventies men were affected more adversely than women by this trend. Although male labour supply was decreasing, male employment declined at a much faster rate. From 1973 the situation worsened for both females and males. Female un-

Table 21-5 Changes in mid-year labour supply, employment, and unemployment, 1951–77 (thousands)

	Males				Females			
	1951–66	1966–73	1973–77	1951–77	1951–66	1966–73	1973–77	1951–77
Increase in population aged 15 and over	+1388	+416	+436	+2240	+1253	+406	+351	+2010
Effect of changes in age structure	−435	−282	−352	−1069	−1231	−549	−333	−2113
Estimated effects of changes in activity rates	−88	−614	+44	−658	+1583	+784	+1054	+3421
Increase in labour supply	+865	−480	+128	+513	+1605	+641	+1072	+3318
Of which: Increase in employment	+700	−873	−487	−660	+1651	+491	+388	+2530
Increase in registered unemployment	+95	+262	+489	+846	−9	+32	+241	+264
Estimated increase in unregistered unemployment	+70	+131	+126	+327	−37	+118	+441	+522

Source: Moore, 1978.

employment, including the unregistered category, in fact rose more rapidly than male unemployment. Between 1973 and 1977, 53 per cent of the increase in total unemployment was among women, while their share of the labour force was only about 40 per cent. Although the number of female employees continued to increase by an average of nearly 100 000 a year, this was no longer sufficient to absorb the accelerating increase in labour supply, amounting to an estimated 250 000 a year. The rapid growth in female labour supply during this period was due to a sharp increase in participation rates. This resulted from the halt to expansion of further education (affecting men as well), the decline in births, and also from increased economic pressure on married women to work.

A disproportionate share of rising unemployment in the major capitalist countries including the UK has been borne by young people. From Table 21-6 it can be seen that in the UK, North America, and France the young unemployed accounted for over 40 per cent of the total and in Italy over 60 per cent, compared with a share of only about 20 per cent in the active population in these countries. Unemployment rates have been particularly high among school leavers. Official figures probably understate actual unemployment among young people because of non-registration.

High levels of youth unemployment have resulted from the cyclical and secular decline in employment opportunities. Inexperienced workers are desired less by employers, and in addition natural wastage policies and seniority rules work against the interests of entrants to the labour market. Older male workers too experience relatively high rates of unemployment because of difficulty in finding new work when made redundant. Unemployment also varies regionally and among occupational groups with the highest rates among unskilled manual workers. Racial minority groups have suffered disproportionately from the rise in unemployment because of discrimination and disadvantage in training. There was a very high level of unemployment among workers of West Indian and Asian origin in the early sixties, when immigration was at its peak, but subsequently there was a

Table 21-6 Unemployment rates by age, 1976

	Per cent of civilian labour force		Under-25s as per cent of total unemployed
	Under 25	25 and over	
US	14.4	5.5	46
Japan	3.0	1.8	23
West Germany	5.3	3.8	24
France	8.0	3.2	40
UK	12.0	3.8	44
Italy	14.3	1.6	64
Canada	12.8	4.2	48

Source: Hughes (1978).

long-term downward trend as new arrivals were absorbed into a relatively full employed workforce. However, this trend has been offset by the opposite tendency for minority unemployment to rise disproportionately with a general rise in unemployment.

Within the racial minorities two groups have experienced particularly high levels of unemployment, both in the period of relatively full employment and in the period of rising unemployment. These are young people and women. In the 1971 census (see Table 21-7) the level of unemployment among women born in the West Indies, India, or Pakistan was 9.3 per cent compared with 5.6 per cent for all women in the workforce. Among men, however, the two figures were very similar (minorities 6.3 per cent, general population 5.4 per cent). Thus even when minority unemployment was near its lowest point it was still disproportionately high among women. And as the unemployment situation worsened for all minority workers it deteriorated particularly sharply for women. Between 1973 and 1977 male minority group unemployment rose by 385.2 per cent, while total male unemployment rose by

Table 21-7 Percentage of the economically active who were unemployed analysed by birthplace, age, and sex, 1971 census

	Total	Age				
		Up to 20	21–25	26–35	36–55	56+
All men	5.4	8.6	6.0	4.6	4.2	6.8
Men born in:						
West Indies	7.7	16.9	12.5	6.8	6.2	8.8
India	5.3	6.9	5.4	4.0	5.1	8.5
Pakistan and Bangladesh	5.8	7.4	6.0	4.6	5.6	9.2
All women	5.6	7.3	5.3	5.7	4.6	6.6
Women born in:						
West Indies	9.5	18.3	9.6	8.8	8.0	9.9
India	8.7	13.8	11.6	9.3	7.0	7.0
Pakistan and Bangladesh	13.1	22.6	14.9	13.7	9.4	7.3

Source: D. J. Smith (1977).

163.9 per cent. Female minority group unemployment rose by a massive 1000.7 per cent compared with 505.2 per cent for total female unemployment (Shah, 1978).

Table 21-7 shows the high levels of unemployment of young workers born in the West Indies and Asia. For those up to 20, unemployment was nearly 20 per cent for girls born in these countries, compared with 7 per cent for all girls in the same age group. Among West Indian boys unemployment was 17 per cent compared with 9 per cent for all boys. (Unemployment among Asian boys was not higher than average.) Young people born in Britain who are from West Indian and Asian families also suffer from high levels of unemployment.

21-5 THE CAUSES OF UNEMPLOYMENT

Having examined the differential impact of unemployment, let us turn to the reasons why it has risen since the late sixties in the industrial capitalist countries and, particularly, in the UK. Marxism, with its emphasis on the class nature of capitalism, provides an analysis of unemployment that is quite distinct from the approaches taken by orthodox economists, which all characterize unemployment as the result of malfunctioning in the economic system. Marx, on the other hand, developed the concept of the industrial reserve army of labour—i.e., a surplus of workers available and needing to sell their labour power to the capitalist class, which capitalism required in order to function normally and profitably. While at certain phases the reserve army would consist of workers engaged in non-capitalist production relations—e.g., peasant production or domestic labour—which were being eroded by the expansion of capitalist production, at other times capitalism needed to create its own internal reserve army by making sections of wage labour unemployed. Whenever profitability declined there would be a tendency for capital accumulation to slow down and a consequent rise in unemployment as a result of the cumulative decline in demand for wage labour. The slump in capitalist production and resultant unemployment provided a mechanism by which profitability could be restored. On the one hand, it would drive out of business the less productive and often smaller firms, reducing competition between capitalists and thus strengthening the market position of the larger capitalists. On the other, it would weaken the bargaining power of labour as competition between workers for jobs increased and trade union organization was undermined. As profitability started to rise again, the demand for labour per unit of output would also be lower as capital stock incorporating the less productive technologies would have been written off in the course of the slump.

While it can therefore be argued that unemployment is functional for the maintenance of capitalist profitability, it may also have social, economic, and political consequences that are destabilizing. Thus while the economic bargaining power of labour may be undermined by unemployment, working class political consciousness may be strengthened in the direction of rejecting an economic system that has such devastating consequences for the mass of the population. Equally, profitability may be undermined to such an extent by the cumulative decline in output that a renewed burst of capital accumulation is indefinitely postponed. It was fears associated with these possible outcomes in the thirties that led to acceptance of the Keynesian theory of unemployment and the need for state intervention to curb unemployment. According to Keynes, the major cause of mass unemployment in the thirties was inadequate demand for the products of industry. The solution was for the state to intervene by boosting demand via fiscal and monetary policy and direct public expenditure. Thus unemployment, caused by malfunctioning of the market system, could be eradicated by correct government intervention and full employment would become the normal condition of capitalist economies.

While Keynesian theory and policies appeared valid to many orthodox economists during the full employment years of the fifties and early sixties, they proved inadequate as unemployment rose again in the inflationary period of the late sixties and the seventies. Social scientists opposed to a Marxist interpretation of these events have adopted one of two theories. The first is the theory of unemployment as 'voluntary', which has roots in pre-Keynesian neo-classical economics. The second relates unemployment to technology and develops the concept of the 'post-industrial', 'leisure' society.

Unemployment is termed 'voluntary' by economists if it arises from unwillingness to work at the equilibrium wage. The view that the increase in the level of unemployment relative to vacancies since 1966 is due to a rise in voluntary unemployment is based mainly on assumptions concerning the effects of higher unemployment benefits. In 1966 an earnings-related supplement to unemployment and sickness benefit was introduced for between 2 and 26 weeks, which raised total benefits for those unemployed from about 60 per cent to 80 per cent of net earnings likely to be obtained in employment. In addition, although less significant because of more limited scope, the Redundancy Payments Act was introduced in 1965. It has also been suggested that a change in attitudes to work and unemployment has occurred, causing a rise in voluntary unemployment. This argument has not only been applied to recent years, it has even been suggested that half of the unemployment in the thirties was voluntary (Benjamin and Kochin, 1979).

A rise in voluntary unemployment would take place either if more people chose to become unemployed or if those already unemployed chose to remain so for a longer period of time. There is no evidence of an increase in the inflow of people becoming registered as unemployed. It has been relatively constant, at about a million each year. The increase in unemployment that has occurred has resulted from a rise in the average duration of unemployment, from about 7 weeks in the mid sixties to 15 weeks in the late seventies.

About 40 per cent of men unemployed for between 2 and 26 weeks (about a half of all unemployed men) receive the earnings-related supplement, and a much smaller proportion of women. Only about 7 per cent of unemployed workers will have received redundancy pay on leaving their last job, and these tend to be concentrated among the higher occupational levels. It has been calculated that, even on the strong assumption that the effect of increased benefits has been to double the length of time each person receiving them remained unemployed, the consequent increase in male unemployment would have been only 50 000 between 1966 and 1974, rising to 100 000 in 1977 (Moore, 1978), or less than 10 per cent of the increase in registered unemployment since 1966. Moreover, while there was an increase in the ratio of unemployment benefit to net earnings in employment in the sixties, the ratio stabilized between 1967 and 1971 and actually declined during the seventies, when the major increase in unemployment took place.

Survey evidence on attitudes and analysis of the long-term unemployed indicates no decline in willingness to work. The Department of Employment Survey of attitudes and characteristics of the unemployed found a decline between 1973 and 1976 in the proportion of unemployed workers recorded as 'somewhat unenthusiastic' in their attitude to work. Of the 26 per cent so recorded in 1976, the vast majority had poor prospects of work because they were older workers, sick or disabled, or women with domestic responsibilities. Only 2 per cent of the total were recorded as having both 'somewhat unenthusiastic' attitudes and good reasonable prospects of work.

The vast majority of unemployment has clearly been involuntary and resulted from a lack of job opportunities. But while it is not difficult to discredit the theory, its ideological impact has been considerable, being used as a justification by the 1979 Tory government for reducing supplementary benefits. It is very useful politically from a capitalist viewpoint for the blame for unemployment to be placed with the unemployed themselves.

The second theory that has gained popularity, particularly in the late seventies with the growing impact of micro-electronic technology, seeks an explanation for unemployment in a changed relationship between work and leisure. According to this theory, technological change is bringing about a permanently reduced demand for labour in industry, resulting in an increase in enforced leisure, which will take the form either of unemployment for a growing proportion of the population or of work-sharing and shorter working hours for the population as a whole. While less insidious politically as an explanation of unemployment than the concept of 'voluntary' unemployment, this approach is ideologically useful from a capitalist standpoint, since it locates the problem in the sphere of technology rather than the social relations of production. If social divisions arise, they are between the employed and the unemployed and not between capital and labour.

Among Marxists there is disagreement about the likely future impact of technological change on employment. However, the unemployment of the seventies as a whole cannot be attributed to labour-saving technology. Instead of a surge in productivity growth, there has been an actual decline since 1973 by comparison with the preceding 20-year period, in all the major capitalist countries and across industrial sectors. The decline in productivity growth has been even sharper in the UK than elsewhere. Thus the low level of demand for labour has resulted from a very slow growth in output rather than from a fast growth in output per head. And the particularly high levels of unemployment in the UK are the result of relative industrial decline and not of relative advance towards the 'post-industrial' society.

Thus the main explanation for the rise in unemployment internationally, as in previous capitalist crises, must be the lower levels of investment and economic growth rates associated with downward pressure on profitability. This does not mean, however, that a renewal of investment activity and economic growth will automatically eliminate large-scale unemployment. For example, it has been estimated for the UK that a growth rate of about five per cent a year would be necessary in the early eighties to reduce unemployment to the level it was at the beginning of the seventies, given the growth in labour supply and the assumption that there would be no significant decline in working hours (Moore, 1978). This would entail growth at a considerably higher rate than the UK has ever achieved in the past, even when the international context for growth was more favourable than it is likely to be in the eighties. This estimate also assumed no massive labour-saving technological change. It is possible that future bursts of investment incorporating new technology may lead to a surge in labour productivity and a lower demand for labour. In the past, labour 'shake-outs' have occurred when a high level of investment has been followed by falling profits and cyclical downswings in demand, as in 1967 and 1971. These factors together encouraged scrapping of old plants and dishoarding of labour.

The likely future impact of investment and new technology on jobs is extremely difficult to assess. As we have seen, at the macro level, whatever tendency there was for technological change to increase labour productivity in capitalist countries was more than offset by contrary tendencies during the seventies. For example, there was a much slower transfer of labour from relatively low productivity agriculture to industry than had previously been taking place. However, the major cause of low productivity growth was probably the low pressure of demand, reinforced by state intervention to combat inflation and the deflationary effects of the oil crisis. This increased costs because of the burden of overheads and the lack of incentive for firms to invest and reorganize production processes.

However, at the micro level during this period there is evidence that a range of labour-saving innovations, based in particular on the micro-processor, were taking place and having a major impact on jobs. The production of many items that previously depended on mechanical moving parts (e.g., watches, cash registers and telephone equipment) has been revolutionized by this new technology. There have been massive increases in labour productivity in such industries, resulting in reductions in the workforce. For example, employment in the production of cash registers halved in both the UK and the US as the electronic machine replaced the mechanical one.

The effects of the new technology have begun to be felt not just on the products affected but on production techniques throughout the economy. Moreover, the most dramatic impact may well be in the service sector, which has previously absorbed labour displaced by labour-saving innovation elsewhere in the economy. In retail distribution a new revolution is under way that may be comparable to the introduction of the self-service supermarket, with the computerized point of sale system that carries out stock control as well as adding up prices of goods purchased. Eventually the reading and ringing up of prices will also probably be done automatically, eliminating the need for check-out cashiers and workers to price individual goods on shelves. Such technological changes may have indirect as well as direct effects on demand for labour in the industry, as the cost savings enjoyed by the large firms place further competitive pressures on small shops, forcing more of these to close and shed labour.

However, the most serious employment implications for the service sector come from the automation of office work made possible by machines such as word processors. Two or three word processors are estimated to perform the workload of ten typists. Technological change here could therefore reduce dramatically job opportunities for women workers, 40 per cent of whom are at present employed in some form of clerical work.

While the jobs of specific groups of workers are at risk because of new technology, it remains uncertain how much unemployment overall will rise as a result of labour-saving technological change. It has been estimated that 16 per cent of the UK workforce—4 million people—would be displaced by the new technology over a 15-year period (Barron and Curnow, 1979). This would imply a growth of productivity directly attributable to new technology of 1.2 per cent a year (cf. the trend growth of 2.6 per cent in UK productivity 1960–73). What happens to productivity overall, however, will depend on the extent to which increases arising from technological change are offset by other factors, such as stagnant output. And whether displacement of labour leads to higher unemployment will depend on such factors as market conditions, capitalist strategy, and the education and training of the labour displaced. Thus in Japan, where technological change has been more rapid than in the UK, the associated unemployment appears to have been lower. There firms often guarantee 'lifetime employment' and are under pressure to find ways of maintaining jobs by expanding or diversifying output.

However, technological change does reinforce another tendency inherent in capitalist economies, and a particular feature of the UK, that of structural unemployment. This occurs where there is an imbalance between the pattern of labour supply and the pattern of labour demand occupationally, industrially, and geographically. It is indicated in a boom period by a coexistence of vacancies in certain areas with unemployment in others and tends to be masked in a slump, when there is a general surplus of all kinds of labour.

Structural unemployment is inherent in a capitalist economy because of the uneven development of regions and industries. It can be alleviated, however, by state intervention in such areas as regional policy, retraining, and assistance to labour mobility.

While it is difficult to estimate structural unemployment, in a period of slump it might be expected to have increased. Even in the boom period of the sixties, when development areas received substantial government support, resulting in the creation there of about 150 000 new jobs, net emigration from these areas continued at a high level. Since the late sixties emigration from these and other low growth areas has declined because of reduced employment opportunities in the Midlands and south-east. This has exacerbated unemployment problems in the less prosperous areas. In addition, regional policy has been less effective in the seventies because overall stagnation in investment has reduced its impact. EEC membership has also exacerbated geographical imbalance, both because of the tendency for industry to be drawn increasingly towards the heart of Western Europe and because EEC policy favours aid to depressed agricultural rather than depressed industrial areas.

It therefore appears plausible that some increase in structural unemployment in geographical terms has occurred. However, a study of structural unemployment found little evidence for its existence on an industrial basis in the UK or a number of other OECD countries (Turvey, 1977). In the period 1963–74 there was little evidence of an increase in long-term industrial structural change. This, however, may no longer be the case, given the current restructuring in steel and vehicles industries, and the introduction of micro-electronic technology elsewhere.

21-6 CONCLUSION

While labour supply factors do appear to have played a role in the long boom and subsequent slump of the capitalist world in the period after the Second World War, labour constraints do not appear to have played a direct role in the deteriorating relative position of UK capitalism.

For the UK, the period falls into two distinct sections. Up to 1965 the growth of the non-agricultural labour force was slow and labour markets were generally tight. However, there does not appear to have been any persistent aggregate shortage of labour. Private services and housewives provided a reserve of labour available for manufacturing in periods of boom. Problems of structural imbalances were present, however, with deficits of labour in the most prosperous areas in the Midlands and south-east and surpluses in the north, Wales, Scotland, and Northern Ireland. Persistent shortages of skilled labour were also present. This, and the fact that booms and slumps were relatively short-lived, encouraged firms to hoard labour, particularly skilled labour. The low level of investment associated with the stop–go cycle meant that scrapping of old plant was discouraged and industry remained relatively archaic and labour intensive, exacerbating labour shortages where these did occur.

Thus in this early period low levels of structural and cyclical unemployment coexisted with localized, periodic, and skilled labour shortages. It is likely that if demand for labour had grown more rapidly and steadily, increased supply would have been forthcoming from higher female participation rates and higher net immigration. The state was also slow to intervene to tackle the structural problems. It was not until the early sixties that attempts were made to develop regional policies and industrial training. This was for a combination of economic and political reasons. The fluctuating and slow rate of economic growth allowed the government, which was also politically opposed to state intervention, to avoid tackling the problems.

From 1966 the situation altered, with a persistently higher level of unemployment being maintained in the subsequent period both in the UK and internationally, rising to particularly high levels from 1973 onwards. The major cause of unemployment has been a slow-down in investment and economic growth rates during this period, which governments, abandoning Keynesian policies, have encouraged rather than sought to reverse, in an attempt to combat inflation. At times the use of unemployment to discipline the workforce and reduce trade union bargaining power, which Marxists have emphasized, has been made explicit by governments that have failed to achieve the same effect by anti-trade-union legislation or incomes policy.

Thus both the 1974–9 Labour government and the 1979 Tory government have stated their intention to curb trade union wage demands through higher unemployment unless voluntary restraint is accepted.

The perspective for the eighties is that unemployment will rise further, given the intensification of deflationary policies associated with the Tory government's commitment to a run-down of the public sector. According to estimates that make no allowance for any significant labour-saving technological change, registered unemployment is likely to rise to about $2\frac{3}{4}$ million by 1985 and to $3\frac{3}{4}$ million by 1990 (*Cambridge Economic Policy Review*, 1979). Other forecasts that assume that new technology will have a greater impact on jobs reach even higher figures. While the overall effect of technological change remains uncertain, it will inevitably reinforce structural unemployment problems, leaving the young, women, and the unskilled with employment prospects that are extremely bleak.

FURTHER READING

For information on unemployment and employment trends see *Labour Research*, *Cambridge Economic Policy Review*, and *National Institute Economic Review*. Other relevant works are McCracken (1977), Rowthorn (1975), Barratt-Brown (1978), Barron and Curnow (1979), and Community Development Project (1977 and 1979).

TWENTY-TWO

CLASS STRUGGLE

Jean Gardiner

22-1 INTRODUCTION

This final chapter in Part Five brings together the conclusions reached in the three preceding chapters and looks at the implications they have for the nature and effectiveness of class struggle. It discusses the impact of working class militancy and strength in Britain on economic growth and changes in the overall balance of forces between capital and labour.

Starting with an examination of the fundamental conflict of interest between capital and labour within the labour process, Chapter 19 showed how shifts in the balance of power between them had occurred in Britain as elsewhere. Relevant factors here were market conditions affecting both products and labour, labour organization and unity, and the nature of controls labour could exert within the production process in the light of technical and managerial developments. It was argued that for a number of historical reasons workers in certain industries, especially engineering, had succeeded in developing job controls that had limited the exploitation of their own labour. However, in a capitalist economy these controls would always be limited by the ultimate power of capital to withdraw in favour of investments elsewhere. The intensification of international capitalist competition from the sixties had in fact resulted in growing threats to the use of job controls.

Chapter 20 examined the nature of the British working class and the relative strengths and weaknesses of the labour movement. The British labour movement has certain clear strengths by comparison with those elsewhere, strengths related to its size, historical continuity, political unity, and roots in the workplace. Nonetheless, weaknesses also exist, such as sectionalism and a relatively low level of political consciousness.

In Chapter 21 the labour market conditions within which class struggle has taken place were analysed both for the period of relatively tight labour markets in the fifties and early sixties and for the subsequent period of rising unemployment. However, the implications for bargaining power of workers, both potential and actual were not examined.

So far most of the analysis has been concerned with the potential influence the British labour movement is able to exert, given its own structural features and the production and market contexts in which it has operated. We now turn to the actual extent and effectiveness of working class pressure in capitalist Britain.

22-2 THE EXTENT OF INDUSTRIAL MILITANCY

The analysis so far has indicated that, especially for the period before the mid-sixties, the British working class was in a potentially stronger position to defend its economic interests than the working class in other industrial capitalist countries. It is more difficult to assess, however, the extent to which potential strength manifested itself as an actual force shaping developments that took place. Measures like the incidence of strikes or the rate of growth of money wages are not satisfactory as indices of working class bargaining power or combativeness, since both reflect the outcome of all the forces at work in the situation. For example, visible signs of militancy, like strikes, may be less frequent when working class bargaining power is at its highest, since the threat of industrial action is sufficient to force concessions from employers. An examination of the trend in the number of working days lost through strike action provides an illustration. While the bargaining power of the British working class was greater in the sixties and seventies than it was in the twenties, the number of working days lost through strike action was considerably lower (see Table 22-1).

Taking account of the limits of those measures that we have, let us consider the trends in strike activity and their implications. In doing this it is important to bear in mind not only that strikes are a very partial indication of industrial conflict, but also that available strike statistics are themselves an imperfect measure of work stoppages. For example, some employers are more scrupulous than others in recording disputes, and the criteria used to determine what is counted as a work stoppage will vary. The official statistics exclude very short strikes (lasting less than a day) and very small strikes (affecting fewer than 10 workers), both of which are thought to have been fairly common in British industry. They also exclude work stoppages that are not concerned with terms and conditions of employment (e.g., political protests against government pay restraint).

From Table 22-1 it can be seen that while the number of working days lost through strike action has generally been lower during the last 50-year period than was the case previously, the number of stoppages has risen. The number of workers involved in strikes shows no clear trend. There has thus been a substantial reduction in the average duration of strikes.

The rise in the number of strikes that has taken place over the last 50 years appears even sharper if coal mining is excluded. In Britain, as in other industrial countries, coal mining has tended to dominate the strike records. Thus for two decades from the Second World War, coal mining provided over half the recorded stoppages in every year. Since then, however, there has been a dramatic decline, from 2224 mining strikes in 1957 (about three-quarters of total) to 212 in 1975 (only a tenth of total). This reduction resulted both from the drastic decline in employment in mines associated with the policy of pit closures and from the abolition during the sixties of piece-work payment, a major cause of disputes. By contrast, all other industries experienced a rise in the number of stoppages, from about 600 in the mid-fifties to an average of 2400 in the seventies.

Strike activity has in fact become considerably more broadly based, spreading from the mid-sixties into previously unaffected industries, such as public administration and professional services. Nevertheless, the ranking

Table 22-1 British strike statistics: annual averages, 1900–79

	Number of strikes	Workers involved (thousands)	Striker-days (thousands)
1900–10	529	240	4 576
1911–13	1 074	1 034	20 908
1914–18	844	632	5 292
1919–21	1 241	2 108	49 053
1922–25	629	503	11 968
1926	323	2 734	162 233
1927–32	379	344	4 740
1933–39	735	295	1 694
1940–44	1 491	499	1 816
1945–54	1 791	545	2 073
1955–64	2 521	1 116	3 881
1965–69	2 380	1 208	3 951
1970–74	3 666	1 573	14 077
1975–79	2 303	1 608	11 592

Source: Hyman (1977), *Department of Employment Gazette*, January 1980.

of industries in terms of strike frequency and strike incidence has remained fairly stable, with five industries—coal mining, docks, motor vehicle manufacturing, ship building, and iron and steel—accounting for a quarter of strikes and a third of working days lost, although they cover only about six per cent of employees. Strike activity has also become more broadly based among occupational groups, with a rise in the participation of non-manual workers since 1966. However, manual worker involvement continues to be much greater, with 85 per cent of strikes in the period 1966–73 involving manual workers alone.

Some studies of concentration of industrial stoppages have been conducted which indicate that, at least as far as manufacturing industry is concerned, strike activity is by no means a widespread phenomenon. In each year from 1971 to 1975 only 2 per cent of all manufacturing establishments and about

20 per cent of all employees were affected by stoppages. These proportions remained remarkably constant despite variations in the overall level of strikes. The picture that emerges is that industrial stoppages are concentrated in a relatively small number of mainly larger plants. In fact, as many as a half of the largest plants employing 1000 or more workers were affected by stoppages on average during the period 1971 to 1975.

It is difficult to assess the significance of strike activity in the UK without some attempt at international comparisons. The comparative evidence must be interpreted with caution since the criteria and methods of data collection differ between countries. The most statistically comparable measure of strike activity is the number of working days lost per 1000 workers. According to this measure Britain holds a middle ranking among both industrial capitalist

Table 22-2 Working days lost through industrial disputes per 1000 employees in selected industries (mining, manufacturing, construction, and transport), 1969–78

	Annual averages
France	297
West Germany	90
Italy	1938
Japan	231
UK	897
US	1282

Source: Department of Employment Gazette, February 1980.

countries as a whole and also among its major international competitors, as shown in Table 22-2. The evidence that exists therefore does not support the strike-prone reputation of British industry. The Ministry of Labour admitted to the Donovan Commission in 1965 that 'the UK's reputation abroad has probably suffered more than the time lost through strikes in comparison with other countries would warrant' (Donovan, 1968).

The cost of industrial stoppages in Britain therefore appears close to average for industrial capitalist countries. It is also relatively low by comparison with other causes of lost production, such as accidents (20 million working days a year) and sickness (over 300 million working days). What has characterized British industry, however, throughout most of the post-war period is a relatively large number of fairly short, spontaneous, unofficially sponsored strikes reflecting and reinforcing the trade union strength in the workplace that characterizes key sections of British industry. However, developments in other Western European countries associated with the sharp rise in industrial militancy in the late sixties and early seventies may be bring-ing the general pattern of strike activity closer to the British model.

To sum up the evidence so far, it appears that there have been a number of shifts in the pattern of industrial militancy as measured by strike activity. In the fifties and sixties in Britain, relatively low levels of working days were lost through industrial stoppages by historical standards, despite the expan-sion in the labour force that took place during that period. However, a new pattern of more frequent, relatively short, and mostly unofficial strikes was established. Industrial stoppages remained concentrated in the traditionally more strike-prone industries and occupations. The period 1970–74 saw a sharp upsurge in militancy, reflected both in frequency of strikes and working days lost. Militancy also became more broadly based during this period, in-volving some traditionally less militant industries and occupational groups, notably those in the public sector. Between 1975 and 1978 there was some reduction in the number and scale of strikes, although the number of working days lost continued at considerably higher levels than those experienced in the fifties and sixties and rose again sharply in 1979.

Both the level and trend of industrial militancy in Britain are fairly typical of industrial capitalist countries as a whole, although strikes in Britain have tended to take a characteristically shorter, more spontaneous, and unofficial form than elsewhere. The differences may be narrowing, however, as pressure for stronger workplace trade union organization develops elsewhere, and longer, official strikes, involving larger numbers of workers, become more common in Britain.

22-3 THE CAUSES AND EFFECTS OF MILITANCY

Traditionally economists have avoided the subject of industrial militancy and strike activity, perceiving it as irrational and therefore of more concern to sociologists than to themselves. This view is based on the assumption that conflict of interest does not exist in industry and that the costs of a stoppage to the strikers themselves normally outweigh the gains.

While these assumptions have continued to dominate the conventional approach to labour economics, two distinct schools of thought have emerged regarding the role played in the economy by the institutional framework of industrial relations. On the one hand, the neo-classical monetarist approach discounts the effects of trade union intervention and militancy as an active force, seeing these as mere reflections of atomistic market forces. In this tradi-tion the Phillips curve explains rises in money wages by reference to the level of excess demand for labour, combined more recently with the rate of price inflation (actual or expected). On the other hand, the institutionalists empha-size the structure and internal dynamics of trade union organization and the independent effect this has on the economy (e.g., via cost-push inflation).

What neither of these approaches recognizes is the economic rationale within capitalist social relations of production for industrial conflict and militancy. More progressive writers have, on the other hand, attempted to develop a political economic analysis of wage militancy. Their arguments will be summarized in this section.

First let us look at certain international trends that have been linked with the upsurge in working class militancy in industrial capitalist countries from the late sixties. Two developments occurred around this period which restricted the share of resources available in the private sectors of these economies for distribution between wages and profits. The first was the growth in state expenditure, which accelerated in nearly all the major industrial capitalist economies during the sixties, resulting in a growing burden of taxation for the private sector. The second was a stabilization in the late sixties and then rise during the early seventies in the terms of trade for primary products. In the fifties and early sixties industrial countries had benefited from the deteriorating position of the primary producing countries. The reversal of this trend meant that primary producing countries were now claiming resources that had previously been available for the private sectors of industrial countries. The oil price rise alone in 1974 was equivalent to around four per cent of GDP in countries like the UK.

It was these two sets of pressures that gave rise to growing industrial conflict in the industrial capitalist countries, as workers and capitalists each resisted bearing the resulting burden. In addition, a number of political and economic factors placed the working class in a newly strong bargaining position within this struggle. The boom years of the fifties and sixties had virtually eliminated the indigenous reserve army of labour in the industrial economies themselves. Labour had begun to be in excess demand, with the result that trade unions were gaining in confidence and organizational strength. In addition, political and ideological divisions, inherited from the Cold War period, which had seriously weakened trade union movements, were breaking down. This combination of factors resulted in a tendency for the share of profits in output to be squeezed in the late sixties and early seventies in the major capitalist countries.

These trends affected Britain, where they were reinforced by specific problems related to the economy's declining international position. In order to analyse industrial militancy in Britain it is convenient to look first at the fifties and sixties and then turn to the seventies.

The period from the fifties to the mid sixties was one in which, as has already been argued, the British working class appears to have been in a structurally stronger position, in terms of both market power and organization, to defend and advance its economic interests than any other. Yet the evidence suggests that little of this potential power was actually exerted. It was certainly a period of relative quiescence by historical standards according to measures of strike activity. It is true that gross income from employment did rise as a percentage of total output. However, this rise was more than accounted for by the rise in the burden of taxation on wages and salaries. Although part of this latter rise reflected improved state social services, benefiting the working class, it is nonetheless interpreted as a deduction by workers increasingly bargaining for net pay. These trends are shown for the manufacturing sector in Table 22-3.

A number of factors may explain the relatively low level of industrial militancy in Britain during the fifties and sixties. The most important factor is probably the historically unique experience of a fairly steady improvement in net real male earnings of about two per cent a year on average between 1950 and 1965. It was not until this rate of increase fell to less than one per cent between 1965 and 1969 that militancy began to build up. The improvement in incomes for many families was probably greater than these figures indicate because of the growth in married women's employment during the period, which meant an increase in the number of two-wage families.

Table 22-3 Wages and salaries as a percentage of manufacturing output, annual average 1953–68

	Gross wages and salaries	Net wages and salaries
1953–56	62.6	57.0
1957–60	63.9	57.1
1961–64	64.7	56.8
1965–68	64.5	54.5

Sources: King (1975), Jackson, Turner and Wilkinson (1975).

The improvement in earnings that did take place during the fifties and early sixties appears to have been less the result of working class organized strength than of a number of favourable economic factors. Low levels of unemployment and labour reserves led to steady upward pressure on wages. Moreover, private sector incomes in Britain not only benefited from the relatively stable levels of taxation and favourable terms of trade enjoyed by the industrial capitalist world as a whole in the fifties and early sixties but were also protected by two legacies of imperialism: an overvalued currency and access to cheap imported food. The fact that foreign trade represented an especially high proportion of output in the case of Britain meant that these conditions were of considerable although short-term advantage. As developments elsewhere in the world undermined them, however, incomes in Britain would inevitably be squeezed.

Political and ideological factors also played a part in reducing class conflict. Both the Labour Party and the trade union movement as a whole supported the renewal of British imperial strategy and subscribed to Cold War politics.

It would be wrong, however, to imply that working class organized strength had no effect whatsoever during this period. Combined with the pressures of full employment, it forced management in certain key productive industries, especially in engineering, to acquiesce in shopfloor bargaining power over wages and other issues, partially eroding their control over the labour process and providing a further disincentive to management to over-haul the means and relations of production. In addition, it could be argued that the potential working class strength, which was known to exist acted as a political threat, underpinning the resistance of the British capitalist class to state intervention and reinforcing their fear that economic planning was the thin end of a socialist wedge.

It is, however, possible that if the working class had exerted more of its organized economic strength during this period and had dissociated itself politically from British imperialism, particularly in the key period 1945–51, the ruling class would have been forced to dismantle its imperial structure and restructure British industry. Thus ironically the conclusion emerges that working class militancy, far from causing the subsequent economic decline, was insufficient to prevent it.

A number of factors that precipitated the upsurge of militancy from 1969 onwards will now be clear. The marked deceleration in net real earnings dur-ing the period 1965–9 already noted was caused by both an increased tax burden on wages and salaries and rising inflation. The single most important factor in price rises at this stage was probably the overdue devaluation of sterling which occurred in 1967. By 1969 inflation had risen from about three per cent a year in the early sixties to around seven per cent.

Another major factor giving rise to a militant working class response was state intervention in the fields of wage control and industrial relations. In-comes policies implemented throughout the post-war period have had both as implicit aim and effect the lowering of money wage increases relative to price increases. From Table 22-4 it is clear that incomes policies when in operation have reduced the rate of growth of real earnings and been invari-ably followed by bursts of income growth secured by faster growth in money wages. Thus, for example, the growth in grass roots militancy in 1969 brought an end to four years of state enforced wage restraint imposed by the Labour government. Equally, attempts by both Labour and Conservative govern-ments to impose legal limits on trade union activity, especially of an unofficial kind, met with a powerful response by the trade unions, culminating in the mass mobilizations of 1972 in support of the Pentonville Five.

The intensity of the militant response in the period 1969–74 can be explained by the differential impact of incomes policies on different groups of workers. New leading groups emerged, not noted either for militancy or even in some cases, for high levels of trade union organization during the fifties and sixties. These were the groups that had actually suffered real reductions in net pay during the late sixties, when earnings on average were only growing very slowly (e.g., the coal miners, electricity workers, and local authority manual workers). Not surprisingly, it was in the public sector, where incomes policies were most rigidly enforced, that resistance emerged most strongly.

Implicit in much of the analysis so far is an acceptance of the view that trade union bargaining behaviour is concerned with target levels, shares, or rates of increases of net real pay. While militancy may not be a major factor in bringing about rising real incomes in a period of boom, aspirations developed in such a period and backed by trade union strength give rise to growing conflict when incomes begin to stagnate.

Table 22-4 Increases in gross earnings, prices, and net real income from employment: periods with and without incomes policy compared (annual compound rate of increase)

	Gross weekly earnings (x)	Retail price (y)	(x−y)	Net real income[a]	Incomes policy
1948–50	4.30	2.87	1.43	1.15	on
1950–56	7.65	5.26	2.39	2.43	off
1956–58	3.76	3.33	0.43	−0.74	on
1958–61	5.96	1.63	4.33	3.04	off
1961–63	4.40	3.09	1.31	1.40	on
1963–65	7.83	3.96	3.87	2.11	off
1965–69	5.92	4.04	1.88	0.39	on
1969–72	12.23	7.35	4.88	4.20	off
1972–76	15.64	15.34	0.30	−1.78	on

[a] Gross weekly earnings adjusted for direct tax and price effects. The tax estimates are based on the standard tax allowances for a married man with 2 children under 11 years of age.

Source: Tarling and Wilkinson (1977).

However, a wage aspirations theory of militancy can only explain part—albeit an important part—of the upsurge of class struggle at the end of the sixties. A number of wider economic and democratic aspirations began to be asserted. The defence of jobs and future of employment began to emerge as a major issue within the trade union movement. However, while some important initiatives were taken at a grass-roots level both of a defensive kind (e.g., the UCS work-in) and of a forward-looking nature (e.g., Lucas Aerospace Shop Stewards Corporate Plan), the trade union movement as a whole failed to develop any coherent strategy. Among public sector workers pressure for more democracy at work and improvements in the quality of public services (e.g., health workers' campaign against private beds in NHS hospitals) developed alongside the wages struggle. Many of the conflicts that developed involved women workers to an extent that was unprecedented. This was linked in turn to a growing militancy of women on issues of equal opportunity and equal pay. The broadening of class struggle in this way was associated with the emergence of a number of new social movements—the women's liberation movement and the environmental/community action movement, for example—which began to organize around class and democratic issues that had been largely ignored by the traditional labour movement.

22-4 INFLATION AND THE STATE

Before completing this analysis of the class struggle and its effects in the seventies it is appropriate here to relate the analysis of inflation and the state developed elsewhere in the book to the role of the organized working class. For it is the role of trade unions in the inflationary process that has been singled out for attack by successive governments and that has been used as the public justification for incomes policies.

During the fifties and sixties a moderate level of inflation was fostered by the state as a means of sustaining corporate profits during a period when a relatively tight labour market put steady pressure on money wage rates. Until the late sixties a combination of moderate inflation and a shift in the burden of taxation from profits to wages and salaries succeeded in keeping the share of post-tax profits, for the manufacturing sector at least, fairly constant. However, in the late sixties this relatively stable situation was undermined by three factors: the acceleration of inflation internationally, the deteriorating international position of the British economy, and the upsurge of working class militancy. Inflation rose from a moderate to an explosive rate. It was the result of intensifying conflict between workers and capitalists over the distribution of resources that were themselves coming under pressure from the state and foreign sectors.

This combination of circumstances meant that inflation, which during its moderate phase had sustained profits, began to erode them. In addition, inflation was becoming politically destabilizing because of its distributional implications. It also had serious consequences for international competitiveness, since by the early seventies prices were rising more rapidly in Britain than elsewhere.

The state was therefore forced to attempt the delicate task of simultaneously reducing inflation and restoring profitability. This could only be done by a combination of policies that sought to control wages and weaken the economic and political power of the trade unions—i.e., state control of wages and rising unemployment.

22-5 INCOMES POLICY

During the post-war period there has been a pervasive although not universal belief that policies to manage demand and supply need to be supplemented by instruments to influence prices and incomes. This influence was exerted through a variety of institutions and types of policy. During 1948–50 the Labour government established a zero norm for pay increases; 1956–7 the Conservatives used the Council on Prices, Productivity and Incomes (the Three Wise Men); 1961–2 they set a zero norm, and in 1962–3 a 'guiding light' of 2–2½ per cent, raised to 3–3½ per cent, monitored by the National Incomes Commission (Tarling and Wilkinson, 1977). All of these policies were nominally voluntary; the government would set a target and try to persuade firms and unions to settle within that target. It would also 'set a good example' in public sector wage bargains.

The Labour government had a 3–3½ per cent limit during 1965–6 and set up the National Board for Prices and Incomes (NBPI), followed by a compulsory six-month freeze and then a zero norm for six months. For the rest of the Labour government there was a series of 'voluntary' restraints, supported by some legal powers of delay. Throughout this period there were a variety of exceptions for such things as productivity improvements, differentials, and low paid groups. The NBPI also extended its role beyond merely monitoring prices and incomes.

For the first two years of the administration (1970–2) the Conservative government had no formal incomes policy, but used restrictions on public sector settlements to try and bring down the general rate of growth of wages. In 1972 they felt forced to introduce a compulsory freeze followed by a Phase 2 maximum of £1 + 4 per cent, with an enforced gap of 12 months between wage increases. The restrictions were enforced by the Pay Board. Phase 3 during 1973–4 allowed a maximum of 7 per cent or £2.25 plus threshold agreements which compensated for inflation. The Labour government elected in 1974 abandoned compulsory incomes policy and replaced it with the 'social contract'. During 1974–5 the policy was that increases should only compensate for price changes between settlements; 1975–6 a £6 maximum with a 12-month rule; 1976–7, 5 per cent, and subsequently various 'norms'. Like the 1970 government, the 1979 Tory government renounced incomes policy.

There were three main ways in which policy was enforced—through legal restrictions, through public sector settlements, and through pressure on the trade unions to comply with the government target. The effectiveness of all this effort is controversial. A recent econometric study (Henry and Ormerod, 1978) concludes that over the period 1961–75

... whilst some incomes policies have reduced the rate of wage inflation during the period in which they operated, this reduction has only been temporary. Wage increases in the period immediately following the ending of the policies were higher than they would otherwise have been, and these increases match losses incurred during the operation of the incomes policy.

The incomes policy 1975–8 certainly held down the growth of money (and real) wages, but as previous experience suggested, this was offset by a subsequent wage explosion. Supporters of incomes policy argue that what the evidence suggests is that it is a mistake to remove incomes policy, but international evidence suggests that it is impossible to maintain incomes policies over the long term in industrial non-communist countries. Countries with highly centralized union structures (such as Sweden and the Netherlands) maintained them for considerable periods, but even there they eventually collapsed.

The issue is essentially in the first instance a distributional one. Given the structure of production and available supply, to reduce inflation requires reducing the claims on available output. Since a policy objective of UK governments is to shift resources to investment and exports, and they have chosen to rely primarily on the market mechanism, profits must be maintained; thus either the claims of wages or government expenditure must be reduced. Incomes policy is the mechanism used to reduce wage claims. But the extent to which it achieves this will depend on the balance of class forces and market pressures.

22-6 THE LIMITS OF TRADE UNION MILITANCY

It will be clear from the foregoing analysis that organized working class action has been a powerful force impinging on the development of British capitalism. It is also clear that the potential power of the working class is considerably greater than any that has yet been mobilized.

Taking wage militancy alone, this can take either a purely defensive or an offensive form. The effects this will have depend on political as well as economic factors, and specifically on the way the state reacts—i.e., whether it pursues inflationary or deflationary policies or intervenes directly to restructure the economy.

What is clear is that wage militancy, which is the predominant although not exclusive form taken by the intensified class struggle of the 1969–74 period, on its own is incapable of bringing about a permanent political and economic shift in the balance of class forces.

By the late sixties international pressures reinforced by the domestic class struggle finally forced the British ruling class partially to dismantle the imperial structure on which it had been based and to seek a new political and economic base in the EEC from which to restructure British industry. Their success in achieving this switch of strategy meant that the heightened phase of class struggle in the early seventies was finally resolved to the capitalists' advantage.

The experience of inflation and response of the state to the trade union militancy of the early seventies left the labour movement without a clear strategy but with a growing consciousness that wage militancy alone is insufficient to defend or advance working class interests. The need for the labour movement to develop a wider political and economic strategy became more urgent with the far-reaching policy changes initiated by the Conservative government elected in 1979. These are matters pursued in the final chapter, which follows.

FURTHER READING

For information on trade union activity useful sources are the annual reports of the TUC, *Labour Research*. Strike series are reported in the *Department of Employment Gazette*. See also Crouch (1979a and 1979b), Panitch (1976), Hyman (1977), Hyman and Brough (1975), Allen (1966), Jackson, Turner, and Wilkinson (1975), Rowthorn (1980), Henry and Ormerod (1978), Tarling and Wilkinson (1977) and Rubery (1978).

TWENTY-THREE

CONCLUSIONS AND PROSPECTS

Sam Aaronovitch

23-1 PROSPECTS FOR THE EIGHTIES

The manuscript of this book was being completed at the beginning of the eighties. In political time, if not in calendar time, the new decade began with the election victory of the Conservative Party in May 1979, but we have had relatively short experience of the new government's policies and their effects; our estimates are therefore necessarily speculative. In our introductory chapter we said that Marxism was not deterministic, in that there was no inevitable outcome independently of what people do; and also that Marxism was developed as a practice in which theories are used, developed, and 'tested' in the course of 'changing the world'. For these reasons this final chapter deals directly with problems of political as well as economic strategy. We cannot do this without some fuller account of the political and economic background, drawing on the detailed economic analysis already made in the preceding chapters.

There are a number of important conclusions to be drawn from our analysis that have a bearing on policies designed to change the direction of the UK economy.

First, the British state has failed (or, more correctly, refused) to carry through the necessary coordination and direction for modernizing and expanding the industrial base of the domestic economy, and in this has been unlike state power in our main capitalist rivals.

Second, although financial and industrial capital have increasingly become intertwined in the UK economy, they are separated in a way that has held back the mobilization of funds for economic growth based on long-term investment strategies. This, too, has been unlike the situation in countries such as West Germany and Japan.

Third, financial capital and increasingly industrial capital have been orientated overseas for many decades; and their preoccupation has been with their world role rather than with the UK domestic economy. The internationalization of British financial and trading capital that began early in British capitalist history has been joined by the internationalization of industrial capital.

Fourth, partly because of this world orientation, the weakened UK economy has been opened up to world competitive pressures, which have led to rising import penetration of manufactures and acute balance of payments constraints. North Sea oil has masked the overall worsening of the UK economy's world position but through raising the exchange rate has weakened the trade balance in manufactures and consequently aided the forces of cumulative decline.

Fifth, British capital has had to deal with a well organized trade union movement with considerable shopfloor strength and substantial defensive power but occupied with sectional interests and having little perspective of an alternative to capitalism.

In spite of the fact that overall the post-war growth of the UK economy has been high by our *own* historical standards, it has been pushed onto the path of *relative* decline. In the two decades from 1960 to 1980 from being one of the richest capitalist economies in Western Europe, Britain became one of the poorer. The trend, if continued, would leave the UK with a 'derelict' economy by the time the flows of North Sea oil dry up. With these conclusions in mind, we can try to make an assessment of the seventies and consider the prospect for the eighties.

Judged overall, the decade of the seventies can be considered one of economic regression for the UK. The past decade has probably witnessed the emergence of a new phase of world capitalism; a phase longer than a business cycle and involving, in comparison with the fifties and sixties, lower average rates of growth of production and trade, with above average rates of inflation and unemployment. The UK economy has been more affected than many other economies by this new phase because of the relative weakening of its position and has entered the eighties with a set of severe economic and social problems: large-scale poverty involving up to ten million people; unemployment rising above two million; acute industrial discontent as expectations of improved living standards strike against the barrier of restrictive and deflationary policies; high levels of inflation; and with no solution in sight to the non-oil deficit in visible trade. So the list could continue.

It could also be argued that the seventies have been a decade of *political* regression for the UK, which reached a new point with the election of the Conservative government in 1979. But political regression also covered the period of the 1970–74 Conservative government and the 1974–79 Labour government. The Conservative election victory in May 1970 occurred as left circles in the Labour Party and in the trade unions succeeded in shifting the Labour Party national executive and its annual conferences towards policies of radical change, as expressed in the 1973 Labour Party programme and at many TUC congresses. This policy shift, which encouraged left-wing hopes of major changes to be carried through by the 1974 Labour government, proved in fact to have only limited significance compared with the shift to the right taking place within the Conservative Party and among Labour and non-Labour people. In considering the prospects for the eighties we need to analyse why this rightward shift took place. Among the most important reasons we would propose the following.

The 1974 Labour government, operating in a slow-growth economy, attempted to reduce real incomes, place legal constraints on trade unions, and weakened the ability of the welfare services to function in the interests of the people. The majority experienced the rising burden of direct taxation as inflation brought them into the tax net, while the health, education, and welfare services that those taxes were financing seemed to be deteriorating; moreover, people experienced—especially in areas such as housing and social security—a sense of bureaucratic insensitivity. Similarly, with regard to the nationalized industries, the many changes of policy imposed on them by government, and their increasing financial problems, created among both employees and consumers a growing disenchantment with nationalization as they experienced it. It was the 1974–9 Labour government that carried out the biggest reductions in the share of public spending in GDP, which in turn contributed to the sharp rise in unemployment of more than half a million. And, of course, inflationary pressures arising from internal and international conflict created within a sluggish economy divisiveness as well as discontent; social tensions increased and a fertile field for racialism was created.

In these ways, a government presenting itself as social–democratic was identified with a kind of 'bureaucratic statism' or 'corporatism', simultaneously involved in increasing the inequality of incomes and wealth and perpetuating slow growth. For all these reasons, the Labour Party as represented by its leadership helped to create a political vacuum. In this situation, what, then, was the position of the left within the labour and trade union movement?

Put bluntly, the left could not occupy the political vacuum. Among the main active force of the Labour Party and trade unions, the basic philosophy of right-wing social democracy was still predominant, and the left itself was fragmented. Although beginning to come together in its critique of the 1974–79 Labour government, it comprised some groups that had simply repeated the basic tenets of socialism without reviewing and developing them in the light of a drastically changed world, as well as groups that saw the need for new strategies but had not yet started to work them out. The policies of radical change, which began to emerge and be influential in the early seventies, were, however, the property of relatively small groups, such as those around the weekly journal *Tribune* and individuals such as Tony Benn. They did not correspond to the mood and level of understanding of the great majority of people, including the majority of organized workers. The left was overwhelmed by the spread of cynicism and apathy and even opposition that was developing, so that even the existence of an emerging left alternative strategy was known only to a small minority of the movement. Undoubtedly, the outcome of the referendum vote on the EEC in 1975 represented a setback for the left, which was further reinforced by the 'devolution' votes in Scotland and Wales in 1978. Right-wing social democracy had failed; the left was relatively weak and isolated.

Who, then, could fill the political vacuum? It was, as we know, filled by the Conservative Party, which was able to wage a sustained ideological campaign, seizing on the worries of the people and attaching them to right-wing ideas on law and order, state, bureaucracy and the individual, and the 'excessive' power of the trade unions as against democratically elected government. But the ability of the Conservative Party to seize the political initiative was also determined by changes that had been taking place within that party. The position of the Conservative Party had weakened in recent decades as part of the weakening of the two-party system. The response within that party was to strengthen both the 'principled' right and the 'populist' right. The 'principled' right represented a theoretical challenge to the predominance of Keynesian thinking; a reassertion of 'liberal' political economy symbolized by the theoretical and political stance of Milton Friedman and developed in the publications for instance of the IEA and the study groups connected with Keith Joseph and other Conservative leaders. The 'populist' right was able to exploit the fears and anxieties of large numbers of people and take advantage of widely held authoritarian and racialist attitudes.

This combination of 'principled' and 'populist' Conservatism (anticipated by Enoch Powell and the initial declarations of the 1970 Heath government) contributed to Mrs Thatcher's election as party leader, gave the cutting edge to the party's election campaign, and has defined the policies of the 1979 Conservative government.

However, this ideological shift was accompanied and 'fed' by a rising wave of impatience among sections of business looking for more drastic action against the trade union movement. This was noticeable in the tough stand of the Engineering Employers Federation and the way their line was carried into the CBI.

How, then, are we to characterize the policies of the Conservative government as they have appeared up to the early part of 1980? Perhaps the best way to start is by attempting to state what we think are its objectives. First and foremost, to shift the balance of strength further towards capital and away from labour. This will facilitate rationalization and reorganization in the interests of greater productivity. Success in this would assure the continuing unity of big business around the party and the debate would then be primarily over tactics rather than the objectives themselves. Of course, if the cost to capital—in the destruction of industries, the further reduction in profitability, and the threat to political stability—is considered too great, that unity will crack. The second objective is to transform the levers of state intervention in the production of goods and services and in the movements of capital; and to limit their possible use by a subsequent Labour government. This also involves dismantling sections of the welfare system, opening the way further for private health and education. This is seen as part of a campaign to change the outlook of millions of people to a more favourable view of the 'cash-nexus' and to elevate the virtues of 'self-help'. The third objective is to offer the widest scope to the global operation of British capital and to increase its mobility (as was done, for instance, in the abolition of exchange controls), even though such mobility carries with it dangers even for a Conservative government.

The measures needed to realize these objectives carry with them enormous risks and the probability, if not the certainty, of damaging conflicts. The deflationary policies of the government must themselves worsen the situation of many sections of capital; if on top of those deliberately inflicted wounds the government fails to intimidate the trade union movement but yet persists in its policies, industrial unrest and political instability must follow. In addition (and this is a point we take up later), if the government is mistaken in its view of the way the system will respond to its measures by way of restoring and improving profitability, tensions must rise among its own supporters.

Such conflicts will include, for instance, conflict between those sections of business whose interests are mainly tied to the economic 'health' of the domestic economy as compared with those operating mainly in the international sphere. Such conflicts have shown themselves with regard to the EEC (for instance, how to deal with increasing import penetration in textiles). A further dimension of conflict will be the growth in hostility of large numbers of small business and professional strata, which constitute an important source of ideological and practical support for the party. None of this is to say that the government is without room for manoeuvre. The rising price of oil will by 1985 provide the government with very substantial revenues; but, of course, there is no need to assume that policies will remain unchanged; and such changes could come from a change by the existing leadership of the party or by changes in that leadership itself.

If, however, the government were defeated in an election, whether at the end of its full term or following a major political/industrial crisis, the election of a Labour government is the most likely outcome. The policy debates within the Labour Party and the Labour movement are therefore of great interest on that account; but also because those policy discussions affect the movement of resistance to Conservative government policies. Before we review these discussions it is convenient to look briefly at the policy debate as it has been formulated among mainstream economists.

23-2 MONETARISTS AND KEYNESIANS: THE POLICY IMPLICATIONS OF THE THEORETICAL DEBATE

The public discussion on economic policy, to the extent that it has taken place, has been deeply influenced by the debate between two main contrasting theories, monetarism and Keynesianism which have been described in earlier chapters. Our concern here is with the policy implications of these theoretical positions, although some of their main ideas will be briefly reviewed. We need to recognize at once that there are differences *within* each of these 'camps' and also that there is a substantial overlap *between* them, partly because of common theoretical roots (in neo-classical theory) and because there are often common political presuppositions. For instance, in so far as some Keynesians regard inflation as the main danger (along with monetarists), they have accepted major assumptions. We cannot deal with every strand in the debate at this stage, nor with those who may be either Keynesians or Marxists but who believe that 'money matters'.

Monetarism

Monetarism has two components. One involves an underlying vision of the economy as self-regulating and tending towards some kind of full employment equilibrium, although full employment is defined as a situation in which everybody prepared to work at the rates offered can find employment. This is essentially a version of the traditional neo-classical view. A second component, which more specifically defines monetarism, involves the belief that there is a clear causal relationship between prices and the money supply, in which the causality runs from the money supply to prices; it follows that changes in price are primarily the result of changes in the money supply. Because of the mechanism by which the supply of money is altered, the key factor in increasing money supply is the rise in the public sector borrowing requirement (PSBR).

The monetarists themselves divide into two tendencies: the 'straight' monetarists and the 'international' monetarists (though the differences should not be exaggerated) and it is the latter who are involved with the Forecasting Unit of the London Business School. The international monetarists believe that changes in the money supply directly affect the exchange rate, which in turn changes world prices measured in sterling. These world prices then determine the prices of goods traded on the home market.

The policy implications of the 'straight' monetarists lead to support for the steady reduction in the PSBR so as to bring about a steady decline in the rate of increase in the money supply. This in turn would alter the public's expectations of future inflation and adapt the growth in money supply to the increase in productivity. This approach fitted nicely into the 'Friedman' vision of the world, which calls for major reductions in state intervention and for a labour market liberated from 'trade union monopolies'.

Monetarists believe that the exchange rate should be allowed to float, determined by the market without intervention. In practice this has resulted in a high exchange rate for the UK as a consequence of the restrictive monetary policies (as well as North Sea oil) thought necessary to bring down the rate of inflation. They are unconcerned that the high exchange rate has priced

British exporters out of many markets. In fact, in their view, the competitive pressures brought about by such high rates may improve efficiency in the UK.

Keynesianism

Keynesians concern themselves with the 'real' economy; capitalism for them is *not* a self-regulating system that will tend towards full employment but, on the contrary, one that can settle down at high levels of unemployment of people and capacity. The main reason for this lies in the mechanisms that reduce effective demand below the level needed for full employment. In the light of this, Keynesians recognize that the government alone can act deliberately to raise the level of effective demand and, if there are unused resources, create high levels of employment. In expanding demand, Keynesians place a heavy weight on fiscal policy. An important Keynesian proposition is that because the labour market is unlike the ideal competitive market of economic theory, money wages are inflexible downwards, and this lends support to cost-push versions of the inflationary process. It follows that wage control is necessary to reduce the rate of inflation.

In broad terms, Keynsians favour expansionary policies as the key to increased investment, productivity, and rising real incomes. They criticize the monetarists on the grounds that they misunderstand the causal relation between money supply and price and are mistaken in seeing the critical locus of inflationary pressure in the PSBR. They argue that prices are determined by 'normal' costs and not by supply and demand, and that changes in demand are met by adjustments in output rather than price. Keynesians generally agree that the high exchange rate of sterling that has been prevalent is extremely damaging to the UK economy. But here there is a divide that has become familiar because it is identified with the differences between the National Institute of Economic and Social Research and the Cambridge Economic Policy Group. The National Institute favours devaluations as the most favoured way of dealing with the balance of payments constraint. For devaluation to work, however, domestic costs must be prevented from eating up the advantage to exporters, and this requires an 'incomes policy'. The CEPG believes that workers will not accept the real wage cuts implied in such a policy and so any competitive advantage will be eroded. That is why they consider that only wide-ranging import controls can be effective.

The Policy Implications

There are obviously very clear contrasting policy differences between the monetarists and the Keynesians, and these differences have played an important part in the public discussion on policy. The relationship, however, between these theoretical arguments and the policies of governments, political parties, and class groupings and organizations (such as the CBI, for instance) is far more complex.

In the first place, policy makers are usually committed to a view of their interests and will use (even seize on) theories that justify or legitimize the policies they wish to pursue. The theories play an ideological role and sometimes leave the theoreticians protesting that they are misrepresented by what is done in their name. But there is a second aspect, which is that policy makers even in formulating their interests must draw on visions of the world available to them providing these are not self-evidently destructive of the society they identify with. Conservative and right-wing Labour governments have drawn freely on monetarist and Keynesian sources (but not on Marxist ones). And third, policy makers have and make choices between strategies that are necessarily related to theories which they find plausible.

Keynesian theory, however, has always had a subversive element; hence the existence of a left-Keynesian tendency from the thirties, symbolized, for instance, in the work and activities of Joan Robinson. It has proved a useful theory and provided a set of practices for capitalist economies in which the state has expanded its role. But because of its subversive possibilities, two things have happened: on the theoretical level, a systematic effort has been made to absorb Keynes fully into neo-classical theory; and on the policy level, the major groups of financial and industrial capital in all capitalist countries and in the international organizations dominated by them (such as the BIS, IMF, etc.) have maintained an 'orthodoxy' which has increasingly reasserted itself as the post-war expansion slowed down and the need and possibilities of reducing working class bargaining power emerged more clearly. For these latter groups, monetarism has provided both justification and the view that its application would do what they wanted.

The Conservative government elected in May 1979 has claimed monetarism as a justification for its policies (the 'ideological' role referred to above), but it also believes that the mechanisms and relationships presented by monetarists (and in particular, the proposition that the causes of inflation lies in the money supply itself primarily fuelled by the PSBR) will hold if used in determining policy. If they are wrong then they will be confronted with results they did not want, but it is likely that they would then, with or without a change in leadership, prove far more eclectic in their policies. But even at the time of writing, the damage done, both intentional and unintentional, is severe. On *unchanged* policies, the prospects for the UK economy throughout the eighties appear desperate in their effects on the lives of the people.

This is perhaps the appropriate point at which to return to the position within the Labour Party and labour movement. The 1974–9 Labour government had already moved a considerable distance towards a version of restrictive monetary policies accompanied by attempts at wage control; as we have seen, it began the 'counter-revolution' in pushing back the share of public spending in GDP. At the same time it practised a halfhearted industrial 'strategy', which we have analysed in Chapter 10. The 'heart' of the labour movement has always been committed to full employment, economic growth, rising living standards, and high levels of social welfare with substantial degrees of state intervention. The failure of Labour governments to bring these conditions about and the degree to which the 1974–9 Labour government prepared the conditions for the Conservative victory have led to a renewed and increasingly urgent debate within the left on radical solutions to the problems of the British capitalist economy. A large part of this debate has centred around the concept of an *alternative economic strategy*.

23-3 THE ALTERNATIVE ECONOMIC STRATEGY (AES)

The subheading is in one sense misleading; there is no single agreed alternative economic strategy. What is under discussion are attempts by various groups and tendencies to find a common policy response to the urgent and deep-seated problems of the economy. Although broadly on the left of the leadership of the Labour Party, the common response has been approached from different theoretical and political positions, which we might classify in the following way.

First, there are those who approach the AES from some version of 'left-Keynesian' theory, an excellent example of which can be found in Blake and Ormerod (1980). Here the emphasis is on the importance of expanding demand as the key to increased output, investment, productivity, and rising standards. The state increases its spending and intervention but the issues of class and class power are either left out of the discussion or remain implicit. Another approach is from the traditional socialist and social–democratic elements in the movement, who go along with the Keynesian approach described but are more emphatic on public ownership and industrial democracy. The third trend is represented by the explicitly Marxist groups and individuals who see the alternative economic strategy as a necessary programme on the road to the fundamental reconstruction of the UK economy on socialist lines. Among these groups, some place the AES within a strategy of working class unity and broad alliances.

Given the variety of approaches, the degree of convergence is substantial but, not surprisingly, there are many unresolved questions, and the degree of agreement and disagreement must influence the character of the resistance to Conservative government policies, the kind of demands currently presented and argued for, and the prospects of widespread support for a programme that could make possible the eventual formation of a left Labour government.

In what follows, we have presented a version of the AES that is the writer's version of what its essential character needs to be (for a detailed analysis and survey, see Aaronovitch (1981)); this is followed by a brief review of some unresolved issues, and we then consider objections to the AES from circles such as the Militant group within the Labour Party.

The significance of the AES is that to the degree it becomes a credible and coherent 'package' and becomes widely understood, it will provide the perspective from which demands for change are currently made; it helps all those who recognize that Conservative policies are damaging to see a possible line of advance; it fights passivity and feelings of impotence. In these senses, its significance is immediate. In another way, however, it becomes part of the policy contest within the labour and trade union movement and can help determine the character of a new Labour government.

The AES must involve, therefore, some clear view of directions, priorities, constraints, and mechanisms. It is put forward as a set of policy proposals that can ensure economic growth, take Britain a long way towards full employment, provide improved standards, reduce inequality, and do this in a way that greatly extends democracy in all spheres of life. Its essence is summarized below.

First, major plans for economic expansion initiated and coordinated by the state and supported by a wide range of instruments. These involve large-scale increases in public spending, with the emphasis on capital spending and extensive employment subsidies. Such expansion could bring quite dramatic improvements in the rate of unemployment.

Second, such rapid demand expansion will raise acutely the problems of imports which we come to below. But it is likely that it would quickly hit against the barrier of productive capacity. For this and other reasons, the acceleration of investment is critical. Because this involves the manufacturing sector especially, which is mainly in private hands including large multinationals, a whole battery of measures will be needed. Major investment of the kind that will lift the British economy out of its rut requires long period horizons as against swift pay-back calculations. The state itself must therefore intervene in a bold way in a number of key areas. By direct establishment of enterprises (e.g., in some sectors of high technology), by extending public ownership (e.g., in oil and chemicals) as well as participation, by providing funds, and by compulsory planning agreements with the dominant firms (involving agreement on their investment plans), a substantial build up of investment would need to take place.

To ensure that financial resources are fully used for the programme of industrial 'regeneration', key sectors of banking and finance would become part of a publicly owned system. Both in relation to the private and expanded public sector, this would facilitate the financing of major long-run investment decisions (as in fact has happened in Japan, West Germany, and France, for instance). Nationalization of North Sea oil would add large revenues available for investment.

Third, the main objectives must obviously arise from widespread public debate and the decisions of democratically elected bodies, but steps would need to be taken towards some basic mechanisms for democratic planning. Whatever its character, such planning mechanisms must involve the largest and most critical enterprises in the economy (public and private); a relatively small number of them account for the bulk of output and investment as well as for a large share of total employment. The biggest need will be for such mechanisms to focus only on major investment and allocative decisions on the one hand, and on the other, to 'incorporate' the needs and proposals from the regions and local authorities.

If a bureaucratic system of state intervention is not to be reconstructed then major measures of democratization will be needed, which will include:

(a) Effective trade union and workers' representation in the publicly owned industries at all levels built into the legal structure of these corporations.
(b) In the private sector, the importance of compulsory planning agreements in defining the objectives to be pursued by the firm, the provision of information (open books policy), to and the monitoring role of the workforce.
(c) The representation of popular organizations at regional level in the public sector organizations.
(d) Pursuit and encouragement of varied forms of local authority and co-operative ownership of enterprises providing goods and services (including trade).

Fourth, in learning the lessons from the collapse of the 1965 National Plan, a left government would need to construct a foreign economic policy that would lift the constraint placed on domestic growth by rising import penetration and meet the requirements of a growing economy. The elements of such a policy would include such measures as:

(a) Import controls, which would be intended to allow imports to grow in a planned way so that they could be matched with earnings of foreign exchange, and so that priorities for growth in imports would be based on the priorities established by overall objectives.
(b) The reimposition of controls on movements of capital.
(c) Negotiation of long-run trade agreements, especially with the less developed countries, but there is also scope for such agreements with other major suppliers of food and materials (such as New Zealand, Australia, etc.) as well as with planned economies.
(d) Through the compulsory planning agreements, to try to reach agreement (based on *quid pro quos*) on marketing export and import strategies of the major multi-national firms and on investment strategies which allow for some measure of import substitution. Effective control and agreement with MNCs also require international cooperation among governments and this would be an important objective.

Fifth and last, there is need now for substantial reforms of the welfare and fiscal system designed in part to attack poverty and to reduce the unequal distribution of income and wealth. For the coming period, North Sea oil, as we have said, can provide very large revenues available for use elsewhere in the economy; economic growth will also increase resources and tax revenues; the corporate sector can certainly pay more tax, and a wealth tax would begin to reduce inequality. Cuts in military spending would, in the medium term, release further resources. There is now a substantial body of writing on the kind of advances in content and structure necessary for social advance (see, for instance, Blake and Ormerod, 1980).

The fact that this has been a necessarily brief account of the main features of the AES should not be allowed to obscure the limitations of the AES and the important areas of debate among its supporters. Here we indicate four.

The first problem relates to wage bargaining. Economic expansion that involves increasing aggregate demand quite rapidly would bring the threat of accelerating inflation, as demand increases faster than domestic supply and productivity. In some sectors, increased demand (especially if imports were restricted) would tempt sellers to increase their profit margins. This would also arise if wages rose faster than productivity and the increased wage costs were passed on and if the same thing happened with raw materials and intermediate inputs. One method of dealing with this kind of problem would be a system of price controls. Short-term price controls can certainly work; the problem of longer-run price controls and their range is more difficult. But far more contentious is the question of wage bargaining. One view of the matter is that if vigorous expansion takes place alongside the other measures in the package then the trade unions will respond accordingly, and free or normal collective bargaining can take place in an atmosphere in which the unions respect the problems and priorities of a left Labour government. The other view believes that the rate of growth of incomes must be subject to some degree of planning as part of the attempt to allocate resources between, for instance, investment and consumption and between private and public consumption. The political conditions under which this becomes an issue are clearly crucial.

The second problem concerns the regulation of foreign trade. There are supporters of the AES who are very doubtful about any kind of direct regulation of imports and prefer a policy of devaluation. But even among those who, not always for the same reasons, consider tariffs and import controls as necessary, there are still important unresolved issues. Most proponents of the AES have tended to argue for selective import control as against generalized import controls; but important questions still arise as to how to control imports without encouraging inefficiency in domestic industries and unduly restricting consumer choice: results that would raise domestic prices and create widespread discontent among consumers. The problem of British trade policy also impinges on attitudes to membership of the EEC. A large section of the British left was against Britain's entry and is for our withdrawal. It considers that the diversity of Britain's world trading connections and its requirements for cheaper food imports and the necessity to regain freedom over its foreign trade policies justify withdrawal. But there are others who believe that while the UK should use its strength to improve the terms of membership, including revision or ending of the Common Agricultural Policy, links between the UK and the EEC are already close and important, and the EEC represents a major centre of power in which a left government could exercise considerable influence with other left forces in Western Europe.

The third problem is how to exercise some control over the multi-nationals, such as Ford, ITT, IBM, Unilever, etc. Even if all their UK operations were to be nationalized at a single stroke (which is not proposed in our version of the AES) there would remain not only the consequent political problems but also economic problems arising from intra-company trade and flows of components, design, technology and patents, overseas markets, etc. The questions of control and cooperation on an international level clearly remain important. Planning agreements at the national level and international government cooperation would be critical; the difficulties are great.

The fourth and perhaps most central group of problems is those raised by the relationships between state intervention, planning, democracy, and the market. The supporters of the alternative economic strategy have not agreed on the degree to which state ownership (whatever the forms) should be extended; the 1973 Labour Party programme spoke of state control of 25 of the largest firms in the country as well as of the dominant banking and insurance companies. There are differences of view as to whether the focus should be on acquiring all the major firms in an industry as distinct from one dominant firm, and as to which industries should be treated in this way. A linked question is the extent to which a central planning body, however responsive to initiatives from below, should concentrate on a limited number of crucial investment and allocation decisions, leaving the greater part of economic activity to the operation of the market under various general constraints. This would seem to be the approach of most spokesmen for the alternative strategy. However, even if good theoretical arguments could be put forward to deal with these problems, everything would depend upon enlisting popular support and initiative, involving the trade unions and cooperatives, the political parties, and, beyond that, a vast mass of voluntary and *ad hoc* associations of citizens. That would only be forthcoming if large bodies of people were struggling for such a new direction in economic policy and could see such a left government as expressing their needs and objectives. Reciprocally, such a movement for change could not come into existence without credible alternative policies to those so far experienced in the UK.

It should be clear from the discussion so far that the AES as a package operates at two levels. On one level, it demonstrates the existence of a credible and coherent alternative to policies currently operated. To the degree that it is supported, it strengthens the resistance to those policies and creates the possibility of shifts in policy by Conservative governments or Labour governments that fall far short of having left programmes. At another level, the AES creates the support for a government of the left and helps to shape the likely programme of such a government.

Many supporters of the AES are deeply concerned as to whether any government that attempted to implement a package of the sort described would be able to survive the hostility and sabotage of world capitalist groups and governments. But before we consider this, there is a political and theoretical challenge to the AES from certain groups on the left, such as the Militant group within the Labour Party, as well as groups outside it.

These groups differ among themselves and their critiques of the AES are not identical, although they often overlap, but we can perhaps distinguish two main strands in their attack.

The first is the starting proposition that successful revolutionary change cannot take place in one country alone but must be successful on an international plane. Britain, especially, so deeply embedded in the international economy, cannot be 'separated off'. There is not a specifically British crisis but a crisis of world capitalism. Programmes like the AES, which focus on shifts in power within one country and offer the prospect of radical change, are therefore misconceived. It promises what it cannot deliver but, even worse, it hinders the important task of building up the strongest international movement. Within this framework, proposals such as import controls are seen as chauvinist measures, exporting unemployment to the workers of other countries. Programmes for building up investment and similar proposals are regarded as incorporating the working class movement into plans for regenerating capitalism; it has been argued that Wedgwood Benn represents *industrial* capital in the UK concerned with its domestic market.

The second strand, often linked with the first, regards the AES as a reformist, milk-and-water set of proposals, which cannot deal with the deepseated problems of British capitalism. This could only be done by a root and branch programme for beginning the socialist reconstruction of the UK, which requires the winning of working class power.

In terms of policy, taking into account the differences between groups, these tend to fall into two groups. First, there is a set of 'immediate' demands—such as the 35-hour week, opening of company books, nationalization of all firms threatened with closure, ending of compensation payments by nationalized industries, nationalization of all financial institutions without compensation. In one version, these demands are won by mass mobilization, which will be able 'to throw the state and Parliament into chaos and when the committees established by the mass movement have taken affairs into their own hands will it really be possible to sort things out' (IMG). The Militant group appear to separate off more clearly immediate demands, such as the 35-hour week, work or full pay, sliding scale of wages with the price index to be worked out by trade unionists, crash programme of public works, open the books. Beyond these immediate demands they pose 'a socialist plan of production' involving nationalization of the 200 monopolies plus finance, worker's control and management, socialist planning, etc (see Glyn and Harrison, 1980). Unless these more drastic measures are carried through, big business would be left with sufficient power to sabotage a left government and organize a reactionary counter-strike.

Such arguments can only be fully discussed in the context of the overall political strategies and objectives of the different groups and parties involved in the debate. Many of the supporters of the AES who regard themselves as socialists (i.e., committed to a democratic society based on social ownership and control of the decisive areas of the economy) see this as arising from a complex and prolonged struggle in which credible alternative policies are necessary to give people the confidence to struggle for change and become involved in forming policies as well as fighting for them. Those who present the ostensibly more revolutionary programme have the 1917 Russian Revolution as their model, in which events lead up to a single decisive battle between classes.

Defenders of the AES would argue that it is not appropriate to pick out import controls from the AES without seeing it as part of an overall package. Import controls could be (and to a limited degree already are) used by a Conservative and also by a right-wing Labour government. But the AES proposal is intended as part of a programme designed to permit the UK economy to grow and increase the level of imports even though its composition would change. In any case, employment in other countries is affected by many other factors, such as domestic stagnation, devaluation, shifts in productivity, etc.

These are arguments that will go on being intensively debated. But it remains important to consider the worries among socialists and supporters of the AES as to whether even such 'limited' strategy would not face hostility and sabotage from capital, both in the UK and internationally. The AES undoubtedly represents a challenge to big business. Would not a left government be compelled to take increasingly drastic action to defend itself or be overwhelmed by economic and political crises?

We can look at the problem in a number of different ways. In the first place, it is the mass of the people who must be convinced that they need the changes involved in the AES; it is that popular mobilization and the alliances to support it which would enable a left government to defend its policies and *extend* them if threatened by sabotage. In so far as the AES can be seen as offering sensible and credible answers, it contributes to that popular support and the will to carry it further. Another approach is to consider the potential bargaining strengths available to a left government provided it maintains popular support.

For a number of advanced industrial countries whose governments and dominant groups may well be hostile, the UK remains a major importer of their manufactures, and this would remain substantially the case if she can expand her economy. For many countries we are major exporters of necessary goods and services. In this respect, North Sea oil would be a major asset to a left government. Because political and economic crises threaten to disrupt the world monetary 'system' and prove expensive to those who provoke such disruption, there is some vested interest in compromise. The UK is also the host to immensely valuable investments by foreign based firms, which are, to some degree, hostages.

A left government, popularly supported at home, need not be thought of as isolated in a hostile world. There would certainly be widespread support and sympathy in the industrially more advanced countries, such as France, Italy, Scandinavia, Japan, and substantial bodies of people in West Germany and the United States. The third world countries would stand to gain by mutually supportive long-run trading agreements; and this would be true also of the planned economies of Eastern Europe.

We cannot say if such a government will come into existence in Britain in the eighties. What does seem clear is that the deepseated problems of the British capitalist economy, which arise from its entire history, will not be dealt with except by major changes, however painfully that realization comes.

FURTHER READING

The matters raised in this chapter are under continuous debate and readers who wish to follow the discussion in 'left' circles can do so in journals such as *Tribune, New Statesman, Labour Weekly*, the annual volumes of *Socialist Register* (ed. R. Miliband and J. Saville), *Marxism Today* (CPGB), *International Socialism* (SWP), and *Militant*. Policy issues are also discussed in Blackaby (1979a) and Major (1979).

Important articles can be found in *Capital and Class* (published quarterly by Conference of Socialist Economists), the *Cambridge Economic Journal* (Academic Press), *Economy and Society*, and *National Institute Economic Review*.

Materials on the economic strategy will be found in the Labour Party conference programmes (see 1973 and onward), TUC annual economic review, and materials published by such unions as ASTMS, NALGO, NUPE, and others.

Relevant books include Dobb (1969), Holland (1975 and 1979), Benn (1979), Blake and Ormerod (1980), CSE, London Working Group, (1980), Socialist Economic Review (1981) and Aaronovitch (1981).

On experience of planning in the USSR and Eastern Europe see Ellman (1979) and Brus (1975). On planning in the UK as practised we have referred in earlier chapters to Budd (1978) and Leruez (1976).

A critique of the alternative economic strategy can be found in Glyn and Harrison (1980).

BIBLIOGRAPHY

Aaronovitch, S., *Monopoly*, Lawrence and Wishart, 1955.

Aaronovitch, S., *The Ruling Class*, Lawrence and Wishart, 1961.

Aaronovitch, S., The Road from Thatcherism: the *Alternative Economic Strategy*, Lawrence and Wishart, 1981.

Aaronovitch, S., and M. Sawyer, 'The concentration of British manufacturing', *Lloyds Bank Review*, October 1974.

Aaronovitch, S., and M. Sawyer, 'Mergers, growth and concentration', *Oxford Economic Papers*, 1975a.

Aaronovitch, S., and M. Sawyer, *Big Business: Theoretical and Empirical Aspects of Concentration and Mergers in the United Kingdom*, Macmillan, 1975b.

Allen, V. L., *Militant Trade Unionism*, Merlin Press, 1966.

Atkinson, A. B., *Unequal Shares*, Penguin, 1974.

Atkinson, A. B., and A. J. Harrison, *Distribution of Personal Wealth in Britain*, Cambridge University Press, 1978.

Bacon, R., and W. Eltis, *Britain's Economic Problems: Too Few Producers*, Macmillan, 1978.

Bain, G. S., and R. Price, 'Union growth and employment trends in the U.K. 1964–1970', *British Journal of Industrial Relations*, November 1972.

Bain, G. S., and R. Price, 'Union growth revisited 1948–1974', *British Journal of Industrial Relations*, 1976.

Ball, M., 'British housing policy and the house building industry', *Capital and Class*, Spring 1978.

Baran, P., and P. Sweezy, *Monopoly Capital*, Penguin, 1968.

Barnet, R. J., and R. E. Müller, *Global Reach: The Power of the Multinational Corporations*, Jonathan Cape, 1975.

Barratt-Brown, M., *From Labourism to Socialism*, Spokesman, 1972.

Barratt-Brown, M., *Economics of Imperialism*, Penguin, 1974.

Barratt-Brown, M. (co-ed.), *Full Employment*, Spokesman, 1978.

Barron, I., and R. Curnow, *The Future with Microelectronics*, Frances Pinter, 1979.

Beckerman, W. (ed.), *Labour Governments' Economic Record 1964–73*, Duckworth, 1972.

Benjamin, D. K., and L. A. Kochin, 'Searching for an explanation of unemployment in interwar Britain', *Journal of Political Economy*, August, 1979.

Benn, A. W., *Arguments for Socialism*, Cape, 1979.

BEQB, 'Measures of real profitability', *Bank of England Quarterly Bulletin*, December 1978.

Berthoud, R., 'Training adults for skilled jobs', *Policy Studies Institute Broadsheet*, No. 575, April 1978.

Beynon, H., *Working for Ford*, Penguin, 1973.

Black, J., *The Economics of Modern Britain*, Martin Robertson, 1980.

Blackaby, F. (ed.), *De-industrialisation*, Heinemann, 1979a.

Blackaby, F. (ed.), *British Economic Policy, 1960–74*, Cambridge University Press, 1979b.

Blake, D., and P. Ormerod, (eds.), *The Economics of Prosperity*, Grant McIntyre, 1980.
Blaug, M., *Economic Theory in Retrospect*, Heinemann, 1968.
Bleaney, M., *Underconsumption Theories*, Lawrence and Wishart, 1976.
Block, F. L., *The Origins of the International Economic Disorder*, University of California Press, 1977.
Bottomore, T., *Classes in Modern Society*, Allen and Unwin, 1965.
Brandt Report, *North–South: A Programme for Survival*, Pan, 1980.
Braverman, H., *Labour and Monopoly Capital*, Monthly Review Press, New York, 1974.
Brittan, S., *The Treasury under the Tories, 1951–1964*, Penguin, 1964.
Brittan, S., *Steering the Economy*, Penguin, 1970.
Broadbent, T. A., *Planning and Profit in the Urban Economy*, Methuen, 1977.
Brown, C. J. F., and T. D. Sherriff, 'De-industrialisation: a background paper, *NIER*, 1979.
Brown, C. V., and P. M. Jackson, *Public Sector Economics*, Martin Robertson, 1978.
Brus, W., *Socialist Ownership and Political Systems*, Routledge and Kegan Paul, 1975.
Buci-Glucksmann, C., *Gramsci and the State*, Lawrence and Wishart, 1979.
Budd, A., *The Politics of Economic Planning*, Fontana, 1978.
Burch, P. H., *The Managerial Revolution Reassessed*, Lexington Books, Lexington, Mass., 1972.
Carrington, J. C., and G. T. Edwards, *Financing Capital Investment*, Macmillan, 1979.
Castells, M., *City, Class and Power*, Macmillan, 1978.
Central Policy Review Staff, *The Future of the British Car Industry*, HMSO, 1975.
Channon, D. F., *British Banking Strategy and the International Challenge*, Macmillan, 1977.
Channon, D. F., *The Service Industries*, Macmillan, 1978.
Chevallier, J-M., *Structure Financière de l'Industre Americain*, Cujas, Paris, 1970.
Cipolla, C. M. (ed.), *The Twentieth Century (Vols. 1 and 2)*, The Fontana Economic History of Europe, Collins/Fontana, 1976.
Cipolla, C. M. (ed.), *Contemporary Economics (Parts 1 and 2)*, Collins/Fontana, 1976.
Clay, H., *Lord Norman*, Macmillan, 1957.
Clifton, J. A., 'Competition and the evolution of the capitalist mode of production', *Cambridge Journal of Economics*, June 1977.
Cockburn, C., *The Local State*, Pluto Press, 1977.
Community Development Project, *The Costs of Industrial Change*, CDP, London, 1977.
Community Development Project, *The State and the Local Economy*, CDPPEC in association with PDC, Nottingham, 1979.
Cornwall, J., *Modern Capitalism*, Martin Robertson, 1977.
Coutts, K., W. Godley, and D. Nordhaus, *Industrial Pricing in the U.K.*, Cambridge University Press, 1978.
Cowling, K., *et al.*, *Mergers and Economic Performance*, Cambridge University Press, 1980.
Cowling, K., *Monopoly Capital*, Macmillan, 1981 (forthcoming).
Crockett, A., *International Money*, Nelson, 1977.
Crouch, C. (ed.), *State and Economy in Capitalist Society*, Croom Helm, 1979a.
Crouch, C., *The Politics of Industrial Relations*, Fontana, 1979b.
CSE, London Working Group, *The Alternative Economic Strategy*, CSE/LRC, 1980.
Currie, D. and R. Smith (eds), *Socialist Economic Review*, Merlin Press, 1981.
Deane, P., *The Evolutions of Economic Ideas*, Cambridge University Press, 1978.
Denison, E. F., *Why Growth Rates Differ*, Brookings Institution, Washington DC, 1967.
Desai, M., *Marxian Economic Theory*, second edn, Basil Blackwell, 1979.
Devine, P., *et al.*, *Introduction to Industrial Economics*, Allen and Unwin, 1979.
Dobb, M., *Political Economy and Capitalism*, Routledge, 1968.
Dobb, M., *Welfare Economics and Socialism*, Cambridge University Press, 1969.
Dobb, M., *Theories of Value and Distribution since Adam Smith: Ideology and Economic Theory*, Cambridge University Press, 1973.

Donovan, Lord, *Report of the Royal Commission on Trade Unions and Employers Associations*, HMSO, 1968.

Dow, J. C. R., *The Management of the Economy 1945–60*, Cambridge University Press, 1965.

Doyal, L., and I. Pennell, *The Political Economy of Health*, Pluto Press, 1979.

Dunning, J., 'The U.K.'s international investment position in the mid-1970's', *Lloyds Bank Review*, April 1979.

Edwards, R. C., M. Reich, and T. E. Weisskopf, *The Capitalist System*, Prentice Hall, New Jersey, 1972.

Elbaum, B., W. Lazonick, F. Wilkinson, and J. Zeitlin, 'The labour process, market structure and Marxist theory: a symposium', *Cambridge Journal of Economics*, September 1979.

Ellman, M., *Socialist Planning*, Cambridge University Press, 1979.

Erritt, M. J., and J. C. D. Alexander, 'Ownership of Company Shares: a new survey', *Economic Trends*, September 1977.

Fetherston, M., B. Moore, and J. Rhodes, 'E.E.C. membership and UK trade in manufactures', *Cambridge Journal of Economics*, December 1979.

Field, F., M. Meacher, and C. Pond, *To Him Who Hath*, Penguin, 1977.

Fine, B., *Marx's Capital*, Macmillan, 1975.

Fine, B., *Economic Theory and Ideology*, Edward Arnold, 1980.

Fine, B., and L. Harris, *Rereading Capital*, Macmillan, 1979.

Fraser, D., *The Evolution of the British Welfare State*, Macmillan, 1973.

Freeman, C., 'Technical innovation and British trade performance', in Blackaby (1979a).

Friedman, A., *Industry and Labour*, Macmillan, 1977.

Galbraith, K., *The New Industrial State*, Hamish Hamilton, 1967.

Gamble, A., 'The free economy and the strong state', *Socialist Register*, Merlin Press, 1979.

Glyn, A., and J. Harrison, *The British Economic Disaster*, Pluto Press, 1980.

Glyn, A., and R. Sutcliffe, *British Capitalism, Workers and the Profits Squeeze*, Penguin, 1972.

Goodrich, C. L., *The Frontier of Control*, G. Bell, 1920.

Gough, I., *The Political Economy of the Welfare State*, Macmillan, 1979.

Government Social Survey, S. Parker, *Workplace Industrial Relations 1973*, Office of Population Censuses and Surveys, London, HMSO, 1975.

Green, F., and P. Nore, *Economics: an Anti-Text*, Macmillan, 1977.

Griffin, K., *International Inequality and National Poverty*, Macmillan, 1978.

Griffin, T. 'The stock of fixed assets in the UK: how best to make use of the statistics', *Economic Trends*, October 1976.

Hall, S., *et al.*, *Policing the Crisis*, Macmillan, 1978.

Hannah, L., *The Rise of the Corporate Economy*, Methuen, 1976.

Hannah, L., and J. Kay, *Concentration in Modern Industry*, Macmillan, 1977.

Harcourt, G. C., *Some Cambridge Controversies in the Theory of Capital*, Cambridge University Press, 1972.

Harris, L., 'On interest, credit and capital', *Economy and Society*, 1976.

Hart, P., M. Utton, and G. Walshe, *Mergers and Concentration in Modern Industry*, Cambridge University Press, 1973.

Hay, D. A., and D. J. Morris, *Industrial Economics*, Oxford University Press, 1979.

Henry, S. G. B., and P. Ormerod, 'Incomes policy and wage inflation 1961–77', *NIER*, 1978.

Hilferding, R., *Das Finanz-Kapital*, Dietz Verlag, Berlin, 1955.

Hill, T. P., *Profits and Rates of Returns*, OECD, 1979.

Hirsch, F., and J. Goldthorpe (eds.), *The Political Economy of Inflation*, Martin Robertson, 1978.

HMSO, *Review of Monopolies and Merger Policy*, Cmnd 7198, 1978.

HMSO, *Review of Restrictive Trade Practices Policy*, Cmnd 7152, 1979.

Hobsbawm, E. J., *Labouring Men*, Weidenfeld and Nicolson, 1964.

Hobsbawm, E. J., *Industry and Empire*, Pelican, 1969.

Hobsbawm, E. J., *The Age of Capital*, Weidenfeld and Nicolson, 1975.

Holland, S., *Strategy for Socialism*, Quartet Books, 1975.

Holland, S. (ed.), *Beyond Capitalist Planning*, Blackwell, 1979.

Holloway, J., and S. Picciotto (eds.), *State and Capital*, Edward Arnold, 1978.

Hood, N., and S. Young, *The Economics of Multinational Enterprise*, Longman, 1979.

Howard, M. C., and J. E. King, *The Political Economy of Marx*, Longman, 1975.

Hughes, J., 'Young workers', in Barratt-Brown (1978).

Hunt, A. (ed.), *Class and Class Struggle*, Lawrence and Wishart, 1977.

Hunt, A. (ed.), *Marxism and Democracy*, Lawrence and Wishart, 1979.

Hutt, A., *British Trade Unionism*, Lawrence and Wishart, 1975.

Hyman, R., *Strikes*, Fontana/Collins, 1977.

Hyman, R. and I. Brough, *Social Values and Industrial Relations*, Basil Blackwell, 1975.

Institute for Workers Control, 'Committee of Enquiry into the Motor Industry', *Capital and Class*, Summer 1977.

Irvine, J., I. Miles, and J. Evans (eds.), *Demystifying Social Statistics*, Pluto Press, 1979.

Jackson, D., H. A. Turner, and S. F. Wilkinson, *Do Trade Unions Cause Inflation?* second edn, Cambridge University Press, 1975.

Jacquemin, A. P. and H. W. de Jong, *European Industrial Organisation*, Macmillan, 1977.

Jessop, R., 'Recent theories of the capitalist state', *Cambridge Journal of Economics*, December 1977.

Kaldor, M., *The Disintegrating West*, Pelican, 1979.

Kaldor, N., *Causes of the Slow Rate of Growth of the UK*, Cambridge University Press, 1966.

Kaldor, N., 'Economic Growth and the Verdoorn Law: comment on Mr. Rowthorn's article', *Economic Journal*, December 1975.

Katouzian, H., *Ideology and Method in Economics*, Macmillan, 1980.

Kay, J. A., and M. A. King, *The British Tax System*, Oxford University Press, 1978.

Kendall, W., *The Labour Movement in Europe*, Allen Lane, 1975.

Kennedy, C., 'Inflation accounting: retrospect and prospect', *Economic Policy Review*, March 1978.

Kilpatrick, A., and T. Lawson, 'On the nature of industrial decline in the U.K.', *Cambridge Journal of Economics*, March 1980.

Kindleberger, C. P., *The World in Depression*, Allen Lane, 1973.

King, M. A., 'The U.K. profits crisis: myth or reality?' *Economic Journal*, March 1975.

Lansley, S., *Housing and Public Policy*, Croom Helm, 1979.

Lenin, V. I., *Imperialism*.

Lenin, V. I., *State and Revolution*.

Leruez, J., *Economic Planning and Politics in Britain*, Martin Robertson, 1976.

Lipsey, R. G., *An Introduction to Positive Economics*, Weidenfeld and Nicolson, 1975.

Maddison, A., 'Phases of Capitalist Development', *Banca Nazionale del Lavoro*, June 1977.

Magdoff, H., *The Age of Imperialism*, Monthly Review Press, New York, 1969.

Major, R. L. (ed.), *Trade and Exchange Rates*, Heinemann, 1979.

Mandel, E., *Marxist Economic Theory*, Merton Press, 1971.

Mandel, E., *Late Capitalism*, New Left Books, 1975.

Mandel, E., *The Second Slump*, New Left Books, 1978.

Marris, R., *The Economic Theory of Managerial Capitalism*, Macmillan, 1964.

Marx, K., *Critique of the Gotha Programme* (Lawrence and Wishart).

Marx, K., *Value, Price and Profit* (Lawrence and Wishart).

Marx, K., *Wage Labour and Capital* (Lawrence and Wishart).

Marx, K., *Theories of Surplus Value* (Progress Publishers).

Marx, K., *Capital* (Vol. I, Penguin Books, 1976; Vol. II, Penguin Books, 1978).

Massey, D., and A. Catalano, *Capital and Land*, Edward Arnold, 1979.

McClellan, D., *Karl Marx: His Life and Thoughts*, Macmillan, 1973.

McCracken, P. (ed.), *Towards Full Employment and Price Stability*, OECD, 1977.

Meek, R., *Economics and Ideology and Other Essays*, Chapman and Hall, 1967.

Meek, R., *Studies in the Labour Theory of Value*, Lawrence and Wishart, 1973.

Meeks, G., *Disappointing Marriage*, Cambridge University Press, 1977.

Miliband, R., *The State in Capitalist Society*, Weidenfeld and Nicolson, 1969.

Miliband, R., *Parliamentary Socialism*, Merlin Press, 1973.

Moore, B., J. Rhodes, R. Tarling, and F. Wilkinson 'A return to full employment?', *Economic Policy Review*, March 1978.

Morishima, M., *Marx's Economics*, Cambridge University Press, 1973.

Morishima, M., and G. Catephores, *Value, Exploitation and Growth*, McGraw-Hill, 1978.

Morris, C. N., 'The Common Agricultural Policy', *Fiscal Studies*, March 1980.

Morris, D. (ed.), *The Economic System in the U.K.*, Oxford University Press, 1979.

Mukherjee, S. 'Government and labour markets', *Political and Economic Planning Broadsheet*, No. 566, November 1976.

NEDO, *The Nationalised Industries*, 1976.

NEDO, *Finance for Investment*, 1975.

Nichols, T., and P. Armstrong, *Workers Divided*, Fontana, 1976.

Nyman, R., and A. Silbertson, 'The ownership and control of industry', *Oxford Economic Papers*, 1978.

O'Connor, J., *The Fiscal Crisis of the State*, St Martins Press, 1973.

O'Connor, J., *The Corporations and the State* Harper, 1974.

Owen, R., and R. Sutcliffe (eds.), *Studies in the Theory of Imperialism*, Longman, 1972.

Panitch, L., *Social Democracy and Industrial Militancy*, Cambridge University Press, 1976.

Parker, R. H., and G. Harcourt (eds.), *Readings in the Concept and Measurement of Income*, Cambridge University Press, 1969.

Passingham, B., and D. Connor, 'Ford Shop Stewards on Industrial Democracy', Institute for Workers' Control Pamphlet, No. 54, IWC, Nottingham, 1977.

Penrose, E., *Theory of the Growth of the Firm*, Basil Blackwell, 1959.

Phillips and Drew, 'Ownership of company shares', 1979, Phillips and Drew, Stockbrokers, Lee House, London Wall EC2.

Pollard, S., *The Development of the British Economy, 1914–1967*, second edn, Edward Arnold, 1969.

Posner, M. V. (ed.), *Demand Management*, Heinemann, 1978.

Posner, M. V., 'Institutions in the financial market', *Bank of England*, November 1979.

Poulantzas, N., *Classes in Contemporary Capitalism*, New Left Books, 1975a.

Poulantzas, N., *Political Power and Social Classes*, New Left Books, 1975b.

Poulantzas, N., *State, Power, Socialism*, New Left Books, 1980.

Prais, S., *The Evolution of the Giant Firms*, Oxford University Press, 1976.

Prest, R. A., and D. J. Coppock (eds.), *The UK Economy: A Manual of Applied Economics*, Weidenfeld and Nicolson, 1978.

Pritt, D. N., *The Labour Government, 1945–51*, Lawrence and Wishart, 1963.

Pryke, R., and R. Rees, *Public Enterprise Economics*, Weidenfeld and Nicolson, 1976.

Radice, H. (ed.), *The International Firm and Modern Imperialism*, Penguin, 1975.

Ray, G. F., 'Structural changes in the economy, 1956–1978', *NIER*, August 1979.

Rees, R., 'The pricing policies of the nationalised industries', *Three Banks Review*, June 1979.

Reid, M., 'The secondary banking crisis—five years on', *The Banker*, December 1978.

Revell, J., *The British Financial System*, Macmillan, 1973.

Roll, E., *A History of Economic Thought*, Faber and Faber, 1973.

Rosdolsky, R., *The Making of Marx's Capital*, Pluto Press, 1977.

Routh, G., *The Origin of Economic Ideas*, Macmillan, 1975.

Rowan, D. C., *Output, Inflation and Growth*, Macmillan, latest editions.

Rowthorn, R. E., 'What remains of Kaldor's Law?', *Economic Journal*, March 1975.

Rowthorn, R. E., *Capitalism, Conflict and Inflation*, Lawrence and Wishart, 1980.

Rubin, I. I., *Essays on the Marxist Theory of Value*, Detroit, 1972.

Rubin, I. I., *A History of Economic Thought*, Ink Links, 1979.

Rubery, J., 'Structured labour markets, worker organisation and low pay', *Cambridge Journal of Economics*, 1978.

Ryder, D., *British Leyland, The Next Decade*, HMSO, 1975.

Sawyer, M. C., *Theories of the Firm*, Croom Helm, 1979.

Sawyer, M. C., 'Concentration in the UK', *University of York* (mimeo), 1979.

Sawyer, M. C., with P. Samson and S. Aaronovitch, 'Business pricing and the inflationary process', *Journal of Industrial Affairs*, 1979.

Scherer, F. M., *Industrial Market Structure and Economic Performance*, Rand McNally, 1980.

Scott, J., *Classes, Corporations and Capitalism*, Heinemann, 1979.

Shah, S., 'The immigrant community', in Barratt-Brown (1978).

Sherman, H., *Stagflation: A Radical Theory of Unemployment and Inflation*, Harper and Row, New York, 1976.

Shinohara, M., *Structural changes in Japan's Economic Development*, Kinokuniya, Tokyo, 1970.

Shonfield, A., *British Economic Policy*, Penguin, 1958.

Shonfield, A., *Modern Capitalism*, Oxford University Press, 1965.

Shonfield, A. (ed.), *International Economic Relations of the Western World, 1959–1971*, Oxford University Press, 1976.

Singh, A., *Takeover*, Cambridge University Press, 1971.

Singh, A., 'Takeovers, economic natural selection and the theory of the firm', *Economic Journal*, 1975.

Singh, A., 'UK Industry and the world economy: A case of de-industrialisation', *Cambridge Journal of Economics*, June 1977.

Smith, D., *The Defence of the Realm in the 1980's*, Croom Helm, 1980.

Smith, D. J., *Racial Disadvantage in Britain* (the PEP Report), Penguin, 1977.

Smith, R., 'Military expenditure and capitalism', *Cambridge Journal of Economics*, March 1977.

Smith, T., *The Politics of the Corporate State*, Martin Robertson, 1979.

Sraffa, P., *Production of Commodities by Means of Commodities*, Cambridge University Press. 1960.

Steedman, I., *Marx after Sraffa*, New Left Books, 1978.

Strange, S. 'International monetary relations', In Vol. 2 of Shonfield (1976).

Swann, D., *The Economics of the Common Market*, Penguin, 1978.

Sweezy, P., *Theory of Capitalist Development*, Monthly Review Press, New York, 1968.

Sylos-Labini, P., 'Industrial pricing in the U.K.', *Cambridge Journal of Economics*, June 1979.

Tarling, R., and F. Wilkinson, 'The social contract: post-war incomes policies and their inflationary impact', *Cambridge Journal of Economics*, December 1977.

Taylor, C. T., and A. R. Threadgold, 'Real national savings and its sectoral composition', *Bank of England*, October 1979.

Terkel, S., *Working*, Penguin, 1977.

Therborn, G., *What does the Ruling Class do When it Rules*, New Left Books, 1978.

Thirlwall, A. P., *Balance of Payments Theory and the UK Experience*, Macmillan, 1980.

Thompson, E. P., *The Making of the English Working Class*, Penguin, 1968.

Thompson, G., 'The relationship between the financial and industrial sector in the U.K. economy', *Economy and Society*, 1977.

Townsend, P. *Poverty in the United Kingdom*, Penguin, 1979.

Townsend, P., and N. Bosanquet (eds.), *Labour and equality*, Heinemann, 1980.

Tsuru, S., *Essays on Economic Development*, Kinokuniya, Tokyo, 1968.

TUC, 'Women workers/1976', Report of the 46th annual conference of representatives of trade unions catering for women workers.

Turvey, R., 'Structural change and structural unemployment', *International Labour Review*, September–October 1977.

United Nations, *Transnational Corporations in World Development*, 1978.

URPE, *U.S. Capitalism in Crisis*, Union for Radical Political Economics, New York, 1978.

Urry, J., and J. Wakeford, *Power in Britain*, Heinemann, 1973.

Usher, D., *The Price Mechanism and the Meaning of National Income Statistics*, Clarendon Press, 1968.

Utton, M., 'The effects of mergers on concentration: UK manufacturing industry 1954–65', *Journal of Industrial Economics*, Vol. 20, 1971.

Vernon, R., *Big Business and the State*, Macmillan, 1974.

Ward, T. S., and R. R. Neild, *The Measurement and Reform of Budgetary Policy*, Heinemann, 1978.

Weisskopf, T. E., 'Marxian crisis theory and the rate of profit in the post-war US economy', *Cambridge Journal of Economics*, December 1979.

Westergaard, J., and H. Resler, *Class in a Capitalist Society*, Heinemann, 1975.

Williamson, J., *The Failure of World Monetary Reform 1971–74*, Nelson, 1977.

Williamson, O. E., *Corporate Control and Business Behaviour*, Prentice–Hall, 1970.

Wolff, E. N., 'The rate of surplus value, the organic composition and the general rate of profit in the US economy, 1947–1967', *American Economic Review*, June 1979.

Wood, A., *A Theory of Profit*, Cambridge University Press, 1975.

World Bank, *World Tables*, Washington DC, 1976.

Wright, E. O., *Class Crisis and the State*, New Left Books, London, 1978.

Young, S., and A. V. Lowe, *Intervention in the Mixed Economy*, Croom Helm, 1974.

Zeitlin, M., 'Corporate ownership and control: the large corporation and the capitalist class', *American Journal of Sociology*, Vol. 79, 1974.

AUTHOR INDEX

SUBJECT INDEX